THE LAND IS OURS

South Africa's First Black Lawyers and the Birth of Constitutionalism

TEMBEKA NGCUKAITOBI

PENGUIN BOOKS

Published by Penguin Books
an imprint of Penguin Random House South Africa (Pty) Ltd
Reg. No. 1953/000441/07
The Estuaries No. 4, Oxbow Crescent, Century Avenue, Century City, 7441
PO Box 1144, Cape Town, 8000, South Africa
www.penguinrandomhouse.co.za

Penguin
Random House
South Africa

First published 2018
Reprinted in 2018

3 5 7 9 10 8 6 4 2

Publication © Penguin Random House 2018
Text © Tembeka Ngcukaitobi 2018

Cover photographs
Henry Sylvester Williams: Wikimedia Commons; **Alfred Mangena:** Museum Africa;
Richard Msimang: Historical Papers Research Archive, University of the Witwatersrand;
Pixley Seme: Swaziland National Archives; **Ngcubu Poswayo:** provided by Poswayo family;
George Montsioa: provided by Montsioa family

PUBLISHER: Marlene Fryer
MANAGING EDITOR: Robert Plummer
EDITOR: Lynda Gilfillan
PROOFREADER: Bronwen Maynier
COVER AND TEXT DESIGNER: Ryan Africa
TYPESETTER: Monique van den Berg
INDEXER: Sanet le Roux

Set in 10.5 pt on 14 pt Minion

Printed by **novus print**, a Novus Holdings company

MIX
Paper from
responsible sources
FSC
www.fsc.org   FSC® C022948

Penguin Random House is committed to a sustainable future for our business,
our readers and our planet. This book is made from Forest Stewardship Council ® certified paper.

ISBN 978 1 77609 285 7 (print)
ISBN 978 1 77609 286 4 (ePub)

Contents

Introduction

In the blazing heat of the Bloemfontein summer of 1943, black intellectuals, acting under the aegis of the African National Congress (ANC), met to deliberate the future of South Africa. Before them was the Atlantic Charter, precursor to the United Nations Declaration of Human Rights. They discussed how Africans might be accommodated in a new world order that could follow in the wake of the imminent victory of the Allied forces in the Second World War. From the discussions, the Africans' Claims emerged. This document served not only as a response to the Atlantic Charter, but also included new normative principles to underpin an imagined South Africa that belonged to all. The group of intellectuals included some of South Africa's first black lawyers. These lawyers were responsible for converting these principles into a Bill of Rights containing basic civil liberties to be enjoyed by all, regardless of race, class or origin. For nine decades, it passed from generation to generation before it found expression in today's South African Constitution.

South Africa's Constitution stands as a monument in the world. For Ruth Bader Ginsburg, a judge of the Supreme Court of the United States of America, it is not the Constitution of the United States of America that is a model for the world, but the South African Constitution. The magnitude of its vision and ambition is unprecedented. Coming after centuries of settler violence, economic exploitation and apartheid racism, retribution is not its animating theme. South Africa belongs to all, it proclaims. The state must facilitate economic justice, the Constitution mandates. The judiciary must protect the Bill of Rights, enforce its promises and monitor the conduct of the government. Yet, despite the admiration of the world, many of the promises contained in the Constitution remain a hollow hope. Millions continue to starve, while a fortunate few enjoy the wealth of the country. Does South Africa really belong to all? In this climate of economic exclusion, and social and political marginalisation, where the winners take all, some question whether the constitutional framework was in fact the correct response to colonialism and apartheid. They ask whether the very idea of a Bill of Rights, which protects individual liberties, is not animated by a fundamentally Eurocentric mindset, one that is unsuited to the African landscape.

In this book I attempt a partial answer, showing that the idea of a Bill of Rights had its origins in South Africa. Not only did the ideas germinate from

South African soil, they emanated from a group of black intellectuals and legal practitioners at the beginning of the twentieth century. The idea of the Bill of Rights was a negation of colonial violence. That black lawyers conceived of it in an era of aggressive colonial expansion brings to the fore the shifting uses of law, from its epicentre in Europe to the lands of the colonised. Law was not always and exclusively an expression of colonial oppression. Sometimes it was an antidote to it, as is true today. Whether law can be an instrument of justice is debatable, with a singularly important factor being the agency of the actors. In the period covered in this book, it was the personal agency of the lawyers that determined whether law was an instrument of oppression or its opposite. This is still the case today.

The Bill of Rights must be enforced by an independent and supreme judiciary. Many argue that this principle, too, is rooted in the legal traditions of Europe. It is indeed so that the fundamentals of racial segregation in late-nineteenth- and early-twentieth-century South Africa were laid down by Victorian politicians and their Cambridge- and Oxford-trained bureaucrats, but it was the colonial judges who cemented and institutionalised racism. Areas such as criminal law, the law of master and servant, the law of property and the very constitution that flowed from the South Africa Act of 1909 were manifestations of colonial power relations. Henry de Villiers, chief justice of the Cape, had a political career before going to the bench, having served as a parliamentarian and attorney-general at the Cape. He presided over the 1908 Convention which decided on the creation of the Union of South Africa, where Africans, despite their protests, were excluded from government of the country. His reward was to be made the first chief justice of the Union of South Africa in 1911. Despite occupying this position, he accepted an acting appointment as governor-general of the Union. His legacy was continued by Chief Justice James Rose Innes, who, in a judgment delivered in 1907, ruled that evidence tendered by white witnesses was more reliable than that of Africans[1] – a view generally held by judges of the apartheid era. Rose Innes presided over a legal system that consolidated pass laws, arbitrary expulsions from land and a compulsory labour system. His successors were no different, and it would be too tedious to recount here their many perverse judgments. The point is not to cast blame on these judges, or to assume a uniformity of judicial opinion at the time. Instead, I seek to demonstrate that, at least insofar as the 'native question' was concerned, there was clear consensus and explicit collaboration between the colonial judges and the ruling elite.

Africans generally encountered the legal system either through the Native Courts or the Magistrate's Courts. Both of these institutions were extensions of the executive. Colonial magistrates were government appointees, but they were also clothed with judicial power. It was African intellectuals who pressed for separation between judicial functions and politics. They believed that only an impartial judicial branch could guarantee their freedoms against the colonial state which sought total control over all aspects of black life. Thus, in South Africa, the idea of a Bill of Rights enforced by an impartial judiciary has a long and solid pedigree. It first emerged in the late 1890s in the writings not of a lawyer, but a journalist: John Tengo Jabavu, editor of the Eastern Cape newspaper *Imvo Zabantsundu*. The circumstances under which this arose warrant a brief examination. In the mid-nineteenth century, when the jurisdiction of the Native Courts was severely restricted, South Africa used a jury system. However, Africans could not be appointed to sit on juries. In his capacity as newspaper editor, Jabavu received a steady flow of complaints about the lack of impartiality of the juries. Upon his own independent investigation, he discovered that it was true that blacks were more likely to receive harsher sentences where the complainants were white. His findings served as a rallying point around which he started advocating for 'an unbiased' judiciary. Accordingly, he proposed that cases be tried by judges 'trained in the law', and that the race of persons involved in the trial should not be taken into account.

Unsurprisingly, the ideas put forward by Jabavu in a marginal Eastern Cape newspaper were ignored by the colonial government of the day. But they found fertile ground in an organisation whose foundations he clearly influenced – the South African Native National Congress (the SANNC, later renamed the ANC). Its founders included three lawyers: Alfred Mangena, Pixley ka Isaka Seme and George Montsioa. (Some historians incorrectly include Richard Msimang in this list, but he was not in South Africa when the organisation was launched in January 1912.) As a London-trained barrister, Mangena had a clear theoretical understanding of the argument in support of an unbiased judiciary. In his constitutional law course at Lincoln's Inn, where he undertook his training between 1905 and 1909, Mangena took particular interest in Baron de Montesquieu, the French philosopher who is credited with the idea of *trias politica* – three arms of government. Personal liberties and freedom, Montesquieu believed, could only be guaranteed if judicial power was separated and insulated from legislative and executive power. Mangena was immediately attracted to the argument, given his own experience of political persecution in the Cape, and indeed the abuse of power by the Natal colonial government in 1906, when martial law was used to justify the deprivation of fair trial rights to the Bambatha warriors.

As a result of Mangena's influence, a central plank of ANC policy in the early twentieth century was the demand for an 'unbiased' judicial system and 'equal' application of the laws of the country, without regard to 'race or creed'. This influence would also become pronounced in the ANC's response to the South Africa Act of 1909 and the 1913 Natives Land Act. The response of Africans to both these pieces of legislation was to work within the 'constitutional' system. In 1923 African lawyers, working under the auspices of the ANC, produced the 'African Bill of Rights for South Africa'.[2] It contained a statement of five rights to be included in the Bill of Rights. The Bantu inhabitants of the Union, it began, have 'as human beings, the indisputable right to a place of abode in this land of their fathers'. Africans, as children of the soil, have a God-given right 'to unrestricted ownership of land in this, the land of their birth'. Yet Africans were not the only ones inhabiting the land. So, 'like the British subjects', blacks have 'the inalienable right to the enjoyment of those British principles of "liberty of the subject, justice and equality of all classes in the eyes of the law" that made Great Britain one of the greatest powers'. Even as they made these demands, the lawyers were not yet sure of their universal application. Their demand, they explained, was for the application of a principle made famous by Cecil John Rhodes, former prime minister of the Cape, for 'equal rights for all civilized men south of the Zambesi', regardless of race, class, creed or origin. The final statement of the Bill of Rights was for representation of blacks by 'members of their own race in all the legislative bodies of the land, otherwise there can be "no taxation without representation". This Bill of Rights would later serve as a galvanising, rallying point for further demands for inclusion into the government of South Africa, and a share in the land. Right from these early days of resistance, black legal intellectuals were concerned about equality, justice, and a system of land allocation and administration informed by legality and fairness.

Consequently, when the Africans' Claims was produced, it included an expansive Bill of Rights. The black lawyers who were part of its drafting included Seme, a practising attorney in Johannesburg, Professor Z.K. Matthews, a legal academic at the University College of Fort Hare, and Lionel T. Mtimkulu, an attorney in Ngcobo, in the Eastern Cape.

Seme had been part of the founding generation of the ANC, being the organiser of the conference of 1912, when the ANC was launched. His friend, Mangena, who was the first black South African attorney to practise law in South Africa, was elected as one of the vice-presidents to John Langalibalele Dube. Mangena and Seme were inspired by the vision of Henry Sylvester Williams, the founder of Pan-Africanism, who practised as the first black advocate in the Cape from 1903 to 1905. George Montsioa, another attorney who was a graduate of Lincoln's Inn, was elected as recording secretary. Though Msimang was not yet in the country when the ANC was formed, upon his return late in 1912, he was thrust into the affairs of the ANC, becoming treasurer and head of the constitutional drafting committee. The pages that follow record the collective experiences of these lawyers and explore the influences that animated them. As activists, they used the law as an instrument against injustice. In an age of aggressive colonial expansion, land dispossession and forced labour, they were not deterred from their goals. Rather than resorting to law *in spite of* the military occupation of the colonial era, they resorted to law *because* a military option was not available to them. Though their impact continues to be felt in today's South Africa, it is a largely unexplored topic. The focus has been the law (and its absurdities) during the apartheid era. However, this leaves a gap in our historical understanding of human rights and their true origins. By focusing on these lawyers, human rights – and constitutionalism – are restored to their rightful place in our current discourse. Constitutionalism – meaning a system of government according to laws that are fair and informed by principles of justice – did not emerge as an alternative to political struggle. Instead, constitutionalism is an integral part of South Africa's political struggle. By examining the lives of the lawyers who practised their profession in the colonial era, before apartheid, we enrich our historical understanding; and in a modern era fraught with the politics of power rather than principle, we also broaden the intellectual basis of our engagement with human rights. Furthersmore, it becomes clear that the unfinished struggle for land can only take place through a framework of law.

By the time the 1943 conference was held, the ANC's human rights tradition was firmly established. Equality before the law constituted the central, organising principle. The Bill of Rights itself was broader than the original 1923 document. Representation was, however, still a point of contention. The 1943 Bill of Rights called for the abolition of political discrimination based on race, and the extension of the right to vote to all adults, to provincial councils and other representative institutions. Judicial institutions were of special significance to the politics of resistance, and the Bill of Rights envisaged the conditions for their legitimacy to function as arbiters. Freedom of the press was seen as important since the press constituted a vital platform for the expression of subaltern perspectives. 'The right to own, buy, hire, or lease and occupy land' was protected by law, without racial restriction. Compulsory education was mentioned, as was freedom of trade and occupation.

The Africans' Claims has stood the test of time. As Albie Sachs reminds us in *We, the People*,[3] Oliver Tambo, the venerated president of the ANC, was committed to constitutionalism. The 1989 Constitutional Guidelines of the ANC also reflect this commitment.[4] Echoing the views of the earlier period in Africans' Claims, the guidelines highlight the role of the Constitution in transforming society: 'the effects of centuries of racial domination and inequality must be overcome by constitutional provisions for corrective action'. While it is not possible to draw a straight line between the writings of early African intellectuals and the present Constitution, the adoption of the Freedom Charter in 1955,[5] conceived by Z.K. Matthews, had a significant impact, and was therefore a momentous occasion. Furthermore, it is clear that the ideas of the first generation of black lawyers provide the intellectual basis from which later generations could draw when imagining the kind of South Africa they wanted for themselves. This still holds good today: if we are to reimagine our present and imagine our future, we should start by reimagining our past.

Part I of this book begins the task of reimagining the past by excavating its remains from the ruins of Empire on the eastern frontier. The story of how the land was lost there provides a useful entry point, illuminating the larger political formation of South Africa. The eastern frontier provides a template for understanding how 'natives' saw themselves in relation to the British Empire. The emergent racial theories of social Darwinism, which gained currency after the end of slavery, were first played out in that part of the world by a man who believed in the supremacy of the white race, Sir George Grey. His friend Thomas Carlyle, a racial theorist of mid-nineteenth-century Victorian England, believed it was a mistake to have abolished slavery. The colonial encounter on the eastern frontier carried special significance because of the expansive network of missionary institutions; their original purpose was upended by Grey when he replaced 'bookish' education with industrial education which was 'suited' to 'native children'.

Part II examines the life of each of the lawyers who constituted the first generation of black lawyers in South Africa. In line with the conventions of biography, which follows sequential developments, I focus on the events that shaped their ideas, and examine their thinking during the formation and development of early South Africa. Because the law was important to their world, I provide a close analysis of the legal cases they took on, the principles of law involved, and how they reconciled the law with political upheavals of the day. In circumstances where legal victories were undermined by politics, I attempt to examine what it was that sustained their fidelity to the idea of the law. By considering each life separately, and drawing connections where they intersect, I try to address the broader question: how can the law be used as an instrument of justice in an oppressive society? In itself, law is never sufficient for justice. What is crucial is a committed group of actors, willing to use the instrumentality of law in aid of the oppressed.

Part III focuses on the collective response of the individual actors in Part II. The response occurred in two phases, the first relating to the establishment of the Union in 1910. While the demand for equality fell on deaf ears, it is noteworthy that the very idea of the formation of the Union emanated from the imperial government's desire to resolve the 'native question'.[6] When the South African delegates convened to deliberate, the expectation was that they would find an acceptable resolution to the matter. Yet with the eventual submission of a draft South African Bill to the House of Commons, nary a word was raised about the exclusion of the native inhabitants from government. The second phase occurred after a series of disappointments, as blacks finally accepted that their struggle for equality depended not on British intervention, but rather on self-reliance. It was during this phase that the Africans' Claims document was conceived, debated and produced. It is my contention that the Africans' Claims document is an anti-colonial statement. Yet it should be recognised that in its very rejection of colonialism, it employs its language – the language of rights, freedoms and equality. Perhaps this is the lesson of this book: the lesson of ambiguity.

PART I

LAND

1

How the land was lost

> *The conquest of the earth, which mostly means the taking it away from*
> *those who have a different complexion or slightly flatter noses than our-*
> *selves, is not a pretty thing when you look into it too much. What redeems*
> *it is the idea only. An idea at the back of it; not a sentimental pretence but*
> *an idea; and an unselfish belief in the idea – something you can set up,*
> *and bow down before, and offer a sacrifice to ….*
>
> – Joseph Conrad, *Heart of Darkness*

The cattle had stopped grazing. Their eyes were swollen, their noses covered in sores. Their breathing was rapid, laboured, and they seemed to experience coughing fits. Their mouths hung open and their tongues protruded. Emaciated, they began to die, one by one. The dying began in the west of the land of the Xhosa. It soon spread across the entire Xhosaland. Once a cow showed symptoms, the entire herd was affected. One death led to tens of deaths, tens led to hundreds. No one knew the cause, though families, clans and entire villages felt the effects. Everyone was worried about the rapidity of the spread, the scale, and the pitiful manner of the deaths. Local seers were consulted, but they were unable to provide answers. Some resorted to practical solutions: if a cow was spotted with the symptoms, it was immediately put down. Others believed the cattle were possessed by an evil spirit. Yet others saw this as ancestral anger at the living.

For more than fifty years, the British had tried to place the land of the Xhosa under colonial administration. While the 1853 war of Mlanjeni had ended in the military defeat of the Xhosa, it did not result in complete subjugation. Nevertheless, it had been a dispiriting and demoralising war for the Xhosa. The man known as Mlanjeni – 'he of the river' – had experienced visions: the dead rising from their graves; the return of the days of Xhosa independence and prosperity; and freedom from British colonial administration. These happenings could not, however, come to fruition because the world was inhabited by evil. So, evil had first to be banished from the earth. Thereafter, the cattle sickness would vanish. The earth, the animals and the people would be cleansed. The dead would rise. News of Mlanjeni's visions soon spread across the land. It was believed that he possessed divine powers, transmitted through the invisible god of the Xhosa, Naphakade, son of Sifubasibanzi.[1] When Mlanjeni declared that traditional medicines and beliefs were witchcraft that should be abandoned, people obeyed him. It was believed that he had the power of 'smelling out' witchcraft (*ukunuka*). People gathered in large numbers at his homestead to witness the performance of cleansing from evil spirits. They were not disappointed by the spectacle. Mlanjeni set up two poles, instructing those present to walk between them. Anyone who did so without shaking or collapsing was not a witch, he proclaimed. Those who trembled or fell as they walked through were possessed. They could be dispensed with, according to the laws of the land. That often meant death, unless Mlanjeni himself declared the hapless victim cured of witchcraft. As the story of Mlanjeni spread, people arrived bearing gifts, and with questions as to life's problems and mysteries. Mlanjeni never failed them, providing answers rooted in traditional and religious belief which could mean everything and nothing at the same time. Nevertheless, the people followed him.

Mlanjeni's cult following eventually came to the attention of the British authorities, who smelt a plot. Anyone who believed in the disappearance of whites and the rise of Xhosa ancestors posed a threat. They believed that Mlanjeni was plotting a war against the British. Mlanjeni eluded arrest, so they approached Sandile, the king of the Xhosa. The governor of the Cape, Harry Smith, gave instructions for Sandile to see him at once. Fearing that he was being set up for arrest, Sandile declined. This act, perceived as defiance, gave Smith the perfect excuse. He stripped Sandile of all power as king, transferring this to the resident magistrate, Charles Brownlee. In a stroke of the pen, the Xhosa now reported to Brownlee. Sandile's lower-ranking chiefs rejected the order, opting for armed resistance. They consulted Mlanjeni, who agreed to prepare the Xhosa for the impending war. A government-imposed magistrate was not acceptable, and war alone would restore their credibility and status. Mlanjeni would not only administer the war medicine, but would also take over the total strategy for the war. He went about the ritualistic cleansing of the Xhosa warriors, which included wearing a particular root known as *ikhubalo likaMlanjeni* around the neck, chewing the stick of the root, spitting it out, and then calling upon the ancestors and Mlanjeni himself. The warriors were assured that if these instructions were followed, the guns of the British would spit water, the gunpowder would not ignite and the ammunition would be harmless. 'Those persons who observe witchcraft will die,' but those who trusted in him and obeyed his instructions would survive, he pronounced.[2]

The actual fighting was, however, led by the great Xhosa military general, Maqoma, who joined Mlanjeni's war because he had suffered personal humiliations at the hands of Smith. Unlike in previous frontier wars, the Xhosa formed a broad alliance with the Khoisan. Historians have explained this as the emergence of a class alliance, as both were engaged in struggles against incorporation into the colonial capitalist economy.[3] But this conception, which focuses on material gains and losses from mutual cooperation against the colonisers, cannot be the complete story. The Xhosa and the Khoisan had, as Jeff Peires argues, lived together and alongside each other for a much longer period before the establishment of the colony.[4] Their material, cultural and spiritual worlds had intersected, overlapped and combined to the point of being indistinguishable. Colonists and missionaries were at times unable to draw a clear line between the Khoi and the Xhosa, applying the term 'kaffir' to both. Nevertheless, with the exception of a temporary victory in December 1850, where the Xhosa killed more than forty British soldiers, the war of Mlanjeni was a disaster for the Xhosa. The guns did not spit water but shot live ammunition. Thousands were killed. Sandile accepted defeat and offered to make peace with Smith, who rejected it. He had given an instruction for the extermination of 'these most barbarous and treacherous savages'.[5] He wished to solicit the help of 'the Afrikaners', announcing that he would be pleased if they named their own commandant, and that 'under him they may go their own way and shoot as they like'. The language of 'extermination' was widespread. According to Roger Levine, the war offered the British settlers the opportunity of a 'permanent settlement' of the Eastern Cape.[6] He quotes the land speculator, William Southey, who wrote: 'All Kaffirs, even to Natal, must be subdued, their lands conquered from them and they themselves made Servants … Urge the active people to arms; there is nothing now for it but an attempt at extermination.'[7] Smith was unconcerned about possible repercussions of his extermination order, noting, 'I care not what the people in England think of my fiery proclamation.' He would allow Afrikaners – known to have engaged in the random killing of blacks – to 'shoot as they like'.[8]

Smith had rejected the peace offering, and Mlanjeni's promises proved to be a hoax. The Xhosa were left no option but to fight to the bitter end. According to Peires, the war of Mlanjeni was 'the longest, hardest and ugliest war ever fought over 100 years of bloodshed in the Cape Colony's Eastern Frontier'.[9] Ultimately, the Xhosa were pushed across the Kei River and removed from their land. Importantly, the Xhosa lost the Amatola, the area around the Tyumi, Keiskamma and Buffalo Rivers, their most prized pieces of land. They were pushed across the Kei River and squeezed into a confined space. A peace settlement had to be found, and with the end of the war the law began to take its course. The British would retain the lands conquered during the war, but they would not interfere with the internal control and leadership of the Xhosa. Although a new 'overseer' was appointed, he would not have the same powers as Brownlee. The Xhosa would rule themselves according to their own traditions and in accordance with their own systems. The war had been expensive for Britain, costing about £3 million. For the Xhosa, however, the cost went beyond money. It was the human cost that mattered: 16 000 Xhosa died, many more were displaced and the traditional structure of government was destroyed. Smith, however, was himself a casualty of the war. The British government held the view that, had it not been for his obduracy, the war could have been avoided. He was soon replaced, and his successor was perhaps the single most important agent of British imperialism in nineteenth- and twentieth-century South Africa – though his name was not Cecil John Rhodes.

Civilising the 'barbarian' races

Sir George Grey landed in Cape Town on 4 December 1854. Before then, he had been governor of New Zealand. His mandate there was to 'civilise the barbarian and hedonist races'.[10] Having suppressed the indigenous people of New Zealand through military conquest and ethnic killing, Grey was sent to the Cape to build hospitals, schools and courts, instruments to impose the will of Empire; as governor, he would establish a government and thereby accomplish the 'civilising' mission. His knighthood came about as a result of writing a constitution for New Zealand, which placed the country under British rule. His new appointment was a promotion, and his vision of the Cape was one where the 'ultimate frontier' was partly native and partly European, where the natives would be 'worn by our exertions to Christianity, trained by us in agriculture and in simple arts … accustomed to our laws and aware of their advantages, attached to us from a sense of benefits received, respecting us for our strength and generosity.'[11]

By allocating finances to education and public works for the Xhosa, Grey believed that he would help to create 'a friendly commerce between the races, based upon mutual advantage and convenience, which, continued for a few years, cannot but tend to cement a lasting union between them'. Grey had an opportunity to express his vision when he addressed the Cape Parliament on 15 March 1855. He set out his grand plan for the civilisation of the native races:

> We should admit that we cannot live in immediate contact with any race or portion of our fellow man, whether civilised or uncivilised, neglecting and ignoring our duties towards them, without suffering those evils which form the fitting punishment of our neglect and indifference; that we should feel that if we leave the natives … shut out from our community of interest with ourselves, they must always remain a race of troublesome marauders, and that, feeling this, we should try to make them a part of ourselves, with a common faith and common interest … a source of strength and wealth for this colony, as providence designed them to be.[12]

These were empty words, however. For Grey, coexistence between the races meant white supremacy, with Africans occupying a servile, inferior position. He would initiate a wide-ranging industrial programme which included agriculture and the building of roads. The workers would be the indigenous population, as in New Zealand ten years before. The Cape Colony, he believed, would be turned into a limitless reservoir of labour. He explained the plan thus: the Xhosa man 'will be marched into the colony under their European superintendents, unarmed and provided only with implements of labour ... and will be marched out of the colony in the same manner when employment ceases'.[13] Although promises of decent remuneration were made, many workers earned a pittance and could hardly make ends meet. Workers had the added burden of seeing to their own needs regarding clothing – which had to be European – as well as food and transport. A central component of Grey's plan was education. He would create industrial training centres, 'native' schools and hospitals. Industrial training and native schools would fall under the control of missionaries. At the time of Grey's arrival in 1854, one missionary school, the Lovedale Institute, established thirteen years before, was catering to the educational needs of native children. It provided training for Xhosa boys in carpentry, masonry, metalwork, wagon-making and agriculture, and Grey made a substantial financial contribution to the school.

Grey's ambitions were matched by the size of his war chest. The British government had provided him with the generous sum of £40 000, with promises of more, to be disbursed at will for his pet projects. Grey's mission was going exceedingly well until his ambitions got the better of him. As part of the settlement at the end of the war of Mlanjeni, the Xhosa could administer their affairs in accordance with their own laws and customs. But this was in conflict with Grey's civilising mission – for instance, he believed that the practice of smelling out witchcraft was contrary to civilisation. Also, he felt unable to fully control the Xhosa if they had their own system of laws, and believed that the appointment of resident magistrates would give him direct power to control them. He began by consulting with the chiefs to accept his plan of deploying magistrates across the Kei, which was now the land of the Xhosa. Certain powers belonging to the chiefs would be assumed and exercised by magistrates. Grey expected resistance, but to his surprise, Sandile, Maqoma and Mhala – all senior Xhosa leaders – accepted the introduction of the magistrates. Another plan was to place the chiefs on the payroll of the government. No meaningful resistance was forthcoming, though the chiefs did enquire in rather polite terms about the return of the lands they had lost during the war. They received no reply. The implication was clear. Grey was not in the mood for returning land. Although he was surprised at the chiefs' meek surrender, the fact of the matter was that the unfulfilled prophecies of Mlanjeni and the brutality of the war, which included the notorious scorched-earth policy of the British and the subsequent loss of land, had completely demoralised the Xhosa. They were tired, weary of battle, and attempting to reimagine their place in a changed world. Quite apart from the effects of loss of land and political authority, a new poverty was settling in. Overcrowding had become the norm, and many diseases were becoming uncontrollable.

A 'decisive moment' for Christianity

The year was 1856. One morning in April, the niece of local Xhosa medicine man Mhlakaza went to chase birds from cornfields along a river known to the locals as Gxara. The girl, who was about fifteen years of age, was called Nongqawuse. According to legend, two strange men appeared to the girl. They identified themselves by name – names known to Nongqawuse – though the men themselves were long dead. They gave her a chilling instruction:

> Maze nisibulisele emakaya, nixele ukuba singo Nantsi abafa kudala. Ze nixele ukuba umzi uza kuvuka wonke ekufeni, nenkomo mazixelwe zonke ezi zikoyo kuba zifuywe ngezandla ezincolileyo, kuba kuko nabantu abapete ubuti. Makungalinywa, makumbiwe izisele ezikulu ezitsha, kwakiwe ne zindlu ezikwa ntsha, kubiywe nenq'ili ezinkulu ze ntlanti kusikwe intsuba, kulukwe neng-cango zobuka zibe ninzi. Zitsho inkosi u Napakade into ka Sifuba-sibanzi. Abantu mababulahle ngokwabo ubuti, bungade bumbululwe ngamagqira.[14]

Everyone must kill all their cattle. They must not plough. They must destroy the food in their possession. All forms of witchcraft must be abandoned. Once this was done, preparations for a new world should begin. New kraals must be built. New houses must be built. If these instructions were carried out, within eight days the dead would arise and the whites would return to the sea. That the whites would 'return' to the sea was particularly significant. Some Xhosa held the belief that the whites had come from the sea. According to Noël Mostert, although the Xhosa had lived along the coast, it had never been their understanding that there were other people living across the ocean. Whatever lived across the ocean, they believed, had been separated from them by God, and would never come into contact with them. Hence, the end of oppression by whites was always linked to their 'return' to the sea.[15]

Nongqawuse returned to Mhlakaza and narrated the men's tale. It was met with mild disbelief and some derision. The following day, with Mhlakaza in tow, she returned to the spot where the two men had appeared to her. The men reappeared, although they 'did not reveal themselves to Mhlakaza'.[16] When they enquired whether Nongqawuse had conveyed their instructions, she replied in the affirmative. They repeated their instructions, and because she was the only one who could 'see' and 'talk' to the invisible men, Nongqawuse conveyed these 'instructions' to Mhlakaza. This spurred his imagination, as the description of the two men matched those of his long-deceased relatives, and Mhlakaza began to take the tale seriously and to act accordingly. When he visited the invisible men again, Mhlakaza was told through Nongqawuse to pass on the message to Chief Sarhili: the Xhosa had to ensure that the cattle were killed, in order to prepare for the coming of new cattle that would be free of all disease. Mhlakaza then began the slaughter of the cattle. This was taken up by his followers.

Amid the confusion, another girl, Nombada, appeared from an area known as Mpongo in Macleantown. She had the same message. If the people wanted to end the suffering, they should kill their cattle. More villagers followed the instruction. But this was not yet a frenzy; instead, there were isolated, sporadic instances. Sarhili's cattle contracted lung disease, and began to die. Coupled with Sarhili's own personal misfortune,[17] the death of his cattle turned cattle killing into a general slaughter across the land of the Xhosa. Sarhili now declared himself a 'believer' in the prophecies of Nongqawuse. Some Xhosa had refused to slaughter their cattle, disputing the veracity, reliability and authenticity of Nongqawuse's visions. But once their king, the respected Sarhili, believed, they too became 'believers'. The slaughter turned into an orgy, then a religion of destruction. Soon the instruction included the killing not just of cattle, but of all living things – including goats and sheep – and the burning of cornfields.

The news eventually reached Grey, who showed little sympathy for the impending poverty caused by the destruction. His main concern was that this might be a plot against the colonial government. If the cattle killing resulted in starvation, that in turn could lead to a declaration of war against the government. Accordingly, he sent a letter to Sarhili telling him that the killing of the cattle would lead to starvation and disorder, and should that be the consequence he would regard him as the guilty party and punish him as the one responsible for the slaughter. Sarhili was undeterred. On 3 November 1856, he replied: 'There is a thing which speaks in my country, and orders me and my people to kill our cattle, eat our corn and throw away all our witchcraft … and not to plant, and to report it to all the chiefs in the country.'[18]

Finally, the eighth day arrived, when the 'new people' would be unveiled. Mhlakaza – who by now had accepted the prophecies – promised that on 18 February 1857, the sun would rise from the east as usual but at midday it would return to the east. Robert Mullins, an English settler, was one of those who went to witness the event. He recorded in his diary on 17 February 1857 that the 'kaffirs say that the sun will set as soon as it rises tomorrow … I feel very restless and do not know what to do.' On 18 February, Mullins noted: 'Mhlakaza's day today.' He also wrote: '[The] first thing I heard was hollering that the sun would set in the east …' His final entry before going to sleep was: 'the sun set as usual'. Frances Brownlee, wife of resident magistrate Charles Brownlee, wrote: 'The sun rose and made the circuit of the heavens closely watched by expectant hosts in vain. He set in silent majesty in the west, leaving the usual darkness over the earth, and the black darkness of a bitter disappointment in the hearts of thousands.'[19]

There would be no 'new people'. The whites would not return to the sea. Life would go on. That night and the following day the Xhosa had to confront their lives as they always had. But the tragedy of it all was that they had lost their possessions. They had lost their land. Their cattle were slaughtered. After the disaster of Mlanjeni, Nongqawuse's prophecies seemed also to have gone up in flames. There was, however, some lingering hope. Some privately believed that Mhlakaza may have confused his dates. Perhaps the day of destiny was still coming. For a while they awoke longing, wishing and hoping for the appointed day. They looked towards the kraals for the emergence of the new cattle. They looked at the sea, waiting for it to open up and swallow the whites. They looked for signs, any signs, of the emergence of the 'new people'. But all was in vain. As Frances Brownlee wrote: 'Oh! The pity, the heart-breaking grief, the sad horror of it all.'[20] Despite all this, Mhlakaza believed that he could rescue his tarnished reputation. In August 1857, he promised another day of resurrection. But this too ended in bitter disappointment.

To the most ardent believers it was by now abundantly clear that the prophecies would not be fulfilled. Some believed the events were evidence of punishment by the ancestors. With no land and no cattle, the Xhosa were a broken people. In January 1857, the Xhosa population in British Kaffraria was recorded as 105 000. By December that year it had shrunk by more than half, to 37 000. It is estimated that between 15 000 and 50 000 died of starvation alone. Thousands more were displaced, in search of a new life.[21] Noël Mostert notes that immediately after this period, thousands of Xhosa left to offer themselves for labour. There was widespread starvation, so much so that a condition of their labour was that they be given food rations for a limited period. Quoting a newspaper report at the time, Mostert records:

> The body of kaffirs which was marched into town … by Mr Hart exhibited a spectacle of famine-gaunt and thin, which failed not to draw sympathy from all who saw them; and although the kaffir has been to us the subject of constant dread and abhorrence … it was impossible to look upon the group assembled in Church Square … without a desire to stretch forth the hand of charity to the poor-starved heathen … Here the tall adult presented a form bearing evidence of muscular strength, but 'sharp misery' has so worn him to the bone, that the joints stood out in hideous relief in his shrunken frame.[22]

The situation presented a new opportunity. White employers and their agents plundered Xhosa villages for labour. They collected hundreds of starving, emaciated people and sold them to farmers and other employers for anything between £1 and £5 per head. The demand for labour broke the ties of family, clan and kinship. One labour agent noted: 'One thing is much required and that is some 30 young boys and girls for the residents in the town of Graaff Reinet ... I should be glad to get the boys and girls separately registered to avoid further disputes; I mean separate from the parents.'[23] In conditions never imagined by Grey, the power of the chiefs was destroyed. The social structure of the Xhosa had undergone irrevocable disruption. Hundreds of thousands left their homes in search of employment. Labour was cheap, and more than 25 000 Xhosa were registered as workers.

Grey now considered the back of the Xhosa resistance broken. Trumped-up charges led to the arrest of the chiefs. After sham trials in which no legal representation was allowed, the chiefs were imprisoned on Robben Island. Grey was finally able to control the land of the Xhosa. Nongqawuse's vision was the final straw, and Grey admitted as much. In 1858 he wrote that the cattle killing was by far 'the most decisive movement in the direction of Christianity'.[24] Yet he knew that its most significant consequence was economic, commenting, 'A restless nation, who for years have harassed the frontier, may now, to a great extent, be changed into useful labourers ... I think that a transference to the Colony ... of a considerable number of destitute persons from Kaffraria, as labourers, will prove highly advantageous to this country.'[25] Bishop Henry Coterill of Grahamstown added: 'But for this event, we might have laboured many years instead of these last two or three, and had very little results.'[26] Not only were the Xhosa turned into wage labourers, but their land was placed under the control of the British government. As 'conquered people', Grey asserted, 'their lands are held only during pleasure. The Crown takes whatever tracts of country it requires ... and requires the people on such tracts of country to move ... Thus throughout British Kaffraria the native has no recognised right or interest in the soil.'[27]

From conquest to modernity
Europe's imagining of Africa was cemented not in Africa, but in Germany. Otto von Bismarck hosted the Berlin Conference, which commenced on 15 November 1884. Under the doctrine of 'effective occupation',[28] acts of conquest such as that in the Eastern Cape were formalised into law. Any European state that could prove effective occupation of African territory was regarded as the owner of that land. With this, the nation state was born in Africa. Prior to 1884, African 'states' effectively comprised independent political entities and polities held together by loose tribal lineages that could be broken at any stage. Now the entire continent would be constituted in the image of Europe. All the land, whether on the surface or

underground, belonged to Europe. Not only the trees, rivers and seas, but also the inhabitants, African men and women, would be controlled by Europe. Solid geographic boundaries were arbitrarily drawn up. Any resistance was met with force, and it is estimated that ten million Congolese were killed when Leopold II of Belgium plundered the Congo Free State, first for ivory and later for rubber.

The German general Lothar von Trotha, a product of the Second Reich, justified the ethnic cleansing of the Herero and Nama people in today's Namibia: 'I destroy the African tribes with streams of blood … Only following this cleansing can something new emerge, which will remain.'[29] Significantly, Governor Theodor Leutwein, who dissented, explained his objection not in humanitarian but in economic terms: 'I do not concur with those fanatics who want to see the Herero destroyed altogether … I would consider such a move a grave mistake from an economic point of view. We need the Herero as cattle breeders … and especially as labourers.'[30] Nevertheless, Trotha lived up to his promise. By the end of the genocide,[31] the Germans had killed more than 100 000 Herero and Nama people, holding thousands more in concentration camps, including the notorious Shark Island camp. The land had been cleared for German occupation. While Germany was displaced by South Africa under Article 22 of the Covenant of the League of Nations in 1921,[32] the oppression and dispossession of the Herero would continue until 1990,[33] when Namibia achieved its independence.

Similarly, Governor Harry Smith regarded the 'extermination' of the Xhosa of the Eastern Cape as 'the only principle to guide us'.[34] Boundaries between and within African states were constructed to suit the imperial wishes of Europe. Foreign languages would be imposed throughout the continent. Families, clans and communities were split down the middle by random borders. Notwithstanding the colonial genocide and plunder of Africa, Veit Erlmann points out that a novelist such as Charles Dickens regarded the period as one of 'great expectations', where people of all classes awaited the arrival of a new age where technology and industry would usher in peace and prosperity, 'a heaven on earth'.[35] John Stuart Mill, icon of nineteenth-century liberalism, saw this new world as 'farther advanced in the road to perfection; happier, nobler, wiser'.[36] However, it was left to Karl Marx to bring home the paradoxes of the moment. To him, everything seemed 'to be pregnant with its contrary', as noted by Marshall Berman.[37] In Berman's own view, the era of modernity was characterised by the 'great absence and emptiness of values and yet, at the same time, a remarkable abundance of possibilities'.[38] He illuminates this paradox by citing Friedrich Nietzsche's 1882 assertion:

At these turning points in history there shows itself, juxtaposed and often entangled with one another, a magnificent, manifold, jungle-like growing and striving, a sort of tropical tempo in rivalry of development, and an enormous destruction and self-destruction, thanks to egoisms violently opposed to one another, exploding, battling each other for sun and light, unable to find any limitation, any check, any considerateness within the morality at their disposal .... Nothing but new 'wherefores,' no longer any communal formulas; a new allegiance of misunderstanding and mutual disrespect; decay, vice, and the most superior desires gruesomely bound up with one another, the genius of the race welling up over the cornucopias of good and ill; a fateful simultaneity of spring and autumn .... Again there is danger, the mother of morality – great danger – but this time displaced onto the individual, onto the nearest and dearest, onto the street, onto one's own child, one's own heart, one's own innermost secret recesses of wish and will.[39]

In an era that might be called the age of paradoxes, the Eastern Cape was the site where the paradoxes of Empire – the explosive battles 'for sun and light' – were first played out in South Africa. It was on the eastern frontier that the British exercised their imperial ambitions, the effects of which would irrevocably shape modern South Africa. By 1878, the Xhosa had lost their land. This was to be a blueprint for the country as a whole. When the last frontier war – the War of Ngcayechibi – ended in 1879, the colonial forces shifted their focus to labour. After the defeat of the Xhosa, the British took prisoners, and these included women and children. However, the previous year, in 1878, it had been decided that no women or children would be admitted to camps in British Kaffraria, so they were released. But with their land being taken, and husbands and fathers either deceased or imprisoned, the question arose as to where they should go.

When Government Notice No. 372 of 1878 was proclaimed, it had two objectives. The first was to remove women and children from the conflict on the frontier so that they would be unable to continue supplying food and ammunition to their men in order to weaken the opposing forces. The second was that these women would be transported to Cape Town for purposes of employment. In May 1878, more than 2 000 Xhosa men, women and children were transported from the Transkei area to Cape Town, forming part of a group of 6 000 Xhosa who were indentured to work in the Cape. In terms of the indenture system, prospective employers could apply to use these labourers through special officers. The officers concerned would then allocate labourers to 'successful applicants'. The working conditions were dreadful, and wages pitiful or non-existent. Without accommodation, the labourers were forced to live like squatters, yet they were not permitted to leave their employers. Any attempt at doing so resulted in imprisonment. In 1879 more prisoners were sent away, this time to work on the Kimberley diamond fields. But when the war ended, those Africans who were sent to the Cape were not allowed to return to their homes. Soon afterwards, large numbers of Africans went to the Cape in search of their relatives. They had obtained temporary passes of up to four months, and although they went looking for relatives, many found it impossible to return home and so they began searching for employment. Quite apart from people directly affected by the war, either through the indenture system or the search for missing family members, the consequence of the war was that Africans were largely rendered destitute. Many went to the Cape seeking employment on the docks, in public works and in the factories.

With the land lost, and Africans unable to resist the military incursions of the British, a new frontier was open – the frontier of ideas. Education, law and religion were the epicentre of this new frontier. The goals of the Empire also shifted from conquest to the needs of the time. Blacks had to be educated in order to acquire industrial and agricultural skills that would be useful to the colonial economy, as administered indirectly from the Cape for the benefit of the Empire. The second goal was acceptance of the religion of the West – monotheism, as embodied in Christianity and its value system – by the local African population. These goals were all-encompassing, making it impossible to be both Christian and traditional. Nor could one be educated and traditional. Acceptance of colonial education and Christianity implied the negation of African values, beliefs and ways of life. Although the conversion of blacks into labourers had begun in the Cape Colony, it was in the Transvaal that capitalism as a system began.[40] There, civilisation would become synonymous with capitalism. At the centre of this project was Cecil John Rhodes and his heir, Alfred Milner.

Black labour and the seeds of a capitalist economy
Cecil John Rhodes was a dominant figure in the diamond trade of the Cape, bringing him much admiration among the British political establishment. With the patronage of the imperial government and financial support of the Rothschild family, Rhodes quickly climbed what Benjamin Disraeli described as 'the greasy pole' of politics,[41] finding himself at the apex of Cape government when he became prime minister for a while. Rhodes the politician, imperialist and capitalist merged into a seamless whole. The state was truly captured by capital. The discovery of gold on the Witwatersrand in 1886 whet Rhodes's grand imperial ambitions. Until that point, the Transvaal was of peripheral interest to the British Empire. With this discovery, Britain prioritised the control of the politics of the Boer republic. Control of government, it believed, would convert to the economic sphere. Rhodes solicited the support of the Chamber of Mines to hatch an audacious takeover in what became known as the Jameson Raid. A rag-tag army, supported and sponsored by the British, prepared to stage an uprising in late

1895, but it ended in spectacular failure. The Boers repelled Jameson's troops, and with this defeat, Rhodes's reputation was irreparably damaged. Many of his local supporters shifted their perception of him. Olive Schreiner condemned the raid as 'a murderous attack on the Transvall [sic] by the Chartered forces'. She also noted that Rhodes 'has believed that with the same ... injustice with which he has handled the natives he may handle the well-armed Boers'.[42] For peace to be secured between the Boers and Britain, 'Rhodes must depart from public life and the Charter revoked'.[43] Schreiner warned that, as long as Rhodes remained, 'there is war to the depth between Dutch and English. To cause that is the one way in which he can yet justify himself and creep back to power. He will do it indirectly, but he will do it'. But she did not believe Rhodes would go quietly, so those opposed to him should be prepared 'to stand by our guns, with pen and tongue'.[44]

That the Jameson Raid was an act of imperialism is hard to refute. But while the Raid was crushed, Rhodes himself was not defeated. Imperial ambitions merely mutated, and a new high commissioner for South Africa was appointed: Alfred Milner. In 1899 he was behind a new war against the Afrikaners,[45] 'a classic example of imperialist aggression prompted by capitalist greed'.[46] The same greed and aggression that had animated Rhodes less than five years earlier was at the centre of Milner's war. Schreiner described the conflict as 'a capitalist war'. She wrote that the war would be one of many, noting that it would recur 'again and again on larger and bloodier fields ... Of course, this war is just as much though in a subtler manner, because veiled behind the semblance of nationality, a capitalist war'.[47] The war ended in 1902, but as Schreiner had predicted, it laid the blueprint for South Africa's capitalist future. The British and the Boers signed the Treaty of Vereeniging in 1902. Despite the participation of 'armed natives', as Schreiner called them, Africans were excluded from the signing of the treaty and indeed from any meaningful participation in the political and economic life of the emergent entity known as South Africa. Milner actively campaigned for settlement by British citizens as a way of ensuring the enduring power of the British over the Dutch and the native populations. His views were expounded in a document entitled 'The Settlement in South Africa: On the importance of attracting a Loyal Population to settle upon and to own the land'. He advocated mastery 'by tenacity and strength ... combined with consistency and justice'. Milner urged the imperial government not to create difficulties for itself 'by attempting to conciliate by concessions'. Importantly,

> unless the predominance of the Dutch in the population of the country districts and as the owners of the land [and therefore] of the country, is largely modified if not destroyed, the security of England's position in South Africa,

and her trust and confidence in it as a loyal and reliable portion of the British Empire will be less than complete.

Milner went on to argue that, unless adequate measures were taken to attract settlers of the right sort to be 'the foundation and the strength of permanent British rule in South Africa, then whatever fabric of Government may be reared, will be but built upon the sand'.[48]

The main concern of the British was control of the mines of the Transvaal. Ben Magubane notes that the British settled generously with the Boers in order to obtain the gold mines, following which the Boers became 'the grudging vassals of British imperialism', to be repaid in land and native labour.[49] With the treaty concluded, processes for the construction of a new state began. A central issue was obtaining labour for the mines, industry and agriculture. Labour was in short supply, as Schreiner notes: 'This is a funny little place: no baker whose bread you can eat, no dress maker and above all no servant ... I have offered a boy 2/6 just to come and help me carry up the coal from the cellar from the stove fire but he refuses. I don't quite see how I am to keep on living here if I can't get any help.'[50]

Milner soon got to work. One of his first acts was to appoint John Buchan as a key member of 'Milner's Kindergarten', a group of bureaucrats trained at Oxford and Cambridge, who were advisors to Milner. Their influence was so profound that even after Milner's exit from the political scene, a number of them remained in office and continued to shape South Africa's policy. Buchan had graduated from Oxford with a degree in the classics. As private secretary to Milner, he became a key player in devising policy and overseeing its implementation and enforcement. The necessity for inequality in social standing and education between Africans and Europeans was one of his chief concerns. In 1903, Buchan published *The African Colony: Studies in the Reconstruction*, which was the main source of policy reference for much of Milner's government. Buchan argued that those who are educated should govern, and since Europeans knew more than Africans, it was justifiable to put them in control. Buchan believed that there was 'no common standard' in the South African community, and therefore no possibility of 'social and political equality'.[51] He explained:

Between the most ignorant white man and the black man there is fixed for the present an impassable gulf, not of colour but of mind. The native is often quick of understanding, industrious, curiously logical, but he lives and moves in a mental world incredibly distant from ours. The medium of his thought, so to speak, is so unique that the results are out of all relation to ourselves. Mentally he is as crude and naïve as a child, with a child's curiosity and ingenuity, and a child's practical inconsequence. Morally he has none of the traditions of self-discipline and order, which are implicit, though often in a degraded form in white people. In a word, he cannot be depended upon as an individual save under fairly vigilant restraint; and in the mass he forms an unknown quantity.[52]

He went on to detail an educational programme he deemed suitable for native children. The teaching of natives, 'if it is to produce any practical good', should be confined to the elements and to technical instruction. This is because the 'native mind' is very ready to learn anything which can be taught by concrete instances, and most forms of manual labour 'come as easily to him as to the white man. When boys are taught everywhere carpentry and iron work and the rudiments of trade, and the girls sewing and basket making and domestic employments, a far more important influence will have been introduced than the Latin grammar or the primer of history.'[53] Buchan's ideas fitted into the grand policy scheme of the nascent country. Mine labour was in short supply. The Anglo-Boer War had reduced the labour force by 50 000, while labour needs were estimated to be in the region of 150 000. A new country and a new economy had to be built. This required road construction, the revival of agriculture and a wide-scale industrial programme. South Africa's potential as the mining capital of the world could only be realised by a constant flow of labour to the Transvaal. Although Africans had been kept out of the political system, the mining bosses were acutely aware that they had to be brought into the economy for the system to function. But as what? The answer was provided in a memorandum drawn up by fifteen mining engineers representing the Transvaal Chamber of Mines, for the attention of Lord Chamberlain and Milner.

The memorandum held that the desire of those 'connected with the Rand' – i.e. the mining bosses – was that 'good wages should be paid to all white employees and at the same time the greatest efficiency and competency should be insisted upon'.[54] This would ensure that the best labour in the world was attracted to the goldfields. If wages paid to the white employees were good, 'the dissatisfied would always be very easily replaced'. Yet the notion of a good white worker being paid the best possible wage was not enough. African workers had to be brought into the fold. The memorandum concluded by pointing out that, if a combination could be found between 'actual muscular work' to be carried out 'by the brute force of the native and the intellectual and skilled work by the white man', South Africa would have 'the happiest condition of affairs for working this great gold mining industry'.[55] In order to achieve this, the entire way of life of the Africans had to be reconstructed. The mining companies put pressure on the colonial government to ensure the availability of labour for the mines, including the disruption of their social and family structure:

The Committee suggests (1) more legal and moral pressure to compel a greater number of natives to work and for longer periods; (2) recruiting over a larger area and with more vigour; (3) importation of Asiatics ... What does (1) mean? What moral pressure is we can understand; but what is legal pressure, when the native does not work, as the Committee tells us, because he does not want the money? Can there be any large number of natives who are released from the necessity of working by the possession of many wives? In all other polygamous countries nine-tenths of the men have one wife only.

The education of Africans needed to fit into the colonial and industrial framework, and Africans had to be educated to know their station in life and not aspire to the European way of life. Milner proved to be the perfect candidate to achieve this goal. Through his efforts in the Anglo-Boer War, the whole country was now under the control of the British. Milner would be given the task of creating a new economy to serve British financial interests. As a bureaucrat, he was talented, and he possessed a sharp intellect. He was 'precise in all matters and possessed a logical and lucid mind. He digested and retained reports of memoranda easily, and was able to see through a plethora of confusing details to the heart of an administrative problem'.[56] Precisely because of these talents, the colonial secretary Joseph Chamberlain gave Milner unfettered control over the shaping of South African policy. At the heart of it was the native question, the related issue of property and the provision of an education fit for the economy. Milner was the man to balance imperial goals, and to do so with rigor and exactitude.

Creating a 'useful and contented' labour force
Milner appointed the South African Native Affairs Commission, which duly commenced its work in 1903. Its preoccupation was the black male body, its control and domination, including control of its mind, its desires. The main target of the commission, apart from the conversion of Africans into labour units in the colonial economy, was to 'civilise' Africans. A civilised native was any native 'holding land in their own right', and a 'barbarian' referred to those 'who still cling to the tribal system and communal occupation of land'. Labour would be a primary instrument for the civilisation of Africans. The commission report seems to imply that *any* form of contact with the European economy constituted 'education' for Africans:

It has been represented to the Commission with some force that the native is more useful and contented when brought under the control of the European and so acquires habits of industry and a knowledge of the simpler forms of the agricultural and mechanical arts. That a process of education in the foregoing sense is actively going on has been made clear. The many thousands of natives constantly employed on farms, railways and public works, and in mines and workshops are inevitably being brought under what is, in the wider sense of the word, an educational influence.[57]

The consensus of opinion among the authors of the report was that, in some instances, education created 'in the natives an aggressive spirit, arising no doubt from an exaggerated sense of individual self-importance, which renders them less docile and less disposed to be contented with the position for which nature or circumstances have fitted them'. Despite this misgiving, the report noted that education was beneficial and of 'advantage to the community' because it had raised the level of intelligence of natives and increased their capacity as workers as well as their earning power.[58] In order to address the perception of educated natives overestimating their self-worth and importance, it was recommended that industrial training be tailored to correctly position the native both societally and economically. The report expressed concern about the potential for arousing the political aspirations of African students who were educated in the 'negro colleges' in the United States.[59]

> The independent native bodies have already sent or have encouraged the parents to send youths to America for a course of instruction in the Negro colleges. The character of the education of these colleges, with the accompanying grant of 'degrees' are low on qualifications and the atmosphere of racial animosity in which the education is acquired, render an extension of this practice undesirable.[60]

While the report makes reference to the low standard of qualifications at such colleges, a prime concern was the 'racial animosity' they allegedly generated. For Africans, however, there was no such animosity. These colleges provided space for Africans to consider their own position in the world. Having conquered by military means, the colonial state aimed not only to turn the black masses into a large pool of semi-skilled labourers, but also to create a docile educated class that would not question the economic and cultural hegemony of Empire. However, as the following paragraphs demonstrate, education, especially in the hands of the colonised, created a sense of awareness that disrupted the consensus of the colonial state. The visit of Fisk University's Jubilee Singers in 1890, after a ten-year political hiatus, provides a vital point of departure. It was during that visit that many Africans began to recover the belief in their ability to resist the encroachment of Empire. Paradoxically, however, the new forms of resistance required the adoption of the ways of Empire, the most significant of which was the law. So, how did this begin?

'We need our own magistrates, judges and lawyers'

Colonialism and imperialism were maintained not only by the force of arms or the forces of commerce, but by the force of an idea: the supremacy of Europe. But ten years after Britain's final military assaults of the late 1870s in Xhosaland and Zululand, a new form of resistance employing the institutions of colonialism emerged. It was driven by Western-educated African intellectuals. The movement began in the Cape, and its circumstances were accidental. In June 1890, an African-American choir that hailed from the Hampton Institute in Virginia arrived at the Cape. Their songs – 'Ethiopian airs' as they were called – were based on the religious movement known as Ethiopianism that has its foundations in Psalm 68, verse 31 of the Bible: 'Princes shall come out of Egypt; Ethiopia shall soon stretch out her hands unto God'. African-American interpreters of scripture read this as a prophecy: one day, God will redeem Africa. As the redemption would take place in Ethiopia, Africa would be the crucible of the new salvation. The choir's mission was to hold a number of fundraising concerts to save its university from threatened closure. The Hampton Institute had been established in 1866 to educate African Americans, following the end of slavery in that country. But the university had run into financial difficulties, and its survival was at risk. It was therefore decided to embark upon a fundraising tour of the world. A choir was formed, and after touring the United Kingdom, Australia and South Africa, enough money was raised to save the university. In the Cape, however, the choir did more than fundraise: it left behind a legacy that would shape the aspirations of Africans for generations to come.

The Jubilee Singers were surprised at the multiracial character of their South African audiences. But outside of the protected environment of the theatre, they discovered that racism was alive. In a letter written by one of the members to the *Cape Argus*, their experiences are recorded thus:

Everyone seemed captivated with the singing; never heard such singing in all their lives, and they said, 'And just to think that black people should do it.' The latter remark will give you some idea of a feeling of prejudice; well, so it is. There is no country in the world where prejudice is so strong as here in Africa. The native today is treated as badly as ever the slave was treated in Georgia. Here in Africa the native laws are most unjust; such as any Christian people would be ashamed of. Do you credit a law in a civilised community compelling every man of dark skin, even though he is a citizen of another country, to be in his house by 9 o'clock at night, or he is arrested ... these laws exist in the Transvaal and Orange Free State, which are governed by the Dutch, who placed every living creature before the native.[61]

Nevertheless, audiences throughout the country were enthralled. Performances usually began with songs like 'Swing Low, Sweet Chariot', 'Still Away to Jesus' and 'Go Down Moses'. The *Cape Argus* noted that singing such as that of the visiting choir had 'never been before heard in this country':

> Their selection consists of a peculiar kind of pipe song, the different voices joining in at most unexpected moments in a wild kind of harmony ... it is without doubt one of the attributes of the race to which they belong, and in their most sacred songs they sing at times inspired, as if they were lifting up their voices in praise of God with hopes of liberty.[62]

The songs were, of course, deeply rooted in slavery and the yearning for freedom. 'Go Down Moses' tells a tale of an instruction from God to Moses to go to Egypt and tell Pharaoh to 'Let my people go'. The lyrics of 'Swing Low, Sweet Chariot' are similarly a call to freedom:

> Swing low, sweet chariot,
> Coming for to carry me home.
> Swing low, sweet chariot,
> Coming for to carry me home.
> I looked over Jordan, what do I see,
> Coming for to carry me home.
> A band of angels coming after me,
> Coming for to carry me home.
> I looked over Jordan, what do I see,
> Coming for to carry me home.
> If you get back to heaven before I do,
> Coming for to carry me home.
> You'll tell all my friends, I'll be coming there too,
> Coming for to carry me home.

The Jubilee Singers were widely popular at the Cape. The governor, Sir Henry Loch, attended one of the concerts and is said to have been most impressed.[63] The choir established a relationship with the local Dutch population. A teacher at a local school, who had previously taught at the Hampton Institute, arranged for the choir to perform in the Transvaal. A member of the audience later wrote: 'It is wonderful to see our staid Dutch people go to ecstasies over them, and our servants who were allowed to go into the anteroom to listen to them were taken right off their feet.'[64] One of the attendees at a concert in February 1891 was the

Transvaal president, Paul Kruger. When the choir sang 'Nobody Knows the Trouble I See', Kruger was moved to tears.[65] Afterwards, Kruger shook the hand of the conductor, Orpheus McAdoo, and confessed that this was the first time he had shaken the hand of a black person.[66]

African audiences responded to the choir with much admiration, particularly its message concerning education, self-determination and political emancipation. *The Kaffrarian Watchman*, a King William's Town newspaper, reported that the local rural audience were also somewhat bewildered, and

> could not quite understand what sort of people they were. Some of them hesitated to class them as kaffirs as they seemed so smart and tidy in appearance, and moved about with all the ease and freedom among the white people that a high state of civilisation and education alone can give. Occasionally, however, a kaffir would salute a 'singer' in his own language, and when he fails to get a reply he would look puzzled, exclaim kwoku! And walk away wondering how his brother did not return the salute.

It is in such encounters that the true value of the Jubilee Singers becomes apparent. Their visit to the Cape coincided with a period of great dismantling and dispossession of societies. New identities were being forged, and a particularly important identity was being established through education. The Singers were seen by the African elite living in the Cape as an example of what education might accomplish for the native races of South Africa. It was also seen as a possible base from which transatlantic alliances could be forged in common struggles. When the choir performed in Kimberley, three educated Africans attended: Josiah Semouse, Patrick Lenkoane and Solomon Plaatje. The choir's last concert in Kimberley was aptly titled 'Natives and Coloured People'. Semouse paid tribute to the 'great American singers' in the local newsletter, *Leselinyana*:

> Gentlemen, I do not find the words to describe the way in which these people sang. Unless I am mistaken, I can say that they sang like angels singing Hosannah in heaven. All the people on the diamond fields agree that they sing better than anybody else, white or black. Today they have their own schools, primary, secondary and high schools, and also universities. They are run by them without the help of the whites. They have magistrates, judges, lawyers, bishops, ministers and evangelists, and school masters. Some have learnt a craft such as building, etc. etc. When will the day come when the African people will be like the Americans? When will they stop being slaves and become nations with their own government?[67]

These sentiments were shared by influential leaders in the black community. Jabavu penned a stirring tribute:

> It would strongly savour of presumption for a native African of this part to venture a critique on his brethren from America, who are now visiting this quarter of their fatherland, and whose position, socially, is being deservedly pointed at on all hands as one that the native here should strive to attain to. As Africans we are, of course, proud of the achievements of those of our race. Their visit will do their countrymen here no end of good. Already it has suggested reflection to many who, without such a demonstration, would have remained sceptical as to the possibility, not to say probability, of the natives of this country being raised to anything above remaining as perpetually hewers of wood and drawers of water. The recognition of the latent abilities of the natives ... cannot fail to exert an influence for the mutual good of all the inhabitants of this country. The visit of our friends, besides, will lead to the awakening in their countrymen here of an interest in the history of the civilisation of the negro race in America, and a knowledge of their history is sure to result beneficial to our people generally.[68]

Semouse, Plaatje and Jabavu were all breaking with the prevailing narrative. Education for Africans did not have to carry an industrial slant, and they could aspire to be 'magistrates, judges, lawyers, bishops, ministers and evangelists, and school masters'. The narrative of missionaries and their vision of black education could be broken. From then on, the Jubilee Singers were flooded with requests from black South Africans for educational opportunities in the United States, which were referred to universities for blacks such as the Hampton Institute in Virginia and Wilberforce University in Ohio.[69]

The Jubilee Singers instil self-belief

The impact of the Jubilee Singers was profound. Their destinations had included the British colonies of the Cape and Natal, where the education of Africans was in a formative stage. In the Cape, the effect of the visits was immediate. In 1891 an African choir was formed, drawing on the same message of self-liberation. Africans in the Cape decided to raise funds to establish their own university which, like the Hampton Institute, would focus on advanced technical education for local Africans. The majority were alumni of Lovedale, and they called themselves the African Native Choir. The members included Josiah Semouse, Paul Xiniwe, Eleanor Xiniwe, Charlotte Manye and Johanna Jonkers. Having raised sufficient funds locally, the choir set sail for England, where, in the words of Semouse, they hoped to gain 'civilisation and education'.[70] With this trip began a broad exchange of culture, education and knowledge. Prior to this, there had been a few isolated instances of South African blacks who were educated in the United Kingdom. The significance of the African Native Choir was the transportation of an entire culture to the UK. Ordinary people in London would interact directly, learn for themselves, and clear their minds of prejudice through exposure to the African Native Choir.

During the trip, Semouse recorded their experiences. He began by informing curious Londoners about the history of his people. Addressing a hotel owner who had shown interest in the background of the choristers, he said:

Africa, on the side of the Indian Ocean, from Natal to near the Portuguese colony, was ruled by a king by the name of Chaka. He was the lion of that whole country. That country in the west was called Embo, its ruler had a son whose name was Tshawe. One day, Tshawe and a young group of men (iboto) and young women went westwards (the young men carrying food with them). After they left, all of the men and the women committed adultery. According to Zulu custom, the whole group, together with the girls should have been killed. None was to be left out, as it should have been a day of total destruction, all should have been killed because of only one person. As a result, the whole group feared to return home and carried on with their hunt, down the coast to what is now known as the Cape Colony. There the iboto met the bushman (baroa). The bushmen named the iboto, Xhosas. Those bushmen came from the west ... Their home country is the Cape; it is there that the whites, when they came to this country, found them. They fled to the north and east of Africa. What is known is that they, like all other African nations, descended from the son of Noah Ham ... The iboto formed itself into a nation, intermarried with the bushmen and then called itself Xhosa. That is why we find in the Xhosa language words which are called 'clicks' in the white man's language ... As a result of their inter-marriage with the bushmen, we find among the Xhosa reddish people with woven lined hair like that of the bushmen.[71]

Semouse continued to write home about his experiences in London. In one *Leselinyana* article,[72] he notes: 'London is a very big place, I have never experienced its end, I will explain it when I have seen where it ends and have thoroughly seen its end.' In a later piece he writes, 'All in all, I can say the things which I can see in this town are big and numerous, if I were to try and explain them, I would go mad.' The African Native Choir was a sensation in London, and their concerts were often sold out. Charlotte Manye recorded her bizarre experiences of British prejudice, as some Londoners commented: 'Look at their short hair, as though they have shaved, their eyes are black and beautiful, they have mouths and noses like people.' Such prejudice was, however, reflective of the time – as Dickens's description of 'noble savages' demonstrates:

> There is at present a party of Zulu Kaffirs exhibiting at the St. George's Gallery, Hyde Park Corner, London. These noble savages are represented in a most agreeable manner; they are seen in an elegant theatre, fitted with appropriate scenery of great beauty, and they are described in a very sensible and unpretending lecture, delivered with a modesty which is quite a pattern to all similar exponents. Though extremely ugly, they are much better shaped than such of their predecessors as I have referred to; and they are rather picturesque to the eye, though far from odoriferous to the nose. What a visitor left to his own interpretings and imaginings might suppose these noblemen to be about, when they give vent to that pantomimic expression which is quite settled to be the natural gift of the noble savage, I cannot possibly conceive; for it is so much too luminous for my personal civilisation that it conveys no idea to my mind beyond a general stamping, ramping, and raving, remarkable (as everything in savage life is) for its dire uniformity. But let us – with the interpreter's assistance, of which I for one stand so much in need – see what the noble savage does in Zulu Kaffirland.[73]

Dickens's attitude is one of utter contempt: 'if we have anything to learn from the noble savage, it is what to avoid. His virtues are a fable; his happiness is a delusion; his nobility, nonsense.'[74]

Although the concerts were spectacularly successful, with one attended by Queen Victoria, the trip eventually turned into a farce. Owing to the financial mismanagement of their agent, Englishman Jason Balmer, the choristers ran out of funds. Semouse accused Balmer of misappropriating funds and leaving the choir stranded. The choir was rescued by Dr James Stewart, founder of Lovedale College. Semouse expressed his debt of gratitude to Stewart: 'The favour and grace done by Dr Stewart to the singers of Africa' would never be 'forgotten by the elders and friends of the African Choir. Had it not been for Dr Stewart, we would have been scattered like sheep without a shepherd.' According to Veit Erlmann, the tour would ultimately be remembered as 'the pilgrimage to the source of light, the all-seeing eye, the very conscience and *theoria* of the world'.[75] Semouse, however, had not found his 'education and civilisation' in England, proving, as Erlmann suggests, that Joseph Conrad was correct when he said that England too 'has been one of the dark places of the earth'.[76]

Having failed in the quest for civilisation in England, the choir launched a second tour, not to Europe but to the United States. But there a further debacle ensued.

After travelling as far as Ohio, they again ran out of funds and were stranded. And no white man would come to their rescue. Instead, they were rescued by a black church, the African Methodist Episcopal Church. Its members had learnt of the plight of the Africans via local newspapers. They arranged funding for six of the singers to attend Wilberforce University, and this opened a new frontier.

In 1892, the Zulu Choir was formed in Edendale, Natal, also owing to the inspiring message of the Jubilee Singers. Edendale had been the site of the 'first enlightenment' in Zululand. It was there that Daniel Msimang opened the first Methodist mission, in response to the entreaties of missionary James Allison. Those who went through the mission went on to be educated at the Healdtown Wesleyan Training Institution in the Eastern Cape. The grandson of Daniel Msimang, Richard William Msimang, would become the first black South African to be admitted as a solicitor in London's Lincoln's Inn, some twenty years after the Zulu Choir first travelled to that city. Edendale became the epicentre for black Christian choral concerts, and a guiding light in the black encounter with modernity. The central figures in this encounter were the Msimangs and Saul Msane, who had been educated at Healdtown. Msane was an important figure in the Zulu Choir that toured London in the 1890s. The Christian converts, generally referred to as *amakholwa*, enjoyed a volatile, and at times ambivalent, relationship with the non-believers. Some Edendale residents had, in the war of 1879, sided with the British against the Zulu. But this did not imply an uncritical support of everything the British stood for. It was Saul Msane, a self-proclaimed convert, who, during the Zulu Choir's London tour, astonished the British by making a public declaration of support for King Dinuzulu ka Cetshwayo's return from exile on St Helena, and advocating for a meeting with Harriette Colenso.[77]

The Zulu Choir returned home in 1893. They had been inspired by what they perceived as the 'normalisation' of England, thereby disrupting – however momentarily – the supremacist mission of imperialism: the English were no longer experienced as distant, exotic and omnipotent creatures. Instead, England was merely a place with its own eccentricities, stupidities and violence. But the Zulu had also left their mark on the cultural make-up of London. The Londoners no longer relied on the jaundiced portrayals of natives from Africa provided by colonial administrators and missionaries. They now enjoyed first-hand accounts from Africans themselves. Twenty years later, when numerous black students began to enter British life, British society would be even more enlightened, and therefore accommodating towards black students from South Africa. The links established by the Jubilee Singers would form the foundation of tertiary studies for black South Africans, in Europe as well as America. By 1906 there were more than 150 black South Africans studying at American universities, including the black colleges in that country. Sebopioa Molema was one of them.

Molema obtained his secondary education at Zonnebloem College in Cape Town. The college was established specifically for the education of children of African chiefs from the Eastern Cape, though it later extended to the whole of South Africa. Molema's father, Silas, was a chief of the Tshidi Barolong, one of the Tswana clans of Mafeking. In August 1904, Molema left Zonnebloem to commence law studies at Wilberforce University in the United States. Just before leaving the college, he delivered a stinging indictment of Zonnebloem. He wrote that his younger brother Modiri should never be allowed to study at Zonnebloem, and should instead be sent to Lovedale – 'by far the best native school I know'. Many boys at Zonnebloem, he noted, 'indulge in liquor'. The speaking of English was 'not enforced as it should be'. Also, because of its close proximity to town, students stood the risk of mixing with 'bad companies'.[78]

Some three months later, in October 1904, Molema arrived at Wilberforce. Bishop Levi Jenkins Coppin, a former teacher at Zonnebloem, welcomed him to America and to Wilberforce, where Jenkins was now a teacher. But Molema was feeling 'very lonely here'. He had hoped to receive regular copies of the Tswana newspaper *Koranta ea Bechuana*, which 'would make me feel at home'. Still, he was pleased to be at Wilberforce, 'this great Negro University where young men from different parts of the globe gather for the cause of higher education'.[79] Education, he noted, was a blessing which he was very keen to acquire. Molema spent a year at the preparatory collegiate of Wilberforce before being accepted to the law degree in 1906. The faculty members to which new arrivals from South Africa were exposed included some of America's foremost black intellectuals. W.E.B. Du Bois lectured in English, German and classics; he had just returned from graduating in Germany. William Scarborough taught classical languages in the School of Theology; he had risen from slavery and become one of America's foremost philologists. Wilberforce was, according to Thozama April, distinguished by 'its underlying faith in the intellectual potential of the black race'.[80] Students were exposed to a full classical curriculum featuring ancient and modern languages, mathematics and science. Rhetoric and composition were included, and proper elocution was encouraged. Candidates in the ministry received training in everything from systematic theology to Hebrew, and the school also boasted a small law department. Four degrees were awarded: Bachelor of Arts, Bachelor of Divinity (awarded to graduates of Pyne's Theological Seminary), Bachelor of Science and Bachelor of Law.

In 1908, Molema completed his law degree. But he did not return to South Africa immediately. Instead, he chose to apply to practise as an attorney in the United States. By 1910, he was able to write home from his new address as an associate attorney with the law firm I.L. Purcell Attorney, 120 West Street, Jacksonville, Florida. This was a momentous occasion. For the first time, a black South African could practise law in the United States. Molema then decided to return to South Africa, where he hoped to put his legal education to use. But he faced a hurdle: South Africa did not recognise qualifications from black colleges of the United States. He returned in 1911 and applied for admission to practise as an attorney in the Cape Colony. While the Americans had accepted him with open arms, this was not the case in the country of his birth. The Cape Law Society rejected his qualification, arguing that it could not vouch for the standard and quality of his degree. If he wished to be admitted as an attorney, he should study afresh. Molema refused, and returned to Mafeking, where he served as secretary to his uncle, chief of the Barolong, a position he held until his death. So, Wilberforce may be said to have produced South Africa's first black attorney, and while it did not produce the second one, namely Alfred Mangena, it did make an important contribution to the latter's decision to study law.

Wilberforce, Charlotte Maxeke and other Eastern Cape lawyers
We now turn to the person who inspired Molema to take up law. Her name is Charlotte Manye, though she is better known by her marital name, Charlotte Maxeke. She was one of the first South African women to obtain a university education, and probably the country's first African female graduate. Like Molema, Maxeke was educated at Wilberforce University. It is worth exploring the wider significance of Wilberforce in producing a generation of African scholars who contributed to the emergence of radical thought in the early nineteenth century. To do that, it is necessary to briefly sketch the period and the personalities. African legal scholars were clearly shaped by, and drew intellectual strength from, these US-educated scholars. America as a fountain of new ideas was important in and of itself. But 'negro' colleges were of special significance. Not only did they use education as a basis of self-awareness and self-reliance, they saw it as a means of waging new struggles for emancipation. The anti-slavery message resonated with black South Africans, and the African-American experience of racial segregation and white supremacy intersected, overlapped and collided with their own in striking ways.

Charlotte Maxeke arrived at Wilberforce in 1895. She was one of five students from the Eastern Cape, including Magazo Fanelo Sakie, James Nxaninxani Kombolo, John Boyson Radisi and Edward Magaya. Maxeke's wish was that 'there were more of our people here to enjoy the privileges of Wilberforce and then go back and teach our people so our home lose that awful name "the Dark continent" and be properly called the continent of light'.[81] Of the group of five students, Maxeke was the only one who graduated from Wilberforce. Magaya graduated from Lincoln University in 1903. April argues that these students were a product of a specific class at a particular historical moment. 'They were drawn from a highly conscious Christian elite in which respectability and commitment to Western education reigned supreme.'[82] But, as they saw themselves as the 'talented tenth' – to borrow a phrase from Du Bois[83] – they had a duty towards their fellow Africans.

Maxeke displayed exceptional commitment to her fellow Africans, both at home and abroad. In 1896, she facilitated the college registration of Chalmers Moss and Henry Msikinya, both from Kimberley. The Moss and Msikinya families were both involved in the legal system. Moss's father, Joseph, was an interpreter at the High Court of Griqualand West. Msikinya's brother, Jonas, was also a court interpreter, at Beaconsfield. Chalmers Moss died within a year of arriving in America, in 1898. Henry Msikinya returned to South Africa in 1901, after completing his degree. Two more students, Charles Dube and Theodore Kakaza, arrived at Wilberforce in 1896. At eighteen years old, they were the youngest of the South African students there. Dube was the son of an ordained minister of the American Board of Commissioners for Foreign Missions (ABCFM), and the younger brother of John Dube, the founding president of the South African Native National Congress, later the ANC. Kakaza hailed from a Wesleyan congregation in Port Elizabeth. They were followed by James Tantsi and Marshall Maxeke, who joined the student body at Wilberforce towards the end of 1896. By the end of the nineteenth century, African Christians from Cape Town and Bechuanaland were filtering back across the Atlantic from Wilberforce.

It was this generation that Maxeke joined when she went to Ohio. She inspired not only Molema, but also Stephen Gumede, though after qualifying in 1910 he did not seek admission to practise in South Africa. Maxeke's return to South Africa in 1901 made national headlines. At the time, Alfred Mangena was active in the politics of the Cape, and after a chance meeting with Maxeke he too embraced the idea of studying law, though he eventually went to Lincoln's Inn in London rather than the United States. Alfred Xuma makes the following mention of Mangena in his biographical account of Maxeke:

> I learn that a certain gentleman who during her return from abroad was treasurer of a certain organization in Cape Town, was so inspired by her achievement that he committed the righteous sin of converting the funds with which he was entrusted to his own use to pay his passage to England and for his education there. Later this gentleman became one of the strongest and ablest black barristers in South Africa.[84]

In a sense, then, Alfred Mangena's decision to study law may be said to reveal the influence of Wilberforce University and other black colleges in America. He was inspired too by Henry Sylvester Williams, a personal friend of W.E.B. Du Bois.

Williams became the first black person to practise as an advocate at the Cape Bar in 1903. Likewise, Pixley ka Isaka Seme was encouraged to study law in the United States by John Dube, whose brother had been a student at Wilberforce.

In focusing on figures such as Mangena, Msimang and Seme, it is necessary to recall the structural and personal circumstances of their lives: the loss of land owing to the colonial aggression of the late nineteenth century; the emergence of black radical thinking during the same period; the influence of Wilberforce; and the individual contributions of Charlotte Maxeke. This book is an attempt to restore the historical record, thereby giving these people and their ideas the recognition that is long overdue, and well deserved.

PART II

LAWYERS

2

'Fair play and no favours'

> Mr Williams is a man of extraordinary pluck. He has built up for himself
> a practice in Cape Colony in the teeth of the bitterest prejudice of the
> whites, to whom the spectacle of the coloured man practising his law as a
> barrister appeared something unnatural and abominable. His professional
> brethren boycotted him. He was shut out from the circuit and bar messes,
> and everything was done by the majority of the bar – Englishmen, by the
> way – to demonstrate how hollow a hypocrisy is in the so-called equality
> of rights under the British flag.
> – William Stead, *Review of Reviews*, 1905

The founder of Pan-Africanism, Henry Sylvester Williams, is a largely forgotten figure, virtually unknown within the local legal community. Yet not only did the Trinidadian coin the term Pan-Africanism,[1] he also founded the African Association in 1897,[2] which spread the message of Pan-Africanism among many nations of the world. In 1903, Williams was admitted to the Cape Bar, and thereafter he practised as an advocate of the Supreme Court in the Cape Colony. He was the first black person to do so. His ideas of Pan-Africanism, which emphasised self-reliance and mutual cooperation among Africans pursuing common ideals of liberation and freedom from all forms of bondage and oppression, including slavery and racism, have radiated across continents and generations. Writing from Victorian England in 1901, Williams described the 'constant request' of Africans as one of 'fair play and no favours'.[3] Since he was not South African by birth, the circumstances of his arrival and his admission to practise law are worthy of explanation.

Between 1875 and 1905, there was a population explosion in the number of black Americans and West Indians living in the Cape Colony. In 1904, 483 people classified as 'mixed/other' were of Caribbean or American origin. This represents an increase of almost 138 per cent over the number reported in 1891. Between 1875 and 1891, the number of 'mixed/other' Americans and West Indians rose by 410 per cent. The overwhelming majority of these immigrants to the Cape were from the Caribbean, with most coming from the British West Indies. Eighty-five per cent of those from the Caribbean were from Barbados, British Guiana or Jamaica. According to the 1904 census, 93 were from the United States, and another 96 were possibly from there.[4] Three main factors explain the presence of West Indians in the Cape. First, West Indians who had fought on the side of the British in the Anglo-Boer War were permitted to reside in the colony. As Robert Vinson notes, around 1895 the majority of West Indians at the Cape were employed as stevedores.[5] The West Indies–born employment agent for dockworkers, James Wilson, was a skilful recruiter. He marketed not only the relatively high-paying jobs in Cape Town, but also its advantages as a 'really modern city' and 'one of the largest and finest cities in the world', comparable to New York or London. This motivated scores of West Indian workers skilled in maritime jobs to seek employment at the Cape at a time when such skills were in short supply. Furthermore, West Indians were economically excluded and oppressed in their native lands. While they had been liberated from slavery, it would take years to reconstruct the economic, social and cultural wreckage caused by the transatlantic slave trade. 'We were black and the only way we could do anything along the lines we were interested in was by going abroad,' lamented C.L.R. James, a native of Trinidad.[6]

West Indians who migrated to the Cape during this era became very well-off. While referred to as 'sea kaffirs' by whites, they were in fact, and in the eyes of the law, far better off than their South African native counterparts. Not only did they have skills that attracted a high level of demand, they were also insulated from the segregationist policies of the Cape. Unlike local blacks, West Indians and African Americans were regarded as 'honorary whites', exempt from the racially discriminatory laws of the Cape.

The material advantages they enjoyed as a consequence of their position of relative equality vis-à-vis the white community soon translated into achievements in the professions. The first black doctor in the colony was Andrew Jackson, a West Indian educated at Edinburgh University in Scotland.[7] It was not long before Jackson ran the most successful medical practice in Cape Town.[8] West Indians had arrived in their utopia – but this would not last long.

The clouds of racial discrimination were gathering. The post-war settlement, competition for jobs with white workers and the hardening of racial attitudes among whites resulted in fundamental changes to the position of West Indians. First, they lost their status as honorary whites. Race now counted more than a person's place of origin. In 1903, Harry Dean, an African American living in South Africa, complained about being compelled to 'carry a pass like a native in his barbarous state'.[9] Second, black dockworkers had to give way to white workers in certain job categories. Third, the position of the native black population was deteriorating. West Indians could no longer enjoy the privileges associated with being white in a country where the screws of racism were tightening. A new ideology was required to communicate black struggles – and it is at this point that Henry Sylvester Williams and his Pan-Africanism arrive on the scene.

'No power of thinking and no exact knowledge'
Williams's date of birth is uncertain; some scholars give it as 1867, while his biographer, Marika Sherwood, claims he was born in 1869.[10] Even his place of birth is disputed. It is generally accepted, however, that Williams grew up in Trinidad, where he qualified as a teacher. Later on, in search of greener pastures, he left for the United States, where he did menial work. Following this, he enrolled at Dalhousie University in Nova Scotia, Canada. He was praised for his oratory, but his overall academic performance was dismal, with one teacher noting that Williams 'had no power of thinking and no exact knowledge'.[11] The result was that he failed the first year of his law studies at Dalhousie Law School, and subsequently abandoned academic studies in Canada.

Williams then travelled to England, where he enrolled at King's College London to study Latin, while preparing to sit for his entrance exams at the Inns of Court. He passed these in 1897, which paved the way for him to enrol at Gray's Inn, where he trained as a barrister.

When Williams was called to the English Bar in June 1902, he had a solid political reputation. Two years earlier, in 1900, he was a key figure in the organisation of the first Pan-African Conference, held in London. More than fifty blacks from Africa and the diaspora attended the conference. They included W.E.B Du Bois and Booker T. Washington, respected figures in African-American history of the time. Walter Benson Rubusana and John Tengo Jabavu, the most influential educated black South Africans of their generation and key proponents of Pan-Africanism, were invited to the conference, but had to send their apologies owing to a lack of funds. Williams was impressed by the contributions of black South Africans who spoke at the conference. He was also distressed by their account of the general condition of the black population in the country, and began to consider the possibility of applying his legal training in South Africa. Later, having qualified as a barrister, Williams would set his sights on Cape Town. But why did he specifically choose the Cape? It is here that we need to turn to a little-known woman named Alice Kinloch.

Alice Kinloch and the foundations of Pan-Africanism
The condition of black South Africans was not a central consideration of the nascent Pan-Africanism – at least, not until a chance meeting in Birmingham, England, between Williams and a black woman from Kimberley in 1897. Her name was Alice Victoria Kinloch, an obscure figure in the historiography of Pan-Africanism. Yet had it not been for Kinloch, South Africa's first black advocate may never have set foot in the Cape, let alone considered the Cape Bar as a professional option. Kinloch was born in Natal, but she took her surname from her mining-engineer husband, Edmund, whose father was Scottish and his

mother Zulu. Alice and Edmund met on the diamond fields in Kimberley, where she worked for the local newspaper.

In 1896 the couple moved to the United Kingdom, where Alice exposed the exploitation of African mineworkers. In one of the public lectures organised by the Aborigines' Protection Society (APS), she described the 'slave-like' conditions on the diamond mines, pointing to the 'two evils' facing black people in South Africa: the greed of the mining bosses and the duplicity of the missionaries.[12]

Immediately impressed by Kinloch, Williams invited her to regular informal meetings among a circle of blacks living in the UK. It was at these meetings that the establishment of the African Association, forerunner to the Pan-African Conference, was first conceived, in 1897. Kinloch's encounter with Williams thrust her onto the national stage, and she spoke on public platforms for a defined constituency, the African Association. On 5 May 1897, the *Yorkshire Herald* carried a report that Kinloch had described the compound system, which held in confinement the 'native labour' without which the Kimberley mines could not survive. The compound system and the conditions at the mines were another form of slavery, a system tolerated because of the proselytising missionaries' support; confined in such compounds, African men were within easy reach of the 'word of God'. Kinloch contended that the churches could not be trusted to prevent the excesses of hard labour and similar abuse. Moreover, racial segregation was promoted by the churches, with missionaries routinely flogging church members. In this way, 'The missionaries followed in the footsteps of the financial man.'[13] She further criticised the pass-law system for restricting the freedom of movement of Africans.

When Kinloch was challenged for generalising with regard to the behaviour of missionaries, she argued that only a small minority treated Africans decently. The majority perfectly fitted her characterisation of duplicity, she countered.[14] Kinloch's influence and activism resulted in the African Association adopting a resolution to protest against the measures used to control the movement of Africans, and to agitate against forced labour. Those resolutions were then sent to the prime minister and the secretary of state for the colonies, or colonial secretary.[15] Under the thinly veiled pseudonym 'A.V. Alexander', which was in fact her maiden name, Kinloch published a pamphlet, *Are South African Diamonds Worth Their Cost* – a devastating critique of the country's diamond trade. She argued that the value of diamonds could not be calculated solely in terms of the financial benefit they brought: the human cost was pre-eminent. The cost to race relations resulting from the appalling conditions and treatment of black workers in the mines was incalculable. Workers were imprisoned for refusing to work and were given unduly harsh punishments for trivial offences. No amount of money, she contended, could compensate for the human suffering that was the *sine qua non* of mining.[16]

Moved by these accounts, Williams referred to Kinloch as 'a woman of our race'.[17] Though her criticism of missionaries did not sit well with some sections of the British public, she remained steadfast in her views. She told the editor of *The New Age* that it was astounding that people in the United Kingdom did not appreciate her criticism of missionaries. She accepted that there were some good missionaries, but these were 'very few'.[18] For a long time, the perceptions of the general UK public were positive towards missionary work, and it was, in part, through the work of Kinloch that a spotlight was shone on the malevolence of much missionary work and its complicity in colonialism.

Kinloch's influence on Williams was immediate, and he referred to the compound system as un-Christian, degrading and illegal.[19] The system was a 'blight' upon Christian England, he charged.[20] Addressing an audience in Trinidad in 1901, Williams contended that African mineworkers were induced to work on contracts for British companies which lodged workers in enclosed compounds, without their wives or children, for periods of three months at a time, at the miserable wage of two pence a day. If they were two minutes late for work they were flogged, and at the end of each shift they were drugged and subjected to a search for stolen diamonds.[21]

Kinloch's campaign soon gained traction beyond the Pan-African sphere of influence. In August 1901, *The New Age* reported that African rebels who had surrendered in Bechuanaland were being 'marched down to Cape Town and hired out to farmers at ten shillings a month'. If this was not a form of slavery, the paper rhetorically asked, what was? Williams, recalling the conditions of slavery of his own people, described these 'prisoners' of the Matabele War as poor and unfortunate. They had been sent to Cape Town by a chartered company and then sold, as in the days of slavery in the United States. The British public, said Williams, was incensed by this. But it was Kinloch who travelled the length and breadth of England, speaking on behalf of indigenous South Africans working in unbearable labour conditions, against their wishes. In this, she was following in the tradition of Dyani Tshatshu, who had travelled across the country in 1836. The tradition was passed on to Sol Plaatje, who spent many years in England engaged in similar activism.

Kinloch's influence on the consolidation of the Pan-Africanist ideology is incontestable. When Williams set about organising the first Pan-African Conference, originally planned to take place in May 1900, it was the plight of the 'natives under British Rule', including those of South Africa, that was uppermost in his mind.[22] While Kinloch exerted an indirect influence over the male planners of the Pan-African Conference, her impact was also direct. The first Pan-African Conference was organised by the African Association, of which she was the founding treasurer. However, by the time the preparatory committee of the Pan-African

Conference met on 12 June 1899, Kinloch had returned to Natal. She had also abandoned her marriage to Edmund, and was now married to a Zulu man. Her influence, however, loomed large. Williams would acknowledge her role, not only in positioning the interests of South African blacks at the forefront of the Pan-African agenda, but also in shaping Pan-Africanism itself. Writing to Harriette Colenso in June 1899, Williams attributed the existence of the association to Kinloch: 'the Association is the result of Mrs. Kinloch's work in England and the feeling that as British subjects we ought to be heard in our own affairs'.[23]

In setting up the preparatory committee for the Pan African Conference, it was decided to include a native South African: J.T. Jabavu. It is unclear whether Kinloch played a role in his appointment to the committee. Jabavu was an important figure in the politics of South Africa as editor of the weekly *Imvo Zabantsundu*. Unlike Kinloch, Jabavu was ambivalent about missionaries. His time at the South African missionary institutions of Healdtown and Lovedale had made him appreciate the benevolent aspects of missionary work. On the preparatory committee, Jabavu worked with internationally acclaimed black thinkers, such as Booker T. Washington and W.E.B. Du Bois.

Along with Kinloch, Williams had been a key figure in the establishment of the African Association, eventually becoming its secretary. In 1897 the Nigerian newspaper, the *Lagos Standard*, carried an article announcing the establishment of the association at a time 'when the voice of black men should be heard independently in their own affairs and that this could best be achieved by an organisation of this kind, having its headquarters in London, the seat of the government'. A further encouragement was 'the treatment of the natives in Africa, principally South, East and West Africa', which had 'not been conducive to the proper welfare of the natives under the English flag and control'. Moreover, in Bechuanaland there was a 'new form of slavery', while actual slavery existed in Zanzibar, Pemba and surrounding countries in East Africa. The article contended that such ills, including the 'illicit traffic in strong drink [were] absolutely against the traditions and constitutional spirit of the Empire'.[24] Expressing the widespread belief that the British political system was essentially a just, constitutional and equitable system, the article went on to argue:

> The time had come when Parliament is required to particularly consider the welfare of the natives, and not to leave them absolutely to the capricious greed of so-called Empire builders. The thinkers of the race fully recognise the fact that British rule has been an advantage to the people, but in no ways are prepared to contend that a system of oppression as enforced in practice in the Empire today is beneficial ...
>
> Students of the English constitution are aware that the Imperial Parliament

is supreme in the Empire, and by a sufficient legislation the eyesores of the Empire can be remedied; therefore the Association thinks British public opinion is a prime force in this matter, and solicits its power, whereby members of Parliament could be instructed that the better treatment of Native Races should command greater attention in Parliament.[25]

Typical of the times, the report is patriarchal in its position, though of course black women were eventually permitted to become members of the association. As noted, Kinloch became a member soon after its establishment.

In her lectures, Kinloch had sought to expose the compound system as well as pass laws that limited the freedom of movement of African mineworkers. She questioned colonial practices and, referring to her involvement in the association, she said in a lecture: 'I have formed a society for the benefit of our people in Africa by helping them to bring some of the dark side of things in Africa and elsewhere to light.' That very night, she stated, the African Association was formed, and it would try to educate people 'in this country in regard to the iniquitous laws made for blacks in South Africa. If the colonies would be strict in regard to the selling of drink to my people it would help us ... but of course they are benefited and enriched by the sale of drink.'[26]

'Savage South Africa'

The conscientisation of Williams regarding the circumstances of blacks in South Africa proved very useful. Not only did it encourage the formation of the African Association, it also helped challenge racial stereotypes prevalent in Victorian England: the inferiority of black-skinned people – 'those who have a different complexion or slightly flatter noses than ourselves'.[27] An event that took place some years after Williams's encounter with Kinloch confirmed the fact that the English viewed Africans not merely as inferior or exotic, but non-human – 'savage', to be precise. In April 1899, Frank Fillis, a promoter of theatre productions and exhibitions, brought to Earl's Court 'over 200 natives of South African tribes, a number of Boer families, representatives of mounted police, and a number of animals'.[28] Among the animals were elephants, tigers, lions, horses and dogs. This cast of people and animals would perform daily shows at the Empress Theatre in Earl's Court, as part of the Greater Britain Exhibition. *The Times* of 9 May 1899 described it simply as a 'capital circus performance'. Yet its intention and effect ran deeper than mere titillation of curious theatregoers. It set out to shock the British public about the 'savagery' of the black races of Southern Africa. Hence the name of the show: 'Savage South Africa'. The main production was the reconstruction of scenes drawn from the Anglo-Zulu War of 1879. Zulu war strategies were enacted, including an ambush of an English army by Zulu warriors brandishing shields and spears. But the show chose not to dramatise ensuing battles, including that at Rorke's Drift, where the British routed the Zulus. Consequently, by 1879, the land of the Zulu people was under the control of the British, and their king, Cetshwayo ka Mpande, forced into exile.[29] Yet the significance of the show lay in sharpening the differences between the world of the 'savage' and that of the 'civilised'. The African soldiers – or 'warriors' as they were called – were presented as carrying shields and spears, in contrast with British armies on horseback, carrying rifles and swords and wearing helmets. Productions like 'Savage South Africa' were useful in justifying the excessive use of violence in the colonies. What the show demonstrated was that the natives of the colonies were not the idealised 'noble savages' of Romanticism; they were dangerous and threatening. Force was therefore necessary, at times, to impose British values on its subjects.

English society was both titillated and disgusted by the show. Leading the charge was the Aborigines' Protection Society, a rights-based organisation that had campaigned for the abolition of slavery in England and its colonies. The APS had an interest in South African affairs, having assisted the Zulu king, Cetshwayo, to meet with Queen Victoria to plead the case of the Zulus in 1884, after the Anglo-Zulu War of 1879 had resulted in the conquest of their territory.[30] Whereas the APS had originally demonstrated ambivalence towards the formation of the African Association, it accepted the association and had a working relationship with it.[31] Williams was a central figure in the establishment of these relations. Several meetings between the two organisations were held between 1898 and 1899. Notably, at the APS annual meeting of 1899, attended also by Williams, the 'native question' in South Africa was discussed. The meeting noted the link between the 'native question' and the 'labour question' in South Africa, concluding that the roots of the native question were to be found in the 'new economic factors in South Africa'. For his part, Williams's contribution at the meeting was that 'the well-educated and cultured men of my race' should be consulted in regard to the 'future status of the South African aborigines'. Echoing Kinloch, Williams urged the abolition of the mine compound system.[32] Probably at Williams's insistence, the APS included on its agenda 'Savage South Africa' – he had been critical of the show. In the report of November 1899, the APS called for an end to the practice of bringing 'uncivilised natives' to Europe as 'commercial exploitation' for the 'profit of their exhibitors'.[33] Williams had helped expose the plight of the Zulu, who were part of the show. In the parliamentary debates that ensued, one of the complaints raised was that the participants had been duped: 'These men had been led to believe that they were to be employed at the Kimberley Mines'. Members of Parliament urged the government to put an end to the exhibition. Joseph Chamberlain, the secretary of state for the colonies, expressed his regret at the exhibition, but nonetheless claimed that the government lacked the authority to intervene:

> Her Majesty's Government have no power to compel the return of the Natives to South Africa. I can only express my regret and disapproval of their introduction. I had not observed that the show was to be opened by the Duke of Cambridge, but I now propose to communicate with his Royal Highness immediately on the subject.[34]

Some five months after the show began, it was closed down. Ironically, racism – the very reason why the show had come to England in the first place – was the reason for its sudden end. Concerns had been expressed about the conditions of the performers. But the *Pall Mall Gazette* raised fears about the impact of these 'primitive natives' on 'civilised' English society.[35] The concern for the welfare of the Zulu performers was not the prime reason why the production was shut down. A story was reported which threatened to blow apart the racial myths of England. The shows had become popular in England, with stories circulating of female patrons being curious to touch the performers on stage, and being constant visitors to the 'Kaffir kraal'. The American *Galveston Daily News* reported on 'vile orgies' at the 'Kaffir kraal', where 'fashionable women' went 'into black man's huts to give them presents'. Adding insult to injury, the paper also reported that an Englishwoman had fallen in love with one Peter Lobengula, 'a former inmate of the kraal', and was planning to marry him. According to the report, this 'little band of savages had brought home to the English people for the first time the seriousness of mixed marriages'.[36] It was in these circumstances that the London Exhibition Company shut down the exhibition and ordered the performers home. A show whose intentions were to showcase the might of the Empire had not only ended in an embarrassing spectacle, but had exposed the fallaciousness of racial hierarchy. Williams's belief in a world where race did not determine one's station in life was reaffirmed by these events. He had challenged English hypocrisy, and shown his solidarity with the black people of South Africa. Though separated geographically from his South African brethren, the universality of race discrimination brought them together. He would next take up the cudgel against one of the most powerful men of the era, Cecil John Rhodes.

Challenging Cecil John Rhodes

At its meeting of 12 June 1899, the African Association asked to be addressed by Lord Grey, who was a director of Rhodes's British South Africa Company (BSAC). He had gone to 'set right' the claims that the company was ill-treating its workers, claims around which the African Association had been publicly campaigning. Grey referred to the 'wonderful treatment' of Africans by the company, and urged the association to stop its public criticism. Williams was by now well informed about the condition of blacks in South Africa and Rhodesia, where the company operated. With that information, he was able to challenge Grey. In his rebuttal, Williams pointed out that a reliable source in Bulawayo had informed him that the natives of that country 'were subject to the same indignities as in the Transvaal. It was not an uncommon sight to see the lash used.'[37] Grey was unable to counter this, instead promising to investigate the allegations. The criticism of the practices of Rhodes and his BSAC in South Africa and Rhodesia did not end there. J.R. Hooker refers to another letter by Williams directly challenging Rhodes and his policies, although he dates it 'most likely from August 1898', addressed to the editor of *The Leader*. Williams commences the letter by noting that he 'belong[s] to the African race'. He then records that the letter is an appeal 'to the thousands of my white brothers and sisters … on behalf of my ill-treated fellow countrymen'. He continues:

> It is scarcely possible to conceive that the present Imperial Government condones the reinstatement of slavery in South Africa under the leadership of Cecil Rhodes … Must the illicit traffic in strong drink by European traders continue to ravage all that is great and noble amongst the simple and ignorant natives … shall quiet, law-abiding and progressive people be goaded into revolt, carnage and devastation through the enactment of questionable ordinances … without a protest from the Christian people of this great nation, who have always been the defenders of the weak?[38]

Challenging Rhodes was no mean feat. He was an extraordinarily powerful man, not only in the south of Africa, but also in England. But Williams was committed to the righteousness of his cause, and unafraid to speak out. Between 1897 and 1900, the African Association was at its most active, publicising its activities, signing up new members and constantly challenging the practices of the Empire in the colonies. Sherwood describes the 'accomplishments' of the association: it attracted a galaxy of members with wide experience, including people who had been engaged in various struggles of black people across the globe; it also arranged meetings with members of Parliament and addressed Parliament in its own right. Its public profile was raised in Britain, Africa, the Caribbean and the United States of America. Sherwood concludes: 'That Williams managed to form an association of black people from around the world was unprecedented. That it had begun to take action on issues affecting black lives in many parts of the world was a stupendous achievement.'[39]

It should be recalled that the primary purpose of establishing the association was to launch a Pan-African Conference. Coined by Williams, the term itself was probably informed by political movements that arose at the dawn of the new millennium, including the Pan-Dominican Movement and the Pan-American Movement. As Williams turned his attention to the launch of the Pan-African Conference, the concerns of South Africa and its native people remained central. As we shall see below, South Africa received a special place in the final resolutions of the conference.

'The problem of the 20th century is the problem of the colour line'

The year 1900 was selected for the launch of the Pan-African Conference. South Africa was, at the time, in the throes of war, with Boers pitted against the British Empire. This proved to be to the advantage of the African Association, providing it with a unique opportunity to foreground the interests of the black people of South Africa, but its main concern remained the treatment of black people by the British Empire throughout its colonies. In the *Lagos Standard* of 5 July 1899, the following report appeared:

> In view of circumstances and the widespread ignorance which is prevalent in England about the treatment of native races under British rule, the African Association, which consists of members of the race resident in England, and which has been in existence now for nearly two years, has resolved during the Paris Exhibition in 1900 to hold a conference in London … in order to take steps to influence public opinion on existing proceedings and conditions affecting the welfare of natives in the various parts of the Empire, viz. South Africa, West Africa and the British West Indies.

The conference took place in July 1900. Kinloch's influence was pervasive in the deliberations, even though she was no longer living in England. The programme would discuss, inter alia, 'organised plunder versus human progress', and that 'Europeans and others are enriched at the cost of Africa; i.e. they take all and give little.' Also, the situation of the missionaries could no longer be taken for granted, and Europe had to 'atone' for the wrongs done to Africa: Christian missions were included among the 'wrongs', and it was proposed that they could not simply 'take the place of Christian communities'.[40]

Not everyone shared in the enthusiasm for the conference, however, and the *Glasgow Herald* carried the following editorial:

> The Pan-African Conference at present being held in London is one of the most curious of the signs of the times. Political animists and novelists with an eye for the striking effects have done their best during the past few years to

familiarise the public with the idea that the black and yellow races may long assert themselves with effects disastrous to the supremacy so long, sometimes so arrogantly, claimed by the white man. We are haunted with the yellow carole in various forms and we are even asked to contemplate what would be the awful results if the great belt of coloured races that girdles the earth were to put forth their strength in unison and drag their pale-faced 'men and brother' from his seat of immemorial superiority ... the Pan-African Association ... represents one race, the negro and persons of African descent ... there is no denying that the negro races and their mixed descendants have displayed wonderful capacity for progress ... the Pan-African Association will show genuine wisdom if it devotes itself mainly to helping on quickly that work of progress and refraining from any ill-advised struggle for social equality which is not worth fighting for, and which must come naturally in the course of time.[41]

The conference heard an array of impressive speakers, including W.E.B. Du Bois. He spoke of the racial prejudice experienced by blacks in the United States of America and elsewhere. Black people, he urged, 'must insist upon the removal of the artificial obstructions that were placed in the way of the black, brown, and yellow boy'. They should have the same opportunities in life as white people. The elimination of racial barriers, he argued, 'should be the central cry of the conference'.[42]

That did indeed become the central cry of the conference, as Williams himself later explained:

It was time some effort was made to have us recognised as a people, and to enable us to take our position in the world. We were being legislated for without our sanction, and without a voice in the laws that were made to govern us. My idea in bringing about some alteration in this respect was confined in the first place to the British Colonies, but the scheme developed into a Pan-African one. Our object now is to secure throughout the world the same facilities and privileges for the black as the white man enjoys ...

And then there is an attempt in the world today to re-enslave the negro race. Especially is this the case in South Africa. We feel we must bring our whole forces together to prevent that and that can best be done by having a representative organisation in England through which to make our protests.[43]

A sub-committee, chaired by Du Bois, was appointed to draw up the conference resolutions. The contents were as prophetic as they were testament to the extraordinary abilities of the people who drafted the document. 'The problem of the 20th century is the problem of the colour line,' it declared. It questioned 'as to how far differences of race – which show themselves chiefly in the colour of the skin and the texture of the hair – will hereafter be made the basis of denying to over half the world the right of sharing to their utmost ability the opportunities and privileges of modern civilisation'. It noted that 'the darker races' are the least advanced in culture according to European standards. This had not, however, always been the case in the past, and certainly 'the world's history, both ancient and modern, has given many instances of no despicable ability and capacity among the blackest races of man'.[44]

The conference was not asking for the domination of the world by the black races. To the contrary, its request was for a shared future and a shared humanity:

> If now the world of culture bends itself towards giving negros and other dark men the largest and broadest opportunity for education and self-development, then this contact and influence is bound to have a beneficial effect upon the world and hasten human progress. But if, by reason of carelessness, prejudice, greed and injustice, the black world is to be exploited and ravished and degraded, the results must be deplorable, if not fatal.

From now on, the conference resolved, 'Let not colour or race be a feature of distinction between white and black man, regardless of worth or ability.' The natives of Africa should not be sacrificed 'to the greed of gold'. Christianity should not use 'the cloak of Christian missionary enterprise' in order to 'hide the ruthless economic exploitation and political downfall' of Africans. The statement was signed by W.E.B. Du Bois, chairman of the committee.

The conference also addressed a petition to Queen Victoria, 'her most gracious Majesty, Queen of Great Britain and Ireland, Empress of India, defender of the faith'.[45] The petition is remarkable for its direct focus on the South African question. It respectfully invited the queen's 'august and energetic attention to the fact that the situation of the native races in South Africa is causing us and our friends alarm'. It tabulated the main concerns:

1. The degrading and illegal compound system of native labour practised in Kimberley and Rhodesia.
2. The so-called indenture system, i.e. legalised bondage of native men, women and children to white colonies.
3. The system of compulsory labour on public works.
4. The pass or docket system used for people of colour.
5. Local bylaws that segregated and degraded the natives, such as the curfew, the denial to the natives of the use of the footpaths, and the use of separate public conveyances.
6. Difficulties in acquiring property.
7. Difficulties in obtaining the franchise.

Lord Chamberlain received the petition on behalf of the queen, and in a tone-deaf manner replied that he wished to assure 'the members of the Pan African Conference that, in settling the lines on which the administration of the conquered territories is to be conducted, her Majesty's government will not overlook the interests and welfare of the native races'.[46] An assurance was given that a copy of the letter would be sent to the British high commissioner for South Africa. The queen's reply was dated 12 January 1901, the day before her death. For Williams, this had special significance. Every black person across the world had reason to be proud of Queen Victoria and to revere her memory, said Williams. Her first act on ascending the throne was to grant the absolute emancipation of their people. And her very last act – the reply to the Pan-African Conference – had a connection with them too.[47]

The impact of the conference was widely felt by Africans across the globe. South Africa launched its own Pan-African Association, under the leadership of Francis Peregrino, the Ghanaian founder and editor of the first black newspaper in the Cape, the *South African Spectator*. Peregrino had attended the Pan-African Conference of 1900, and it was there that he had first met Williams. South Africa was Peregrino's adoptive home, where he had come to settle towards the end of 1900. His vision was to spread the doctrine of Pan-Africanism,[48] and it found expression in his attempt to counter the prevailing racial ideology in the Cape, with its rigid racial categories of 'coloureds' and 'natives' – people who, in Peregrino's view, were African.

On 23 February 1901, the *South African Spectator* announced the establishment of the Pan-African Society in the Cape, which aimed to 'secure to Africans and their descendants throughout the world their civil and political rights'. But its mission was not confined to South Africa, since it also proposed to 'ameliorate [the] condition of our oppressed brethren in the Continents of Africa, America, and other parts of the world, by promoting efforts to secure effective legislation'. The society aimed also 'to foster friendly relations between the Caucasian and African races'. In order to achieve its ends, it would set up a 'Bureau as a depository for collections of authorized productions, writings, and statistics relating to our people everywhere'. While the Pan-African Society gained prominence in 1901, it soon faded into obscurity, however, and by 1903, when Williams arrived at the Cape, it had virtually ceased to exist.

Henry Sylvester Williams at the Cape

In 1903, Williams's practice at Gray's Inn was beginning to pick up. His reputation as a legal activist in cases involving the inferior social conditions of blacks was entrenched in the public mind. But he was concerned at the slow growth of his legal practice. He had a young family to support, with a child who was barely a year old. His success as an organiser of the African Association (later the Pan-African Association) had not translated to success as a barrister. He therefore considered relocating his practice to Cape Town. At the time, advocates admitted to practise in London could apply to be admitted in either of the British colonies, the Cape or Natal. A few years earlier, a young man named Mohandas Gandhi had applied for admission as an attorney of the Supreme Court of Natal, and despite an objection by the Cape Law Society – that a person of Indian origin was not fit and proper to practise law – the court admitted him. Gandhi's admission, and the decision of the Natal Law Society, made news in London. Williams must surely have been aware of this when he made the decision to move to Cape Town, with the intention that his family would join him there later.

In October 1903, Williams set sail for the Cape. Although this was his first visit, he considered himself well informed. Jabavu, Kinloch and Peregrino had kept him apprised of political developments. But even for such a keen follower of politics, nothing could have prepared him for what he was about to encounter. In the first place, the Anglo-Boer War had recently ended. Thousands of Africans had participated on both sides, as unarmed soldiers and auxiliaries, but they received no financial compensation for the losses they sustained. Their partici-pation in the war and their internment in concentration camps is meticulously recorded by Stowell Kessler in *The Black Concentration Camps of the Anglo-Boer War, 1899–1902*.[49] Though conditions in the notorious concentration camps for Boers were bad, it is clear that the situation was far worse in camps that held blacks. The total losses in the Boer camps amounted to some 26 000 women and children, while the camps for blacks held large numbers of men. By the end of the war, 21 000 black men, women and children had perished in camps established by the British. In addition to this number, the Boers conscripted, without pay, some 10 000 black men to assist their commandos in the war. For their part, the British employed about 100 000 blacks, with only 10 000 being issued with fire-arms. The actual number of blacks who died in battle was never recorded.[50]

Williams had, thus, arrived in a colony trying to come to grips with the aftermath of war. Thomas Pakenham has written about the irony of the whites-only post-war settlement. The British government arranged for £35 million to be borrowed from the British private sector for investment in South Africa, particu-larly in the Transvaal. There was a further promise of £30 million in development finance which was guaranteed by Wernher-Beit, the pre-eminent mining com-pany of the era, with links to Cecil John Rhodes (though the company was never called upon to make good on the guarantee).[51] Perhaps one of the most decisive interventions of the post-war era was the establishment of the Public Debtors Commission – today's Public Investment Corporation. Annual reports of the Pub-lic Debtors Commission during this period reveal that one of its key roles was to acquire the debt of Boers experiencing economic distress. The commission set up the 'Armefonds' – the poor man's fund enabling Boers to continue the business of farming on beneficial terms. As such, not only were the Boers directly compensated, and therefore able to buy property, but their debts and liabilities were taken over by a state fund.

The British provided no similar compensation for the thousands of Africans who perished in the war. Instead, what took place was complete betrayal. In the establishment of the Union of South Africa in 1910, which incorporated the two Boer republics of the Orange Free State and the Transvaal and the two British colonies of the Cape and Natal, there was no place for blacks. They would play no part in the administration or government. Their own affairs would be placed under the administrative control of the secretary for native affairs. As the key demand of Johannesburg – the new mining centre of the world – was labour, the main preoccupation was converting black men and women into wage labourers. Over time, blacks would indeed become labourers, with their movements strictly monitored through systems such as pass laws. Inequality in wages, categories of work and working conditions was rife. White workers in the mines of the Transvaal and Kimberley earned roughly eight times more than their black counterparts. Living conditions were vastly unequal. Describing the life of the diamond diggers of Kimberley, Josiah Semouse writes: 'Diamond diggers and civil servants alike work all day, without rest. I have travelled all over the Cape Colony, I saw towns and cities, but I have never seen a city as bad as Kimberley. And its laws are also bad.'[52] He elaborates:

> Black people are pushed around like animals. They are being chased around the city like locusts and put into jail when they have no pass. Because if they have no means to get a pass, they are not given a pass. I have never seen such a calamity. The diamond diggers work naked, their back is exposed to the sun. After work you are searched, searched thoroughly, turned upside down in a disgraceful manner, the argument being that you are hiding diamonds.[53]

The resultant human suffering was dreadful. There were 'many different kinds of diseased people in Kimberley', and Semouse records the trauma: 'One had no feet, only the body and jumped around like a frog. One day, when he was jumping through the streets, he saw horses approaching him. I thought that they would stop in front of him. But he just looked up and at precisely that moment he made a giant leap forward so that his forehead, nose and mouth touched the ground.'[54] Williams had first learnt about the pass system, the labour compounds in the mines and racial inequality in the Cape from Kinloch. Now he was about to witness it for himself. At the time, black West Indians living in the Cape were not directly affected by discriminatory laws, even though they were often subjected to racist behaviour. Apart from his nationality, Williams was distinguished from most local Africans by the fact that he was an educated man, a barrister. He was thus unique in South Africa. As one of the few educated blacks, he felt a special duty towards those who were marginalised. He was numbered among Du Bois's 'talented tenth'. Ironically, it was this special responsibility which, he felt, would prove his undoing.

The 'talented tenth'

When Williams embarked on his journey to the Cape, he was fulfilling not only a personal mission but also a generational one. W.E.B. Du Bois was the first black person to graduate with a PhD from Harvard University, and his concept of 'the talented tenth' signalled the duties of the educated class of blacks towards the less-privileged members of their race.[55] In his eponymous 1903 essay, Du Bois explained the responsibilities of the educated few, 'the talented tenth', to their society. 'The negro race,' he began, 'is going to be saved by its exceptional men.' He argued that the problem of education 'among negroes must first of all deal with the talented tenth; it is the problem of developing the best of this race that they may guide the mass away from the contamination and death of the west, in their own and other races'. Du Bois then posed the question:

> Can the masses of the negro people be in any possible way more quickly raised than by the effort and example of the aristocracy of talent and character? Was there ever a nation on God's fair earth civilised from the bottom upward? Never; it is, ever was and ever will be from the top downward that culture filters. The talented tenth rises and pulls all that are worth the saving up to their vantage ground. This is the history of human progress; and the true historical mistakes which have hindered that progress were the thinking first that no more could ever rise save the few already risen; or second, that it would be better the unreason to pull the reason down.[56]

His prescribed solution was to school the best and most capable of the youth. However, Du Bois noted that the question of human education 'is not simply a matter of schools'. It was more 'a matter of family and group life'. The 'black boy of the south' would be taught by 'the group leaders of the negro people – the physicians and clergymen, the trained fathers and mothers, the influential and forceful men about him of all kinds; here it is, if at all, that the culture of the surrounding world trickles through and is handed on by the graduates of the higher schools'.[57]

Williams clearly saw himself as being numbered among the talented tenth, not only in the Western world, but also in the African diaspora. After all, three years earlier, his vision was to organise Africans of the world, not only of the Western world. He would take his experience, his education, his knowledge, skills and talents, and use them for the upliftment of the natives of South Africa. He was one of the few 'exceptional men', and he had a duty to rise and pull others up with him. Yet when he arrived in Cape Town, he did not find people waiting to be saved. Africans in the Cape had been organising since at least 1882, when *Imbumba Yabamnyama* was formed to unite black people in their fight for their 'national rights'.[58] The founders of the organisation were concerned not to allow religious differences to divide them on political matters. They noted that 'the white people are solidly united when it comes to [political] matters'. To be effective in their organisation, Africans also had to forge unity, among the churches first, and also in the broader political sphere.[59]

The South African Native Congress (SANC) was launched in 1890 as a platform to articulate black grievances and channel black concerns. In 1903, it presented a statement to Joseph Chamberlain, secretary of state for the colonies, titled 'Questions Affecting the Natives and Coloured People Resident in British South Africa', which represented the most comprehensive rejection of British policy by Africans up to that point.[60] The statement addressed the administration of justice, and was critical of the jury system on two grounds. First, 'the frequent cold-blooded murders of natives so uncommon even among the most barbarous races, and the difficulty of securing convictions under the jury system, is having a marked effect on lowering the high prestige of the bench'. Furthermore, the jury system 'has too often degenerated into a mockery from its frequent abuse in cases between white and black'.[61]

Jabavu addressed the inequities of the jury system in *Imvo Zabantsundu* after receiving a steady flow of complaints about its lack of impartiality. It was true, he noted, that Africans were more likely to receive harsher sentences where the complainants were white. His writings served as a rallying point as he started advocating for an independent judiciary. To prevent bias, he proposed that cases be tried by judges 'trained in the law'. The race of the accused should not be a factor in the administration of justice. He also recommended that the question of the administration of justice involving white and black should receive the consideration of the British government.[62]

With Williams, a black advocate, about to join the Bar, expectations rose. Though he might never ascend to a judicial post, he had joined the hallowed ranks of advocates, and there were hopes for even-handedness in the administration of justice. Williams would play a role that no advocate had played before. Not only would he represent the individual causes of his clients, he would also be a representative of the race.

Representing the race

In 1901 Williams made contact with Peregrino, the aims of whose newspaper included the achievement of 'black unity, sobriety and respectability', and which referred to itself as Pan-African, in line with ideas put forward at the Pan-African Conference of 1900. On arrival at the Cape, Williams was provided with an office by Peregrino, though he later moved to his own offices at Metropolitan Chambers in Church Street. A few weeks after arriving, Williams wrote to his wife, Agnes, telling her: 'It is impossible for me to write at length as I have two heavy briefs, both marked £25 each, which comes on this session. One is for "forging", the other is for "attempting to poison".'[63]

Williams was aware of the weight of expectation, and felt that many people were looking to him to ensure justice. For this reason, he felt the need to 'see to it that my debut in the criminal arena will be memorable'. He spoke of the friends who had written to him from London celebrating his admission as an advocate at the Cape Bar. These friends included 'an old colleague' from Gray's Inn who wished him well and gave him tips for survival at the Cape Bar. Money, it seems, was hard to come by, though this was not a cause for concern, he wrote: 'Please do not fear for me on the score of leaving myself bare – I shall always try to keep a Pound by me.' He had been hopeful that he might send his wife some money, but he had not yet received any payment. When payments were made, Agnes could 'expect another draft'.[64] He was optimistic about his prospects at the Cape Bar, something he had not felt in London. He told Agnes: 'I am wishing myself back in London again, but there seems a chance here for me to make a little cash and so I shall abide the flow of time.' Nevertheless, he recognised the difficulties he was facing: 'At present it is very hard.'[65]

It is not known what transpired in the two 'heavy briefs' referred to in his letter. But in December 1903 he appears to have defended a coloured wagon driver accused, along with others, of four counts of theft of tarpaulins in Woodstock, Cape Town. The defence of his client was that he had acted merely as a carrier and was not an accomplice. This was rejected by the jury. Two of the accused were discharged, while the main accused (a white person) and Williams's client were found guilty. Williams's client was sentenced to nine months' hard labour. The white accused was sentenced to 'such hard labour as he was capable of doing'.[66] The disparity in the sentences is clearly evident. In another case where Williams represented a Jewish immigrant charged with theft of government property, he was again unsuccessful and his client was convicted.

Williams's practice took him to the Supreme Court at a time when it was unheard of for a black person to appear there as counsel. The *South African News Weekly* of 15 June 1904 reported the case of *Basson* v. *Basson* in which Williams appeared for Mrs Basson. Williams was also involved in a case involving Samson

Afrika, who had opened a shop in the grounds of Saron Mission where coloured people lived under missionary supervision and were required to conform with the rules laid down by the mission. The allegation was that Afrika had broken the rules regarding the opening of shops on mission lands. Williams knew that on technical grounds his client had probably violated the rules. He decided to challenge the problem at its source. It was the rules, he contended, that were unlawful. The basis for the illegality was that the rules were not authorised by law. Moreover, the rules did not treat coloured people living on missionary land in a manner similar to the way missionaries themselves were treated. Two principles of law were accordingly at stake. The first was that any rule drawn up by the mission could not be contrary to the laws of the country. The second was the principle of equality, i.e. rules must apply equally and without distinction.

Williams lost in the lower court. When the matter was taken on appeal, different counsel replaced Williams. Still, the appeal did not succeed. Having failed on the legal front, attention turned to the political front: there was an uprising against the mission stations, relating to their laws. The uprising resulted in a petition being presented to the attorney-general. The residents at the mission argued that they did not know whether they were 'British subjects, free men or slaves and whether [they] are bound by the laws of the land'.[67]

One reported case where Williams appeared, *Van Boom* v. *Visser*,[68] involved a dispute about land. Williams acted for a client who was alleged to have encroached upon a piece of land that did not belong to him. The land owner applied to court for an order compelling Williams's client, Visser, the defendant, to remove buildings which had been built on the applicant's land. The defendant did not appear in court when the matter was first called. However, Williams appeared on his behalf to ask for an opportunity to submit the correct set of documents before court – in that case a statement under oath. When the matter was called, it appears that the correct documents had not been submitted. The application for the ejectment of Williams's client was allowed. In a judgment that was critical of the manner in which Williams had handled the case, Chief Justice Henry de Villiers stated the following:

> On the last occasion when the matter was mentioned an affidavit was produced on behalf of the defendant in which he stated that he had been served with a summons, but that he was not aware of the contents, and that all the subsequent proceedings against him were taken entirely without his knowledge. These statements of his are now entirely denied by the attorney whom he employed in the country, and, so far as they can deny them, by the attorneys in Cape Town. But it is said that this man is an ignorant man living in the country, that he has a good defence to this action, and that some consideration

should be shown to him. This is just what the court is anxious to do; to show him every consideration, and for the purpose of showing him that consideration, counsel was informed on the last occasion that when he applied again he should produce an affidavit from which it might be fairly inferred that the man has a good, honest defence to the action. If such an affidavit had been produced today, there would have been no difficulty whatever in granting the order which is asked for. The applicant, however, has not taken advantage of this opportunity. He has not filed any affidavit of merits as indicated by [the rules of court]. He has had ample time to do so, and under these circumstances it is impossible for the court to grant him any relief. The application must be refused, with costs.

The application to introduce evidence by way of a petition was, accordingly, rejected. Nevertheless, Williams attempted to represent the defendant in the subsequent trial where evidence was to be led in person and not in written form. But this attempt was also rejected by the chief justice, finding that Williams had no legal standing to represent his client. With Williams having left the court, the plaintiff led evidence, which was uncontested. Despite the fact that it was accepted that the building in question 'looked as if it had stood for a long time', the court found in favour of the plaintiff. The effect of this was that Williams's client was instructed to demolish the structure or pay an amount of £25 to the land owner in exchange for the encroached part of the land, together with £10 in damages with costs. The implications of the judgment were severe and punitive to the client represented by Williams. For an advocate whose concern was justice, the substance of the judgment must have indicated that law was not always infused with justice. On a personal level, the criticism by the court would surely have stung him. Here, the man who believed that he would take on the legal system of the Cape was having his mistakes exposed by the very system he hoped to change. What magnified his mistakes was not only his race, but also the implications this had for those he represented. Many imponderable questions must have struck him: would it have made a difference to the outcome if, for example, he had been more diligent in the conduct of the case? The injustice of the outcome for his client, however, struck him forcefully. If the law could not be relied upon to provide justice, what else was there? To provide an answer to this question, Williams began to shift his focus to the source of the law: politics.

The legal is political
Williams's approach to the law was not limited to advocacy in the courtroom. He believed in an integrated legal system, where mobilisation and advocacy outside the courtroom could be employed to secure greater and sustainable social and

political change. The question of racism within the jury system had occupied Africans since Jabavu first addressed the issue on the pages of *Imvo Zabantsundu*. In 1904, Williams led a delegation to meet with the attorney-general of the Cape Colony concerning the issue of black jurors. They asked for the appointment of jurors on a non-racial basis. This did not succeed. But Williams did not believe that the approach would in any event have changed the attitude of the British government. He was aware of the many instances where promises had been made, only for them to be rejected. While the commitment to making jurors more representative failed, it was significant that the only black advocate in the Cape had taken up the cudgels for representation directly in the administration of justice.

Towards the end of that year, a nasty surprise awaited Williams. He had been aware that the white members of the Cape Bar would probably exclude him on a social level. But he never expected that this would affect his earnings as an advocate. However, he would soon learn that the Cape Bar proposed resolving that, henceforth, only counsel who had been approved by majority vote were permitted to travel on circuit. Since the seat of the Supreme Court was in Cape Town, in order to reach far-flung areas of the colony, the court travelled to selected towns or villages. For the advocates, the circuit practice was both substantial and also financially rewarding. The normal practice was that any advocate could go on circuit. But the new majority ruling of the Bar had changed this. Williams never put his name up for consideration, as he probably thought the odds were stacked against him. For him, the very idea of majority approval for the 'privilege' of circuit work was a clear signal of exclusion, on racial grounds, in a Bar whose membership was exclusively white. There was, of course, a personal irony in this. His wife, Agnes, was a white woman, and by now the couple already had two children. Still, the members of the Bar – who were all, of course, white – refused to socialise with Williams. By proposing the change in the circuit rules, the Cape Bar Council clearly sought to starve him financially by withdrawing its vote each time he might be required to undertake circuit work.

Williams was not only deprived of circuit work, he was also boycotted – both professionally and personally. Life at the Bar became intolerable; he would later relate these experiences to William Stead, publisher of the *Review of Reviews*, who commented:

Mr Williams is a man of extraordinary pluck. He has built up for himself a practice in Cape Colony in the teeth of the bitterest prejudice of the whites, to whom the spectacle of the coloured man practising his law as a barrister appeared something unnatural and abominable. His professional brethren boycotted him. He was shut out from the circuit and bar messes, and everything was done by the majority of the bar – Englishmen, by the way – to demonstrate how hollow a hypocrisy is in the so-called equality of rights under the British flag.[69]

Williams's earlier optimism was replaced by a new realism. He now accepted that, despite the Cape's claims concerning equality, race ultimately determined one's personal destiny and professional destination. He began to focus on political work, and planned to leave for the United Kingdom, where he wished to advocate against the Cape Bar's exclusionary practices. By changing the wider political landscape, he hoped to effect change at the Cape Bar. Sol Plaatje's *Koranta ea Bechuana* of 9 November 1904 reported that Williams would 'temporarily' return to England to represent the coloured people and to espouse their cause with the British Parliament. It is apparent from Plaatje's report that Williams intended to return to the Cape. Upon learning of Williams's impending departure, *Imvo Zabantsundu* reacted with dismay:

> Who had made this novel request, who presumably will be accountable for the expenses which cannot be trifling? That as yet there is no hope in South Africa for a coloured man as an advocate, it has always appeared to us patent and clear; and no doubt it is this fact our friend has discovered after a few months experience at the Cape Bar. We are rather sorry Mr Williams should have to leave … as in our opinion he would have been of great service to the coloured people in instructing them on right lines politically.[70]

Williams's brief though memorable sojourn at the Cape Bar had come to an abrupt end. But his relationship with South Africa had not. During his time in South Africa, Williams had met Alfred Mangena, who was at the time secretary of the local Dock-Workers Association, and their relationship would prove important in the founding of the new resistance movement. Williams also claimed to have a personal friendship with Pixley ka Isaka Seme,[71] who was a friend of Mangena. In March 1905, the *Review of Reviews* gave a glowing account of Williams: he had returned to London, said Stead, in order to prevail upon his colleagues at Gray's Inn that the Cape Bar should relax its boycott. Williams was now back in the Empire as 'the British negro barrister'.

In two lectures, published as *The British Negro: A Factor in the Empire*,[72] Williams criticised government policy relating to black citizens in the British Empire. He believed that the same standards of justice, education and 'civilisation' accorded to other racial groups should be extended to black people.[73] By now, Williams had seen for himself how the British Empire treated native peoples in its colonies across the world, and he continued his activism for change. He addressed a meeting in London regarding the South African situation, and the excerpts below testify to his extraordinary ability to make a case against injustice to a foreign audience:

> The natives of South Africa are now kept back by the white man, but they would come to the front in the future, and he knew that intelligent English people desired that they should rise from the state of lethargy in which they had been buried for some time. The coloured man had his mission in life and he was convinced by his travelling in South Africa that the Africans heard.
>
> As a native of Trinidad he found that he was looked upon as an undesirable in South Africa ...
>
> The education of the native was insufficient ... in South Africa a native could not buy an inch of land in his own name and the only way out of the difficulty was representation in Parliament....
>
> English people in South Africa had boycotted him and tried to prevent him getting on as a barrister while the Dutch held out the hand of friendship.[74]

At the end of 1905, Williams was back in South Africa. This time he went to the Transvaal, where he worked with Walter Rubusana, author of the seminal 1906 work, *Zemk'inkomo magwalandini*.[75] The issue was land restrictions in the Transvaal Republic. Until 1905, the view that germinated during the days of the Transvaal Republic, that ownership of land could not be registered in the name of a native, still held sway. The practice was justified with reference to the Transvaal Volksraad Resolution of 14 August 1884 and Article 13 of the Pretoria Convention of 1881, which ended the war between the British and the Boers concerning the status of the Transvaal as a republic. The relevant clause of the Pretoria Convention stated that 'leave shall be given to natives to obtain ground, but the passing of transfer of such ground shall in every case be made to and registered in the name of the Commissioner for Kaffir Locations hereinafter provided for, for the benefit of such natives'. In practice, Africans were not allowed to have land registered in their own name. Where they bought land, it was registered in the name of the 'Commissioner for Kaffir Locations' to be held in trust for the benefit of Africans. A case, however, which went to the Supreme Court of Transvaal, brought by a prominent black leader in the Transvaal, Edward Tsewu,[76] decided that there was nothing in law prohibiting the registration of land in the name of Africans.[77] The practice was, accordingly, unlawful. Writing the judgment, Chief Justice Rose Innes noted the prevailing practice 'of not allowing transfer of land to be made direct to any native, but insisting upon transfer being taken in trust for him by an official appointed by the State'. Yet this practice had no basis in law. State officials could not assume powers not granted to them by the legislature. 'It is for the legislature to deal with the matter if it is thought right to make special provisions in regard to natives. When we find nothing in the statute book which would warrant us in drawing any distinction we are bound to draw none'.[78] The effect of this judgment was dramatic. Many Africans lined up asking the government to register land in their own names, a practice which – even though not the law – appears to have continued well after the passing of the 1913 Natives Land Act.[79] William Windham, the Transvaal secretary for native affairs, reported in his annual report of 1907 on the 'growing tendency amongst the natives generally to acquire land in individual or partnership title, as opposed to the communal tribal acquisition, which, until the decision of the Supreme Court in the application *ex parte Tsewu* ... had been almost universal'.[80] The government tried to put an end to this practice by introducing a ban on individual land registration for Africans.

It was in these circumstances that Williams entered the fray. Since he had been out of the country for a while, he consulted firstly with the local leaders, including Rubusana and Tsewu. Williams was acutely aware, based on his own experiences, that the court victory in the Tsewu case would not be sufficient. Any court victory had to be cemented with a clear political strategy. Accordingly, he consulted with colonial officials to ensure that the proposed ban on private African land ownership was not passed. Williams and Rubusana were ultimately granted audience with Lord Elgin, British secretary for colonies, who duly informed Lord Selborne, the British high commissioner for South Africa, that he was not prepared to endorse the passing of 'restrictive legislation on this subject by a nominated legislature'. The monarch, King Edward VII, was advised to disallow the legislation which had been proposed in the Transvaal. The United Kingdom overturned the law upon the advice of Selborne. For a while, the courts and the politicians were aligned on the issue of land ownership by blacks. Blacks could acquire land in their own name. But this would not last for long.

In response to the Tsewu judgment, the Transvaal government, upon attaining self-government in December 1906, made a fresh proposal to pass a law to ensure the outright prohibition of natives from holding individual title. Some three years earlier, Sir Godfrey Lagden, the commissioner for native affairs, had produced a report into the structure of native title for land ownership in the Transvaal. The report, titled 'Report Relative to the Acquisition and Tenure of Land by Natives in the Transvaal'[81] concluded that blacks should be allowed to hold land, but on a communal, rather than individual, basis. When acquiring land, it should be registered in trust. Land title for blacks, it was proposed, should be 'vested in the Commissioner for Native Affairs in trust for the owners, who cannot, therefore, encumber or dispose of their interests without the consent of the Government'.[82] In 1907 the Transvaal government dusted off the Lagden report and sought, once again, to restrict the ability of blacks to register land in their own name. To this end, it passed an Executive Order in Council, in 1907. With its own elected legislature, the Transvaal government was empowered to pass its own laws without the sanction of the British government. The courts, having earlier identified the defect as the absence of legislation, could not intervene. From 1907 onwards, the legal position remained that blacks were not legally allowed to hold individual title without the permission of the government. Feinberg, however, notes that in reality, for some Africans, acting either jointly or individually, the Tsewu decision did represent a real opportunity to effectively acquire land. Between 1905 and 1909, Africans were able to buy more than a hundred farms, even when not registered in their own names. As such, it is apparent that a dual system of land ownership emerged – some Africans bought land in their own names, while others resorted to the trusteeship system.[83] It remained the case, however, that Africans experienced grave difficulties in acquiring land. A theme which underpinned the strategy of the Transvaal government was to render that part of the country a white man's country. Political activism without political power, it seemed, did not provide the full answer for Williams. But Williams was not about to give up. If the racial injustice of the Transvaal could not be prevented, the racial cruelties of the colony of Natal had to be exposed.

In 1906, Bambatha ka Mancinza, one of the chiefs of the Zondi clan in Zululand, took up arms together with his men against the Natal colonial administration. In the broader context, three factors caused the uprising: the shortage of land resulting from colonial occupation, the shortage of farm labour in Natal, exacerbated by the demand for labour in the mines of Johannesburg. The immediate context, however, was a decision of the Natal colonial administration to impose a poll tax on all 'able-bodied' Zulu men. With no land, young Zulu men were compelled to work on farms. Bambatha decided on an armed resistance against the tax. The uprising was widely reported in the British press, with references to it as a 'rebellion'. Williams took an active interest in the uprising, following reports from Alfred Mangena. Mangena had written to major newspapers across the world, bringing to their attention the plight of Zulu warriors. Williams added his voice in an article titled 'The Black Peril: Why the Zulus are threatening rebellion', published in the *Manchester Daily Dispatch* of 5 December 1907. In the piece, Williams presented a defence of the Zulu 'rebels'. He criticised the colonial government in Natal for the manner in which its inspectors were regulating the lives of Africans, particularly by depriving chiefs of their traditional powers, thereby dislocating the centre of power and disrupting the hierarchy of the Zulu nation. He pointed out that white farmers had taken all the land belonging to the Zulu people and evicted them, allowing them to remain only as labourers. The protests of the chiefs went unanswered, and the government imposed taxes and employed unfair tax-collection methods. As a result, the people trusted neither the government nor the chiefs. But they did trust their own hands – and this had resulted in 'the last upheaval which convulsed the land of the Zulus under Bambatha'.

A further complaint was the fact that the Zulu had no means of expressing their complaints in the legislative council, where laws affecting them were being debated. Williams levelled another charge against the Natal authorities. Presumably based on information he had gathered from Seme, Williams alleged that the authorities had attempted to influence the University of Oxford not to admit Seme as a student, despite the fact that he was qualified for admission. As a result of the uprising, the king of the Zulu, Dinuzulu ka Cetshwayo, was indicted by the Natal government on charges which included treason. The indictment of a man of Dinuzulu's stature caused outrage among the Zulu. The British government was also criticised for turning a blind eye to the conduct of its surrogate government in the colony of Natal. In his newspaper article, Williams had focused on these treason charges, questioning their veracity and suggesting that an ulterior motive lay behind them. Dinuzulu had won a defamation case against a white woman, and it was this triumph which was 'resented by Europeans in Natal generally', and had led to the false charges of treason and an attempt to 'crush' Dinuzulu. Williams was not the only person to raise public concern about the fate of the warriors of Bambatha. While Bambatha and his men were ultimately crushed by the Natal government, and the British government proved ineffective in protecting the individual rights of the Zulu, who also counted as British subjects, it was the exposure of the injustice and the indifference of the British government that ultimately mattered – and Williams's article had drawn attention to this.

The return of the land of the Batlokoa and Bakhuluwe
On 19 January 1907, *The Scotsman* carried a report titled 'The Basutos' Claim'. It noted the following:

> Reuters Agency learns that Mr Sylvester Williams, on behalf of the Basuto deputation, now in London, yesterday handed in at the Colonial Office a statement of the Basutos' claims. The statement particularly urges the repeal of the old Dutch Ordinance of 1893, which was re-enacted by the British Government in 1903, and which prevents natives from either owning or leasing land.

The 'Basutos' referred to were not from Lesotho but from South Africa. They formed part of the various sections of the Sotho-speaking people who had splintered from the main Basotho groups and settled in South Africa in the early nineteenth century. They belonged to two branches of the Basotho, the Batlokoa and the Bakhuluwe. While busying himself with the fight for justice in South Africa, Williams had also entered local politics, winning a seat in the London borough of Marylebone – notably beating a South African contender, Reverend John Michael Dwane. He would, he hoped, now gain access to the London ruling elite. Yet, characteristically, he would not use those official channels for personal benefit, but for the black races everywhere in the world. It is unclear whether the Batlokoa and Bakhuluwe were aware of Williams's position as a local councillor when they approached him for help with their deputation. They wanted him to take up their cause. Owen Charles Manthurin speculates that the choice of Williams was probably because of his earlier visit to King Lerotholi of Lesotho in 1904.[84] But this is unlikely, as Lerotholi was based in Lesotho, not South Africa. Although both groups share the Sesotho language, they had grown apart during the nineteenth century. The person who is most likely to have raised the possibility of approaching Williams was Josiah Gumede. Whatever the case, Williams's proximity to political power, flowing from his position as a local councillor, undoubtedly facilitated the audience with the government.

Gumede was a familiar face in the United Kingdom. In 1892, he had been a member of the Zulu Choir that visited England. While the choir's mission had been fundraising, they were surprised to learn that they were also required to take part in an exhibition 'to reproduce their native customs, especially their war songs and dances' for the amusement of the British public. Their initial reaction was to reject the request, until the intervention of the Church of England, which persuaded them that it would be 'morally right' for them to include the exhibition as part of their programme.[85] By 1906, Gumede was a land agent at the Natal law firm Thackeray Allison and Albert Hime Solicitors. An educated man who had graduated from the Healdtown missionary institution in the Eastern Cape, he also translated English documents for his Sotho-speaking clients. As the latter role grew, he effectively took over certain cases, assuming the traditional function of an attorney. By 1906, some three years after the original Basotho claims were made, there was still no resolution. Gumede suggested that they approach the imperial government in London, making direct representations concerning the return of the land. After all, he argued, it was precisely because Africans had sided with the British that the Boers were now refusing to return their land. Gumede was aware of the position taken by the British in relation to the land in its three protectorates, Basutoland (now the Kingdom of Lesotho), Bechuanaland (now Botswana) and Swaziland (the Kingdom of Eswatini or Swaziland). They had not been incorporated into South Africa, and discussions concerning the unification of South Africa suggested that they would remain British protectorates. Gumede, then, believed that the British would assist the Basotho. In December 1906, Gumede, together with two chiefs of the Basotho, Chief Lisa Moloi and

Chief Lequila, travelled to the United Kingdom to make representations in support of the land claim.

The case of the Basotho presented a challenge similar to what Williams had encountered in the Transvaal Colony. There, he had succeeded in persuading His Majesty's government to throw out the law as formulated by the Transvaal government. Could he now do the same for the Orange Free State? Unlike the factual situation in regard to the Transvaal, here the facts were complex. A 1907 newspaper reported[86] that a deputation of Basotho had arrived in London under the care of Williams, who said that they had 'settled in the Transvaal in 1866' and fought alongside the Boers 'in native warfare'. As a reward, the Basotho were offered land in the Orange River Colony – under Boer control at the time – for which they paid 7 000 cattle. The Basotho fought on the side of the British in the First Anglo-Boer War of 1880, which was fought over Transvaal independence. When that war ended, with the signing of the Pretoria Convention in 1881, Britain agreed to recognise the independence of Transvaal. Once the Transvaal and Orange Free State became independent republics, Africans could no longer expect Britain to intercede on their behalf. Afrikaners turned their focus to their own developmental needs, which required land. They then turned on the Africans, ejecting the Batlokoa and Bakhuluwe from land in the Orange Free State.

In the Second Anglo-Boer War (1899–1902), the Basotho again fought on the side of the British. When the British won, the Basotho chiefs expected the return of the land they had lost in 1881. But this was not to be. Instead, the British government, which now controlled the Orange River Colony, invoked a Dutch law that had been used in the Orange Free State, stating that Africans could neither own nor lease land. The offer made to the Basotho was that they could return to the farms as labourers. The offer was rejected on the basis that the just thing to do was to return to them the land taken from them after 1881. The Batlokoa and Bakhuluwe discovered that political allegiance – and military support – counted for little. With Britain's focus being the consolidation of relations between English and Afrikaner, it was clear that race was the overriding concern.

Williams and his clients were granted audience with the British government on 29 January 1907. Leading the delegation from the British government was Lord Elgin, who attended with four other members of Parliament. While *The Scotsman* of 30 January 1907 reported that 'Lord Elgin [was] understood to have made a sympathetic reply' to the case presented by Williams, the discriminatory law was not in fact changed. There was no restoration of land. The prohibition of land acquisition by blacks did not change. Some five weeks after the delegation left, Lord Elgin sent his reply. Although disappointing, the response was not unfamiliar. His Majesty's government refused to interfere with the rights of the white inhabitants of South Africa in the manner suggested by Williams. The preservation of

English and Afrikaner relations was not the sole motivation for Britain's decisions concerning South Africa. Britain wanted to retain its dominance in global economic trade, and gold was central to this scheme. Sound political relations with the Transvaal Afrikaners were therefore imperative in ensuring mineral exploitation of the area. Britain was facing competition in Europe, especially from Germany, and key to British economic strategy were her colonial policies. Through these, she could ensure that political control over the colonies translated to trade.[87] Hence, for Britain, Africans were dispensable, but Afrikaners were not.

'A most unsavoury influence in Liberia'

Williams found himself back in Africa in 1908, though this time in Liberia. The National Bar Association of Liberia had invited him as the main speaker at its annual meeting. He was given something of a royal reception, with the president of Liberia present upon his arrival. Williams was introduced to the Supreme Court of Liberia by the attorney-general and several high-ranking government officials and judges. He gave an address on 19 January 1908, which was reported on in the newspaper *African League*:

> Mr Williams held his audience spell-bound as he described his own experience and the treatment of the Negro in South Africa by the Englishman. No one who had attended that lecture can admire the English in their treatment of Negroes in the colonies. It indicates that the kind treatment they give the Negro while in England is but the superficial treatment accorded a visitor. Mr Williams is a man of wisdom and courage – a defender of the rights of his race. He could give the Liberians invaluable assistance in many ways in London.

On 5 February 1908, Williams addressed the annual meeting of the Bar Association. In his lecture, he expressed his political views and also outlined the role of the association. He reminded his audience that West African states had been wiped out and 'made to swallow the debt of scorn, contempt and even slavery at the hands of the pretentious invader'. Notwithstanding their sixty years of liberation from slavery, Liberians were neither free nor safe. The prejudices against Liberians were 'based upon jealousy and a strange antagonism'. Liberia, he argued, had a duty to the world and its people to maintain its integrity as an example for the rest of the continent of Africa. To achieve this, Liberians needed to form links with black people in the United States, Brazil and the West Indies. The success of the Bar Association depended on 'honesty and sincerity' among its members. As with the Bar Association of England, it was necessary that it should be watched over by members of the profession. The 'most objectionable offence' would be an allegation of unprofessional behaviour. Judges, he emphasised, 'have always been beyond the reach of temptation', and he hoped that the same applied to the Liberian judiciary.

These statements, and the popularity Williams enjoyed in Liberia, brought him once again to the attention of South African authorities. In March 1908, enquiries were made by the colonial office to the Transvaal government concerning 'the subject of a West Indian negro named H. Sylvester Williams'. The secretary for the colony, Sir Edward Grey, wished to know of 'any information in the possession of the Earl of Elgin regarding the career of this individual in South Africa'. This request was triggered by a declaration made by J.L. Harris, who described himself as 'a subject of the United States of America domiciled in England'. Since 10 January 1907, he had been living in Liberia, and was employed as an engineer for the Liberian Development Company. He had attended a meeting addressed by Williams in the capital, Monrovia. At that meeting, he heard Mr Williams, 'who described himself as a member of the English Bar', deliver an address:

> The address, so far as Great Britain and the British Government were concerned, was treasonable. He said that the British Government in South Africa treated the natives like serfs. He referred to the last Zulu War and said that the War had been forced upon them (the Zulu) by the British Government. He stated that if the native slept in a town without permission he was sent without trial to work at the mines for five years. He told the people to resist with all their power anything English. He added that England wanted this country and he could procure discontented West Indians to come to Liberia and help to build up the country.[88]

Sir Edward Grey, however, was of the view that, although Williams was 'exercising a most unsavoury influence in Liberia', it was not possible to take action against him. Nevertheless, enquiries would be made in South Africa.[89] An intelligence report procured on a 'confidential' basis was obtained. It contained inaccuracies, however, alleging that he had once been arrested on a criminal charge. While the report confirmed that Williams was admitted as an advocate of the Supreme Court of the Cape of Good Hope on 29 October 1903 and had spent some time in the Transvaal, he was never arrested on any criminal charge, and, as pointed out by Grey, 'nor was he involved in any trouble with the exception that he was a witness in a murder case'.

The police reported information from a Major Cadell, 'who by chance saw and recognised the man here, having come across him during the war in South Africa'. Cadell went on to record further untruths about the whereabouts of Williams. He claimed that he had been 'deported' from the Transvaal for attempting to incite the natives against the British, 'and he was a very prominent agent of the Ethiopian society'. Cadell's account became even more fanciful, with claims that 'the attorneys in the Transvaal combined to have [Williams] excluded from practising in the courts' and that the advocates in Johannesburg and Pretoria refused to have anything to do with him. The further claim was made that Williams 'subsequently travelled about South Africa spreading the doctrine of the country for the black races alone. He is believed to have afterwards passed into Swaziland.' These reports[90] appear to have been discarded by the colonial office, as no further enquiries were made – and nor were any further steps taken against Williams in Liberia.

Williams's period as an advocate at the Cape Bar was brief, a mere two years. Yet it was decidedly significant. He shattered the barrier of race, though he was unable to destroy racism. It would be another fifty years before a black advocate would gain admission to the Bar and practise in South Africa. Williams was admitted because of the liberal laws in the Cape, which drew no distinction on the grounds of race. But the fact that he could not realise his dream of practising as an advocate proved that the removal of the official barriers was merely a first step. He suffered social and economic exclusion, and for such racism to be dismantled, a new culture needed to be fostered.

As a lawyer, Williams transcended traditional boundaries. He understood that law was itself an empty shell if not suffused with justice. For no other reason, this is why his life is worth exploring and understanding. His vision of racial equality was ahead of its time. Henry Sylvester Williams was a brave man, willing to make important choices at great personal cost. In 1912 he passed away, and his bones lie buried in his country of birth, Trinidad. But his ideas of Pan-Africanism live on in his adoptive country, South Africa.

3

'We don't want to swamp the white man in Africa'

One of the difficulties confronting educated Africans in South Africa is that of a choice of career. When a white young man is considering his life's work, he has the whole wide world to choose from for a career. He can enter any profession he wishes as long as he has the ability to acquire the necessary qualifications. Not so with the African young man. The choice before him is very limited. For many a long year such a young man had only two choices open to him, either to preach or to teach – to enter the teaching profession or the ministry of the Church. These are noble professions but goodness knows not every African has neither the inclination nor the necessary ability … For that reason great credit must be given to those who have broken away from the easy road and have decided to blaze a new trail, to break new ground, to start on entirely new careers not previously entered by their fellow Africans. One of the men to whom such honour must go is Advocate Alfred Mangena. . . Today, when the number of Africans in the legal profession is steadily increasing, it is well for us to do honour to the man who led the way.

– Z.K. Matthews, *Imvo Zabantsundu*, 3 June 1961

Alfred Mangena was admired by many during his lifetime, and despite being slandered by some, the significance of his life and ideas was never in doubt. This remains true today, though there is greater urgency in the fact. Mangena was a deep thinker, who took ideas seriously. And while he was conscious of the virtue of an English legal education, he abhorred the racial prejudices of the English. A revolutionary to the core, he pioneered the use of the law as an instrument of revolution. The land of the Africans had been taken by force. But the law, if justly applied, could create the conditions necessary for coexistence and a shared prosperity among the races. His vision of a non-racial society, based on equality and the rule of law, is now commonly accepted. But this was not always the case. Colonial military aggression, exploitation of black labour and European imperialism shaped his era. But for Mangena, injustice could only be fought with justice; illegality with legality; and colonialism with constitutionalism. Mangena's value system was shaped by African society, whose humanism was underpinned by justice. When he encountered British legal training, which spoke of equality for all, he could relate it to his own experience of the inherent fairness in African traditional courts. Yet the hypocrisy of the British experience was not lost on him: English legal education was based on equality, the rule of law and the separation of powers, but in the colonies the reality was vastly different, as he well knew. There, racial inequality, abuse of power vested in colonial magistrates and rule by decree were standard practice. For Mangena, these represented an uncivilised way of life; true civilisation was not possible in the absence of equality and justice.

Unfortunately, Mangena's legal activities came to a premature end, and there are indications that this was precipitated by the authorities. While we shall never know what he might have achieved had colonial South Africa been a different country, it is possible to reconstruct aspects of his life, as well as his ideas, from sources such as newspaper reports. That we know so little of a figure once so influential is an indictment not only of South Africa's history, but also of historical writing.

Early years

The Mangena clan, the amaZizi, had left Zululand during the Mfecane wars[1] to settle in the Eastern Cape. Alfred Mangena's grandfather, however, had remained in Zululand, where his son, Stomela, became a general in Cetshwayo ka Mpande's army. Cetshwayo had led the Zulu in the wars against the British in 1879, a year that remains etched in Zulu memory because of their victory against the mighty British army at the battle of Isandlwana. However, it was in the subsequent battles, including Rorke's Drift, where the Zulu were ultimately vanquished. Their land was taken from them and put under British control. The authority of Cetshwayo, the Zulu king, was drastically curtailed on the instruction of Queen Victoria. Zulu laws were replaced by the iniquitous Code of Zulu Law, and scores of young Zulu men were forced to find work on the mines of the Transvaal, where their labour was cruelly exploited. Once military conquest had subjected the Zulu to British rules and laws, their only means of resistance were the institutions of Empire – and foremost among these was education.

The year of Alfred Mangena's birth is unknown, as it was never officially registered. In his latter years, Mangena guessed that he was born either in 1880 or 1881. When he was about four years old, his parents, Stomela and Victoria, left Zululand for Pondoland, in northern Transkei. Two years later, the family relocated to the Transvaal. Even though his parents were not Christian converts, they sent young Alfred to be educated at Clarkebury, a mission school in the Eastern Cape. The education of their eldest son – the first of their children to attend school – represented a turning point in the Mangena family.

First steps to a legal career

Mangena's broader education began before he attended English missionary schools. As a young boy, he was told stories of the wars between the Zulu and the British and how the land of the Zulu people was lost in military wars. He took great interest in debates, and regularly attended Zulu traditional courts where he witnessed the intellectual exchanges of his people. In London, many years later, while he was studying at Lincoln's Inn, Mangena recalled that the practice of law 'was born in me' and 'came naturally'[2] – a result of his early witnessing of proceedings in Zulu courts.[3]

Mangena obtained his secondary education and teaching qualification at the Clarkebury Institution in Ngcobo, Tembuland. The first missionary school in the Eastern Cape, Clarkebury was opened in 1830 by the Wesleyan Church, and William Hargreaves was appointed as principal. Although it started as an industrial school, by the time Mangena arrived Clarkebury had shifted its focus to classical English education, which was described by Sir George Grey as too 'bookish'.[4] Mangena graduated as a teacher before travelling to Johannesburg where he briefly worked on the mines. After his sojourn, Mangena returned to the Transkei. This time, he settled in Qokolweni, a suburb of Mthatha. He soon became frustrated, not only with the monotony of teaching, but also with his repeated failure to prevent colonial encroachment on native land. In 1895, he had witnessed the introduction of the Glen Grey Act, a comprehensive piece of legislation brought into being by Cecil John Rhodes. The Act introduced the requirement for a poll or 'hut' tax, and placed significant restrictions on land ownership by natives. The last Frontier War, in 1878, had ended in military defeat for the Xhosa, so the only practical avenue for challenging the enforcement of restrictive laws and practices was the political arena and the judicial system. While most disputes were resolved by courts, the difficulty remained that there were no black lawyers trained in the craft of law to act as representatives for blacks. Mangena decided to enrol for a law degree, but he had limited financial resources. Cape Town presented itself as an option, as across the Eastern Cape there was news of expanding employment opportunities in the city; the opportunity of making a decent living as a dockworker appealed to Mangena. A dockworker's wage would be an improvement on the salary of a native teacher. He left for Cape Town, with the object of making enough money to enable him to study law in England.[5]

Bubonic plague: origins of residential segregation

Mangena arrived in Cape Town in 1898, on a recommendation from a Kimberley headman, Mr Pongala. Finding a job was, nevertheless, a challenge. Mangena became self-employed, teaching Zulu to white people who wanted to visit Zululand. At the same time, he decided to gain a qualification to work in the civil service, and attended special training in the evenings. He was also a lay preacher at Saint Barnabas Chapel, where he met Reverend Owen Davies, who offered him accommodation at the rectory. Mangena stayed there for five years, and during that time he taught at a night school for natives run by Davies, and also assisted in general missionary work.[6]

The year 1901 was a turning point in Mangena's political life; the reason for this can be traced back to the previous year, in August. That month, the son of Dr A.J. Gregory, chief medical officer for the Cape Colony, noticed eight dead rats within a few yards of one another in the North Quay of the docks. Dr Gregory was informed of this and sent a message to the local police to report any further such instances. He received no further reports about dead rats, but in January 1901, he received a telegram from Dr Matthew Hewat of Mowbray. It read: 'suspicious case Bubonic Plague at Rondebosch Cottage Hospital. When shall I meet you?'[7] That same month, E.A. McCallum, a white thirty-year-old military clerk employed at the South Arm of the docks, complained of pain and swelling in the groin, the result, he suspected, of jumping from a tramcar. But Dr Hewat diagnosed this as very severe typhoid and sent him to the Rondebosch Cottage Hospital, where he was admitted on 31 January 1901. He was found to have 'all the features of a case of the bubonic variety of plague'.[8] Upon further enquiry, Dr Gregory learnt of 'a very large mortality of rats' during the month of January. About 200 rats were found dead, and '[i]n the majority of cases the rats were fat and well nourished'.[9] Later tests proved that McCallum was infected with bubonic plague. Two other employees at the South Arm were later found to have been infected: Andrew Eldy, aged thirty-four, and J. McCarthy, aged seventy-seven. But the very first case, reported on 26 January 1901, was that of a coloured man, Joseph Gobert (or Jonas Galleo).[10] Within two weeks, sixteen more cases were reported. By February, the Cape was in the grip of the plague. An official response was urgent.

The response of the Cape government was political. The plague was a problem caused by black people, and the solution necessarily entailed their removal. Thus, the first racially segregated native location in the Cape was born. Yet the historical antecedents of residential segregation should be acknowledged. For years after the discovery of diamonds in the Cape, Africans lived in the squalor of single-sex compounds, with their atrocious social and health conditions. Residential segregation also enjoyed political support, as evidenced by an address to the Cape Parliament in 1899 by liberal prime minister William Schreiner in favour of a pass and compound system for Africans. He stated that his government was concerned that transient Africans were learning 'all sorts of bad habits' by living in close proximity to European and coloured surroundings. The solution, suggested Schreiner, was a system whereby transient Africans would be in the city for the duration of their employment contracts, whereafter they would be 'sent home'.[11] He was not the first politician to make such a statement. Four years earlier, introducing the Glen Grey Act before the Cape Parliament as prime minister, Rhodes had expressed his support for separate residential areas for Africans.[12]

While consistent with the political sensibilities of the era, the notion of segregated living presented economic and practical difficulties. Africans could not simply be sent 'home' to the Eastern Cape. Many had been settled in Cape Town for years. Also, their cheap labour was in demand. The solution was to create separate residential locations on the periphery of the city. While racial separation in schools, hospitals and many other facilities was the norm, for the majority of whites the central problem remained that of interracial mixing in the city. Businesses, however, saw the matter differently, and regarded the cost and inconvenience of segregation as unnecessary. Their concern was the accessibility of the native workforce. Nevertheless, the municipal council went ahead with its plans. C.W. Downing proposed the adoption of the Native Locations Act for Cape Town in 1898. Uitvlugt was identified as a possible location for natives. The Cape Times expressed approval, stating that the location of Uitvlugt would be 'not only in the interests of the white population, but also in the interests of the aborigines themselves'.[13] By September 1900, preliminary plans for the location had been drafted. Consistent with the policy of the government, no attempt was made to consult with Africans themselves. And on the part of the white population, the plans were met with little resistance.

The ravages of the plague gave impetus to the plans for racial segregation of the city, providing medical justification. Medical experts were brought in to justify an Act that was politically expedient. Medical and 'scientific' explanations were trumped up for pushing black people out of the city. Blacks were being blamed for the spread of the plague, and they were to be removed from the city and placed in a confined area in order to contain the spread of the disease. Myron Echenberg points out that, in strategies for plague control, 'black Africans were designated as major targets'.[14] The Plague Advisory Board of the government employed a cleansing gang to complement the work of the medical practitioners. The gang comprised 160 unskilled European workers, 100 Africans and 280 criminal convicts from Breakwater Prison. Their job was the forced removal of Africans. Sam Ntungwana, who resided at Horstley Street, District 6, made the following statement on 15 April 1901:

I have my goods packed up and ready to be loaded. I could not get the wagon in the morning. The soldiers came to me in the afternoon just as I was taking one of the boxes out and told me to leave it alone and they forbade going into the house again. They told me to bring back all the things which I had already taken out. I went out and I locked the room. After three days I went back to fetch my things: I could not find them and I was told they were burned. [15]

In addition to widespread eviction, anyone suspected of infection was isolated. But the isolation and confinement took place at a new location, in Uitvlugt, where temporary corrugated-iron structures were erected for the purpose. By this time, large numbers of Africans had been marched out of the city and forced to live at Uitvlugt. But this was not all. Travel restrictions were imposed, with Africans being the target, though for employment reasons these restrictions could be relaxed. Remarkably, the vast majority of the evictions were carried out in terms of the Public Health Act of 1897, as an emergency measure. In order to carry out this 'emergency' relocation, the police and the army were brought in. Echenberg explains:

> African dock workers who reported for work as usual on March 12 were told to return to their homes, where they found their possessions either burning in bonfires or thrown into the street and a force of 100 sanitation workers busily scrubbing and spraying their belongings with carbolic solution. By day's end, the police and the army had corralled nearly a 1000 Africans from District 6, District 1 and the dock area. A military escort paraded the helpless dispossessed to the train station for the short trip to the Cape Flats and Uitvlugt. [16]

A new location, the first of its kind, had now been established. Africans would later call it Kwandabeni – place of tales – after a nickname they had given to Walter Stanford, former native commissioner of the Eastern Cape.

In his memoirs, Stanford recalls the establishment of Kwandabeni[17] as coming about because of the large influx of natives from the Eastern Cape who were seeking employment. No provision had been made regarding their accommodation, and the situation became urgent. A commission, chaired by Stanford, which included two medical officers and the chief of police, was established. Stanford consulted various leaders, and among them was Reverend Elijah Mdolomba of a Wesleyan church serving the African population. He records that leading men among the natives 'heartily supported' the suggestion that, on a site away from the city, a location be established by the government to meet the needs of African people.[18] After inspecting various sites, a portion of the forest reserve at Uitvlugt was proclaimed under Government Notice No. 237 of 1901. This legislation, a prerequisite for the establishment of native reserve locations in or near urban areas, had recently been passed. It granted the necessary powers to the governor, and Uitvlugt was designated as a native reserve location.

The location having been proclaimed, a key issue was religion. Churches were allowed to conduct religious work among the natives, and schools were opened. Reverend Mdolomba was one of the first churchmen to establish a church in the area. But the population soon grew beyond the capacity of the land available. There was resistance among some natives to leaving the city, and Stanford explains this as in 'no small measure ... due to the efforts of the white landlords who nationally opposed their removal'.[19] Stanford did, however, recognise that, up to the time of the bubonic plague, there was no law that could compel the forced removal to Uitvlugt.[20] Once the plague broke out, the government used section 15 of the Public Health Amendment Act No. 23 of 1897, which provided that:

> In cases of urgent necessity arising from the prevalence or threatened outbreak in any district of infectious disease, mentioned in section 38 [e.g. smallpox, cholera, etc.], it shall be lawful for the Minister to make and proclaim such regulations to be in force within such district as may be required to prevent the outbreak, or check the progress of, or eradicate such disease.

It was under this provision that, according to Stanford, 'the slums were finally cleared of these people'.[21] Stanford recalls how the name of Uitvlugt was changed at the request of the African population. A deputation was sent to him to ask if the location could be renamed Kwandabeni, which was the name he was generally known by. Though somewhat sceptical, he raised no objections. Stanford presented the proposal to Schreiner. This is how he recalled it:

> We said to the Prime Minister that we wished to submit a request to him for a native name to be given to our location. He asked what name we had thought of. We replied 'Kwandabeni'. 'What does that mean?' asked the Prime Minister. They replied: 'You know Sir, the meaning of "Ndaba" – place of news; Kwandabeni is taken from that.' 'Oh, yes,' said the Prime Minister. 'I see now. You mean the place where I have had talks with you and discussed affairs?' 'Yes Sir,' the reply came.

Stanford also recalled the establishment of a native location outside Port Elizabeth, called New Brighton, under the same law as for Kwandabeni. Stanford described what transpired upon his return to Cape Town after the Anglo-Boer War in 1902:

> On my arrival in Cape Town I found the Ndabeni location much overcrowded. Dock labourers and other natives not in permanent employment had been removed under the provisions of the Health Act to Ndabeni. The only way out was to send these people back to their locations in the Eastern districts or the Transkei territories. This was done, precautions being taken to send away

only those who were clear of any plague infection or contagion. Difficulties were raised in East London. These however were overcome and the evacuation took place.[22]

'A quagmire inside and out'

Resistance to the forced relocations was building. The most prominent leader was Alfred Mangena. Although he was not living at Kwandabeni, the community had elected him secretary of the Dock-Workers Association, whose activities were mostly in the Kwandabeni area. Some months before taking up this position, Mangena had written to the *South African News* to register his protest at the harsh, unfair treatment meted out to Africans who were evicted.

> We are sent out, but foreigners are invited to come and take possession ... we deserve better treatment from a government that boasts of equal rights for all men, irrespective of creed or colour. Our homes are being broken up, furniture soiled and spoiled, and in many cases destroyed.[23]

The *South African News*, whose editorial outlook was anti-imperialist, was sympathetic to the position of the Africans. Not only did it provide a platform for those who opposed the forced removals, it also sounded a word of caution about the removals, arguing that the future prospects for Cape Town were 'grave'. A report on 9 February 1901 contended that, instead of preventing the spread of the plague, the removal of Africans would result in new breeding spots for the disease. But the white population was not prepared to rise up in support of Africans. The same was true of some of the leaders of the coloured community, the most significant of whom was Dr Abdullah Abdurahman. Their reason for not opposing the removal of the Africans was partly because the relocation to Ndabeni primarily targeted Africans rather than coloured people. It is not clear what position was adopted by the Indian community. However, Mohandas Gandhi, their most prominent leader, was of the view that the British government was making a mistake in treating Indians the same way as 'raw kaffirs'.[24] If these views were reflective of the general Indian sentiment at the time, the Indians would have been an unlikely ally for Africans.

Africans realised that they were on their own, but because of the use of the army and other coercive means, they were unable to resist the relocation. It was only after the forced settlement at Kwandabeni that new ways of resistance began to emerge. There were many false promises: for example, William Sipika, who supported the relocation believing that it would enable him to own his plot, build a home and even run a business, was soon disappointed. At Kwandabeni, none of that would happen. Instead, to make a living Sipika would be forced to make himself available to the city as a labourer. Unsurprisingly, Sipika joined a resistance movement. Living conditions at Kwandabeni were appalling, and with insufficient land available, people crowded into huts and shacks. James Jolobe, the first African minister of the Dutch Reformed Church, described the location as 'a quagmire inside and out, once the rains in May had worked their way through the earth floors of the huts'.[25] In June 1901, the colonial government decided that Africans should pay their own rent and also train fares to get to the docks. It was this decision that propelled Mangena to the fore of the resistance movement. As secretary of the Dock-Workers Association, Mangena championed the cause of the dock-workers and residents of Kwandabeni. In a letter published by the *Cape Times* in 1899, he had called for universal franchise. And now he questioned both the legality and moral basis of the authorities' decision concerning Kwandabeni: 'Is this an established location or merely a disused bubonic camp utilised for a temporary purpose? ... By what legal process or right of the law or equity have you ... acted?'[26] To channel the people's resistance, a committee was formed, and Machine Wakani was elected treasurer.

The establishment of Kwandabeni had been justified on medical grounds by the authorities. Dr Gregory had claimed that the native location was necessary for health purposes, and it came into being under legislation that purported to prevent the spread of infectious diseases. Gregory also claimed that the spread of infection was partly due to overcrowding, and that he had 'seen as many as 14 natives sleeping in one small apartment'. While Kwandabeni was meant to be a medical solution to the overcrowding that caused the spread of the plague, the overcrowding did not abate. Instead, it grew worse: contrary to official promises, no housing was provided in Kwandabeni. As Gregory noted, there were merely structures constructed of 'corrugated iron and shaped like the huts erected by the permanent laymen'. Seemingly oblivious to the irony, Gregory continued by describing the houses as having a 'comical shape'. The 'great complaint' was that the houses were too low on the ground, and so they flooded in May when the heavy winter rains came, and 'were damp'.[27]

It was in these circumstances of overcrowding, poor sanitary conditions and inadequate corrugated-iron housing that an African named Arthur Radasi was convicted for refusing to pay rent. He was sentenced to three months' imprisonment with hard labour or the option of paying a fine. The case, reported as *R. v. Radasi*, came before the Cape Supreme Court,[28] where Chief Justice Henry de Villiers overturned the conviction, finding that the municipality did not have the legal power to pass the regulations in terms of which Radasi had been convicted and sentenced.

The victory sent shockwaves along the corridors of power. But it was met with jubilation by the native population. Mangena became aware of the judgment, and in June 1902, with his attorney and an advocate named Wilkinson, he addressed several meetings in Kwandabeni where he explained the implications of the Radasi case. The message was clear. Since the regulations had been declared *ultra vires* and therefore illegal, they were unenforceable. As such, no one was forced to pay rent, or, for that matter, transport to and from their jobs at the docks. This initiated a boycott, and there was widespread resistance to paying rent. Workers also refused to pay train fares. Mangena was the key spokesperson for the resistance to rental payment. Together with Wakani, he addressed several meetings, calling upon Africans to resist paying rent until such time as the quality of the houses and the general sanitary conditions were improved. Mangena's call was for equal treatment, based on the promise of the British government that all its citizens would be treated equally. In the wake of this resistance, there were widespread arrests. There was an immediate clampdown, and fourteen Africans were arrested, convicted and sentenced to imprisonment with hard labour. A further twelve were later arrested and imprisoned.

Mangena began to raise funds for the defence of those arrested. On 29 June, he and Dr Seller, who was brought in to assist the Africans, addressed more than 500 people at Kwandabeni. They explained that it was illegal for the government to impose the rental requirement. Mangena also informed them that he would be leaving for England to pursue his law studies. The following day, the people refused to buy train tickets and picketed at the station to prevent others from doing so. Empty trains pulled out of the station with many windows broken. While there was no attempt at collecting fares the next day, extra police were deployed and the boycott was crushed. There were widespread arrests and Wakani and eleven others were charged and sentenced. From then on, the dockworkers regarded 30 June 1902 as 'Mangena Day'.

In the midst of all of this, there was internal opposition to the resistance. Reverend Mdolomba, a Cape administration sympathiser and a supporter of the relocation, resented Mangena's popularity with the residents. He was later to make accusations about Mangena having improperly pocketed funds meant for the community, though the charges proved groundless, as becomes clear below.

'Third university of England'

Mangena was on his way to a legal career, headed towards Lincoln's Inn, one of London's four Inns of Court, where barristers are trained. The Inns of Court had long been regarded as the 'third university of England', a term that goes back to the sixteenth century, before English law was taught at Oxford and Cambridge. In those universities only civil, Roman and canon (church) law were taught. So the only place where English law could be studied was at the Inns of Court. But when Mangena arrived at Lincoln's Inn in the early twentieth century, it had been placed under the Council for Legal Education. Before admission, applicants were required to pass an examination, either the matriculation examination offered by the University of London, or the Oxford or Cambridge Senior Local Examination. Mangena passed the matriculation examination, thereby qualifying for admission as a student at the Inn. When he filled in his registration form, Mangena described his father as 'a landed proprietor'.

At Lincoln's Inn, Mangena took courses in Roman Law and Jurisprudence, International Law, Constitutional Law and Legal History, the Law of Evidence, the Law of Procedure and Criminal Law, the Law of Real and Personal Property and Conveyancing, the Common Law, and the Law of Equity. These were new subjects to him. Roman Law covered the Institutes of Justinian and Gaius, the Digest and the Code, and explored the impact of Roman Law on the English legal system. On Mondays, Wednesdays and Fridays, Mangena attended courses on the development of Roman Law and Jurisprudence, which also compared it with English law and traced its effects on current legal systems. Topics discussed included Roman Legal History and the Modern Importance of Roman Law. He also learnt about the natural law, with special reference to Austin's analysis.[29] Various courses covered legislation, its role in the ordering of society and its development. Tuesday lectures included Private International Law and Conflict of Laws. Emphasis was placed on the English doctrine, with courses on British nationality, British naturalisation, domicile, status and legal capacity to enter into legally binding contracts, and family relations.

Constitutional Law classes focused on the title to the crown; the prerogative powers of the monarchy; the councils of the crown, particularly the cabinet system; the ministry and the departments of government; and the revenue service, focusing on collection and expenditure and parliamentary control over taxation. Lectures were also given on the role of the established church, the armed forces, the civil service, and the colonies and their constitutional status. On Saturdays, Mangena attended classes on the Law of Evidence, Procedure and Criminal Law, which examined the procedure in civil action, with practical illustrations taken from actual summonses, pleadings and procedures of court. The Wednesday classes included elementary courses in Criminal Law and Procedure, with the Law of Real and Personal Property and Conveyancing being taught on Thursdays. In respect of Tort Law, the general principles and exemptions were taught, and personal disability, including that of infants and married women, was also covered. The acts of state, being judicial and executive acts, were also in the syllabus. In addition, Mangena was instructed in the Law of Principal and Agent, the Law of Master and Servant, the Law of Remedies, the Calculation of Damages, and the Statute of the Limitation of Actions. The Law of Equity, also referred to as the Law of Limited Companies, focused on prospectuses, underwriting, rescission of contracts, the winding up, reconstruction, amalgamation and dissolution of companies, as well as the general practice and procedure in actions and matters relating to companies.

In addition to this rigorous legal training programme, Mangena was required to attend a specified number of dinners at the Inn. Not all students enjoyed the experience of pupillage, however, as exemplified by Lord Bowen's description in 1858:

> I will recollect the dreary days with which my own experience of the law began, in the chambers of the once famous Lincoln's Inn conveyancer; the gloom of a London atmosphere without, the whitewashed misery of the pupils' room within – both rendered more emphatic by what appeared to us the hopeless dinginess of the occupations of its inhabitants. There stood all our dismal textbooks in rows ... calculated to extinguish all desire of knowledge, even in the most thirsty soul. To use the language of the sacred text, it seemed a barren and a dry land in which no waters was. And, with all this, no adequate method of study, no sound and intelligible principle upon which to collect and to assort our information.[30]

Students were required to pass examinations in Roman Law, Constitutional Law and Legal History, Evidence, Procedure, Civil and Criminal Law, as well as an elective in English Law and Equity. Students could present themselves for examination at any time after admission at the Inn, though the final examination required council approval, unless the student had spent six terms at the Inn.

At one point, Mangena lived at 242 Ladbroke Grove. There were a number of West African, Caribbean and Indian students at the Inn, and by 1900 nearly half of all students were foreign students.[31] In the two-year period after his arrival in 1903, Mangena spent a quiet time studying and preparing for his future role as a lawyer and leader of his people in South Africa. In addition to the rigours of the Inn, Mangena immersed himself in work with other South Africans. In March 1906, he conceived the idea of forming a new association for 'coloured' people coming to England. The diversity of those who responded to the call is notable. *The Gold Coast Leader* of 10 March 1906 noted the following:

> A circular letter signed by Mr Alfred Mangena, (Student at Lincoln's Inn, and South African) was sent round sometime last week convening a meeting of the 'coloured' folk residing or resident in London. A meeting was accordingly held on the 9th inst. at the Saracens Head Hotel, Holborn, Viaduct, W.C. and among those who were present were Messrs J.J. Brown, Frederick Iris (West Indies), Moses Taylor, Gosford Sawyerr (Sierra Leone), Alfred Mangena (South Africa), T.A. Wilson, A. Boehm, John Theo. Harm (Barrister at Law),

P.E. Sampson, Joe E. Eminsang, and A.S. Cann. I understand the object of the meeting was to discuss ways and means by which a Society or Association could be formed in London to promote friendly intercourse amongst 'coloured' races coming to Europe, to render mutual help, discuss social and political subjects connected with the race and to work in such other ways as the society may think when formed, would be conducive to the progress of Africans and to the advancement of the interests of Africans.

Mangena was soon to be thrust into the national and international spotlight by events not in London, but in the land of his birth, Natal.

'You can shoot us. We will not pay you the money'

The year 1906 is remembered for the uprising of Bambatha, the result of a clash of values and also of civilisations. It is a little-known fact, however, that Bambatha himself enjoyed support among the Christianised and educated black elite. Before venturing further, certain facts need to be noted. On 28 August 1905, the Natal government passed the Poll Tax Act.[32] Section 2 of the Act compelled 'every male person of the age of 18 years and upwards', unless exempted, to pay an annual poll tax of £1. The exceptions were set out in section 14, significantly that of section 14(4), which provided that any person 'who shall prove that he is unable through poverty to pay the tax shall be excused therefrom for the time being but the excuse shall not prevent a subsequent prosecution or action if such person shall afterwards become able to pay the tax and fail to do so'.

All able-bodied African men from Zululand were, accordingly, required to pay the tax. This meant they would either need to sell some of their livestock or, if they owned no livestock, look for employment. The primary place where employment was available on a large scale for a mainly uneducated population was on the mines in the Transvaal, or on white-owned farms. The poll tax coincided with the clamour of the mines for large numbers of unskilled workers, and so the claim that it was motivated primarily by the greed of the mining companies seems valid. It was they who influenced the passing of the law in order to compel African men, perceived as being idle, to leave Zululand and to find work on the mines.[33] The charge seems especially valid if one has regard to the demand for black labour after the end of the Anglo-Boer War. Indeed, when the Poll Tax Bill was debated, the minister for native affairs explicitly stated that the tax was 'justified, since for the last 20 years the inhabitants of the Colony have been asking for increased hut tax in order that there may be a greater supply of Native labour'.[34] But the poll tax was also a strategy of consolidation on the part of the imperial government. After the defeat of the Zulus in 1879, the tax was a means of exerting control, and its sole purpose was to force allegiance to, and compliance with, the institutions of government.

The trouble began in 1906, when the colonial government attempted to enforce the law. Although the tax was due from 1 January 1906, it was expected that the enforcement of the legislation would only commence at the end of May 1906. Yet by February the government was already sending out tax collectors. One of these was Duncan McKenzie, who thus threatened chiefs at Ixopo who resisted: 'I want 15 herd of cattle … This is the last chance. He need not come to me with a few assegais; I will go and collect them if he does not bring them all and I will take every beast he has got and then his kraals if the cattle and assegais are not there.'[35] As the refusal to pay the tax gained momentum, the government used police to enforce tax collection. In one incident, near Byrnetown, fifteen policemen set out to crush the resistance. The police intelligence was that more than twenty African men were instigating others to resist the payment, including by arming themselves. The mandate of the police was to arrest these men. Confrontation was inevitable. The rebellion was subdued, followed by a court martial. Mbadi, one of the accused, stated the following in his evidence at a subsequent trial:

> We noticed that they had drawn their revolvers, they were in front of us, so we drew back to the rocks, saying we had done no harm in the location. They said: 'You have been carrying assegais.' We said: 'There is no harm in that.' [...] They told us to lay down our assegais and we said, 'How can we do so when you have drawn your firearms?' The others then shouted, 'You have come here for our money; You can shoot us. We won't pay,' and 'We would rather die than pay.'[36]

These threats simply served to fuel an already flammable environment. There was restlessness across Zululand, and suspicion as to the true reasons behind the imposition of the tax. The issue of the tax also split people, creating two camps: Christian converts and non-believers. The primary resistance was among the non-believers. One of the chiefs who resisted was Tilonko, chief of the Abambo people, in the Richmond area. It was reported that, on 12 February, Tilonko's people had taken up arms and assembled at the chief's homestead. Europeans in the area were moved into a protective laager. But Tilonko and his people did not immediately cause anyone harm, and by April the Abambo had paid all their taxes. Despite the fact that Tilonko had not been prominent in the disturbances, it was decided to bring him before the minister for native affairs, where he was tried before a court martial, without a defence lawyer, on charges of sedition and public violence. He was found guilty and fined 500 head of cattle, though this was later reduced to 250. He was also deposed from his position and exiled to the island of St Helena. Sympathisers, including Harriette Colenso, daughter of

Bishop Colenso of Natal, attempted to move the government to reduce the sentence on the grounds that it was too harsh, given the relatively insignificant role Tilonko had played in the disturbances. The campaign failed, however, as did a petition to the Natal Supreme Court.

The news of the charge for sedition and public violence reached Mangena in London, who was at the time in his third year of study and relatively confident of his legal abilities. Mangena prepared an urgent petition to the Privy Council, in his own name, acting on behalf of Tilonko. The petition charged that there was no evidence against Tilonko, and that the trial was unfair since it took place under the auspices of the native affairs minister, and not an ordinary court of law. Had Tilonko been a British subject, he would have been tried before a criminal court, where he would have been accorded all the rights of an accused person. Mangena's petition failed. And while Tilonko was among the first of the Bambatha leaders to be arrested and subjected to a trial, more was to come. The enforcement of the sentence led to a bloody revolt, at the centre of which was Bambatha ka Mancinza, chief of the Zondi clan in the Weenen area. The government had deposed him a few weeks before the rebellion on the basis of the prominent role he had played in the resistance to the poll tax. When Bambatha discovered that his uncle had been appointed in his place, he kidnapped him. The magistrate and police sent to conduct an investigation were shot on sight, and government troops were sent in to find and capture Bambatha. But by the time they arrived he had fled his home at Mpanza Valley. He then hid in the forests of Nkandla, where he built an army of resistance. For more than a month he stayed in hiding, and was joined by other chiefs from the area, who provided supplies and intelligence. He conducted a guerrilla war against the white troops in the area. Informants from Nkandla eventually betrayed him, which ultimately led to his arrest and beheading, with major casualties being suffered by his people. Dinuzulu ka Cetshwayo was accused of providing Bambatha with support, information and supplies, and he too was exiled to St Helena. At the end of the rebellion, twelve Africans were arraigned before a court martial and pronounced guilty of treason. Alfred Mangena asserted that 'the natives were not the aggressors' and went on to comment as follows on the rebellion and its causes:

In many cases payment of this tax was an impossibility. The Zulus wealth is reckoned in cattle, and their herd is held by the members of a family in common. Individual properties scarcely exist. The tax, therefore, fell not upon one man, but upon his whole family. And its severity can be judged from the fact that five Dollars represents more or less the earnings of an able-bodied Zulu for ten weeks.

The Government knew this. And my opinion is that this tax was deliberately put so high that the Zulus would be quite unable to pay it, working under ordinary agricultural conditions.

The reason for this lay close at hand. The gold mines – the curse of South Africa – needed labour. The mine owners feared the Liberal Government in England would dispense with the Chinese cheap labour. They knew that the natives would not work for the slave wages paid to the Chinese, and consequently they devised some plan to induce the natives to work whether they like it or not.

The Poll Tax seemed to provide this incentive. Apparently the Government and the mine owners played into one another's hands.

... [T]he tax was not to be collected until May 31. But a police force was sent down to collect it at the beginning of February, four months before it became due. This illegal process was carried out. One native – a village Hampden[37] – protested against payment. He was shot. Thereupon the natives thought they were being attacked under no pretext whatever, and in self-defence as they thought, they attacked the police, and an Englishman, Inspector Hunt, was killed.[38]

Mangena went on to mention his 'futile attempts' at petitioning the Privy Council, on behalf of Tilonko and the 'Natal rebels', to intervene so that those arrested in connection with the rebellion were charged under the ordinary courts, rather than the military courts. Mangena's insistence on the use of ordinary criminal courts was not merely about a change in forum. Ordinary criminal courts provided everyone with the procedural rights to a fair trial, including the right to representation by counsel, particularly if the crime carried the death penalty. Martial courts, on the other hand, were military tribunals, set up to try 'rebels' and prisoners of war.

Bambatha at the Privy Council
Once the Bambatha rebellion had been suppressed, reprisals followed. Twelve Africans considered to be the leaders of the rebellion were lined up before a military tribunal, sitting in Richmond, Natal, to face accusations of treason. They were duly convicted and sentenced to death. While they awaited their date with the firing squad, Mangena sought to make a final stand on their behalf. On 2 April 1906, he filed an urgent petition to the Privy Council, urging it to overturn both the conviction and sentence of the tribunal.[39] Martial law, he submitted, was not called for in the Natal Colony, where '[t]here never was a state of war or rebellion'. Moreover, the appellants, on whose behalf the petition was submitted, 'were never at any time taken in open resistance or charged with any overt act of rebellion'.[40] Mangena charged that the true reason for the imposition of the poll tax could be gleaned from the comments made by

the minister for native affairs when the Poll Tax Bill of 1905 was introduced. As already noted, the minister had argued that the poll tax was justified. In his concluding submission, Mangena pleaded for the intervention of the Privy Council, to save the warriors from the impending execution at the hands of the Natal government.

Mangena's petition was remarkable not simply because it brought to the attention of the highest judicial body in the British Empire the fate of the rebels who were 'now lying under the sentence of death in Natal': he had moved in his own name to act 'as the next friend of the Appellants' in defence of a larger community, people who were not present, or were unable to act for themselves. In a judgment of just one paragraph, delivered on the same day as the petition, and apparently without much deliberation, the Privy Council dismissed the petition:

> Having heard the appeal, their Lordships are unable to advise His Majesty to grant the Petition. It is not an appeal from a Court, but in substance from an act of the Executive. Evidently the responsible Government of the Colony consider that a serious situation exists, for Martial Law has been proclaimed. The Courts of Justice in the Colony have not been asked to interpose; and, apart from questions as to jurisdiction, any interposition of a judicial character directed with most imperfect knowledge both of the danger that has threatened or may threaten Natal, and of the facts which came before the tribunal of war, would be inconsistent with their Lordships [sic] duties.[41]

This judgment might strike one as odd, bearing in mind that Mangena's very complaint was that the matter should not have been tried under martial law, but through the ordinary criminal courts which offered greater procedural protections. Nevertheless, the petition having been dismissed, martial law applied. The Bambatha warriors were executed.

Mangena was not alone in bringing to the attention of the world the conditions of these natives. In a letter to *The Star*, F.W. Pethick Lawrence warned: 'there is a considerable number of white men and women in South Africa who actually want to see a native war'. This was 'openly avowed' during his visit to South Africa, as the agitators aimed 'to break up the native locations and take away the native's land, and so render him less independent and more available to the doctrine of the "dignity of labour" in the mines and elsewhere'. Lawrence went on to argue that the war 'would also be welcome to many because it is thought it would (1) unite the Dutch and English races; (2) be good for trade, on account of the expenditure in the colonies for the British troops'. He accused the 'white races' of having been the main provocateurs in the Natal unrest. Lawrence's sentiments were supported by the newspaper's editor, who listed acts which, he said, were 'all deliberately provocative'. These included the imposition of the poll tax, the burning down of native churches and torching of villages, the shooting of fifteen men in the presence of their relatives, the arming of 'loyal natives', and putting a bounty on the head of the rebel chief, an act which was 'contrary to all law, as well as to all ideas of morality'. The editorial also noted the impossible situation in which Dinuzulu had been placed. He had proved his loyalty to the British government. But the government was still not satisfied. English morality, the editor concluded, was not consistent with 'these desperate efforts to provoke the Zulus', and it was the responsibility of the Liberal government to 'checkmate to jingoes and to avert a calamity which will cost the British tax payer 50 millions of money. We are sick of wasting our money on South African follies. We do not believe that it is necessary to govern the natives by machine guns. Treat them fairly, and there will be no trouble.'[42]

Mangena's campaign to bring Britain's attention to the situation in Natal did not end with the execution of the Bambatha warriors. On 4 August, Mangena published a letter in *The Fort Wayne Daily News*, headed 'The Native's Side of the Natal Row'. He explained that the so-called rebellion of Bambatha was 'nothing more than his attempt to escape to a place of safety', and that the fighting was simply 'self-defence on the part of the natives', 3 000 of whom were 'mowed down, while the British casualties scarcely exceed a score'. He went on to plead:

> Now, as to the future; discontent there is and has been among the natives, but we have no anti-European feeling. All we ask for is justice. England prides itself as the champion of the oppressed against the oppressor. Let her then guide us against the rapacious mine owners.
>
> We don't want to swamp the white man in Africa. But we desire a share in the country and some political rights.

If the law were carried out 'without fear or favour', wrote Mangena, 'there will be no further native trouble in Africa'. In another petition to the Houses of Parliament, prepared a few months after the executions, Mangena called for an inquiry into the government of Natal. Questioning the need for martial law in Natal, Mangena suggested that an inquiry be set up. Having set out the events that had transpired since February 1906, when a decision was taken to begin tax collection, Mangena concluded that it was vital to the well-being of the 900 000 natives who lived in Natal, and to the colony generally, that allegations respecting native unrest and general seditious tendencies among the native tribes, as well as evidence justifying martial law, 'should be the subject of an impartial investigation conducted in Natal on the part of the Imperial Government'.[43]

The 'indispensable condition' for the proposed inquiry would be that 'the natives should be afforded unrestricted opportunities' by the imperial government so that they could counter 'any suspicious circumstances that might be set up in support of the theory of sedition'. Mangena was aware that his petition would probably be met with the response that such an action would undermine the authority of the 'Supreme Chief of the natives', the governor of the Natal Colony. After all, when the imperial government had earlier tried to intervene in respect of the trial of the Bambatha warriors, the Natal government threatened to resign en masse. It was only after this threat that the Liberal government decided to adopt the policy of non-interference in colonial affairs. To counter a possible argument along the same lines, Mangena contended that it is a 'mischievous doctrine' to suggest that

> the prestige of the supreme chief will be injured by the natives being made aware that the sovereign, whose troops are ready to crush them if need be, is himself also prepared to intervene and to hear impartially the case of subjects who are without representation in the colonial legislature. As a matter of fact, it is nowadays simply impossible to keep the broad truth of these matters back from the intelligent native. He has sufficient elementary knowledge of the constitutional position, so freely canvassed in the local newspapers, to understand his obligations to those who represent his Majesty the King.[44]

Rather than causing 'alarm', a decision to set up an independent investigation in Natal 'would be regarded with profound satisfaction by many persons of position and special experience in the Colony'. Mangena concluded by asking for a resolution 'affirming the desirability of an investigation to be conducted on behalf of the Imperial Government' in order to verify the 'allegations of seditious intention on the part of the native inhabitants of the Colony of Natal'.

The role of Winston Churchill in the executions

By this stage, the world was generally familiar with the events of Bambatha, and Mangena had played a central role in making them known. Yet there appeared to be little appetite for an intervention by the British government. It is worth exploring why this was so. The answer is perhaps to be found in internal documents exchanged between the imperial government and that of Natal concerning the issue.[45] Winston Churchill, at the time the undersecretary of state for the colonies, was of the view that official actions were 'preposterous', and he opposed the declaration of martial law: 'The proclamation of Marshall law over the whole Colony, causing dislocation and infinite annoyance to everyone, because two white men have been killed, is in itself an act which appears to be pervaded by an exaggerated excitability.' Elgin concurred, lambasting the press for publishing 'vague and alarming rumours' and using 'censorship', which he regarded as a useless tactic in circumstances involving a local native uprising.

When the threatened execution of the twelve Bambatha warriors came to the attention of the imperial government, Churchill sent a telegram requesting that they be suspended:

> Continued executions under Martial law certain to excite strong criticism here. And as H.M.G. are retaining troops in colony and will be asked to ascend to act of indemnity, necessarily to popularise the action taken, trial of these murder cases by civil courts greatly to be preferred. I must impress upon you necessity of utmost caution in this matter, and you should suspend executions until I have had opportunity of considering your further observations.

Churchill's actions were entirely consistent with the law at the time. The powers of the governor included the power to disallow a decision to impose martial law, either in full or in part. But the Natal government threatened to resign on the grounds of interference with a decision of the executive council of a self-governing colony. Once this threat was conveyed, a further telegram was sent: His Majesty's government had clearly changed its tune:

> H.M.G. have at no time had the intention to interfere with action of the responsible government of Natal, or to control governor in exercise of prerogative … [but were] entitled, and where in duty bound to obtain full and precise information … In the light of the information now furnished, H.M.G. recognise that the decision of this grave matter rests in the hands of your ministers and yourself.[46]

Thus placated, the ministers withdrew their resignations. The Bambatha warriors were not saved from execution on 2 April 1906. The matter was then taken up in the House of Commons, and the question asked whether or not the government had sanctioned the executions. When Churchill suggested that the decision rested with the Natal government, Elgin proposed that the safest answer would be a plain 'no, sir'. Churchill was on the back foot, having to explain the executions. Ultimately, he said, no colonial secretary confronted by the threat of mass resignation could have acted otherwise. This response appeared to strengthen the position of the Natal government, which became increasingly oppressive towards the native population, resulting ultimately in the trial of Dinuzulu. After Elgin expressed the private hope that the governor would find a 'first rate lawyer' to defend Dinuzulu against charges of treason, Schreiner was appointed as counsel.

But Dinuzulu was found guilty of some of the charges and sentenced to four years' imprisonment and a fine of £100 for harbouring rebels; also, his position as a government *induna* – or chief – was withdrawn. These events were simply the start of an escalation that demonstrated on the one hand the weakening of the control of the British government over its colonies, and on the other the unspoken alliance in Natal and elsewhere that aimed to place Africans under white control and domination.

Dealing with defamation

Mangena had brought wide attention to the atrocities of the Natal government against the native population. These included allegations that Africans were routinely flogged for minor offences by officials of the government and employers on the farms. The floggings were often carried out in public, and not even chiefs were spared. They were sometimes flogged in the presence of their subjects, as fathers were in front of children. Women, too, were often beaten up naked. Rather than the promised order, martial law produced the opposite – an outlaw state breeding lawlessness. The agent-general of Natal, William Arbuckle, was extremely embarrassed by the publicity, and tried to contain the damaging allegations. Subsequently, a statement was published in London by, among others, *The Daily Chronicle* and *The Times* in an attempt to tarnish the reputation of Mangena by accusing him of fraudulent claims as to his identity. It was alleged that, contrary to his claims, Mangena was in fact not Zulu, but Mfengu. Arbuckle had written to the editor of *The Daily Chronicle* enclosing 'an authoritative statement of Mangena's character'. He implored the editor to 'please publish it in your columns with the hallmark of my official position as representative of the Natal government. True it relates to matters that occurred many years ago, but as the plaintiff is petitioning the King against the Natal Government, I wish, through the medium of the press, to denounce the petitioner and to cover him with infamy.'[47]

Mangena was also accused of misappropriating funds during his time in the Cape. It was alleged that he had absconded with £150, falsely claiming that he would represent some Africans in the Supreme Court, but he failed to bring the case. By publishing the letter, Arbuckle believed that he could minimise the impact of Mangena's criticism of the Natal government. However, he had no personal knowledge of the events referred to in his letter and relied on a witness to back up the story, Elijah Mdolomba – Mangena's old foe from the Cape. It was Mdolomba who had made the original accusations: Mangena was not a Zulu, but a Fingo, who had instigated the 'heathen natives' of Ndabeni to boycott rental payments in 1902; after some were arrested, Mangena collected funds, ostensibly to bring a case before the Supreme Court to challenge the arrests; a total amount of £150 was collected, but Mangena 'absconded', and for a while his whereabouts were unknown. 'This cowardly act greatly exasperated his followers. How he got the money to go to England is a mystery, as he was very lazy to work,' charged Mdolomba.[48] Now, Arbuckle sought to give the accusations credence by publishing them and expressing his support. But he did not bargain for what happened next.

Filing a defamation suit, Mangena cited Arbuckle as a defendant. The newspaper responsible for the publication, *The Daily Chronicle*, was co-defendant. Arbuckle was caught off-guard. Not only his own reputation, but also that of his government was now at stake. Mdolomba, as it turned out, was not such an impeccable witness, and he had relied on hearsay. The imperial government refused to provide financial support to Arbuckle, and in a desperate scramble he sent officials in search of witnesses to the Cape. These efforts drew a blank. Only a handful of witnesses were prepared to give evidence. His lawyers informed him that they had had 'great difficulty in keeping in touch with the witnesses who are continuously shifting from place to place'.[49] Only two of the original witnesses at Uitvlugt location could be contacted. The rest had left for 'Germany, South West Africa, Johannesburg, Kimberley, Prince Town, etcetera'. The defamation trial was held in London. Yet because the allegations were made in South Africa, evidence had to be collected there. This was done by way of a commission, set up to take evidence in South Africa so that a report could be sent to the trial court in London. Reverend Mdolomba had been requested to attend the commission, which was held in Natal, a week before the commencement of the evidence gathering so that he could identify the relevant witnesses and if necessary persuade them to provide the evidence. However, he did not attend. In their report to the magistrate in charge of the commission, Arbuckle's lawyers recorded that 'the natives all seem rather lukewarm and we think it is essential to the success of the Commission that the Rev. Mdolomba should use his influence with them, otherwise it is possible they will not attend the Commission without pressure being brought to bear'.[50]

In 1907 Mangena travelled to the Cape to assist in the gathering of evidence, where, reportedly, he was warmly received.[51] In a memorandum drawn up in support of Mangena by those who knew him from Ndabeni, the accusations made by Arbuckle were rejected as false and unfounded.[52] In their view, Mangena was being persecuted for exposing the racial hypocrisy of the Natal government. It is telling that the report of *Ilanga Lase Natal*, which carried the article concerning the trial of Mangena and Arbuckle, reproduced Mangena's petition to the Privy Council, which called for the establishment of a commission of inquiry into the Natal Colony, in its entirety. Its editorial noted that 'those who know him in Cape Town say he is Zulu, and that he did not squander the money of which is accused by Mdolomba'. A 'mass meeting of natives' was held on 21 August 1906 under the auspices of the Cape Town and District Zulus Association. Three resolutions were passed: the charges pressed against Mangena were false and without foundation; Mangena had not squandered any monies; and the resolutions of the South African Native Congress to support the actions taken by Mangena in relation to the Natal crisis were endorsed. Two more meetings were held, on 4 and 27 September, where these resolutions were approved. In the latter meeting, close attention was paid to the allegations of money squandering, with the following being resolved:

> Whereas it has been brought to this public meeting, that a report has been published to the effect that Mr. Alfred Mangena has fraudulently appropriated to himself the sum of £150 belonging to the various Natives of Ndabeni Location, that he afterwards absconded to England and that the said Natives threaten revenge the day Mr. Mangena returns to South Africa. Wherefore be it resolved that this meeting respectfully and emphatically protest against such wild and loose statements which are without foundation in as much as Native inhabitants of Ndabeni both Christians and Heathens have not been consulted in the matter nor have they made such accusations against Mr. Mangena nor have his legal adviser's account Books been referred to in order to substantiate such charges.

Arbuckle's case was crumbling. Not only were there no reliable witnesses, but his claims were labelled as groundless. Mangena's support, on the other hand, was increasing. Yet although Arbuckle had no witnesses, he was not without supporters. The *East African Standard* of 20 October 1906 carried an attack on Mangena for being on a 'warpath' against Arbuckle, and expressed the 'hope that the genial Agent General for Natal still contrives notwithstanding the facer[53] he has received, to keep his pecker up'. Apparently unaware of Mangena's personal history and his tenacity, the paper ventured that 'it would be instructive to know who is behind Mr Mangena in this matter'.

Arbuckle's requests for funds from the imperial government had been met with cold silence. And now, on 18 January 1908, he was advised by the Natal government that it would not pay for any portion of the costs incurred in the defamation claim. On 8 February 1908, Arbuckle expressed 'astonishment' at the decision, arguing that the letter which had become the subject of the lawsuit was written 'in his capacity as the Agent General for Natal and in the interests of the Government and the Colony'. Moreover, the letter had been fair comment on information officially supplied to the Natal government, the accuracy of which he had no reason to doubt. He had written the letter as agent-general, and not as William Arbuckle. Since the letter had been written in his official capacity, the government was responsible for the costs thereof, particularly since at no point had he been repudiated in relation to the manner in which he had acted. He therefore requested reconsideration of the decision, but he was turned down and was personally liable for the costs of the litigation.

At the trial, Mangena gave a lucid and comprehensive account of the events pertaining to his involvement with the activities of Ndabeni location. Initially, a bemused English bench seemed not to appreciate the possibility that someone from the amaZizi clan could also be Zulu, and even more confounding was the fact that a person could be both Mfengu and Zulu. Having introduced the judges to the ambiguity of Zulu identity (one could be both Zulu and Mfengu), Mangena dealt with the business of the case. Regarding the funds, he explained that, during the resistance in Ndabeni, he was responsible for arranging legal representation for the community. He served as an interlocutor between members of the community and the legal team. He therefore collected funds, which were paid to the attorney, though he was also remunerated for services rendered to the community. This was openly done. The community knew that he was being paid for his services, as did the legal team. Nothing untoward had happened to the funds. As the trial proceeded, it became clear that the allegation that Mangena had falsely claimed to be a Zulu could not be sustained, and nor could the claim that he had absconded with the sum of £150. Arbuckle himself would ultimately buckle. On 13 May 1908, *The Standard* carried the following report headed 'Zulu's Action against Sir W. Arbuckle':

> In the King's Bench Division, yesterday, before the Lord Chief Justice and a special jury the hearing of Mangena versus Arbuckle action for libel was continued, and before it had proceeded much further, a settlement was arrived at. The plaintiff was Mr Alfred Mangena, a coloured law student, and he sued Sir William Arbuckle, the Agent General of Natal, alleging that in a letter to various newspapers ... the defendant had libelled him by imputing that he had taken part in certain disturbances in South Africa, and had also absconded to this country with money belonging to natives, subscribed to prosecute a certain appeal to the Supreme Court. It will be remembered that, in consequence of native outbreaks in Natal, and the murder of some policemen, Martial law was proclaimed, that subsequently an act of indemnity was promoted, and that the plaintiff, on behalf of a native chief and himself, and also others in this country, presented a petition to the King, praying that he would not sanction the act of indemnity. While the petition was pending, Sir William Arbuckle had communicated with the papers, and he now pleaded that what he did was fair comment on a matter of public interest and privilege ... Mr Bankes K.C. referred to the cases against the 'African World' and the

'Times' which arose out of the same matter, and said an arrangement had been come to, under which there would be consent judgment for the plaintiff for £50, upon terms agreed.

Arbuckle duly capitulated. Mangena had defeated him in a courtroom – and the news quickly spread throughout Natal.

Two cases that arose from this episode – *Mangena* v. *Wright*[54] and *Mangena* v. *Lloyd*[55] – may be found in English law reports in support of two legal propositions which are now part of the English common law and the British legal education. In *Mangena* v. *Lloyd*, it was held that a defendant could not justify a defamatory statement on the grounds that it had been made on a privileged occasion – such as parliamentary proceedings – unless he or she provided evidence to that effect. Thus, the newspaper could not simply rely on a statement made in Parliament without proving that Parliament was in fact a privileged occasion and the statement had been made therein. In *Mangena* v. *Wright*, it was established that, where a defamatory statement was factually untrue, a defendant could not claim fair comment, unless the occasion where the statement was made was privileged – such as in Parliament. It would be up to the defendant to show by evidence that the statements were made on a privileged occasion. These cases are still taught today in English law schools and universities, as both established the principles of defamation law in England and Wales.

In the last term of 1907, Mangena sat for his final exam. He passed, and though he was immediately entitled to move for his admission to the Bar, for some reason he chose not to do so. Perhaps he needed to spend more time in England, particularly in the light of the fact that there were impending discussions about the new South Africa Bill that was being debated. A key aspect of that Bill concerned the exclusion of Africans from government. Whatever the reason, it is significant that, in later years, Mangena was a representative of the Transvaal Native Congress in a deputation that opposed the Bill.

First native advocate
On 1 July 1908, Alfred Mangena was called to the Bar, paying the obligatory sum of £50. Of those called with him that day, Mangena was thirty-sixth. His name was proposed by Cecil Henry Russell, who at the time was treasurer of the Inn – a fact that reflects the level of esteem Mangena enjoyed. None of the other admissions were at the time proposed by a person holding a position of executive responsibility at the Inn. Mangena was now a barrister. This was the first time an African person born in South Africa had achieved the honour of admission as barrister. On 14 August 1908, *Ilanga Lase Natal* published a seminal article by Pixley ka Isaka Seme, who was at the time training to be a barrister at Middle Temple Inn:

It has not yet happened in history that the Zulus have had an occasion to celebrate a hero like mine. In saying this I am not denying the fact that the African race too has sent stars to the galaxy of heaven. Yes, indeed ... the records of history reveal the fact that genius is like a spark which concealed in the bosom of a flint bursts forth at the summoning strokes and that it may arise anywhere and in any race. We can count among those of pure African blood many great in wisdom and profound learning; those whom ages call 'the wise', professors of eminent distinction in great universities, kings of independent nations which have burst their way to liberty by their own vigour. In fact history says with a clear and positive voice that in both church and state Africa has made conspicuous and imperishable contributions. However, to the Zulus my hero stands out in a singular record. Without an antecedent he has achieved for our ambitious youth a new star upon which to fix their compass in their journey through these hard and perilous seas. He is a Zulu and therefore his example forms for us a real and positive encouragement and his success we can make our own. ... He came to England in August 1902. His purpose being to start law with this view of returning to his people to serve them in the capacity of a constitutional lawyer. Because he with us believes that the Constitution and not the revolution contains for us the only open door for progress and to prosperity [...] On July 1st, 1908, having passed all examinations, he was called by the honourable society of Lincoln's Inn to become Barrister at Law. Hats off to Alfred Mangena of Lincoln's Inn esquire and Barrister at Law.

Mangena's admission made national news in South Africa. *Izwi Labantu* expressed pride in his achievement, though its editorial warned that his career was doomed to fail: white attorneys who had the exclusive right of access to clients would never 'take their cases to a black man despite the wishes of a client'. The editorial recalled the case of Henry Sylvester Williams, who was 'starved of work by white attorneys', deprived of social contact, and ultimately driven back to England. It suggested that Mangena should follow the same route as Gandhi, who had 'demoted himself' and become an attorney, thereby gaining direct contact with clients. But whatever Mangena chose, the editorial concluded, he would be a pathfinder and open the way for black legal practitioners.[56]

The *Indian Opinion* of 5 September 1908 carried a brief though complimentary article titled 'A Successful Zulu'. It read as follows:

Alfred Mangena, a pure-blooded Zulu, has a record of which a white man might be proud. His father, Stomela, was a veteran of Cetshwayo, and fought with his tribe against the British in the Zulu War; and Mangena was born near Ladysmith, in Natal, afterwards educated at Clarkebury Mission Station, Cape Colony; next served an apprenticeship with the Roodepoort Mine to become an assayer; and was after that at the Collegiate School, Cape Town. 1902 he went to London, and has now been 'called' by the honourable society of Lincoln's Inn, and is entitled to be addressed Alfred Mangena Esquire, Barrister at Law.

Mangena was now able to practise law in the United Kingdom, if he so wished. But that was never his plan. His intention was to acquire sufficient knowledge in constitutional law which, he believed, would help to reverse the political losses of Africans – and also their land. As Seme noted with regard to Mangena, it was 'the Constitution and not the revolution' that held the prospect of 'progress and prosperity'. The Transvaal Native Congress passed a resolution on 24 June 1909 which 'instructed Mangena and Seme to work in cooperation with Schreiner, J.T. Jabavu, Mohandas Gandhi and other delegates' in representing their interests in the South African Native Delegation that was due to present a petition at the British House of Commons. While Mangena's name does not appear in the official records of the delegation, it is probable that, together with Seme and Henry Sylvester Williams, he met with the delegates and was involved in the strategic decision-making concerning approaches to be taken. Mangena, it should be recalled, had gained expertise in British constitutional law, having learnt to navigate the British constitutional system through the petitions and lawsuits brought in his name in connection with the Bambatha warriors. It is likely that his counsel would have been sought by the native delegation.

The delegation did not accomplish its ultimate mission, and the South Africa Act was passed in its original form. The British government elected to stay out of the 'internal affairs' of South Africa. It was, however, noted that the 'native question' needed urgent attention, and it was hoped that the Union government would soon attend to it. This was not the first time that the British government had used the language of non-interference to ignore the aspirations of Africans. This language is, however, deceptive, for what was at stake was British expansionism and the commercial interest of firms associated with the Empire. By refusing to intervene, the imperial government was simply safeguarding its own position. Its strategic goal at the time was to appease the Boers and to consolidate its hold over the economic resources of South Africa. The native question was not a priority. Conscious of the duplicity of the British, Mangena had campaigned around this topic in his 1906 writings. And now, with the completion of his legal qualification, he was ready to return to South Africa to turn his knowledge into action.

In 1910, Mangena returned to South Africa. Rather than to his birthplace, Natal, or the Eastern Cape, where he had been schooled, he returned to the Transvaal. On 18 April 1910, he filed his application to be admitted as an attorney of the High Court. Although he had qualified as a barrister in England, for black people in the Transvaal, no provision existed to practise as such. But in the Cape, where he had cut his teeth as an activist, the situation was different, and so the process of application should have been uncontroversial – as, indeed, his application indicates. He noted his admission to the Bar and elevation to the degree of 'utter barrister' on 1 July 1908 in England. He attached a certificate issued by the secretary of the Inns which records the following: 'Alfred Mangena of Cape Town, South Africa, the second son of Stomela Mangena of Umtata [Mthatha], South Africa, landed proprietor, was admitted into the honourable society of this Inn on the 5th day of October [1903] and was called to the degree of an utter barrister on the 1st day of July 1908 hath paid all dues and duties to the Society, and that his deportment therein hath been proper.' The treasurer of the Inn signed the certificate. Annexed to the application was a certificate issued by the Council for Legal Education which simply affirmed that Mangena had satisfactorily passed his examination, qualifying him to be called to the Bar. Notwithstanding this, the Law Society of the Transvaal saw fit to oppose Mangena's application for admission. Its president, Hendrik Lodewyk Malherbe, filed an opposing affidavit claiming that 'in the present state of society in the Transvaal there is no possibility of a native finding work as an attorney among its white population, and that he would have to make a practice among his natives'.[57]

The Law Society argued, furthermore, that the policy of the Transvaal government 'in the administration of justice among the natives is to discourage litigation among them and to encourage them to come to the minister for native affairs and his native commissioners with their grievances in order to have them settled as far as possible amicably or by means of the native courts'. Clearly endorsing this policy, the Law Society contended that 'it would not be in the interests of the natives of the Transvaal to create among them a class of native practitioners'. It went on to explain that such a native practitioner 'would be beyond the control of the society who would find it difficult to exercise its discipline over him'. Counsel was briefed on behalf of the Law Society, and the matter was argued. Mangena appeared in person, whereas a Mr B.A. Tindall was briefed on behalf of the Law Society to oppose Mangena's application. Making short shrift of the Law Society's argument, Judge Smith ruled as follows:

> Where an applicant possessed the statutory qualifications the court would not be justified in refusing to admit him merely because he belonged to one of the native races. The court could not assume that the applicant was going to encourage litigation among natives, and that he was going to be guilty of

unprofessional conduct. The fact that there was no precedent in the Transvaal was not sufficient ground for excluding the applicant. If for any reason it might be desirable not to allow natives to be admitted, that was a matter for the legislature.[58]

The court had struck a brief but telling blow against the blatant racism of the Law Society. But importantly, the court also recognised that there was no precedent for its ruling. Mangena had achieved what no one before him had managed to do – and the first South African–born African lawyer was now on the roll of practising attorneys.

Adding colour to the courtroom

At the beginning of February 1910, Mangena appeared in the Magistrate's Court, Doornfontein on behalf of a criminal accused. Upon his arrival, the court orderly – a white policeman – refused to allow him to sit among the attorneys, who were all white. When the magistrate arrived, Mangena rose to speak from the public gallery. Upon enquiry from the bench, Mangena explained that he had been prevented from sitting with the attorneys by the court orderly, upon which the magistrate apologised and invited him to sit among his colleagues. Later, the policeman concerned attempted to apologise. But he did not do so himself, and instead sent an intermediary. This was rejected by Mangena, who made the following statement:

> There is no desire that white men should apologise to natives, but there must be a limit to the insults which are put upon the more respectable natives in particular, and the only way of making this clear is that the men who deliberately maltreat them should themselves apologise unless the white man puts himself in the wrong. If a man has any sense of common decency he should apologise even to a dog.[59]

One of the few cases that Mangena took on was on behalf of a member of the Wesleyan Church, Phillip Tolanku, who was charged with theft and misappropriation of church funds. The question for trial was whether or not the accused should be committed to trial, or the charges be dismissed on the grounds of vagueness, which is what Mangena argued before the magistrate. The *Rand Daily Mail* of 27 August 1910 reported: 'A further picturesque element was imparted into the case by the presence of attorney Alfred Mangena, a young Swazi lawyer, practising at Pretoria, who claims to be a barrister at law.' As the hostility towards his client became clear during the course of the hearing, Mangena reserved his defence to be presented at the trial.

Native attorneys in Native Courts

Mangena established his own law firm in 1910, with offices in Johannesburg and Pretoria. He was generally well known and also highly regarded, so his practice was soon bursting at the seams. The majority of his clients were people affected by the growing labyrinth of native laws, rules and regulations. Mangena faced a key obstacle, however: white prejudice against a black attorney appearing in the Magistrate's Courts. Mweli Skota, the celebrated black publisher of the early twentieth century, brought the difficulties experienced by African lawyers in the Transvaal into sharp relief with a tale about Mangena. On one occasion when Mangena went to defend a client, he entered the courtroom with his books under his arm and a smoking pipe in his mouth. Two white policemen, who were wait-ing for the arrival of the white magistrate, suddenly and without a word threw him out of court, and he stumbled and fell to the ground. He picked himself up, collected his books and his pipe, and returned to the courtroom. One of the policemen appealed to the magistrate, who by that stage had arrived, to order him out of court. But the magistrate refused. Recognising 'Mr Mangena', he invited him to take his seat alongside the prosecutor, at the lawyer's bench – to the consternation of the policemen 'who thought Mangena to be a blundering Kaffir, intruding in the Court'.[60]

The Supreme Court was the exclusive preserve of white men. But many Africans were tried in the Native Commissioner's Courts, which were specifically created to cater for Africans. They fell below the Magistrate's Courts in status, though the latter routinely heard appeals from Native Commissioner's Courts. Thus, the use of the word 'court' was anomalous. These courts were no more than an extension of government bureaucracy rather than an independent arm of the state.

As the only available African attorney, Mangena tended to focus on the inter-face between black people and the colonial government – an area administered by the native commissioner's office, which in turn fell under the minister for native affairs. Generally regarded as being outside the civil legal system, 'natives' fell under the executive and administrative arms of the state. This meant that the work of a black attorney largely comprised representations on behalf of black people to officials in the native commissioner's office. When these failed, appeals could be made to the Native Courts, which themselves were adminis-tered from the executive centre, rather than as part of the judiciary. But there was a difficulty. The rules of the Native Courts did not permit appearances by attorneys or advocates. Yet these courts held extensive powers over the lives of black people. With Mangena being barred from the Native Courts, the majority of his clients would be denied legal representation. A test case to challenge the exclusion presented itself when Mangena was instructed to appear on a matter in

Hammanskraal, at the office of the native commissioner. Upon arrival, he was informed that attorneys were not permitted, and he asked to be provided with the applicable rule, whereupon Rule 3 of the Rules for Native Courts was cited. After making a copy of the rule, he asked for an adjournment of the inquiry, which was granted. Back at his office, upon due consideration, he was struck by the fact that the rule made no distinction between civil and criminal matters. Yet the jurisdiction of the Native Courts covered both. The law in the Transvaal was that a criminal accused was entitled to legal representation. If the rule was applied so as to exclude the right to legal representation in all cases, it would be *ultra vires*, i.e. contrary to the legal guarantee in accordance with the prevailing laws of the Transvaal that any criminal accused is entitled to representation by a lawyer. Native commissioners, he reasoned, had no powers to make rules which went against the law of the land. Mangena then began to prepare a challenge to the rule in the Supreme Court. But first, he had to exhaust domestic remedies, and so he prepared to make representations to the commissioner for native affairs, submitting that it was illegal to exclude attorneys from criminal matters at the Native Courts. He noted that, according to the law of the Transvaal, his clients had a right to legal representation in criminal matters. Since the Native Courts had jurisdiction to try criminal cases, they could not, by the mere passage of rules, exclude attorneys. And since the rules were incompatible with the common law and, indeed, the statute, they were unenforceable. Consequently, the Native Courts could not exclude attorneys from appearing in them. This objection had never been raised before, despite the routine exclusion of attorneys from the Native Courts. Yet it was as compelling as it was irrefutable.

Unable to answer Mangena, officials at the native commissioner's office wrote to the minister for native affairs for advice. In turn, the minister referred the complaint to the secretary for justice. On 30 December 1910, a reply arrived, and it was a stunning victory for Mangena:

> It seems probable that rule 3 referred to was designed to prevent the encouragement by unscrupulous practitioners of litigiousness amongst natives. As there can be no such danger in criminal cases the rule could not have been intended to apply but, in any case, could not be enforced, for every man must be allowed to plead before the court his defence to a criminal charge in the most advantageous manner.[61]

The native commissioner's office and Native Courts were now open to legal representatives, without the necessity of acquiring prior permission or approval before they could appear. Through the strategic use of the law, Mangena had opened the system and created a platform for launching further challenges to power. When he appeared for his client in the Hammanskraal case, the charges were promptly withdrawn.

Mangena's reputation grew, and he soon needed assistance. He did not have to wait for long. The following year, in 1911, another British-trained legal practitioner, Pixley Seme, returned to South Africa, and five years later, in 1916, Mangena and Seme formed a law partnership. The only other legal practice that was not white was that of Mohandas Gandhi, namely M.K. Gandhi, Attorney at Law,[62] located in Rissik Street, opposite the offices of Mangena and Seme. Though the seeds for the formation of the Union government were planted after the end of the Anglo-Boer War, the full implications for Africans only became evident after 1910. Having been excluded from power, conditions relating to land and labour worsened. With evictions rife in the Transvaal, and forced labour commonplace, many looked to the legal system to counter these effects.

While in London, Seme and Mangena had conceived the idea of consolidating the various provincial-based native congresses into a national organisation. When they set up their law firms in South Africa they also set in motion the process for the formation of the South African Native National Congress. This had become an urgent matter, given the government's proposed legislation, the Natives Land Bill, which made it clear that racial segregation and land dispossession would be legally entrenched, and Africans living in areas designated for white settlement would be forcibly removed. Mangena and Seme joined the preparatory committee for the launch of the SANNC, whose elected leader was John Langalibalele Dube, formerly the leader of the Natal Native Congress. Mangena and Seme were given the responsibility of drawing up a constitution, as well as formulating a legal response to the Natives Land Bill. The drawing up of a constitution only came to fruition, however, when the third black lawyer to practice in South Africa, Richard Msimang, accomplished the task in 1918. In the meantime, though, Mangena and Seme drew up the foundational documents for opposing the Natives Land Bill, though the delegation to Britain that challenged the legislation met with little success.

In 1911, Mangena returned to London for the four-day Universal Races Congress. He accompanied John Tengo Jabavu, who spoke on 'The Native Races of South Africa'. The aim of the conference was to discuss 'in the light of science and the modern conscience, the general relations subsisting between the peoples of the West and those of the East, between so-called white and so-called coloured peoples, with a view to encouraging between them a fuller understanding, the most friendly feelings, and a heartier co-operation'. It was attended by influential black intellectuals across the world, including the highly respected W.E.B. Du Bois. Topics ranged from the question of race, its scientific justification, to its political significance.[63] An important discussion point concerned the origin of the human species, and behaviours arising from external factors. For most of the nineteenth century, proponents of the notion that a natural racial hierarchy existed had bolstered their theories by referring to 'science' – which was exposed as duplicitous at the congress. When Mangena returned to South Africa, he was armed with knowledge that scientifically based excuses for racism were a sham. But racism, as he soon realised, continued to thrive in the hallowed corridors of courtrooms.

'UMangena noMlungukazi'

In April 1913, what appeared to be a banal criminal trial gripped the attention of the quiet town of Germiston. Typical of the time, the town's social and economic structure was based on the rigid separation of the races, with whites in control of government structures. Justifying this was an imagined threat of black violence, with white women in particular under threat from black men, around whom stereotypes were formed and disseminated. The case in question brought into the open the fears and absurdities of racism. A white woman had accused a black man of indecent assault. No physical interaction was alleged. The complaint was that the black man had proposed love to the white woman, causing the white community of Germiston to react sharply, and bringing its racism out into the open.

When the case was heard in April 1913, the court was full, with whites expecting that blacks would once and for all be reminded of their place in society. *Ilanga Lase Natal* reported it as 'Ummeli uMangena noMlungukazi eGoli' (Attorney Mangena and the white woman in Johannesburg).[64] Mangena represented the accused. During cross-examination, Mangena's questions suggested that the white woman may have been a willing participant in the alleged verbal exchange. The woman became indignant and refused to answer, explaining to the court, 'I do not like answering questions from a kaffir.' Mangena maintained his calm, reminding the complainant of her role as a witness, under oath to answer questions put to her by counsel. As tempers flared in the courtroom, the magistrate intervened, making it clear to the complainant that Mr Mangena was entitled to ask questions in cross-examining her, and that an accused was entitled to legal representation in any criminal trial. The court fell silent. One of their own, a white magistrate, had committed an unforgivable sin: requiring a white woman to answer questions put to her by a black man. What was ignored, however, was the fact that the black man was an attorney, in an incident that serves to demonstrate the truth of Robert Knox's assertion, 'Race is everything.'[65] The woman refused to answer any further questions, and, left with no option, the magistrate promptly discharged the accused and cleared him of the charge of indecent assault. Outside the court, there was jubilation, though the police were quick to put a stop to it. The case brought to the surface the irrationality of racism, and it also cemented Mangena's reputation as a lawyer concerned with racial injustice.

Pass laws and prison labour

Mangena and Seme went into legal partnership in 1916, forming Mangena & Seme Solicitors, with offices in Johannesburg and Pretoria. Though there is little remaining evidence either of their work or of the nature of their practice, the case of one Johanes[66] is worth recounting. Not only does it provide a glimpse into the work undertaken by black lawyers at the time, it also illuminates how the state used the law to enforce black labour. Johanes had been charged with attempting to escape from detention, and Mangena was instructed in the matter. As Mangena investigated the matter, a different, more sinister tale began to emerge. Johanes had been a farmworker in the eastern Transvaal, but because of the harsh conditions to which he was subjected, he escaped. This was regarded as a crime, since Johanes had violated the pass laws. Johanes was then arrested under the pass laws operative in the Transvaal. While in detention, a message was delivered to him by the police. The government was looking for 'gangs' and 'boys' to work on road construction. Johanes was considered eligible, and although a decision was made without his involvement or consent, he did not originally object to the idea. Labour and job training, with the prospect of regular meals, were perhaps a preferable option to the grim routine of prison life. A heavy mobile police guard took a selected number of detainees to the construction site in Pretoria. At such sites, security was generally lax, and escapes were fairly commonplace. Johanes tried his luck, but he was apprehended within days of escaping. Charges of escape from 'detention' were laid, and Mangena was instructed to represent him. During the investigation process, Mangena discovered that the use of awaiting-trial detainees as labourers was a common practice of the government. Unlike the scenario where convicts provided labour as part of their sentences, here the government was using detainees as labourers without any law permitting it. Other prisoners had been deployed in the construction of government buildings and the rail network.

It is clear that the use of prison labour was integrally connected to the enforcement of pass laws, and so Transvaal prisons became a large reservoir of labour. The use of detainees as labour was sanctioned by the government as early as 1902. That year, for example, the attorney-general's office wrote to the secretary of the Native Affairs Department with the following enquiry as to the availability of labour: 'What procedure you propose to adopt in investigating the antecedence of natives handed over to your department and for how long it is proposed to detain such offenders pending investigation and otherwise?'[67] A similar enquiry was made by the Public Works Department in 1908. By then, large construction works had begun in the Transvaal, and there was an urgent need for labour. It was decided that blacks detained for infringement of pass laws would be made to work in the public works underway. But the Public Works Department informed the secretary for native affairs that 'convicts have been employed for some months on road work and the saving effected by using them in place of free paid labour is not such as we would be led to expect'. A suggestion was made to build a portable prison which could be moved along as the roadworks progressed. The government needed 'other lockups' such as these, but it first needed to get legal advice:

> To avoid the possibility of creating criminals through the incarceration in prison of natives convicted for a breach of the pass laws and of the native tax ordinance the Minister for Native Affairs would be glad of your views as to the feasibility of the establishment of public works and other lockups in which natives convicted for such offences could be kept entirely separate from the criminal class.[68]

In a move that clearly advantaged the government's public works plan, the letter went on to propose that '[a]ll natives arrested for contravening of the pass laws be transferred to be handed over to officers of this department who would detain them under investigation and only cause habitual transgressors to be prosecuted'.[69] Thus, the implementation of the pass-law system and the criminal prosecution pursuant thereto would serve an entirely different purpose. It would not serve as a deterrent to crime, but would be deployed for economic reasons. The constant flow of 'criminals and offenders'[70] would create a steady and reliable supply of labour. On 2 May 1908, Lord Selborne, the British high commissioner and governor of the Transvaal, was informed that 'as many as 150 natives' were imprisoned in Johannesburg every week. The ease with which the pass-law system became an instrument of forced labour is evidenced by many internal documents of the Native Affairs Commission, with numerous examples illustrating the absurdity of the enforcement of the pass laws. For instance, on 9 September 1907 the following was recorded:

> Three raw kaffir boys came from a farm near Rustenburg. They went to their chief for a pass, but he said they were too young to need passes. They were all three given the choice of fine or imprisonment, which to moneyless pikininis means prison. I gave up noting particulars after September 10 as they were so troublesome – but I remember that on January 2nd there were a number of boys arrested who had been unable to get passes on January 1st (bank holiday). The police confirmed the statement, the Magistrate gave nominal fines ... thereby making each a criminal who had been convicted ... On Easter Monday an ex-policeman of excellent character came to me because the pass which he held expired on Sunday night. To keep on the right side of the law he ought

to have renewed it on Saturday morning. The pass office had given him this without comment. I gave him a 'special', but if he had not known me he would have risked arrest on Easter Monday. Numerous boys go out with passes endorsed 'waster', 'abominable'. I know one case in which the master endorsed a pass 'lazy and good-for-nothing' because the boy would not continue in his service ... the pass endorsed 'abominable' was given (so the boy said) by a man who was always drunk. Such passes ought to be reported at the Pass Office and verified by the man who so endorses them.[71]

The strategy of turning convicted persons into wage labourers was neither new nor unique to South Africa, however. In *Gulag: A History*, Anne Applebaum explains the commercial rationale behind the establishment of the Russian prison camps under Lenin. The camps, which became known as the Gulag, had their origins in Lenin's ambivalence about forms of punishment in respect of two categories of criminal. The first category consisted of the common criminals, such as thieves, pickpockets and murderers, while the second contained a different type of criminal: the 'class enemy' or 'enemy of the people'. Criminals falling into the latter category were harder to identify because they had not committed 'crimes' *per se*, i.e. crimes against other persons. Lenin's Soviet Union saw the class enemy as more dangerous and harder to reform, unlike the common criminal. So, when people deemed guilty of committing 'political acts' were classified as criminals, there was usually confusion as to what to do with them following their arrest. It is noteworthy that '[i]n the interim they could be made to do forced labour, often digging trenches and building barricades'.[72]

There are echoes of the Gulag system in what transpired in the public-works programmes of the Transvaal in the first decade of the 1900s. People perceived to be in breach of pass laws were usually those evicted from land which had previously belonged to them. The land, which had been occupied through a political act, enforced by law and heavily policed, was now no longer accessible to them. To travel anywhere, these evicted people required official permission. So, while simply walking from one place to another would have been perfectly legal twenty years earlier, this was now illegal. A political ideology had become a harsh system of laws. Breaches of the pass laws could, however, not be regarded as 'criminal' *per se*, and so the government found a strategy for dealing with a burgeoning prison population: the prison labour system. It was in these circumstances that the detainee, Johanes, became a criminal suspect. In criminal law, an escape from detention is generally regarded as a more serious offence than a failure to carry a pass. But the logic of the Transvaal authorities determined that, since black labour was a high-value commodity, criminal law should be turned on its head. It was therefore more important to enforce the pass laws, given the positive economic outcome that resulted from policing the labour of Africans on the farms and the mines. If pass laws were breached, this would constitute a criminal act. But the chain of labour and commerce would not be broken. Instead of working for farmers and mine bosses, Johanes would labour for the state. The obsession with the exploitation of black labour in this period is demonstrated by the fact that Johanes was ultimately acquitted of the charge of attempted escape from detention. But still, his labour was a necessary commodity. He was therefore required to return to the farms of the eastern Transvaal, where he was once again under the control of white farm owners.

Anna Victoria Mcobela

By this stage, Mangena had fallen in love with Agnes Mehlomakhulu, a young woman from Boksburg, near Johannesburg. She was one of the few African nurses at the time. Because Mangena led a very busy life, their relationship suffered strain. Despite his professional and political commitments, he entertained friends whenever he found the time, and enjoyed hosting parties over weekends. One of his close friends was Selby Msimang, Richard's younger brother. Selby later had a sexual relationship with Agnes, resulting in the birth of a child. Agnes complained to Selby that Mangena had 'no time for her'.[73] After the disappointment of Agnes, Mangena became involved in a relationship with the enterprising Anna Victoria Mcobela. 'AV', as Anna was known, was born at Kwamapumulo mission station. She was educated at Inanda Seminary School. Unlike many other missionary schools of the era, Inanda was started by American rather than English missionaries, by a couple named Daniel and Virginia Lindley. Its goal was to educate girls at a time when the only missionary school available in Natal, Adams School, catered exclusively for boys.[74] While teaching was popular among her peers, after her schooling, Anna elected to train as a nurse. The only place where such training was available was at Victoria Hospital at the Lovedale mission in the Eastern Cape. While the hospital became an important site for the training of African women in the nursing profession, its mission was rooted in the 'civilising' ideas that were prevalent at the time. Dr Neil Macvicar, the missionary who was hospital superintendent when Anna arrived, rejected traditional notions of Christianity and held the view that science should replace 'superstition'. He found a fertile ground in Africa, where he could preach to his students to reject traditional methods of medicine and healing. Thus, his training was not only scientific, but also sought to eradicate beliefs which he termed 'superstitious' or 'primitive'. His intention was that, with the right training, Africans could help create a new society founded on Christianity and Western forms of medicine.[75]

Anna qualified in 1910, but she did not stay in the Eastern Cape. Instead, she found employment in Pretoria, becoming the first qualified black nurse in the

Transvaal. It is not clear when she met Mangena, but they married in 1916 – the same year that Mangena formed a professional partnership with Seme. Anna relocated to Johannesburg, and when Mangena left Johannesburg for Mthatha in 1920, Anna remained in Johannesburg. It was four years later, after the death of her husband, that she moved to Port Elizabeth. The city was a hive of activity, and pioneering nurses such as Dora Nginza and Cecilia Makiwane practised there. However, in the 1930s, Anna returned to Johannesburg, where she found employment at the city council in Pimville. It was here that Anna excelled, becoming a leader in her own right, at the Methodist church and in service to her community. Anna employed the principles of science and Christianity in her approach to nursing. But unlike her mentor, Macvicar, she did not believe that African beliefs were rooted in superstition, but rather sought to apply Western medicine in the context of African belief systems. When she died in 1961, many years after the death of her husband, and without having married again, Skota, who wrote a biographical dictionary of Africans in the Transvaal, only had words of praise for Anna Mangena, describing her as 'very clean, industrious, tolerant, obedient and kind to all patients'.[76]

Mzilikazi's last stand

Disputes about land were also experienced in the territory that was renamed Rhodesia in 1895 (today's Zimbabwe). It was under the control of the British South Africa Company, which had been established by Cecil John Rhodes to exploit local mineral resources, with an eye also on lands to the north. In one noteworthy instance, the BSAC had awarded land to a community of Xhosa-speaking Mfengu (known as Fingoes) in Rhodesia, in an area called Umbembesi. The history of this community may be traced to 1899, when Rhodes enticed several groups of Mfengu, led by their chiefs, including Sojini and Hlazo, to travel to Rhodesia in search of new pastures. The Mfengu, who were among the first Xhosa to be converted to Christianity, had collaborated with the British against the Xhosa during the frontier wars of the Eastern Cape.[77] Subsequently, when Rhodes embarked on an imperial mission for gold in the land of the Ndebele and Shona, he forged alliances with the Mfengu, hoping to draw on their support in the event of conflict with the Ndebele and Shona over gold-mining concessions. However, this proved unnecessary as the Ndebele chief, Lobengula, agreed to several concessions that allowed Rhodes to exploit the minerals in Rhodesia. The Mfengu stayed on as domestic and manual labourers in the employment of Rhodes and the BSAC.[78] Since the Mfengu regarded themselves as British subjects, they requested that the land allocated to them by the BSAC be registered according to the same rules as were applicable in respect of British citizens, i.e. individual title. Then, in 1909 the community sent a petition to the high commissioner asking for exemption from the pass laws, as well as permission to carry guns, and other privileges. The petition read as follows:

> The Fingoes are a very small number in this country and also are unfriendly to the people of the country although they have never been in quarrel with us. Our only friend is the British Government who kept our grand-fathers and now is still looking upon us, and he serves us with good hands and his mouth is full of love to his children under his power.[79]

The petition did not receive the response the community expected. Instead, they were reminded that they had been under 'civilised rule' for a longer period than the local Ndebele people. Consequently, it was their duty to show that they had 'benefited' thereby. Moreover, to prove their loyalty, they were required to display 'an amicable demeanour towards those who have not enjoyed the same advantage.'[80]

Thus rebuffed, the community shifted their focus and sought new allies. Two prominent families, the Hlazos and the Sojinis, sought assistance beyond the borders of Rhodesia. They desired security of tenure on land that was registered in their name. So, in 1918 these families approached Alfred Mangena for assistance. It is important to note, however, that contact between the Mfengu of Rhodesia and leaders of the SANNC had begun earlier – and not in Africa, but in Europe. In 1914, the Privy Council began hearings relating to the case of ownership of land in Southern Rhodesia. European missionaries and the members of the APS wanted to arrange for legal representation for the Africans of Rhodesia. They turned to the leaders of the SANNC who were in England at the time to protest the Natives Land Act of 1913. That contact resulted in a petition drawn up and signed by leading figures of the SANNC, including Sol Plaatje, Walter Rubusana and John Dube, president of the SANNC. On his return to South Africa, Dube tried to visit Rhodesia to help the Mfengu there pursue their claims to land, but he was denied entry. Thus, by 1918, the leaders of the Sojini and Hlazo families were acquainted with the leaders of the SANNC, including Mangena.

It was in his capacity as a lawyer that Mangena's services were required in Rhodesia. Unlike Dube, Mangena was allowed entry to Rhodesia. He came as a lawyer, not a politician. His Mfengu clients asked that he also approach the family of the late Lobengula with offers of assistance to reclaim the land of the Ndebele people. Lobengula's land had been taken by the BSAC through a combination of trickery and force, and the Ndebele were keen to follow the South African example of sending deputations and representations to the British government. Mangena would later write that he had met with the royal family of Lobengula and had been received 'with open arms'. Nyamanda, the king of the Ndebele, was impressed after his meeting with Mangena, and undertook to follow his advice. What happened next was somewhat unexpected. The colonial authorities became aware of Mangena's presence, and owing to his connections with the SANNC, he was suspected of being in the country for political reasons. He was deported from Rhodesia at once. Upon his return to South Africa, Mangena alerted Richard Msimang to the case and together they discussed a strategy. It was decided that, because Msimang did not hold high political office, he would travel to Rhodesia and consult with King Nyamanda. Subsequently, in 1919, a petition was drawn up. Mangena was involved in the process, and when it was finalised the petition was taken to Rhodesia in draft form. The draft petition read as follows:

> Referring to native laws and treatment, your petitioners have experienced with great regret that High Commissioners and Governors General, who are the true representatives of your Majesty, have merely acted as disinterested spectators whilst responsible government parties of various names and associations are interpreting the laws in class legislation to suit their purpose. Your petitioners pray that in case Rhodesia is granted any form of government the Imperial Government take over the Administration of Native Affairs in that Country in the same manner as is the case with regard to British Basutoland, British Bechuanaland and Swaziland. Your petitioners are further aware that the judicial committee of your Majesty's Privy Council has found that the so-called unalienated land belongs to the Crown by reason of an alleged right of conquest and the dethronement of the late King Lobengula. The right of justification of that alleged conquest your petitioners do not seek to discuss here; but in the interest of righting justice, and in pursuance of the fact that the right of conquest … is now repudiated by the civilised world, your petitioners pray that Your Majesty be pleased to hand back the so-called unalienated land to the family of the late King Lobengula in trust for the tribe according to Bantu custom, and the right of chieftainship therein to be restored and acknowledged.[81]

For years afterwards, the petitioners and their lawyers went back and forth, making representations to the British government. By 1923 it had become clear that the campaign was a failure. The British were not going to accede to the requests relating to fair government and the land. Instead, the powers of chiefs were drastically curtailed. So, too, were their resources. Mangena himself was never paid for his services. And though his legal expertise was very much in demand, it was precisely this that led to his eventual demise.

Decline and fall

The work that Mangena and Seme engaged in put them under great personal and professional strain. Not only was it politically risky, it also interfered with their efficiency as legal practitioners. Clients began complaining about the time it took for cases to be finalised, or in certain instances that cases were not receiving any attention at all. One such client was James Hokolo.[82] Describing himself as a Thembu resident at Seplan, district of Cala, he instructed Mangena to sue for the recovery of money, and paid a deposit of £5. Later, Mangena asked for an additional payment of £3, which was duly made. Despite numerous enquiries from his client, Mangena simply never did the work. He frequently missed appointments with Hokolo, advising him that the matter was under consideration. Hokolo recalled that he was repeatedly told 'to wait and [Mangena] said that he would deal with the matter'. Two years had elapsed since the instruction was first given to Mangena. Then, in September 1916, Hokolo showed up at Mangena's offices without an appointment. Mangena happened to be there, and after a lengthy explanation and numerous excuses as to why the matter had still not progressed to court, Mangena came up with another plan. He would instruct counsel to handle the matter, but required another payment of £12. Hokolo refused, and asked for a return of all the monies paid to Mangena up to that point. However, Mangena replied that he was unable to refund him. Nor could he provide any proof of work done.

Another complaint came from Ephraim Mogorosi of Mabieskraal in Rustenburg, who complained on behalf of his neighbour, Mabe, about the despotic behaviour of a local chief. The chief had dispossessed Mabe of his land and confiscated his cattle. Mabe therefore instructed Mangena to recover the cattle and to challenge the land dispossession and the powers of the chief. After paying the substantial amount of £102 to Mangena, he made repeated enquiries about the progress of his case. He was sent from pillar to post. Finally, he lodged a complaint with the secretary for native affairs. By 1916, Mangena seems to have gained much notoriety for alleged sharp practice, to the extent that the director of native labour was convinced that 'the firm of solicitors referred to is exploiting natives in a most undesirable manner and the conduct of Mangena has already been unfavourably commented on by a judge of the Supreme Court'. By 22 November 1916, the Department of Native Affairs had collected a number of statements from clients complaining about their cases, as evidenced by the following: 'On numerous occasions in the past natives have made complaints at this office in regard to Mangena's questionable conduct, and during the current year two cases have come to the notice of this office when natives of Vereeniging and Middleburg, appeared to have been victimised by Mangena and Seme, who is now his partner.'[83]

The matter was subsequently reported to the Law Society, which concluded that there was insufficient evidence to pursue the complaints. The clients of Mangena and Seme were advised to pursue individual claims for damages or to ask for the return of their money, but these claims were never pursued. By this stage, however, the days of Mangena & Seme Solicitors were numbered, with the dissolution of their partnership being announced soon afterwards, in the May 1918 edition of *Imvo Zabantsundu*. This marked the end of the first black legal partnership in South Africa. With its dissolution, Mangena's life took a turn for the worse. Though a further attempt to have his name struck off the roll of attorneys did not succeed, he was nevertheless driven out of the profession.

Alfred Mangena died in 1924. By then he was living in Mthatha, though the circumstances of his leaving Johannesburg are not clear. Selby Msimang suggests that Mangena fled his practice and his life in Johannesburg when circumstances became unbearable, given the number of creditors pursuing him. He says too that, by the time Mangena left Johannesburg, he had been struck off the roll of attorneys for professional misconduct.[84] Whatever the case, it is a sad fact that Mangena ended his days not as an attorney, but a 'cattle dipper' – a rather menial job of disease prevention in cattle. Mangena had no children with Anna, who had not relocated with him to the Eastern Cape. When his estate was wound up, it comprised three immovable properties registered in his name. These were situated on the corner of Wein and Prinz Streets, Pretoria, and in Lady Selborne township, in Pretoria. For all his misfortunes, Alfred Mangena had managed to secure three pieces of urban land.

In a stirring obituary, tribute was paid to Alfred Mangena by Davidson Don Tengo Jabavu, one of an emerging group of young intellectuals:

> We never thought he would be cut down so early in life. However short his work may have been, he certainly delivered to South Africa a high and new message for the budding Native life and inspiration. He denied once and for all the idea that the Natives of this country were destined for ever to be hewers of wood and carriers of water. Advocate Mangena was born leader of men. He was a man of great courage who nourished a greater love for his country, for which he felt that no sacrifice would ever be too great. I mourn his sudden death, and I am sure that the heart of all his people is deeply wounded by this blow. May his soul rest in peace as surely as his name takes its just place in final history.[85]

4

The 'most gentlemanly' Richard Msimang

Many old supporters of the Taunton Rugby Club, who remember Mr R.W. Msimang LLB, a most popular player of the Club 25 years ago, will be sorry to hear of his death at Orlando, Johannesburg, at the age of 49. 'Oomsi' as he was known to the crowd, was not only a very fine fly-half, but his popularity was such that sometimes he had to leave the ground by a side entrance. Of sturdy build and full of pluck, he always viewed the game in the spirit which is peculiarly English. Mr Msimang was the son of a Zulu Methodist Minister. He came to Queens College in 1903, learnt rugger and also played for the school first XV, at outside left for many years. At that time, Messrs E.E. Shorrocks and C.C. Salway, two masters of Queens College, were playing in the Taunton three quarter line, and the Club has never had two finer players. Having matriculated at the school, 'Oomsi' served his articles with Messrs Guide and Broomhead. He passed the final law examination in 1912, and then returned to South Africa. He became a learned native attorney, and as a member of the Joint Council of Europeans and Africans he was an upholder of native welfare. Of a quiet and unassuming nature, he attracted friends in all walks of life.

– The Courier, 21 March 1934

The Msimang family features strongly in the history of South Africa. Best known, perhaps, is Selby Msimang, whose statue stands like a colossus in Pietermaritzburg, where a street is named after him. In the Msimang family home in Edendale, KwaZulu-Natal, a large picture of an earnest-looking Selby adorns the sitting room. Many proudly claim kin, and visit his grave in Pietermaritzburg in a form of pilgrimage, for spiritual renewal and connection to a past world. Material relating to the African National Congress is littered with the name of Selby Msimang, as one of the founders. In 2015, a doctorate was awarded by Wits University to a student whose thesis focused on the political life of Selby Msimang. And yet, there was a time when an older Msimang dominated newspaper pages, not only in South Africa but also in the United Kingdom. His name was Richard William

Msimang. He was one of the first two students to be registered at Ohlange Institute, the first school run by a black person in Natal. As a young man, while he was engaged in legal studies in England, he became a well-known rugby player.

Richard Msimang qualified as a solicitor of England and Wales in 1912, becoming the first black South African to do so. When he returned to South Africa later that year, racial discrimination was on the rise, compelling him to focus on its defeat. Given the fact that his training was in the field of law, he put his skills to use in confronting discrimination. The most pernicious legislative instrument that entrenched this discrimination was the Natives Land Act of 1913. Msimang devoted much of his life to working around the legislation, and dealing with its effects on the lives of Africans. In doing so, he was proposing an alternative way in which black and white South Africans could coexist in the land that had once belonged to Africans. Given his considerable contribution to the shaping of South Africa, it is regrettable that Richard Msimang is today a largely forgotten man. It is this wrong that these pages seek to redress.

Richard Msimang's life must, first and foremost, be located in a time and place where there was broad acceptance of Christianity among Africans. Indeed, his grandfather, Daniel, was the first black convert, and he set up a mission station for the Wesleyan Methodist Church of South Africa in Swaziland. Richard's own father, Joel Msimang, followed suit: his mission station was also located in Swaziland, where, as a child, Richard spent much time. Upon Richard's return, as an adult, to Swaziland, the king of the Swazi, Sobhuza II, entrusted him with important matters of state pertaining to land encroachment by the British government. That relationship would, however, end in recrimination, precipitating the demise of Msimang's professional life, and his death as a pauper.

A pertinent question is posed by the character Orlov in Anton Chekhov's novella, *The Story of an Unknown Man*:

> Why do we, who start out so passionate, brave, noble, believing, become totally bankrupt by the age of thirty or thirty five? Why is it that one is extinguished by consumption, another puts a bullet in his head, a third seeks oblivion in vodka, cards, a fourth, in order to stifle anguish, cynically tramples underfoot the portrait of his pure, beautiful youth?[1]

These questions are especially relevant to the life of Richard Msimang. In his thirties, Msimang turned his attention away from the world. It is possible that he collapsed under the weight of expectation – both personally and professionally. Towards the end of his life, Msimang had lost control of his marriage, his law practice and his finances. He sued his clients, and they in turn sued him. He fell behind with his subscriptions and dues with the regulatory body of lawyers, the

Transvaal Law Society, which had in any event been looking for an excuse to strike him off the roll of practising lawyers. While this did not happen, judgments were entered against him. One of these was the sequestration of his estate resulting from a failure to settle his debts. Msimang turned to alcohol – seeking 'oblivion in vodka' – and abandoned his legal practice. On his death, at a relatively young age, there was a sense of emptiness about his life. Left destitute, his wife was compelled to ask family members for financial assistance, which proved fruitless. Despite the tragic end to his life, its early phases help to provide some insight into the making of the man who nevertheless has the distinction of being the first black South African to be admitted to practise as a solicitor of England and Wales.

The Amakholwa of Edendale

Richard Msimang, son of Joel and grandson of Daniel, was born in Edendale, in 1884. His mother, Johanna Mtimkulu, was related to the royal family of the Hlubi, who had once occupied north-western Zululand. Some years before Richard's birth, in 1873, a conflict over land broke out between the Hlubi, led by Langalibalele, and the British forces of the Natal Colony. Langalibalele's followers had acquired firearms through their work on the diamond fields of Kimberley, and so they were able to match the firepower of the British. Ultimately, however, the Hlubi were overpowered and Langalibalele was exiled on Robben Island, from where he was later moved to Uitvlugt, in Cape Town. Johanna and her family had fled the conflict and came to settle in Edendale. The migration of the Msimangs had, however, taken a different path, and may be traced back to Reverend James Allison, a Wesleyan missionary. For a while, Allison had stayed in Richmond, spreading the gospel and converting the local native population. But he soon found himself in conflict with the church authorities, and in the 1840s decided to move southwards. More than 200 people of different ethnicities followed him, united in their belief that Reverend Allison had been wronged. Upon arrival in Edendale, the group bought a piece of land called Welverdiend, owned by Andries Pretorius, a Voortrekker leader. The acquisition of Welverdiend, in the Zwartkop Reserve, through donations by Allison and his followers was hugely significant. The land was subdivided among the new owners, who comprised groups such as the Griqua, the Barolong, the Basotho, the Batlokwa, the Hlubi and the Swazi. Through the wars of the Mfecane, Daniel Msimang's family had been displaced from north-western Natal; they fled to live among the Batlokwa in an area that was later included in the Orange River Colony, later known as the Orange Free State. Daniel was among those who followed Allison to Edendale in the 1840s.

Then, in 1867, Allison left Edendale. Subsequent to his departure, it became apparent that the land had not been fully paid for, and hence did not belong to his followers, which placed their interests in jeopardy. The owner could now take back the land, and leave the African purchasers landless. By sheer good fortune, Sir George Grey, governor of the Cape Colony and Natal, came to Pietermaritzburg at about the same time. The story of the precarious nature of the followers' ownership of the land was relayed to him – as was the fact that these were African Christian converts. This fitted snugly with his vision of creating a class of Africans that was culturally English. He donated the funds necessary to finalise the acquisition of the land. The land was now owned by Allison's followers, who were African and multi-ethnic. Their settlement was renamed Greytown, after Sir George Grey. An important aspect of individual title to the land – Christian conversion and the multi-ethnicity of the settlement – also represented detachment from traditional Zulu life.[2] The Greytown residents established a committee of their own to manage matters related to governance. Henry Msimang makes the following noteworthy observation regarding prevailing mores:

> When our ancestors established a committee of their own to look after their own affairs, it was such an orderly community that most of the town's people like, at weekends, to pay visits out this way, and they admired the way the area was under control. So they got the Governor of Natal to visit the place. When the Governor got here he was struck by the development that had taken place and the way that the little town was controlled. Then he chose the chairman of that Committee with the status of chief, gave him the position of chief. Our forefathers accepted that on one condition, that he became a member of the church and that his function would be to see to it that life in the community was a Christian life. I know that the first chief who was appointed had to be sent away. He started becoming a polygamist and when they got to know this they said 'you are doing nothing' and even confiscated his land.[3]

The system of native administration introduced by Sir Theophilus Shepstone was one of indirect rule, with Africans organised into various tribes or kraals. Each kraal had its own head, and each tribe had its chief. Chiefs (*amakhosi*) and heads of kraals (*iinduna*) were government appointees. Though the largely Christian community of Edendale defied the imagination of colonial administrators, they were nevertheless subject to native law: according to the Natal Code of Zulu Law, all native people had to live under the control of government-appointed chiefs. They could, however, be exempted from the application of native law, subject to approval by the governor. The Msimangs were among the first families to apply for exemption. They argued that native law was not applicable to persons such as themselves: they wished to be free from associations with hedonism, and to be governed by laws that were Christian in content – on that basis, they rejected polygamy. In support of their application, they offered to take an oath of allegiance signifying that they would be faithful and bear true allegiance to Her Majesty Queen Victoria, her heirs and successors, according to law.[4]

The Msimang family was relatively prosperous, with Daniel a trader in addition to being a church leader. He owned two houses, ninety acres of land in Edendale and more than ten plots of land in the village of Driefontein. As a farmer, he owned two wagons, one plough, one harrow, twenty-six oxen, twenty cows and a hundred goats. It was in 1883 that Daniel was asked to set up a mission station in Swaziland. There, he revived the Mahamba mission, which was used as the church headquarters. He established a school and recruited teachers from among the Christian converts. Eight years later, his son Joel followed him to Swaziland. Together with his wife, Johanna, they established the Makhosini mission station which was responsible for the eastern region of Swaziland. Joel not only built schools, he also made it possible for chapels to be used as schools on weekdays. Soon, Joel would take after his father, not only spreading the gospel, but also setting up businesses. One of the first and most prosperous was a bus company that transported workers between Johannesburg and Delagoa Bay.

By this time, in 1891, Richard was seven years of age. There was a mission school at the Makhosini station, which he attended. The family home was a typical European-style brick house with five bedrooms and a separate dining room. From a young age, Richard straddled the two worlds of Christianity and African traditionalism. His native language was Zulu, though he also spoke the closely related Swati, the mother tongue of most other children who attended the missionary school. He was also fluent in English, the language of instruction at the school. John Langalibalele Dube had just opened his Ohlange Institute, the first of its kind, modelled on Booker T. Washington's Tuskegee Institute for children of liberated slaves in America.

Ohlange, the place where 'boys gave up their liberty, but girls discovered it'
Ohlange's focus was industrial education rather than the liberal arts. In that, it was no different to Tuskegee, which concentrated on practical skills such as carpentry, brickmaking, animal husbandry, pottery and dressmaking. In this sense, the school perfectly fitted the model that Sir George Grey and other colonial administrators had conceived for African students. Notwithstanding this, when the school applied for funding from the government, the application was declined, thereby exposing the extent of the colonial plan, which was one of direct control.

Richard Msimang was one of the first pupils at the institute, whose imposing stone boarding school building still stands. Dube ran the school with an iron fist. Ohlange was neither a mission school nor a state school. It was an independent African school. Its first board of trustees included John Dube, John Mdima, Madikane Cele, Chief Mqhawe and Bryant Cele. The teaching staff was racially diverse, and in addition to Dube and his wife, Nokhutela, it included John Mdima, Soffe Dhlula, Thomas Khoza, as well as Reynolds Scott and his wife, Nancy Dhlula. Ohlange, unlike the established schools in Natal, offered an education for both boys and girls. Ohlange also innovated in respect of the rules for boys and girls. Whereas the typical missionary-school approach was that girls were essentially trained to become dutiful wives to the educated boys, there was a different approach at Ohlange. Boys were required to do chores that were traditionally the task of girls. These included gardening, cleaning and cooking. One American missionary remarked that at Ohlange, 'boys gave up their liberty, but girls discovered it there'.[5]

Because Ohlange had no governmental or missionary support, fees were paid by parents. Boys who lived on the premises were required to pay a fee of £5 per annum. Students were expected to see to their own needs in respect of food by growing vegetables, keeping chickens and ploughing cornfields. They were also expected to help with building work, the making of desks and beds, the repair of equipment such as ploughs, and general maintenance of the property. In a sense, their education cross-pollinated their actual lives. Dube's biographer, Heather Hughes, points out that students' chores were not simply a matter of exigency, they were integral to Dube's philosophy of self-help. She rejects the notion that such a school was merely preparing pupils for subservient roles in a racially defined society; instead, she points out that shortages of funds resulted in physical labour playing a crucial role 'in promoting an ascetic, hard-working and virtual standard of civilisation'.[6]

As noted, Dube ran the school in a highly disciplined manner. The day started at 6 a.m. in the fields and in workshops, and it ended with evening lessons. Often there were complaints that pupils were not getting enough food, but Dube showed little sympathy. In his autobiography, *Let My People Go*, Albert Luthuli vividly recalls Dube's response to one such complaint.[7] Dube simply asked the boys if he should rather return their fees and let them look after themselves. His wife, Nokhutela, had just graduated in music at Brooklyn College, in the United States of America – which resulted in a broadening of Ohlange's practical curriculum: she taught music, both vocals and instruments, which eventually turned out to be a vital element of the school. Music was popular among the students, and Nokhutela's creative teaching methods were well received. The school soon formed choirs, which proved to be an effective means of fundraising – in the same way as the fundraising choirs of the 1890s were helpful to the Hampton Institute. The Ohlange Choir frequently held concerts in Durban and sometimes even in Johannesburg. Its audiences were especially appreciative of its strong African vocals.

Impressed by Reverend Allison's tales of education in England, Joel Msimang hoped that Richard and his younger brother Selby would have the opportunity to study in the United Kingdom. But he could not arrange this through contacts at Ohlange, since Dube's connections were mainly concentrated in the black universities of America. Joel Msimang then decided on a local missionary school, hoping that it would improve the prospects of his sons being educated in England. The place he chose was the Wesleyan missionary school in the Eastern Cape – Healdtown.

The missionary school boy
Healdtown was established to educate the children of the Mfengu.[8] This was their reward for loyalty to the British government in the Eighth Frontier War of 1850–1853, fought against the Xhosa. The school is situated some ten kilometres from the town of Fort Beaufort. It was established by the missionary Reverend John Ayliff. In 1855, Sir George Grey, then governor of the Cape Colony, had visited Ayliff. Consistent with his plan for native children, he proposed that an industrial school be built. A substantial sum of money was provided, with one donor being James Heald of Liverpool, whom the school's name commemorates. The school officially opened in 1857. Its primary goal was to produce tradesmen such as mill-wrights, wheelwrights, blacksmiths, carpenters and cobblers. Industrial education was a major goal of the school, but it was by no means the only one. The conversion of the students to accept the Western way of life was its unspoken but central aim. By 1906, Ayliff could boast that the school had a beautiful church that could accommodate 600 worshippers, a number that continued to grow. In the typical paternalistic language of the time, he reported that 'our sons and daughters' attending the school were cared for by 'our Minister' or his family and were 'taught habits of cleanliness and industry, being instructed, fed and clothed in the house built for them'. The trades, he said, would not only be useful to the students, but would also be 'of great benefit to the entire settlement'. A watermill was running, which, Ayliff claimed, was 'the first ever' watermill in a native settlement, inducing 'our people to sew wheat largely instead of Indian corn and kaffir corn'. As the needs of Empire changed, so, too, did the curriculum of the school. Education with an academic slant was introduced, and by 1880 the school was training native teachers and clergy. In 1896 a girls' section was opened, and girls were also permitted to live on the school premises.[9] By the time Msimamg attended Healdtown, it was no longer a predominantly industrial school. Thus, the origins of Healdtown were not dissimilar to the origins of Edendale. Also, like Edendale, Healdtown eschewed tribalism, and took pride in a professed religious tolerance.

The making of a 'black Englishman'
It was at Healdtown that Joel Msimang's dream of providing his elder son with the opportunity of an education in the United Kingdom came into fruition.

The person who provided the necessary contact was the school principal, Mr Honebroek, who showed no hesitation in recommending Queen's College, a school in the sleepy town of Taunton, in Somerset. The school, which had been established by the Methodist Church in 1841, was one of the most academically prestigious schools in the United Kingdom.[10] While it attracted talented pupils from the UK and its colonies, in the years that Richard Msimang attended, he was the only student from Africa. In 1904, he took the long voyage by steamer, and after docking at Liverpool he took a train to Taunton, arriving in September in time for the start of the academic year. He noted that, in his entrance form, he was described as the 'son of Joel Msimang. A native of Natal.'[11]

Education in England did not come cheap. Joel was forced to sell some of his cattle to pay for travelling costs as well as school fees for the first quarter. But he was no longer the wealthy cattle owner of five years before. The rinderpest that struck in the years 1899 to 1902 had destroyed half of his livestock. Though not on the verge of poverty, he certainly lacked the funds to send his two sons to be educated in England. It is a curious fact that the school records indicate that Richard's fees were not paid for the remainder of his stay at the school. Each year, the records showed his fees as 'owing' or 'oustanding'. It is possible that the fees were written off, which would not be inconsistent with the Christian ethos of the school. As was suggested to me, 'one must remember Richard's outstanding contribution to the school, its culture, its sporting achievements, and its reputation. It is most likely that the school decided to keep him on regardless.'[12] Richard adapted well to his new environment, especially so to the local weather. As a young child, he had suffered chest ailments that showed features of asthma, but the weather conditions of Taunton seemed to suit him well, and his symptoms disappeared.

When Richard Msimang arrived at Queen's College in the autumn term, his teachers and fellow pupils were curious to know about him and his country. Two years prior to his arrival, the Anglo-Boer War had ended. The image of the Boers as the enemies of the English was still prominent in the minds of many people. He was asked to write an essay about his country, an exercise intended to test his English-language abilities. By writing about 'A Boer farmer', he was making a calculated choice. 'A Boer,' the essay begins, 'has a pleasant countenance.' But this is one of the few positive things that he has to say about the Boer. In the next paragraph, he describes the Boer farmer as personifying 'useless idleness'. The Boer lives on his farm comprising hundreds of acres on which he keeps a large herd of cattle and a flock of sheep. Yet these are 'almost entirely under the care of those whom he employed'. The Boer never digs a well, never makes roads, and nor does he bother to grow corn in the land of the Transvaal, with its 'soil of great fertility'. What little that is cultivated is usually the maize grown by his farm labourers – tellingly, the Boers regard people schooled in agriculture 'with supreme contempt'. These attributes ultimately boil down to the fact that, apart from being schooled in the Bible, the typical Boer farmer 'is not educated'. And even that Biblical understanding is usually taken 'in its literal interpretation'. Msimang had been raised to believe that, as an educated African, he occupied a special place in the civilised world, but he did not believe that Boer farmers shared in this, since they lived 'the most degraded life of any race with pretentions of civilisation'. Towards the end of the essay, Msimang remarks on the hunting skill of Boer farmers, who can 'shoot an eggshell off the palm of one's hand without hurting even the skin. I have myself seen a Boer shooting an eggshell on a horse's back and hitting it without injuring the animal.'[13]

Msimang's contempt for the Boer farmers did not flow specifically from their exploitation of black farmworkers, who were primarily responsible for carrying out virtually all the farm labour. His main thrust was the lack of education, the lack of 'civilisation' of the Boers. Whether this was a calculated strategy to gain acceptance into the dominant culture of the school by mocking a common enemy is not clear. Also, his status as a newcomer at the school probably explains some of the harsh language he used. For, as we shall see, as he grew in stature, intellectual development and maturity, his language became more restrained.

For its part, the school expressed no criticism of the essay. Quite the contrary. The report by H.S. Morgan, honourable secretary of the Debating Society, which Msimang joined upon his arrival, noted that Msimang 'opened public business by reading an interesting essay on "a Boer Farmer", which was very instructive, upon which SA Wilkinson congratulated the honourable member'.[14] Having delivered his inaugural speech as a member of the Debating Society, Msimang had earned his right of passage. He was now a member of the society and could participate in its debates. On 26 November, the final meeting of 1904 was held. The debate topic was whether or not parliamentary franchise should be extended to women. When the matter was put to the vote, thirteen members voted against the motion, with only eight in support. No record survives of Msimang's vote.

The debater

On 21 January 1905, Richard Msimang was unanimously elected to serve as a member of the organising committee of the prestigious Debating Society. He had the responsibility of setting up the debates and also participated in the selection of topics. The first debate of the year was held on 28 January,[15] and issues debated included the Russian revolt, the surrender of Port Arthur and the decline of rugby football. Msimang was a keen and active participant in the debate concerning the decline of rugby football. At Healdtown, he had played both soccer and rugby, and rugby would be among his greatest passions at Queen's College, bringing him considerable fame.

On 4 February 1905, Msimang played a prominent role in a debate as to the existence of supernatural beings. As the single most controversial issue in relation to African converts to Christianity, it was a topic close to his heart. As a child, he had often listened to his father discussing the interconnection between African religious beliefs and Christian beliefs. Many years later, Selby Msimang recalled this family story:

> The Swazi Queen was reported to be a great rain maker.
>
> When this part of the country, extending to the Mbono Mountains was stricken with drought, the Swazis living there could petition the Queen of rain. To do this a given number of cattle would be driven to the induna, who would, in turn, drive them into the royal grave place. This was an open circular place with the graves in the centre. The induna, who would be alone at this ceremony, would recite the praises of all the deceased kings of the Swazis and pray that they would be pleased to intercede for the supplicants to the Great Umvelinqange for rain.
>
> The supplicants would be waiting outside at the gateway to the real ceremony to receive the cattle when the induna nkulu had gone through the ritual. Invariably rain would begin to fall almost immediately. Upon herding the cattle back to the owners he would instruct them to go to the royal residence of the Queen, no one dare look back.
>
> My father told us, when we wanted to know who 'Umvelinqange' was, that his father, the Reverend Daniel Msimang had, at one time, visited the Queen Mother and questioned her about her power of causing rain to fall. She told him that it was not she who caused the rain to fall but Umvelinqange with whom were all the ancestral kings. She appealed or prayed to the ancestral kings to intercede on behalf of her people who were in need of rain. The Umvelinqange was the creator of all life, and as the spirit of her ancestors were with him, they alone could pray for us.[16]

Such stories were not only about the spirit world – the world of the supernatural – they were also about the linkages between the living and the dead, the living and the natural world, as Selby Msimang makes clear:

> The belief among the amaSwazi is that man does not die but his soul migrates to another world where it continues to live with Umvelinqange ... whose name is Unkulunkulu. The departed who are generally referred to as idlozi are believed to be mere Umvelinqange. After a funeral of a member of the family a ceremony is held, known as 'Ukubuyisa' – meaning that the spirit of the departed is invited back to watch over the welfare and wellbeing of the

living. He is believed to intercede or plead for the village before Umvelinqange. The departed are believed to return in the form of a snake, enter the heart and coil itself at the back of the interior of the heart. A diviner is called to disclose the cause of its visit. Invariably the diviner would identify whom the snake represents or who it is who has come in the form of the snake and what he wants.

This was the broader world in which Richard Msimang grew up. While his family were converts, the belief in African traditional systems had not been entirely jettisoned; on the contrary, many such beliefs were practised. Strict lines drawn between believers and non-believers tend to obscure this world of ambivalence. A Christian identity, at least from the perspective of Africans, did not always signify negation of African traditional beliefs. Africans did not perceive acceptance of Christianity as necessarily incompatible with African traditional beliefs. Thus, the embodiment of the two worlds in one was common. And so was migration between the two worlds. Msimang, therefore, was convinced of the existence of a supernatural world, as represented by the ancestors and also the God of Christianity. It is noteworthy that, when the debate was put to the vote at Queen's College, it was defeated by ten votes to four, with two abstentions.[17] The irony was not lost on the debaters, with one on the losing side wryly observing that it was ironic that in a Methodist school, supernatural beings were seen as non-existent.

A broad range of topics were debated. The 11th of February 1905 was set aside to debate whether or not the execution of Mary, Queen of Scots was justifiable. As one of the speakers, Msimang had to brush up on the history of the period. The majority voted in favour of the motion, with four against and two abstentions. The following week, a topic of special interest to Msimang was put up for discussion, which focused on volunteer fighters in Tennessee and Texas, and the role they played in the formation of states and annexation by America. Naturally, the debate about annexation elicited much interest in the student from the colony of Natal.[18]

In 1906, Msimang graduated from Queen's College. He showed an interest in law studies. At the time, as a preliminary to entering into articles of clerkship, it was necessary to sit for an examination, though there was no strict requirement to pass. Nor was it necessary to have a formal legal degree, since a matriculation sufficed. The date set for the preliminary examination was May 1906. Msimang was among the ninety-two candidates, and one of the sixty-five who passed.[19]

Despite the fact that Msimang had matriculated and qualified for his articles of clerkship, he remained at the school, playing in the rugby team and participating in the activities of the Debating Society. In April 1907, he was elected secretary of the Debating Society, an excellent achievement, recognising not only his intellect, but also his leadership and exemplary character. As secretary, he directed the entire programme, and had the final say on topics for debate. On 9 February, he proposed the topic: 'Chinese labour is detrimental to the interests of the Transvaal'. This was a topic of great relevance in South Africa at the time. Faced with labour shortages following the discovery of gold, and the ravages of the Anglo-Boer War, mining companies began recruiting labour from China. But this labour was seen as competition for the white working class, who had come to regard skilled positions as their own. There were warnings that the move by mining houses would escalate labour tensions. It is against this background that Msimang put forward the provocative topic.[20] He was neither on the side that affirmed or opposed the proposition, but instead was involved in judging the arguments. Since the discussion was 'so keenly contested', a decision was taken that it be adjourned until the following meeting.[21] On 2 March, the proposition was debated, presumably at the urging of Msimang, that civilisation had been conducive to the happiness of mankind. Those who affirmed the proposition were defeated, gaining only nine votes against the opposition's twenty-two. For Msimang, this must have been a particularly pleasing outcome, bearing in mind that the previous year the 'civilised' British had killed thousands of his countrymen in the Bambatha uprising, and executed many more.

As secretary of the Debating Society, Msimang produced an end-of-term report and also suggested a final proposition for debate: 'That in the opinion of the house, the present government has lost the confidence of the country.' At the time, there was general anxiety about the Liberal Party government, which, in Msimang's view, had been reluctant to take a clear stand in relation to its colonies, in particular South Africa. Another proposition that interested him, and which he was keen to debate, was the failure on the part of the British government to control its officers in the colonies. That term, the society inaugurated a reading society which focused on texts relating to the debate programme.

Msimang's term as secretary came to an end in July 1907, though he remained a keen participant in the activities of the society. On 30 November, a debate was proposed concerning the execution of Charles I and whether this was justified or not. On what was to be the last time he took part in the Debating Society, Msimang was afforded two opportunities to address the house on the basis of his 'sound and weighty arguments'.[22]

'Clever work' on the football field

It was in January 1908 that Msimang began his articles of clerkship, at G.H. Kite Solicitors in Taunton. While no longer eligible for participation in the Queen's College Debating Society, he did however continue to play for its football and rugby teams. He distinguished himself in a football match on 11 March 1909, where Queens A beat Taunton Queens by three goals to nil. Msimang played in the position of striker, and a match report noted approvingly: 'Msimang was responsible for some good dashes along the wing ... Msimang scored the third goal with a good shot.' Before this, between 1907 and 1908, Msimang was a member of Taunton Rugby Football Club (RFC), one of the leading black teams in the west of England. According to historian Brian Willan, Taunton RFC, though not as strong as larger clubs such as Bristol or Plymouth, still fell comfortably within the tier below.[23] The Courier reported on a tough game that Taunton RFC lost to Bridgewater, noting that 'Msimang dribbled half the length of the field' even though this was to no avail.[24]

On 11 March 1908, The Courier reported on a match against Weston. Msimang was central to the game, taking the ball from scrum and distributing it among his teammates, and providing crucial tackles in the game. Taunton ultimately prevailed. Another game was played on 1 April, against Wellington. Taunton won the game eight points to five. Msimang was praised for 'good footwork' and for putting in 'a clever combined dribble'.[25] At the end of the year, on 30 December, there was a game between Taunton and Old Monktonians, a side considered to be very strong since it 'had the assistance of two of the Wallabies'. Neither side had an advantage 'until Msimang secured in midfield and kicking across gave Duckworth a chance, which he failed to utilise'. After another attack by the visiting side, Taunton 'again became aggressive, and, after a passing movement close up, Msimang got possession after Duckworth had dropped his pass, and literally dived over the line, amid the cheers of the spectators'.[26] In the second half, Msimang was again back in the action, and by 'clever work', he placed Taunton in a good position. Msimang, who was playing fly-half, 'was always in the thick of the fray' in a game that ended with one try to nil.

Msimang's talented rugby moves brought him much acclaim in the small town of Taunton. After a game in which he played fly-half, The Gazette reported: 'Msimang has become very popular with the crowd. In fact the old Queens boy was one of the shining lights of the afternoon, and made quite a number of sprints on his own, which would have resulted in his scoring on at least two occasions had he possessed more pace.'[27] The Western Daily Press gave the following glowing report: 'Taunton have got an excellent recruit in R.W. Msimang, a young coloured gentleman, who, after having undergone the course of study at Queens College, Taunton, is now training with a local firm of solicitors for the legal profession. He proved wonderfully alert on Saturday, and made a most useful half.'[28]

Msimang's busy law practice and preparation for his qualification exams did not interfere with his sporting activity. In 1910, he was described in the school magazine, The Wyvern, as 'one of the most gentlemanly players that ever donned a jersey', with the hope that he would secure a place in the county team.[29] Throughout 1911, newspapers repeatedly reported on games where Msimang played fly-half. By now, he was vice-captain of Taunton RFC. In The Courier of 11 January, when Cinderford visited, it was reported that 'Taunton figured out a strong team', which included its celebrated fly-half, Msimang. Two months later, on 2 April, *The Courier* reported on a game played at Bridgewater that ended in a nil-nil draw, with Msimang being credited for playing 'capitally'.

A final club dinner was arranged for Richard Msimang in May 1912. *The Gazette* of 11 May 1912 reported on Taunton RFC's annual dinner, where a committee member paid tribute to the efforts of the captain, Mr H. Gummingham, and Mr R.W. Msimang, 'both of whom had done much to create a spirit of unity among the players. (Hear, hear)'. From this moment on, after nine years in the United Kingdom, Richard Msimang would turn his full attention to his legal studies, before returning to his native country.

Solicitor

By 1909, Msimang was fully immersed in his legal studies. The intermediate examination was approaching, and after passing it he could present himself any time after twelve months of being articled. The examinations were held at the Law Society Hall, at Chancery Lane in London. Msimang sat for the exam, and was granted a pass by the Law Society of England and Wales. At the time, two other notable South Africans were living within walking distance of Chancery Lane – Pixley ka Isaka Seme and Alfred Mangena. There is no record that Msimang met either of them during his time there, but it is more than likely that he did.

Msimang was now left with one final examination before he could qualify as a solicitor for England and Wales. Over a two-day period in 1912, on 17 and 18 June, Msimang sat for his final examinations. He was examined in four areas of the law:

1. The principles of the law of real and personal property, and the practice of conveyancing;
2. The principles of law and procedure in matters usually determined or administered in the Chancery Division of the High Court of Justice;
3. The principles of law and procedure in matters usually determined or administered in a King's Bench Division of the High Court of Justice, and the law and practice of bankruptcy;
4. The principles of law and procedure in matters usually determined or administered in the Probate, Divorce and Admiralty Division of the High Court of Justice; ecclesiastical and criminal law and practice; and proceedings before justices of the peace.

Richard Msimang passed his examination and was duly admitted as a solicitor in England and Wales. On 8 November that year, his friends and colleagues arranged a farewell for him. It was a sad occasion for all, and the mood was captured in the following report:

> Mr R.W. Msimang, the well-known fly-half of the Taunton Rugby Club, who has had a playing career of considerable brilliancy, and has made himself extremely popular with all his colleagues, is leaving England on the 16th instant to return to his home in the Transvaal, where his father is a native Wesleyan missionary. Mr Msimang came to Taunton eight and a half years ago as a pupil at Queens College and was afterwards articled to Messrs Dwight, Broomhead, and Kite Solicitors, of Uptown. He recently passed his final legal examination, and is now a fully qualified solicitor. It is his intention to practise his profession in the Transvaal, and his numerous friends hope that he will experience a very successful career there.
>
> At a gathering of the supporters of the Taunton Rugby Club at the London Hotel on Wednesday night, Mr Msimang received from them a very handsome farewell present in the shape of a gold watch chain with a pendant bearing the inscription: 'Presented to R.W. Msimang on his leaving Taunton'.
>
> The presentation was made by the President, Mr E.H. Claridge, who spoke of the excellent sporting qualities which the recipient had displayed during his seven years connection with the club, and of the excellent comradeship which had ever existed between him and the other members.
>
> Mr H.J. Morse, the honorary secretary, added a few words, and remarked that Mr Msimang was always as ready to play away as at home.
>
> Mr Msimang returned thanks and said he would always have pleasant recollections of his stay in Taunton, and of his association with the Club. He very coyly acknowledged all the kindness he had received from the members.[30]

On 16 November 1912, Msimang set sail for South Africa. Debating had sharpened his analytical skills, his ability to interrogate opposing arguments and his powers of persuasion. He had also learnt the virtue of patience and tolerance. From his experiences, it is clear that he was never a victim of racial discrimination during his student days at Taunton. But was this enough to prepare him for what he was about to experience in South Africa? Just eleven months prior to his leaving Taunton, the SANNC had been established in response to the formation of the Union of South Africa, which excluded blacks from government.

Return to South Africa
After disembarking from the *Armadale Castle* on 9 December 1912,[31] Richard Msimang travelled to his birthplace, Edendale, where he had spent his early childhood years. But South Africa was now a very different world to the one he had

left behind, particularly since race relations had worsened considerably during the nine years of his absence. His intention was to establish a law practice, either in Durban or Pietermaritzburg. But the authorities informed him that, because his qualification was obtained in the United Kingdom, he would again have to undertake articles of clerkship. He objected to this, and decided instead to go to Johannesburg.[32] Almost immediately, he experienced racism: in Charlestown, on the train journey to Johannesburg, white police officers arrested him for travelling without a pass. He explained his situation, but this was rejected and he was locked up until the following morning, when the police let him off. Arbitrary arrests for minor infringements, including failure to carry a pass or to produce one on demand, were commonplace. On arrival in Johannesburg, he met up with his brother Selby, who was at the time employed by Pixley Seme as an administrative clerk, and whose wedding in the winter of that year he had missed. Richard stayed with his brother for a couple of months while preparing for his admission as an attorney and later setting up his offices. Seme considered going into partnership with Msimang, but eventually decided against this, and set up his own practice.

Attorney of the Supreme Court of South Africa

When Msimang was admitted as an attorney, Mangena and Seme were the only other black attorneys in the Transvaal. Even though they had been practising for a while, a black attorney was still regarded as a rarity, and even a curiosity. When black attorneys appeared in court, the court would be crowded, filled with curious white lawyers and black spectators. Many white lawyers came to witness the spectacle of a black lawyer in court, while blacks attended as a gesture of support. The admission of a third black lawyer in the Transvaal would not change anything. The date was set for 23 June 1913, and for the Msimang family, it was an occasion of great pride. Not only had their elder son been educated in England, but he had achieved tremendous success. Richard did not only belong to his family, however – the people claimed him too. Much was expected of him. South Africa was rapidly changing, and segregation was being legislated. It would be up to Msimang to navigate the two worlds of white and black, and to lead his people to a new and uncertain world.

On the morning of 23 June 1913, the air around the Palace of Justice in Pretoria was pregnant with expectation. The Msimang family were the first to arrive in court, and took the front-row seats. Seme, Mangena and others of the black educated class also came to witness, and soon the court was full to the brim. In his application for admission, Msimang was represented by his attorney, I. Lappin. In the very first paragraph of his application, he informed the court that he was 'admitted as a solicitor of his Majesty's Supreme Court of Judicature in England'. His certificate, dated 1 April 1913, issued by His Majesty's Supreme Court, confirmed that he was 'duly qualified to act as a solicitor of the Supreme Court of Judicature of the United Kingdom'. It also noted that the records of the Law Society of England and Wales 'contain nothing to his discredit'. The Law Society of the Transvaal did not oppose his admission, as it had done with Alfred Mangena. The registrar of the High Court duly entered Richard Msimang's name in the roll of practising attorneys of the Supreme Court of South Africa. Msimang then took the oath: 'I, Richard William Msimang, swear that I will be faithful and bear true allegiance to his Majesty King George V, his heirs and successors, according to law. So help me God.' By swearing allegiance to the king, Msimang earned the right to practise as an attorney of the Supreme Court of South Africa.

In this way, Richard Msimang became the first African qualified to be admitted as solicitor of England and Wales and admitted to practise as such in South Africa. The two attorneys, Seme and Mangena, who had been admitted before him, had been barristers in the United Kingdom. Now Msimang had conquered both jurisdictions. He was a solicitor of England and Wales and also an attorney of the Supreme Court of South Africa.[33] Msimang's admission marked 'a further step in the history of the Bantu race', as *Abantu-Batho* reported in its edition of 5 July 1913:

> We offer our heartiest congratulations to Mr R.W. Msimang, who has been admitted an attorney of the Supreme Court of South Africa (Transvaal Provincial Division). The application for admission was heard last Monday, June 23rd, at Pretoria, before Mr Justice Mason and Mr Justice Gregorowski. Msimang when entering the Palace of Justice, was accompanied by the Reverend R. Twala of Pretoria (his brother-in-law); the court was then delivering judgment in an appeal case, at the conclusion of which the Registrar of the Court announced that there was an application by a Richard William Msimang to be admitted to practise as an attorney of court. The Bar was crowded with counsel and solicitors, and Mr Msimang walked up to take the usual oaths before the Registrar, after which he signed his name and the application was granted.

The newspaper expressed high hopes for Msimang, noting that he had 'a remarkable, popular and genial personality' and throughout his schooling had been well liked by his friends. Noting also his rugby success, the newspaper reported that Msimang had 'no intention to play football again'. Selby suggests that his decision may have been influenced by the expectations of society; as a solicitor, he would be entrusted with a great deal of responsibility. Time spent on the rugby field might trivialise his newly acquired status, not only as an educated black man, but as one of only three black lawyers in the country.[34]

Activist lawyer

Richard Msimang chose 98 Anderson Street, Johannesburg, as the premises of Msimang Solicitors; he was the sole director and proprietor of the firm. At the time, he was still living with his brother, Selby, who had been elected to serve as recording secretary at the founding meeting of the SANNC in January 1912. He tried to persuade Richard to join the SANNC and to take up a leadership position. Although reluctant at first, Richard eventually relented. Soon afterwards, a meeting was convened where it was proposed that a constitution be drafted for the new organisation.

Richard Msimang was appointed chairman of the Constitution Drafting Committee of the SANNC. From that moment, his life took a different trajectory as he became an activist as well as a lawyer. Rather than recoiling from the problems of race, he dedicated himself to solving South Africa's race problem. At the time, the burning issue was the draft Natives Land Bill. It was enacted in June 1913, and in July Msimang joined a delegation of the SANNC to meet with Prime Minister Louis Botha. At that meeting, the effects of the new legislation were discussed. Botha wished to uphold the main provisions of the Act and to press ahead with residential segregation. He would only consider an expansion of the land allocated to Africans after a report of the Beaumont Commission, established under the Act. Given this intransigence, an answer would be sought by combining legal and political strategy. The SANNC, which had been founded to advance the interests of Africans, had to go beyond political methods, as Selby Msimang explained:

> You see, the ANC was unfortunate … It was established in 1912. In 1913 before it had settled as an organisation, perhaps drawn up its plans to organise and run the whole show, the government introduced the Land Bill, which was a great sensation. It meant that every effort must be made to fight against the Bill. So everyone of us, some of us had to give up our jobs, and go out organising – explaining to the people what this new Bill contained and eventually we decided to send a deputation to England in protest after the government had passed the Bill. It meant all of us should go out into the country collecting funds and my brother was very much interested in collecting information of the developments after the Act had been passed. There was a great deal of upheaval, particularly in the Free State. African farm labourers were uprooted, sent away. All conditions of employment were changed under this Act. You would see a number of families driving their stock in the country not knowing where to take them to. So my brother's job was to go, follow up with families and keep a record and send whatever he had got to the deputation in England to show them what was taking place in this country.[35]

The consensus between the Afrikaners and the English had resulted in the creation of the new South African state in 1910. The passing of the Natives Land Act in 1913 represented a consolidation of that pact. Apart from political power, land would also be distributed along racial lines. Richard Msimang clearly faced a monumental task in the wake of the Act. South Africa could not be a country whose prosperity was shared by all races while racially discriminatory laws remained in place. If a new society was to be created, unjust laws had to be challenged. This would now be his goal.

'Cruel and careless injustices'

Together with journalist Solomon Tshekisho Plaatje, Richard Msimang was tasked by the SANNC with documenting the experiences of Africans under the Natives Land Act, for submission to the South African government. Plaatje recorded the experiences in *Native Life in South Africa: Before and Since the European War and the Boer Rebellion*, published in 1916 with the now legendary opening sentence, 'Awaking on Friday morning, June 20, 1913, the South African native found himself, not actually a slave, but a pariah in the land of his birth.' Msimang opted for a narrower yet equally effective explanation of the facts in a 1916 article later published as a pamphlet, *Natives Land Act 1913: Specific cases of evictions and hardships, etc.*[36] His immediate purpose, Msimang noted, was 'to vindicate the leaders of South African Native National Congress from the gross imputation by the Native Affairs Department, that they make general allegation of hardships without producing any specific cases that can bear examination'.[37]

The SANNC, he continued, had been wrongly accused of making 'wild statements of existing hardships which they failed to support by concrete facts'. Because the charges emanated from the Native Affairs Department, they should be treated with suspicion, as 'from our bitter experience, that Department was in the habit of making prejudiced statements' in order to 'blind' the misinformed European public. So, he asked, what were the real facts?[38]

He began by describing the proceedings of a meeting held in July 1913, in Pretoria, to protest the new law. Despite the fact that the Act had only been in force for six weeks, there were already numerous instances of evictions. One of these had occurred in the vicinity of Pretoria, while in Natal people were being driven out of their homes and their 'ancient residences'. The Native Affairs Department had pleaded ignorance of the evictions, despite the fact that they had with them eighty names of people served with eviction notices. The government's strategy was to deny knowledge of such instances of evictions from homes and farms. The prime minister, Msimang charged, had also repeated the lie. Evictees had directly reported their plight to him, and he had simply turned a blind eye. In Thaba 'Nchu, people who had been evicted addressed the secretary for native affairs during his tour of the Orange Free State. His advice to them was 'to sell all their stock, and return to the farms to labour in capital as unpaid servants!' Otherwise, they should go to the reserves (even though he was aware that there were none apart from Thaba 'Nchu, which was already full to capacity). The same stance was taken by the prime minister in Cape Town when he claimed that vague allegations were made without evidence. Msimang exposed the lie by stating a bald fact: '79 and 100 individuals or more families at Peters and Colwoorth respectively are BEING EJECTED BY THE GOVERNMENT itself in anticipation of the supposed requirements of this law. Yet, without providing land for them. These are the cruel and careless injustices under which our people suffer, and against which we ask relief.'

The government's defence was to deny that the evictions were taking place in terms of the Natives Land Act. Instead, it claimed that the evictions were the result of the Squatters Law Act of 1895. This law, which was applied in the Orange Free State, prohibited farmers from employing more than five African house-holders on one farm without government permission. The law also prohibited Africans from living outside reserves. However, it proved to be ineffective, as land companies repeatedly broke the law. Here, however, the problem, as noted by Msimang, was that the Natives Land Act of 1913 had entrenched the provisions of the Squatters Law Act of 1895. Thus, Msimang's response to the government was that its argument was 'a mere subterfuge'. The evictions, he said, were deliberately made 'with the sole intention of debt-enforced labour, as provided in the Act. White farmers know full well that since the Act, natives are no longer free to obtain land or to make terms for occupation of land.'

Msimang's study focused on two provinces with large numbers of squatters. In Natal there were 436 000 squatters, and in the Free State about 80 000 squatters. These people would soon be driven off the land. In Natal, most of them had already been given six months' notice to vacate the land, while in the Free State the average notice period was five days, and in two cases he was aware of people were given 'one hour's notice to leave and trek'. The removals were capricious and amounted to 'loss of buildings without compensation, and reduction to a state of vagabondage with no prospect of permanent settlement'. The blacks he had interviewed had given him the number of livestock they possessed, and this indicated the extent of the losses that they would sustain. Thus, the effect of the Act was not merely removal from the land, but deprivation of cattle and other livestock, the people's only means of wealth and livelihood.

Having set out his general comments, Msimang went on to deal with specific instances of notices that he described as only 'a few specimens': Jantje in the Free State was told 'to leave the farm within eight days to seek a place'; William was given two days 'to seek a place not to remain an hour in the farm'; Jacob, Piet and

Melka, together with twelve cattle and twenty sheep, were instructed to leave in four days.

Apart from individual cases such as these, there were also group evictions that affected large communities. Msimang recounted one such instance in the district of Ladysmith. Chief Sibisi and his people had for many years lived as squatters or tenants on the farm known as 'remainder of Brakfontein sub A and remainder of Weltevreden sub D', a property owned by the government. The notification to leave affected seventy-nine families, including that of Chief Sibisi. The families were told to leave by way of the following notice addressed to Vellem Sibisi, the 'kraal head' residing on the farms:

> Take notice in terms of section 4 of law 41 of 1884 that you are required to remove with your kraal and inmates from whichever of the said farms you may be residing on six months from this date.
>   The aforementioned farms having all been purchased by the government for closer settlement purposes.

The notice was signed by the assistant magistrate of Ladysmith. Upon receipt of the notice, the chief was required to leave the area. When the matter was reported to the magistrate, the latter advised the tenants that they could remain, provided they agreed to work as labourers for the new farm owner. Msimang then resorted to legal argument, focusing on the details of the law. The notice was purportedly written under the Squatters Law Act, but it was effectively implementing the provisions of the Natives Land Act; not only were natives being ejected from land, but there was no alternative land which they could hire. The undertaking that they could remain on the land provided that they worked for the owner was equivalent to slavery, and in any event made no sense for 'an old man like Chief Sibisi'. The perversity of the enterprise, Msimang pointed out, was demonstrated by the fact that people were being evicted by the government in the full knowledge that there was no alternative land for them.

The same applied in the case of Mgemgeni Hlonuka, an *induna* at Rooiport Farms in Ladysmith. He and his people received notice to vacate, but on appeal to the authorities the magistrate informed them that they could 'go where you like or stay there and work on the farm as labourers'. They left the farm, but indicated that they had nowhere to go and would therefore be squatting as they moved from one place to another. The same fate awaited the families at Stokville Farm, Colworth, where hundreds of people were uprooted and left stranded with their livestock. The government itself was ejecting people, an action 'most disquieting in the native mind', so people inevitably asked: 'can we believe the … promise that we shall be given land, when it is the government that is evicting us from our residences without even attempting to provide temporary places for us pending the settlement of areas.'

Blacks clearly had no hope of being granted any land. In the district of Weenen, where there were 120 families, the municipal office ejected Chief Noxaka Mbhele and all his followers, giving them three months to pack and 'trek'. Any failure to leave as instructed would result in 'steps' being taken against them. Msimang also cited the affidavit of Chief Sandanezwe Mcunu, from the district of Dundee:

> I have livestock consisting of 50 sheep, 30 goats, 30 herd [sic] of cattle and seven horses. If the time of notice expires before I have found another farm for myself and my said afflicted people, I fear I shall have no place to which to go and shall be obliged to sell or dispose of my said livestock at a loss for which I shall have no place in which to store them for grazing. My said people are appealing to me to find a place for themselves, their families and such stock as they possess. But I do not know where to go under the circumstances. The farmer tells us to sell all our livestock.

Upon reporting the situation to the magistrate, Chief Mcunu was advised that he should come to an arrangement with the farm owners 'whereby we must agree to work on the farm for nothing and without pay according to the new law'.

The situation in the Free State was no different. Many people who were evicted were simply told to go to Basutoland. After Zachariah Doge was evicted, he was forced to wander about with his family and the twenty cattle and forty sheep they owned. Anbooi Molele was evicted, but he returned as a labourer after selling his stock at a loss. People were usually given about a week, or at most ten days, to vacate a property. Some disappeared and were never heard from again. John Bhaka was one of these: he went to Basutoland, but his family reported that he had not been seen or heard from since. A large number of people were simply recorded as 'whereabouts unknown'. On the farm Kienzi, in Kroonstad, the Maphike family informed Msimang that 'the conditions under which we live are that we and every member of the family have to labour in the month by month in the year without pay or other remuneration except that we get in return small pieces of land to till for ourselves'. Jacob Maphike described the circumstances in which he lost his livestock:

> About three months ago, our master came to us in the farm, called us together, asked us to collect our stock, which we did. He then counted the aggregate number of livestock belonging to each person squatting in his farm. After counting the stock: cattle, sheep, horses, he said to each of us, you have too

much stock, I have not sufficient room or place for them in the farm. You must sell or dispose of your stock, or you must leave this farm.

Many people had no option but to give their livestock to the very farmers whose land they were working with no pay. Msimang noted that these people were given notice to leave if they refused to sell their livestock. The farmers knew full well that they would not find other farms to live on, so it was a 'good opportunity to make them life serfs'. This was the inevitable outcome: the farmers were aware that as long as Africans were able to own property, they could maintain their independence.

Msimang concluded that the Natives Land Act had created 'slavery, persecution and vagabondage'. Citing the case of Sethlogo Merabe, with his wife and eight children, he noted that while they were on the farm, Merabe and his children were forced to work on the farm every day, with no pay. During the rainy season they ploughed up to ten acres, with each field being 300 by 20 yards. He received no compensation, and afterwards the farmer simply decided to evict them all. Arbitrary periods were given for such evictions, and reasons were often absent in the notices to vacate. An especially pernicious effect was vagabondage. Merabe had 48 head of cattle, 192 sheep, five horses, one wagon, two ploughs and a few other implements. After his eviction he tried to find a new farm where he could settle, but 'every farmer he has approached seeking residence tells him to dispose or sell his stock first and thus be reduced to poverty and be without property or other means of independent subsistence'. He refused the option of becoming a farm labourer, and was instead 'moving from place to place in search of a new home'. In many cases, property was arbitrarily appropriated by the farm owners. Jacob Maroe of Geluk Farm in Kroonstad eventually parted with his property under compulsion. When a farmer wanted to buy his 'hamel' (wether), Maroe refused to sell the animal. The farmer reportedly told him: 'If you do not sell me the hamel then you must leave the farm at the end of the month.' Maroe then agreed to sell the wether for ten shillings. The farmer rejected this, but made no counter-offer. Maroe then suggested nine shillings, which the farmer accepted. But that money was never paid, despite the wether being given to the farmer. To make matters worse, at the end of May 1914, Jacob Maroe was given notice to leave. He told Msimang that he did not know where to go; it had been extremely hard to find an alternative place to settle.

In similar vein, Foreman Ranope revealed that he had once owned 200 head of cattle and had access to grazing land which was suddenly taken over and given to a white farmer. He was then 'employed' by the farmer as a sheep shearer. Because he had no time to inspect the fields and look after his cattle, he discovered one day that his crops had been eaten by cattle. But these were not his own cattle, they belonged to the farmer. He then 'went to the baas and asked why he destroyed our crops like that'. The farmer's response was that he was forced to do this as there was a drought and 'he would not let his cattle die and let the natives live'. After a further confrontation, the farmer told him to leave within three days. When he left, his entire herd of 200 cattle was impounded by 'Mr van Niekerk', the farm owner. Not only had he worked for no payment, he also had his livestock and his land taken from him, and he was left to roam across the Free State.

In some cases, the police enforced the Natives Land Act. In the case of Simon Teatea of Leeuwkuil Farm, he had been evicted from the farm where he had been staying as a squatter, and after six days of wandering about, he found a place to live called Jacob's Farm, which was in the Senekal district. In return, he and his children were expected to work for the farmer. Since there were twelve in the family, including his wife and his ten children, the farmer was keen to allow them to stay on the farm. One day, without any notice, the farmer complained that the girls were lazy and not working according to instructions. When Teatea denied that his children were lazy, the farmer called the police to arrest them for insubordination. On arrival, the police accused Teatea of being insolent simply because he was able to read and write and also owned property. They told him that they would 'put him right' and make him walk all the way to the Basutoland border. They then summoned one of the girls, Eliza, and when she appeared a policeman took a sjambok and started thrashing her. Teatea intervened and the policeman stopped, but he warned that worse was to come. The next day, the farmer arrived with a notice giving them eight days to pack up their belongings and leave. By this time, Teatea had already built seven huts for his family, but he was told that, before leaving, they had to pull down all these huts.

Richard Msimang's accounts constitute what are probably the most vivid and graphic illustrations of the effects of enforcement of the Natives Land Act. By using individual stories of eviction, hardship and deprivation, Msimang was able to demonstrate that the Act achieved three interrelated outcomes. First, the loss of land and the drastic curtailment of security of tenure with black people being evicted at the whim of government or any white person. Second, the loss of property, particularly in the form of cattle. The accounts show that the cattle were not 'lost', but were instead confiscated and taken away by white farmers. Often, sham transactions were entered into, in terms of which blacks were compelled to 'sell' their cattle in order to have a place to stay. The third outcome was the overnight conversion of black people into a class of labourers. But importantly, the stories in Natal and the Orange Free State show that these were no ordinary labourers. They were unpaid labourers, operating in an environment equivalent to forced labour, which resulted in many leaving to settle in Basutoland. Physical punishment was commonplace, and as a rule there were no consequences. Like *homo sacer*, the metaphorical figure of Roman law, a white farmer could kill a black worker, but the killing would not count as murder.[39]

Law as politics

After nine years in the bliss of Somerset, the experiences Richard Msimang recorded opened his eyes to the reality of South Africa. They altered his perception so that he now saw what was truly at stake. Later in 1914, when the SANNC sent a deputation to London, they envisaged that the Natives Land Act would be scrapped altogether. By then Msimang had carefully explored the implications of the legislation. He drew up a letter headed 'Natives Land Act, 1913: An Appeal to the People of England'.[40] In this, Msimang analysed the provisions of the Act, and showed how its application prejudiced native South Africans. Its first clause prohibited the sale, lease or acquisition of land by natives 'from a person other than a native'. Further, the Act provided that a person 'other than a native shall not enter into any agreement or transaction for the purchase, hire, or other acquisition from a native of any such land'. The transactions referred to would only be permitted by the governor-general. At face value, the Act appeared to prohibit everyone, natives and Europeans alike, from such transactions. But as Msimang's document pointed out, for Europeans 'this is a restriction on paper only as the natives have no land to sell'. As a result, 'the provisions of the Act really operate only against the natives'.

The result of these restrictions on land transactions was that natives were immediately rendered homeless when their period of leasehold or tenancy came to an end. In order for them to remain on farms, they had to be servants of the farmer. Section 5 of the Act made it a criminal offence for any person to hire or lease or sell land to a native. Upon conviction, such person could be fined up to £100 and, in the event of a default of payment, imprisoned for a period not exceeding six months. Msimang noted that the implementation of the Act had produced several classes of sufferers, including: persons under notice to quit (since they could not voluntarily enter into free transactions to acquire land); persons actually evicted from farms (since they would have nowhere to settle upon eviction); migrants to territories outside the Union (such as those forced to flee to Basutoland in search of land); homeless wanderers with families and stock in search of new homes; persons who had to leave their crops unreaped; and persons who were compelled to put their labour at the disposal of farm owners for no payment. These were the consequences of legislation that removed natives from farms without making provision for their settlement elsewhere. A foremost concern was the racial discrimination openly promoted in the Act, whose impact was severely felt by natives excluded either from the free purchase of land, from entering into leases or from dealing in land. As Msimang noted, the Act interfered with rights that natives had long exercised under colonial rule:

> In particular they interfere with rights the natives have as British subjects of bargaining with the owners of these farms. In effect this produces a condition of slavery. This is due to a provision which encourages the farmer to exact unpaid services from the native tenants. In the event of eviction, the tenant is unable to settle upon any other farm, except as a farm servant, and therefore is forced to accept almost any conditions the farmer likes to impose upon him. This we claim is slavery.

The point about slavery was particularly relevant in an appeal to the United Kingdom, a country that had pretentions as a bastion of civilisation, having turned its back on forced labour by abolishing slavery in 1833. Ultimately, the objection to the Act was that it entirely excluded natives from occupying or owning land in the Orange Free State. The appeal was put forward in the name of Dr Dube, who was at the time president-general of the SANNC. Msimang had broken down the elements of the Act for Dube, who had been his teacher at Ohlange Institute. In its sharp analysis of the implications of the Act, and its persuasive legal arguments, it was clear that the student had turned teacher, and the teacher become a student. The Natives Land Act came under scrutiny during a House of Commons debate in 1914, following the arrival of the South African delegation which had come to protest the Act. Echoing the complaints documented by Msimang, Liberal Party member Percy Alden stated:

> I wish to bring to the notice of the right honourable gentlemen the question of the native lands of South Africa … If we take away the land from the Native we take away his liberty. In reference to the Natives Land Act of 1913, I want to put two or three points before the right honourable gentlemen. In the Union of South Africa, blacks own about 4,500,000 morgen of land, and the white [sic] own 14 times as much land as the blacks, though, of course, they are very much smaller in number … It has been said over and over again in South Africa that this law applies equally to Europeans and whites as well as to the Natives. There is, they say, no injustice. The European is estopped from this purchase of land, just as the Native is estopped. All I can say in answer to that is that the fallacy is shown the moment you begin to ask what land the Natives have to sell. The native areas are already overcrowded, and they positively have no land which they could sell. When once a Native leaves his farm or is evicted, or has to quit for any reason whatever, the Act does not allow him to purchase, hire or to lease anywhere else for farming purposes except from Natives, who

have not the land to lease or to sell. He therefore must become a servant on the farm. There is absolutely nothing else for him to do but to become a servant.[41]

In reply, Lewis Vernon Harcourt, who was at the time secretary of state for the colonies, stated that the question of the South African Land Act was not a 'sudden inspiration of the Botha government'.[42] He went on to defend it as follows:

It is the outcome and result of a commission appointed by Lord Milner some years ago, presided over by Sir Godfrey Lagden. The Commission was appointed: 'in view of the possible federation of the South African colonies to gather accurate information as to native affairs so as to arrive at a common understanding on questions of native policy'.

That Commission sat for two years. It had upon it representatives of every colony and territory. It arrived at what I believe as a unanimous report, and this Act is practically doing no more than carrying out its recommendations. The Act has already been in operation for 12 months. The Commission of Inquiry, which was to be instituted under the Act, is now sitting. It is bound by the terms of its appointment to report within two years, and will probably report by Christmas next. The whole of this Act is a temporary measure until that Commission reports.

A native deputation has come over and seen me, and I believe many other members. That deputation left Africa against the advice of General Botha, and against almost the entreaties of Lord Gladstone. They knew that the Act would not be disallowed, because it had been announced months before in South Africa. The day the deputation saw me the period of 12 months during which that Act could be disallowed on my recommendation had already expired.

Britain had long envisioned a racially segregated South Africa. During his term as high commissioner, Lord Alfred Milner had appointed Godfrey Lagden to chair a commission of inquiry to present recommendations on future policy on black affairs in South Africa. No Africans were appointed to the commission of eleven members. Two members were from Rhodesia and Bechuanaland. Lagden presented his report in 1905. Its most significant policy recommendations, which became the blueprint for the 1913 Land Act, were threefold. First, the commission considered it necessary that certain measures be adopted to 'safeguard what is conceived to be the interests of the Europeans of this country' in relation to land. Second, the commission recommended certain restrictions upon the purchase of land by Africans in areas to be defined by legislation. Third, it was recommended that purchase of land which may lead to tribal, communal or collective possession by Africans should not be permitted, outside certain areas designated for African occupation. The commission recommended that areas referred to as locations or reserves must be 'defined, delimited and reserved for Africans by law'. The reservation of land for African occupation in reserves and native locations, the commission recommended, must 'be done with a view to finality in the provision of land for the Native population and that thereafter no more land should be reserved for Native occupation'.[43] The British government had endorsed Lagden's report and recommendations. In some circles, the 1913 Land Act was considered to be a culmination of Lagden's recommendations. Thus, for Harcourt, the contents of the 1913 Land Act were no more than a manifestation of British native policy as recommended by Lagden. The true complaint, that there was no land for African occupation, was conveniently ignored. No changes were made to the Land Act, which would apply exactly as intended by the Union government.

The other view was that the 1913 Land Act was a temporary measure. It would apply until the government agreed on a long-term policy for land occupation by Africans. As these debates were taking place, another commission of inquiry was at work. General Louis Botha had appointed Sir William Beaumont to investigate a long-term solution to African land occupation. It was on this basis that Harcourt had, rather disingenuously, referred to the Act as a 'temporary measure' – despite the claim that it 'would not be disallowed'. Beaumont's commission had been sitting for over a year. Msimang was invited to sit as a representative of the SANNC, giving evidence and motivating why the 1913 Land Act should be scrapped. He introduced a further dimension to the discussion of the Act, hinting at a progressive non-racialism. He told the commission that, far from being opposed to sharing the land, natives supported a dispensation in which the land was shared on an equitable basis, subject to the needs of each racial group. He was opposed to violent agitation, for rather than each person being a law unto themselves, the issue should be dealt with by means of a legislated process.

William Beaumont delivered his report in 1916. He did nothing, however, to alleviate the plight of Africans. The key tenet to the Natives Land Act would not change. Territorial segregation would remain. The report recommended the strengthening of 'native reserves', which were already an integral aspect of the Act. He considered it 'absolutely essential' to develop a 'workable scheme for the territorial separation' between blacks and whites. Motivating for racial exclusivity in land occupation, Beaumont added that the restriction of Africans to reserves would help them gain experience in local administration and government. Additional land for African occupation, he reasoned, could not be accomplished owing to the objections of white farmers. As such, the commission's approach to the area of land to be assigned for African occupation had been determined by 'European objection'.[44] The restriction on the purchase of land outside the reserves was consolidated in 1936, with the passing of the Native Trust and Land Act, and while there was a marginal increase in the amount of land allocated to blacks, from 7 to 13 per cent, this figure was not realised.

Because of his involvement in the land issue, Richard Msimang's legal practice suffered. As his brother Selby noted, many activists of their generation were forced to abandon their formal employment. Richard Msimang did not neglect his personal life, however. He married Grace Mbelle, daughter of Horatio (Bud) Isaiah Mbelle, a respected educationist who was elected general secretary of the SANNC in 1917. Grace was herself a woman of extraordinary achievement, having qualified as one of the first black nurses in the Transvaal. It was a challenge balancing his private, professional and political lives, and soon after his marriage, he was called to attend to a case in Rhodesia.

The Rhodesian connection

In many ways, the land question in Rhodesia paralleled that of South Africa. The Ndebele (Matabele) had been conquered by a combination of deception and military force, but by the early twentieth century there were stirrings of revolt. At the centre of this was the royal family of Lobengula. Though the family itself was, at the time, in a state of flux, with several claimants to the throne, Nyamanda, the eldest son of Lobengula, succeeded to the throne in 1896. In so doing, he led a rebellion against the colonial authorities. In 1918, with the assistance of the Mbengu clan who had moved northwards and settled in Rhodesia, he made his first contact with the founders of the SANNC. Nyamanda needed to deal with the land issue, and one of the strategies considered was purchasing land. But because the Natives Land Act forbade this, he was advised by the Mbengu family to approach Alfred Mangena. When Mangena travelled to Rhodesia, the colonial authorities regarded his presence as suspicious because of his SANNC links, and deported him. Mangena then referred the case to Richard Msimang, who helped draw up a petition to the British monarch, which was finalised on 10 March 1919. Essentially, the petition requested that, in the interests of fair and responsible governance, Rhodesia be granted self-government – as with Basutoland, Bechuanaland and Swaziland (see page 112 for the draft petition).

That March, Msimang advised Nyamanda on strategies of taking the case forward, its aim being for Britain to 'hand back the so-called unalienated land'. But first, funds had to be collected to travel to England. As discussed in Chapter 3, the petition did not succeed. The colonial office would not budge. The advantage of holding on to Rhodesia was clear, and it would not be abandoned. Ultimately, the campaign by blacks petered out, and Southern Rhodesia was established as a whites-only self-governing Crown colony in 1923. Now that the tactics of a direct appeal to London had failed, new strategies had to be devised. For Msimang, however, the entire episode ended in recrimination. His organisation, the SANNC, could no more save the Africans in Rhodesia than it had been able to protect its own people against the 1913 Land Act. Msimang's clients ran out of funds, and his bill was not paid. Several letters demanding payment were ignored. He had covered some of his expenses from his own personal funds, but this was never refunded. Thus, the relationship with Lobengula ended in disappointment.[45]

Drafting the SANNC constitution

In 1919, Msimang was asked by the SANNC to draft its constitution. He did so, outlining a basic decision-making structure, and setting out its aims. These aims included the education of 'Bantu people on their rights, duties and obligations to the state and to themselves individually and collectively; and to promote mutual help, feeling of fellowship and a spirit of brotherhood among them'. It encouraged mutual understanding, and the bringing together 'into common action as one political people all tribes and clans of various tribes or races and by means of combined effort in the united political organisation to defend their freedom, rights and privileges'.[46]

The aims of the SANNC were to 'secure the elimination of racialism and tribal feuds' as well as 'jealousy and petty quarrels', and to do so through education and 'goodwill'. The SANNC opposed the 'colour bar' in all its aspects, and it did so by various means, from deputations to protests. It also resorted to educational means, such as lectures and the dissemination of information, in the belief that the time would arrive when it could field its own candidates for election to structures of national, provincial and local government. With this in mind, it elected people to various positions at provincial congresses, in district and local branches, agricultural and educational societies, industrial unions, and any other bodies closely aligned with the objectives of the SANNC. The organisation reserved a special place for hereditary kings, princes and chiefs. The draft constitution was adopted at the 1923 congress. In the meantime, Msimang turned his attention back to his law practice, where he would soon be dealing with three significant cases involving land.

Tribal affiliations, squatters and the law

Previously, Msimang had written about the effects of the Squatters Law Act of 1895,[47] but he would now encounter them in practice. In the first of three cases focused on here, the circumstances were not what he would have anticipated. The case was atypical. It did not involve a white landlord and a black squatter. Rather, both sides were black.[48] The dispute was not about land, but rather tribal affiliations and chiefly allegiances. Paswane was a chief of the Mpafuri tribe, which owned a piece of land described as Sterkstroom No. 18 in Zoutpansberg, in the north-eastern Transvaal (today's Limpopo province). When Paswane ascended to the chieftaincy, there was internal dissent. Ralulime was prominent among those who disputed Paswane's chieftaincy. He announced that he would not recognise Paswane as the chief. In retaliation, Paswane expelled Ralulime from the tribe. He also wanted to eject him from the land, but he lacked the authority to do so. Thus, he approached the native commissioner, but despite an order from Paswane and the office of the native commissioner, Ralulime refused to budge. He would not leave. A formal notice was then delivered. In terms of section 8 of Law 21 of 1895 – the Squatters Law Act – the native commissioner gave Ralulime three months' notice to leave the farm. The notice read: 'The third farm Sterkstroom is tribally owned by the Mpafuri Tribe and this notice is given at the request of and on behalf of Chief Mpafuri and councillor.'[49]

The refusal to leave the farm, as ordered, constituted a crime. Under section 7 of the Act it was an offence for 'the head of a native family' to stay on a farm without a permit from the owner. In terms of section 9, the law stated: 'A number of house holders not exceeding five shall be allowed on farms possessed in ownership by natives in the same way as on farms belonging to white persons, which house holders shall receive their written permit of residence from the Superintendent of Natives, and shall then not fall under the provisions of article seven of this law.'

Ralulime was charged in the Magistrate's Court and found guilty under section 7. His attorney, Msimang, advised an appeal. But the argument on appeal took a different approach. The terms of the statute were against Ralulime. The land was tribally owned. The chief, Mpafuri, was the head of the tribe. Being the head of the tribe, it appeared that he was entitled to order removal of any person from the land. For Msimang, these consequences appeared perverse. The law had never been designed with the intention of being used by blacks to eject other blacks from land, given the precarious nature of their land tenure. In reality, the law was part of a package of laws designed to give effect to the dispossession of Africans of their land, hence the absurdities in its application in the context of the facts before him. Therefore, in the appeal documents, the contention was that the law did not apply to land that was held on a communal or tribal basis. The intention behind the law was to protect individually held title. The argument seemed cogent and was likely to win the case, Msimang reasoned with his counsel. Yet to advance it required an acceptance of the racist logic of the law. The purpose of the law was to protect white land owners with title against black squatters who had no title. But the facts before them, in this case, were different. There was no title. And the pre-eminent dispute was about tribal political power, not land. Ultimately, there was a calculated acceptance, however tendentious, of the inner logic of the law. This was necessary, however, to advance the argument on behalf of Ralulime.

Judge Tindall, who presided, accepted the argument. As his departure point, he narrowed the issue before court to whether 'these sections, 7 and 9, apply to a case like the present, where the farm is not owned in the ordinary way by a native or several natives, but is tribally owned'. He then reached the following conclusion:

> In my opinion, it is quite clear that these sections do not apply to a case of this kind, where the farm is tribally owned, and where the head of the family that was prosecuted was one of the tribe before steps were taken to expel him. That being so, I think the chief had no right to invoke the Squatter's Law for the purpose of getting rid of this recalcitrant induna. It may be that the chief is entitled to get rid of him in some other way, but certainly not by invoking the Squatter's Law. The conviction, therefore, was not justified.

Msimang's client was duly acquitted. But there was also a larger victory. The case had established that the law could not be interpreted in a literal manner. Its primary purpose needed to be taken into consideration. Moreover, the potentially arbitrary nature of chiefly rule was curbed. Chiefs could not resort to the drastic action of expulsion from land to resolve internal political disputes or to enforce discipline. By indirectly striking a blow against the arbitrary deployment of chiefly power, Msimang effectively attenuated governmental power. By this time, under the Native Administration Act No. 38 of 1927, tribal chiefs, *indunas* and headmen were government appointees. Instructions could be channelled through them to individual members of tribes perceived to be politically undesirable. The exclusion of the entire application of the Squatters Law Act from communally owned land was therefore not only a limitation on powers of chiefs, but a check on the powers of government. But to secure this victory, Msimang had to forego his principal – and principled – objection to the law itself. That could wait for another day – and an opportunity presented itself in a case again involving Mpafuri, discussed below.

'Despotic powers' exposed
With the passage of the Native Administration Act, the government had proposed a far more radical solution for 'native affairs'. Instead of exercising power over Africans through the indirect method of appointing chiefs, it would reserve for itself absolute authority over the social, political and legal institutions of Africans. The Act proclaimed that it was intended to be 'for the better control and manage-

ment of native affairs'. Its opening section provided that the 'Governor-General shall be the supreme chief of all natives exercising all such powers as may be vested either by custom or by law in a paramount chief, and that he may appoint officers under him to administer native affairs'. By so doing, the government not only elevated the governor-general above customary law institutions, processes and practices, but rendered him the ultimate source of legal and political authority over Africans. Included in the powers of the governor-general was the power to remove any tribe or portion thereof, or any native, 'from any place to any other place within the country on any conditions he may determine'. The only restriction on such power was that the governor-general had to deem it 'expedient in the general public interest'. If the governor-general wished to remove an entire tribe from its land, he first had to obtain the approval of Parliament. Individuals failing to obey instructions of the governor-general were guilty of an offence and were liable upon conviction to imprisonment or a fine.

A case presented itself to Msimang to test the provisions of the Native Administration Act.[50] Munjedzi Mpafuri of Mpafuri's location in Louis Trichardt, Transvaal, was given an order under section 5 of the Act. The government deemed him politically undesirable – owing to his unwillingness to serve as a government stooge, it transpired. On 5 December 1927, Mpafuri received the following order, signed on behalf of the governor-general:

> By virtue of the powers conferred upon me by section 5(1)(b) of the Native Administration Act, 38 of 1927, I do hereby order you, the native Munjedzi Mpafuri presently residing in Mpafuri's location in the district of Louis Trichardt forthwith to leave the location aforesaid and to remove to Crown Land in Section E in the district of Barberton as may be indicated to you by the magistrate of Barberton, or alternatively to such place as may be prescribed by the Minister of Native Affairs.

Mpafuri refused to leave his home. It was a criminal offence to refuse to obey an instruction under the Act, so he was duly charged. The magistrate entered a finding of guilt. Msimang, who had previously been his attorney before the Magistrate's Court, took the matter on appeal. The strategy now shifted somewhat. Instead of finding and exploiting gaps and contradictions in the law, the focus would be on the purported exercise of authority under the Act. This entailed a close examination of the terms of the administrative order. Did the order clearly communicate to the recipient where, when and why he was being removed from a particular area? If it was an essential component of the principle of the rule of law that the law should be clear, then governmental decisions taken pursuant to a law had to comply with the same standard.

The reason behind the argument was to prevent potential abuses of the law. In the case of Mpafuri, evidence given before the magistrate was that the order had been personally served on him. It was interpreted for his benefit. He was instructed to report at the office of the native commissioner, where 'a free warrant and ticket would be given to him to go to Barberton'. Precisely where in Barberton, was, however, the question that occupied the court on appeal. Yet the court was acutely aware of what was truly at stake. The real challenge concerned the extent of the power granted to the governor-general. In a moment of admirable judicial clarity, the following was noted:

> The power given to the Governor-General is certainly drastic because a native may possibly be removed without any opportunity being given to him to be heard in his defence. It is an order which may be despotically issued by the governor-general because the only thing he has to consider in issuing such order is the fact that he deems it expedient in the general public interest to order such removal. That is the only limitation insofar as a single native is concerned, which the Act places upon him in the exercise of his powers. It is a matter which is entirely in his own discretion, and he may exercise his discretion on informal evidence which is placed before him and not on such evidence as is adduced in a court of law; and from whatever source that evidence is derived he is entitled to take it into consideration and it seems to me that no court would be justified in such circumstances in interfering with an order so made.

It was precisely this consideration that drove the court to consider that, to protect the liberty of the subject, a court should scrutinise carefully the terms of the order issued and the procedure followed by the governor-general. In an era where the substantive validity of official decisions fell outside the purview of judicial review, the base line for the vindication for the rule of law was procedural fairness and strict compliance with the terms of the statute. The court concluded that, where the power is exercised under the statute, it would be necessary that the order should 'strictly comply' with the provisions of the section. A consideration that drove this conclusion was the possibility of criminal sanction in the event of non-compliance. Strict compliance entailed, at a minimum, that 'the place to which such removal is ordered should be definitely specified'. If the order was faulty in this respect, it had to be struck down. The mere fact that a clerk charged not with issuing the order, but with interpreting it to an accused person, had done so in benevolent terms, could not save the order from invalidity. The court was not concerned with the action of the person handing the notice to an accused person, but with the action of the governor-general to whom the original statutory power was vested. An ambiguous order issued by the governor-general could neither be ameliorated nor altered by an administrative official. The interpretation of the order also had to be approached from the perspective of the accused person. Could he understand what the order stipulated him to do? And if he failed to do as ordered, was he aware that he rendered himself liable to criminal prosecution? The order was defective, the court concluded, and therefore unlawful. It failed to specify a place where the accused person had to be removed to. The court noted:

> For example, [the order] says [Mpafuri] has to remove to Crown Land in Section E in the district of Barberton as may be indicated by the magistrate of Barberton. 'Section E' is definite enough and so is 'Crown Lands' and if one takes it that the magistrate is merely to act as a guide or messenger for purpose of indicating the exact place, no one would quarrel with such a direction. But one has to read the order, not piecemeal, but as a whole, and it is all very well to say that we should cut out a portion of the order and if such portion were cut out the rest of the order would be a sufficiently precise indication of the place to which the accused had to remove. … The accused is entitled to say: 'What do you wish me to do? You ask me to remove to Barberton and you ask me to remove to some place which may be specified by the Minister of Native Affairs. Now what must I do?'

Based on this, the court concluded that it had to give a holistic interpretation to the order, and it had to hold the governor-general to the strict terms of the legislation. Bearing in mind the extraordinary powers granted by the Act to the governor-general, there was no reason to read the order with any level of generosity towards the governor-general. It would have been easy for the governor-general to have specified a definite place. On the facts, the order had been issued in December 1926 and only served in May 1927. No discernible excuse could be tabled on behalf of the governor-general as to why a particular place was not selected. The conviction was accordingly struck down. The case proved another point for Msimang. Even where a law is unjust at its core, the process of interpretation could yield just outcomes. Mpafuri's actions, defiant as they were, may have been disobedient, but they were not unlawful. The source of the illegality was elsewhere. By failing to follow its own laws, the government had deprived itself of the advantage it had sought to gain by passing the law in the first place. Perhaps of greater significance for Msimang, as an activist and a lawyer, was the stinging judicial rebuke, with the legislation being described as entrusting the governor-general with 'despotic powers', thereby justifying judicial supervision as a means to prevent abuse and protect liberties.

There was, at the time, an urgent impulse to clear land for white occupation, and the government resorted to various legal instruments. One of the most odious was the Trespass Act of 1906. In 1929, Msimang took on a case where he had to contend with the terms of this legislation.

Trespassing and the law

Both the Squatters Law Act of 1895 and the Native Administration Act of 1927 had altered the status of Africans from land owners to squatters, vagabonds and criminals. Yet there was another little-known piece of legislation, the Trespass Act of 1906, which had introduced the term 'trespassing' into the lexicon of dispossession. Section 2 of the Act provided that any person found trespassing on Crown land might be required to quit such land forthwith, and 'to take with him all goods and persons brought with him thereon and to state his name and ordinary place of abode'. The authority for the administration of section 2 was conferred on magistrates, justices of the peace, police officers and constables. Any person they told to leave a piece of ground, and who refused, was liable to a fine or imprisonment. The result was that many Africans were randomly stopped by police and required to prove, on pain of being fined or imprisoned, that they were not trespassing.

Of course, the very crime of trespassing had its roots in the politics of the day. Overnight, people who were customary owners of land found themselves trespassers, simply because of a change in the law. Through no action or indeed fault of their own, and at the stroke of a pen, many found themselves in a position where, officially, they might easily switch from law-abiding citizens to criminals. Once an area was proclaimed for white settlement, any black people found in that area were committing a de facto crime. Police officers had the power to stop, interrogate and detain them. Land that had previously belonged to them was now regarded as 'Crown Land'.

In the case of Ramkumba,[51] this is what befell him: on 10 October 1927, a notice was delivered to him signed by the native sub-commissioner. It read: 'This is to advise you that in terms of section 8 of law 21 of 1895 you are hereby given notice to quit Crown Land situated within the Zoutpansberg district within three months from date hereof.' Ramkumba refused, and because refusal was a criminal offence, he was charged with a crime. His attorney was Richard Msimang. His defence was that Ramkumba was not a squatter, but a tenant of the land he had been told to quit. The state's case was that his tenancy had come to an end, rendering him liable to being ejected on the basis of the Squatters Law Act. The magistrate found Ramkumba guilty of the offence.

The matter then went on appeal, and arguments were raised in Ramkumba's defence. Msimang attacked the indictment, arguing that it failed to disclose an offence and contained no factual evidence to substantiate the charge. The entire scheme presupposed trespassing, and a person could not be charged under the ordinance if he was not in fact a trespasser on Crown land. Arguing this way imposed a double requirement on the state. First, the state would have to prove that a person was a trespasser. Second, it would have to prove notice to quit and also disobedience. These requirements considerably increased the onus on the state, thus lessening the likelihood of conviction. Msimang's argument was, however, rejected. The judge found that it was not necessary for an indictment pursued under the ordinance to contain allegations relating to trespass. He acknowledged that the charge sheet contained no express allegation of trespass. But he found that this was not a material defect because the charge did inform the accused that he should quit the property within a period of three months. Provided that this was clear enough, and the accused person failed to comply therewith, there could be no legitimate objection to the charge.

Another argument raised on behalf of the accused was that section 8 did not apply to his circumstances. He had been a tenant, not a trespasser. He had paid rent. It was only after the expiry of his tenancy that he was regarded as a squatter. The purpose of the ordinance, it was submitted, was not to penalise persons who were once lawful on the property and who were rendered unlawful as a consequence of the expiry of their lawful tenancy. The purpose was to deal with instances where the occupation was unlawful from the onset. But this argument did not find favour with the court either: it noted that such alleged purpose was not apparent from the terms of the legislation. Msimang's final point related to the terms of the notice. He argued that the ordinance made no provision for a person other than the owner of the land to give notice to quit. As such, the notice issued by the native sub-commissioner was invalid. But the judge found that native sub-commissioners were appointed to preside over the natives, and to carry out orders and instructions issued by the government, including those relating to Africans. Accordingly, a notice stating that a person's tenancy has terminated must be regarded as a valid notice. The appeal was accordingly dismissed.

While the court decision resulted in disappointment, there was no disillusionment: in exposing the arbitrariness of the exercise of bureaucratic and official power, the case had illuminated the definitional ambiguities concerning trespassing. By identifying the core of the case as the imprecise definition of 'trespasser', Msimang had shone a light on a pivotal issue of the times. The line between legality and illegality was often blurred. In June 1927 Ramkumba was a lawful tenant, and by December he was a squatter, liable to expulsion from the land. Black people had in a matter of months moved from tenant to trespasser. The case also brought to the fore the necessity for objectively determinable rules. The ordinance reserved significant discretionary powers for police officers. It was they who decided on a case-by-case basis whether or not a person was a trespasser. Judicial proceedings followed only at a later stage, after the initial determinations had not only been made, but – as in many cases – acted upon. The law, as it stood, did not set out a clearly determinable standard.

It is therefore understandable that, from his own perspective, Ramkumba had committed no offence. He had lived in the same area his whole life, performed the same work for the same employer, and considered himself law abiding. Although he disagreed with the introduction of rental payment, he had in fact complied and paid his monthly rent. As cases such as his navigated the complexities and contradictions of the country's judicial system, they inevitably developed social and political dimensions. Courts were often filled with large numbers of people who found themselves in the same circumstances as the accused; many courtrooms became sites where broader political messages were communicated, mediated and calibrated. Socially, politically and legally, these were difficult times. Black lawyers of the era, such as Msimang, often understood the effects of the laws not only from tales conveyed by clients, but also from personal experiences. More than intellect and passion, Msimang brought compassion, empathy and understanding to the cases of his clients. Yet the perversity of the law, the scale of human suffering, the helplessness of it all, was slowly devouring him. So much was expected of him, but so little was in fact possible. Now in his thirties, the soul of the man who was once burning with ambition would begin to unravel. The process began with his practice, and ended with the man.

Chekhov's prophecy comes to pass
Msimang's practice was taking strain. The Transvaal Law Society complained that he was behind with his dues, and he was unable to settle the required amount of £10. In addition, his political activities had brought him to the attention of the authorities, and the screws were being tightened. On 8 December 1925, the Law Society brought an application against him for an order compelling him to pay his outstanding dues as well as the costs of the application. Rather unexpectedly, and perhaps disproportionately, the Law Society also asked for an order suspending Msimang from practice as an attorney until such time as he had paid the required amount. While the application was opposed, it was ultimately granted. On 17 December 1925, Judge Gey van Pittius granted an order directing Msimang to pay the Law Society the amount owing. He refused, however, to grant the order concerning the suspension of Msimang from practising as an attorney, and specifically stated: 'That no order is made regarding the suspension of the respondent for practising as an attorney'.

Not only was Msimang struggling to keep up with his subscriptions to the Law Society, he was also unable to pay his creditors, some of whom were his own clients. Pauline Klatzky, a creditor who appears to have lent him some funds, obtained three judgments against him, relating to the monies lent. When none were settled, she brought an application to sequestrate Msimang. Though a provisional sequestration order was granted, it was not made final, it seems. At the same time, Msimang had taken on a case representing the Swazi king, Sobhuza II. The case was a sequel to a number of cases related to South Africa's annexation of a section of Swaziland territory. Msimang had, together with Seme, given legal advice to Sobhuza. But no payment was forthcoming. Ultimately the matter ended in a lawsuit filed by Msimang against Sobhuza in relation to payment of the outstanding legal fees. In response, Sobhuza denied liability, raising a technical objection that the services had been rendered for the Swazi nation, and not for him in his personal capacity. He asked for the dismissal of Msimang's claim. While the litigation ultimately proved inconclusive, the fact is that Msimang never received payment for his services. Financial problems such as these took a toll on Msimang. They also impacted on his relationship with his wife, particularly after he began resorting to alcohol.

One of Msimang's clients, Ms Mbanjwa, lodged a complaint with the Law Society relating to deposits made to Msimang for work that was allegedly never done, and the money never returned. The Law Society promptly began an investigation, and the complaint was withdrawn after Msimang agreed to sign an acknowledgement of debt to make regular payments to settle the outstanding amount. Despite such difficulties, Msimang managed to publish an analysis of the Medical, Dental and Pharmacy Act of 1928, and its implications for Africans.[52]

Richard Msimang passed away on 29 May 1933. No children were born of his marriage to Grace, and his estate was insolvent. Grace approached the native commissioner's office with an enquiry relating to her husband's inheritance from his father's will. Selby's rather unhelpful reply to the enquiry by the native commissioner was that, as far as he was concerned, Richard had left no immovable assets.[53] Yet in an earlier case brought by Ms Klatzky, it appears that Richard Msimang had in fact been named as a beneficiary in the will of his parents, Joel and Johanna, and that, as such, he was heir to immovable property. For all this apparent failure, he did however receive acclaim upon his death. *Umteteli Wabantu* made a public announcement on 6 December 1933, and at his funeral service in Orlando, Soweto, the Leake Hall was packed with more than 500 mourners. The funeral service was led by Reverend P. Judgie of the Independent Methodist Church of Africa, who noted that Msimang was held in high esteem not only by the congregation, but also by members of the broader community, both black and white. The SANNC was represented by Mr Mvabaza, who paid tribute to Msimang for the valuable work he had done for the 'Bantu' cause.

Richard Msimang's remains lie in the Nancefield cemetery in Klipspruit, Soweto. On his headstone are the words 'Lala ngoxolo Mdengentonga' (rest in peace Mdengentonga). His nickname, Mdengentonga – 'he who is short of stature, but long in action' – is a fitting tribute to a gentle, unassuming soul who left an indelible mark on the history of his troubled country. A particularly significant contribution was his documentation of the indignities suffered by Africans as a result of the 1913 Natives Land Act. While this piece of legislation has over the years gained notoriety for dispossessing Africans of land, Msimang shone a light on the reality of human suffering that was its cruel consequence. Msimang was the first to recognise that the reach of the Act went beyond land dispossession. Africans lost cattle, they lost possessions, and they were condemned to the status of captive labour units. When the land dispossession is viewed through the experiences of those affected, a richer narrative emerges. It is from realities such as these that a new future may be reimagined for South Africa.

Henry Sylvester Williams, the first black man to be admitted as an advocate at the Cape Bar. He is seen here in his advocate's robes

Booker T. Washington, founder of the Tuskegee Institute. His ideas of self-reliance played a pivotal role in shaping the Pan-Africanist views of South Africans such as Pixley ka Isaka Seme

W.E.B. Du Bois, who was the first African American to graduate with a PhD from Harvard University. He also taught Charlotte Maxeke at Wilberforce University in Cleveland, Ohio

PAN-AFRICAN CONFERENCE.

WESTMINSTER TOWN HALL,

ON THE

23rd, 24th and 25th JULY, 1900.

This Conference is organised by a Committee of the African Association for the Discussion of the "Native Races" Question, and will be attended and addressed by those of African descent from all parts of the British Empire, the United States of America, Abyssinia, Liberia, Hayti, etc.

YOU ARE CORDIALLY AND EARNESTLY INVITED TO ATTEND.

CONFERENCES—Morning, 10.30 and Evening, 8.

H. S. WILLIAMS, *Hon. Sec.*,
139, PALACE CHAMBERS, S.W.

Henry Sylvester Williams was a key organiser of the first Pan-African Conference held in London in 1900, three years before he came to South Africa

Alfred Mangena, the first black attorney to be admitted to practice in the Transvaal

Anna Victoria Mcobela, the first black nurse in the Transvaal. She married Alfred Mangena in 1916

Richard Msimang, the first black South African to be admitted to practice as a solicitor of England and Wales

Pixley ka Isaka Seme, robed as a barrister. Seme was educated at Columbia University, where he attained a BA degree and registered for the BCL degree at Jesus College, Oxford

Richard Msimang was a talented flyhalf, playing in Somerset for the Taunton Rugby Football Club 1st XV, 1909–1910

Pixley Seme (right), with Paramount Chief Montsioa of the Barolong (seated), who was George Montsioa's uncle, in 1916

George Dick Montsioa as a young barrister in 1911

Montsioa as an attorney in Pietersburg in 1918

Ngcubu Poswayo as a newly qualified barrister in 1913

Beatrix Kule, the first black female teacher at All Saints Mission, Engcobo, Eastern Cape. In 1916, she married Ngcubu Poswayo

Charlotte Maxeke, first black woman to graduate with a university degree at Wilberforce College, Cleveland, Ohio. She would later influence Alfred Mangena to take up law studies in the United Kingdom

D.D.T. Jabavu, a fierce critic of the government of Jan Smuts and a president of the All African Convention

Dr Alfred Bitini Xuma, who was president of the ANC when the Africans' Claims document was published

Anton Lembede, who entered into a legal partnership with Pixley ka Isaka Seme, known as Seme & Lembede Solicitors. Lembede was the founding president of the ANC Youth League in 1944

AFRICAN NATIONAL CONGRESS. N3.9

"ATLANTIC CHARTER" COMMITTEE.

1. TERMS OF REFERENCE:

(a) To examine and report various suggested
schemes for post-war reconstruction in
Africa with special reference to Southern
Africa.

(b) In the light of the foregoing to formu-
late a statement of principles and a programme of action with a view of ensuring
that African needs and aspirations in regard to different aspects of African individual and social life receive adequate
attention in the post-war development of
South Africa.

2. MEMBERSHIP:

In terms of the resolution passed at the
Annual Conference of the African National
Congress, the President-General has invi-
ted the following Africans to serve on the
"Atlantic Charter" Committee:-
(see attached list)

3. PROCEDURE:

(a) In order to facilitate the work of the
Committee the President has divided the
General Committee into the following sub-
Committees, each one of which will be
entrusted with the task of preparing
preliminary draft proposals in regard to
the subject coming within their purview.

(b) The draft proposals of each Sub-Committee
shall be submitted to the General Committee
for consent and approval.

(c) Finally, a comprehensive statement will be
drawn up by the Committee embodying the
recommendations of the different Sub-Committees
and the African's demands for full citizenship rights in the land of his forefathers.

(d) Calling of a Convention to ratify the statement of recommendations and demands as set
out in the Committee's report, and, signing
of the ratified report by members of the
Committee.

(e) Publication of the document and its presen-
tation to the Union Government and the United
Nations as the just, fair, and considered,
claims of the African people.

Under Xuma's leadership the African Charter Committee drew up the Africans' Claims document, which became the blueprint for the ANC's Bill of Rights

Sub-Committees.

(1) Post-War Reconstruction [Schemes]
(2) General Principles
(3) Political Aspect
(4) Economic
(5) Educational
(6) Health [Social] Services
(7)

Z.K. Matthews
G.A. Mbeki
Rev. Geo. Molefe
Mr. Selby Ngcobo
Mr. Hubert ...
R.V. Selope Thema
S. Mac Lefolesa
Rev. Z. Mahabane
Rev. Mvambo
L.M. Mafikela
Mr. Mofutsanyana
R.H. Godlo

Economic { Land, Industry, Commerce, Labour }
Mabude
Kotane
A.W.G. Champion
R.H. Qwaka
Selby Ngcobo
G.A. Mbeki
Trade Union Representatives —

Health & Social Services {
Dr. Silgee
Dr. J.S. Moroka
Dr. R.T. Bokwe
Dr. S.M. Molema
Dr. Innes Gumede
Dr. Sellogelo
}

Educational { Scholastic, Technical, Professional }
Z.K. Matthews
Don Mtimkulu
Jacob Nhlapo
Mr. Mkize
Mr. Sl. Seloedi

President-General of A.N.C. is ex-officio member of all
sub committees. Personal representatives of Paramount Chiefs of the Paramount
chiefs, of Chiefs Councils, and the Transkeian Council and
Ciskeian Council will be assigned to Sub-committees
...

The last page of the Africans' Claims document shows the names of the members of the drafting committee, which included three early African attorneys: Pixley ka Isaka Seme, Don Mtimkulu and Professor Z.K. Matthews

5

'In all races, genius is like a spark'

[The] man of wig and gown must walk very warily to avoid the countless pitfalls of etiquette that mark his path to the woolsack. However, an empty purse may tempt him; he must accept a professional fee that falls short of the irreducible guinea with a half-a-crown added for his clerk, whether he has one or not. Some professional men may tout for clients, but not so the barrister.

– Pixley ka Isaka Seme, *Imvo Zabantsundu*, January 1912

Pixley ka Isaka Seme was not only an original and imaginative thinker, but also a magnetic figure. The force of his personality was an undeniable virtue. But it was also something of a vice, weighing on his shoulders and threatening to undermine his legacy. At crucial moments he was, however, able to draw on the potency of this magnetism, which complemented his foresight and clarity of thought. In this way, he has claimed a space in the national consciousness.

Seme has been described as 'the moving spirit'[1] behind the emergence of the African National Congress, in its original guise as the South African Native National Congress. Its organising principle was that of anti-colonialism. The immediate manifestation of colonialism was the formalisation and entrenchment of land dispossession of black people. While colonial wars were responsible for the status quo, local legislation had yet to give full recognition to the dispossession. The Natives Land Act of 1913 was the central legal instrument that confirmed native geographies as well as identities forged in the expansion of Empire. The ANC, a political movement formed by Africans, was charged with coordinating resistance to the Act. Yet 'Africans' as such did not exist. Instead, as Seme observed, there were Zulus, Xhosas, Sothos, Swazis, Fingoes and many other tribes that held fast to their identities. While these tribal identities pre-dated the colonial era, under colonialism they were reified and reinforced as the centre of African power. Through the tribal system, the colonial government could exert hegemony over vast residential tracts, economic zones and ethnic polities. And precisely because of these linkages with the colonial system, tribal elites could access political power and acquire material wealth by collaboration with the local representatives of Empire. By capturing political power and economic privileges, tribal elites were able to enhance their standing and create opportunities for the economic advancement of the tribe. These dynamics ultimately created a network of tribal (and multi-tribal) affiliation that fused with economic patronage and was able to disperse political control, both vertically and horizontally, in seemingly mystifying ways. All too aware of this, Seme's prime and urgent aim was the destruction of tribal identity. Out of the fragments of the tribe, a nation would be born. An African nation. African societies had traditionally been built around a leader whose authority was bestowed by consensus. Seme proposed to use these traditional authorities as a central pillar in the new organisation. While a special house would be created for them in the SANNC – the 'Parliament of African People' – their role would be advisory, ultimately subject to the will of the majority.

The forging of a broad African identity required the deliberate elimination of narrow tribal affiliation. However, as Seme recognised, such affiliation was not merely an economic and political issue. The tribe represented belonging – in emotional, cultural and spiritual senses. Tribal identity was the means of connecting people to their natural and spiritual environments. By proclaiming, for example, his Zuluness, an African was not merely asserting a claim to the land, but his very reason for being. An African identity could therefore not be forged by the simple negation of tribal identity. Instead, tribal identities had to be destroyed yet simultaneously used as pillars upon which the new identity would be constructed. Seme acknowledged the paradox: tribal chiefs, whether collaborators or not, were perceived as essential to the new African movement. But as members and affiliates of the SANNC, it was important that they were perceived as members of a broad platform for the liberation of all Africans and not separate ethnic groups. In this sense, the tribes would be the foundation of the African nation, rather than its negation. The SANNC was an anti-colonial movement – but how could its aims be realised if it was established by colonially educated African elites? It was here that Seme's vision and imagination came into play.

Intellectual influences on young Seme
When Seme was at Oxford University and at Middle Temple Inn, between 1906 and 1909, the study of constitutional law included writings such Montesquieu's monumental study of political theory, *The Spirit of the Laws*, and the works of constitutional theorist A.V. Dicey. Law students voraciously read and discussed Dicey's writings. His important study titled *Introduction to the Study of the Law of the Constitution*, made the case for the rule of law, and rejected the monarchical system. Texts such as these shaped the thinking of law students of Seme's era. Montesquieu, who had written in the eighteenth century, was an ardent supporter of the republican form of government, founded upon the virtue of equality:

[It] is to be observed that what I distinguish by the name of virtue, in a republic, is the love of one's country, that is, the love of equality. It is not a moral,
nor a Christian, but a political virtue; and it is the spring which sets the
republican government in motion, as honour is the spring which gives motion
to monarchy. Hence it is that I have distinguished the love of one's country,
and of equality, by the appellation of political virtue.[2]

Montesquieu believed in a government of laws. Every nation should be governed
by a 'polity or civil constitution' since '[no] society can subsist without a form of
government'.[3] Dicey's first volume in the law of the study of the constitution was
published in London in 1885. By the early 1900s, it was one of the most widely
read books in constitutional law and political science at the English universities.
In the book Dicey identified three principles that undergird the rule of law. The
first was that 'no man is punishable or can be lawfully made to suffer in body or
goods except for a distinct breach of law established in the ordinary legal manner
before the ordinary courts of the land. In this sense the rule of law is contrasted
with every system of government based on the exercise by persons in authority
of wide, arbitrary, or discretionary powers of constraint'. The second was in truth
a principle of equality: 'every man, whatever be his rank or condition, is subject
to the ordinary law of the realm and amenable to the jurisdiction of the ordinary
tribunals'. Finally, Dicey noted that the rule of law was intrinsic to the UK legal
system because rights to personal liberty resulted from judicial decisions. This
was in contrast with countries where such rights could be taken away by political
conduct. Dicey elaborated on the meaning of the rule of law as follows:

It means, in the first place, the absolute supremacy or predominance of regular
law as opposed to the influence of arbitrary power, and excludes the existence
of arbitrariness, of prerogative, or even of wide discretionary authority on the
part of the government. Englishmen are ruled by the law, and by the law alone;
a man may with us be punished for a breach of law, but he can be punished
for nothing else. It means, again, equality before the law, or the equal subjec-
tion of all classes to the ordinary law of the land administered by the ordinary
Law Courts; the 'rule of law' in this sense excludes the idea of any exemption
of officials or others from the duty of obedience to the law which governs
other citizens or from the jurisdiction of the ordinary tribunals ... The 'rule
of law,' lastly, may be used as a formula for expressing the fact that with us
the law of the constitution, the rules which in foreign countries naturally
form part of a constitutional code, are not the source but the consequence of
the rights of individuals, as defined and enforced by the Courts; that, in short,
the principles of private law have with us been by the action of the Courts and

Parliament so extended as to determine the position of the Crown and of its servants; thus the constitution is the result of the ordinary law of the land.[4]

The notions that especially impressed young Seme were the following: equality is intrinsic to the law; government should be ruled by law; individual rights cannot be removed without following due process before an independent judiciary; and the government should not behave in an arbitrary manner, and should abide by clear rules. These resonated with the ideals of African society founded on notions of fairness and respect for others. In the lecture theatres of Oxford, Seme's anti-colonial spirit was being shaped by ideas that found fertile ground in him. He reasoned that, if the English valued equality and universal adult suffrage, exercised political power by means of elected parliamentary representatives, and rejected arbitrary monarchical power, they would understand that the same held good for the native races of South Africa.

Facing challenges

Seme's anti-colonial consciousness was directed at the political as well as the economic sphere. The Natives Land Act set aside areas for native occupation, known as 'reserves'. These reserves were, however, dumping grounds for dispossessed people, and their true value was economic. Farmers, mines and industry drew their labour from the reserves. And because laws were crafted along racial lines, black workers were unable to bargain in a fair manner. Accordingly, exploitation was rife. While the Land Act was all-encompassing, it did permit some exceptions. Blacks could, for instance, acting communally, acquire property in certain areas; such purchases would not be affected by the prohibitions against black property ownership that were an essential aspect of the Act. Spotting an opportunity, Seme started the South African Native Farmers Association. Through this association, two farms, Daggakraal and Driefontein, were acquired in the eastern Transvaal (today's Mpumalanga). Land title was officially granted. Subsequently, there were attempts to impose chiefly rule over the area, but the land titles prevented the government from carrying out evictions. The Native Farmers Association enabled black property ownership and therefore black participation in commercial agriculture.

As a student, Seme's favourite subject was constitutional law, and he had a deep appreciation of the logic of Dicey's ideas on the subject. But, as South Africa proved to him, the nexus of race, power and money functioned to outweigh equality and fairness. And if the rule of law was incapable of overturning the unjust system of colonial government, its foundational notions might be put to use in the defence of individuals and in pursuit of specific causes. Hence, in cases discussed here, Seme soon emerged as a leading thinker in the formulation of legal arguments. Land dispossession became a preoccupation, and he gradually mastered the subject, on a theoretical as well as a practical level. As time has shown, however, the law is frequently used to enforce racial segregation, as was the case in colonial South Africa. Yet the rule of law, at least in the sense envisioned by Dicey, was also an antidote to colonialism. In Seme's world, the practice of law to defend black people required imagination, foresight and clarity of thought. Even though success could not be guaranteed, the cogency of one's argument was paramount. Yet the force of argument in an unjust world did not suffice, despite justice being central to the theory and praxis of the law. Owing to the paucity of reportage in the lower courts, the Native Courts and even the High Courts, it is not possible to draw up a complete and accurate account of all the cases in which Seme was involved. But from the scraps that remain, a picture of his thinking and strategy may be sketched.

From the moment of his admission as an attorney, Seme made a statement about the equality of the races: a black man, he had received his training at the most venerable of institutions – Oxford University. On the day of his admission, there was something of a 'stir' in the courtroom, which was full to capacity, and the air heavy with expectation. The presiding judge enquired whether the Transvaal Law Society was 'aware of this' (i.e. his admission). Seme's forthright reply was 'all the papers are in order M'Lord', the subtle message being that the question was absurd. The judge retreated and said, 'take your order Mr Seme'. The symbolism of the exchange was unmistakable. Thus began one of the most remarkable legal careers of early-twentieth-century South Africa.

Over the years, Seme took on several complex and politically fraught legal disputes. These included the defence of the Swazi nation against the aggressive land-grabbing practices of the South African government; acting as legal advisor to King Dinuzulu during a delicate period in Zulu history; and defending political activists in an era where political opposition was criminalised. For Seme, there was no rigid separation between the law and the political context in which the law functioned. And in South Africa, many legal disputes were rooted in politics. Hence, a broad understanding of the basic political framework was indispensable to a lawyer. But politics and the law were not the same thing. The judicial system, with its peculiar biases, could not be counted upon to resolve many of the urgent problems that confronted the black race. Instead, political action needed to be taken. Seme believed that, in the long term, a political settlement in which 'the Native and European races of South Africa' were equal in the eyes of the law, and blacks were entitled to acquire and own and use land on the same terms as whites, would be unavoidable.[5]

Seme is often praised for his role in the formation of the ANC. But he is also much maligned for presiding over its decline. Two charges are generally levelled against him: the first is lethargy and neglect, and the second is stubbornness. I will not seek to counter these criticisms, for there is truth in them.[6] I do, however, wish to place Seme's life in context to allow for a broader understanding of the complexity of the era and Seme's role in the near demise of the ANC. There were two contributing factors that might explain the decline of the ANC during Seme's era. The first was external: Swaziland's need for legal assistance. Given Seme's commitment to fairness and liberty, he could not refuse the case, but his work as president-general of the ANC suffered as a result of demands on his time. The second factor was the waning financial fortunes of the ANC following the Wall Street crash in 1929. The effects of the Great Depression were especially catastrophic for black workers in South Africa. The demand for South African commodities dropped. Maize exports declined by as much as 80 per cent. Urban unemployment increased drastically, and wages dropped. The response from the Union government was predictable. Urgent solutions had to be found for white poverty and unemployment. Most importantly, white labourers had to be protected from competition from black workers, whose jobs were the first to be terminated when the need arose. Whites had to be first in any employment queue. So far, the principal fundraising organ of the ANC was the chiefs, who collected money from their communities. But the chiefs had gradually become disenchanted with the ANC, as they derived little benefit from the organisation, and many had found that there were advantages to collaboration with the white authorities. The result was that ordinary members, ravaged by unemployment, simply discontinued their subscriptions.

With the ANC in decline, new organisations began to emerge. Foremost among these was the All Africa Convention (AAC), which presented a formidable threat to the ANC. The first AAC conference was a spectacular success, and the organisation posed a very real threat to the ANC. At this crucial moment, Seme's strategic insights saved the ANC: key to its rescue was membership, which needed to be mass-based, with individual members entitled to join. By contrast, the AAC's membership was federal in nature – limited to affiliating organisations, with no individual members. The ANC was a key affiliate to the AAC, and Seme himself served on the Land Committee of the AAC. When the AAC conceived the idea of grassroots recruitment, it consulted with Seme as leader of the ANC. But when the leaders of the AAC asked to campaign for direct membership, Seme baulked. This was a moment of strategic genius. In 1933 the AAC was at its zenith, while the ANC was moribund. Had the AAC been allowed to recruit individual members, it may well have decimated the ANC's support base. While Seme's manoeuvre did not save the ANC from its internal weakness, it succeeded at least in preventing a fatal haemorrhaging of support.

Having given a glimpse of Seme's intellectual contribution to South Africa, it is now necessary to focus on the details of his life, which are outlined below.

'This Zulu is destined for lofty heights'

On 13 April 1906, a virtually unknown Seme was suddenly thrust into prominence when the *Rhodesian Herald* reported that he had been awarded the Curtis Medal for excellence in public speaking at Columbia University. Later on, *Ilanga Lase Natal* also carried a report on his achievement.[7] The news travelled far and wide. On hearing about Seme, Alfred Mangena, who was at the time studying at Lincoln's Inn, remarked: 'This Zulu is destined for lofty heights.' He was elated when he learnt that Seme intended to study law at Oxford, and made plans to meet with him 'upon his landing on these shores'.[8] Henry Sylvester Williams remarked that Seme had joined the pantheon of Pan-African intellectuals, which, though small in number, was growing in influence.[9]

The competition, run annually by juniors and seniors of the university, was tough. It selected the winner 'based on excellence in substance, literary form, and manner of delivery'. The judging panel came to a unanimous decision and awarded first prize, a gold medal, to Seme for his speech titled 'The Regeneration of Africa'. Second prize was a silver medal, which was awarded to Maurice G. Ellenbogen, who would later become a leading Republican politician. On the afternoon of 5 April 1906, there were four orations. The first was that of Bernard A. Rosenblatt, who spoke on 'Class Rule in America', stressing the importance of keeping up a keen interest among citizens, as a prerequisite for democracy. Harold K. Bell followed with a talk on 'The Public Services of Edward M. Stanton', focusing on the statesman's zeal, watchfulness and patriotism, as he saw the nation through the Civil War. Seme was the third speaker, and the *Columbia Daily Spectator* reported:

> Being a native of Zululand, [Seme] was inspired by his subject, 'The Regeneration of Africa.' He spoke of the existing conditions of the nations both north and south of the Sahara Desert. How the conflicts and strife were rapidly disappearing from the anterior nations. How Africa refused to stay on the border of industrial work and the African's unimpaired genius assured their existence. He pleaded that intelligence and the higher attainments of this life would be introduced into Africa in this great age. That the country's sons, studying in all the prominent universities, might promote and elevate their nation as they desire.

The last speaker, winner of the silver medal, was Maurice G. Ellenbogen; he spoke on 'John Marshall's Influence on the Constitution', arguing that it was to this lawyer, judge, soldier and diplomat that the United States was indebted for its Constitution.

When Seme spoke, the judges were impressed not only by the force of his speech, but also by its fluidity: 'I am an African,' Seme began. 'I set my pride in my race over against a hostile public opinion.' He then turned to the theme of 'equality', according to which men of all races were the same, and which in reality denoted *sameness*. This form of equality, 'if by it we mean identity', is an impossible dream, Seme asserted. Man shone in his own unique glory, and 'is a mystery through all ages and for all time'. Yet the concept of race was itself deeply problematic. Within each race, individuals were free, unique and different: every race is 'composed of free and unique individuals', he said. Any attempt to compare individuals – or races – on the basis of 'equality' could only be unsatisfactory. 'Each is himself,' he declared. 'My thesis stands on this truth; time has proven it. In all races, genius is like a spark, which, concealed in the blossom of flint, bursts forth at the summoning stroke. It may arise anywhere and in any race.'

Africa should not be compared to Europe, Seme contended. Any such comparison would 'humiliate' Africa. Then, arguing that there was no common standard, he cited the example of Egypt, with its 'venerable ruins, and the gigantic proportions of its architecture [which] reduce to insignificance the boasted monuments of other nations'. In stating that nothing in the world compared with the pyramids of Egypt, he cut through the supposed advancement of Europe over Africa. If the Egyptian pyramids stood as monuments of civilisation, it was clear that Europe could not claim any superiority over Africa in terms of civilisation. The same was true of the pyramids of Ethiopia, which, though smaller in size, were aesthetically more pleasing than those of Egypt. Seme argued that colonial conquest had in effect reversed Africa's gains in relation to civilisation. Africa, he submitted, had 'sunk beneath the western horizon' in a world which it had enlightened and continued to sustain.[12]

Despite these years of conquest, the giant of Africa was awakening: 'From the four corners of the earth, Africa's sons, who have been proved through fire and sword, are marching to the future's golden door bearing the records of deeds and valour done.' There were many Africans who had shown signs of genius and sufficient character to redeem the race from charges of indolence and barbarism. But those who levelled these charges should recall that no one could emerge from a period of such sustained influence unaffected by the contact. Any contact between the 'backward and the advanced' was bound to leave an indelible mark. The contact between the two – though Seme did not explain who was backward and who was advanced – meant 'the very essence of efficient progress and of civilisation'. There was ample evidence, Seme argued, that progress was upon the continent of Africa. Everywhere south of the Sahara, in Bechuanaland, in Abyssinia and in Zululand, there were signs that the 'African race is evidently a part of the new order of things that belong to this new and powerful period'. Science, religion, commerce and education would be the defining features in this new order of civilisation.

By 'regeneration', Seme meant 'the entrance to a new life, embracing the diverse phases of a higher, complex existence. The basic factor, which assures their generation, resides in the awakened race-consciousness.' And it was precisely this 'race-consciousness' that would give Africans a clear perception of their needs and their powers. Regeneration would therefore lead to 'the attainment of that higher and advanced standard of life'. African people had a common destiny, which was being inhibited by poor inter-tribal relations and wars. Instead, a new spirit of cooperation lay ahead, and Africa's 'greatest source of inspiration' was its 'ancestral greatness, the unimpaired genius, and the recuperative power of the race'. Education would play a crucial role in rediscovering the past, overcoming present difficulties and laying the foundations for a new form of civilisation, while educational institutions would be the pillars upon which regeneration rested. Seme concluded as follows:

> The regeneration of Africa means that a new and unique civilization is soon to be added to the world. The African is not a proletarian in the world of science and art. He has precious creations of his own, of ivory, of copper and of gold, fine, plaited willow-ware, and weapons of superior workmanship. Civilization resembles an organic being in its development – it is born, it perishes, and it can propagate itself. More particularly it resembles a plant, it takes root in the teeming earth, and when the seeds fall in other soils, new varieties sprout up. The most thoroughly spiritual and humanistic – indeed a regeneration moral and eternal.[13]

Seme's speech shattered barriers of national and tribal identity. His language was unashamedly Pan-African. It was not the Zulus or South Africans who faced the crucible of a new order. It was Africans, in the broad sense of the term. The speech also broke new ground in its understanding of the notion of civilisation. Till then, no African intellectual had located civilisation within the grand and sweeping narrative of ancient civilisations such as Egypt and Ethiopia. In fact, African history and culture were generally ignored or dismissed, with African scholars endorsing the claim that Europe constituted the benchmark for civilisation. Seme upended this notion, and questioned the very meaning of civilisation. In his allusion to the 'spiritual and humanistic', Seme reminded his audience of an oft forgotten aspect of civilisation. For him, the European adventure in Africa was disruptive, interfering with progress and bringing about moral corruption. Regeneration should recognise the spiritual, cultural, moral and physical aspects of a new dawn. At the heart of any civilisation lay a respect for humanity. Many years later, Steve Biko, the respected founder of the Black Consciousness Movement, would return to Seme's theme:

We reject the power-based society of the Westerner that seems to be ever concerned with perfecting their technological know-how while losing out on their spiritual dimension. We believe that in the long run the special contribution to the world by Africa will be in this field of human relationships. The great powers of the world have done wonders in giving the world an industrial and military look, but the great gift still has to come from Africa – giving the world a more human face.[14]

Seme's speech made international news. One newspaper reported that a 'Zulu, full-bloodied and of the race of Cetshwayo and Lobengula who gave England the hardest fighting John Bull ever had in South Africa, not excepting the Boers, yesterday won the George William Curtis gold medal, the highest oratorical award conferred by Columbia University'. It recorded Seme's self-assured remarks: 'It's easy for me to learn and I can do anything I make up my mind to do.'[10] In May 1906, an article appeared in the US *Century Magazine*, with Charles Francis Adams arguing that black peoples of Africa were inherently primitive and incapable of assimilation into civilised societies. The claims were based on 'scientific research' allegedly conducted by the author during a few months spent in Sudan. The magazine editor, William Henry Ferris, an African-American graduate of Yale and Harvard, rejected these conclusions as pseudoscience. Ferris referenced Seme's 1906 speech to buttress his argument that inferiority was not inherent in the black race, and that Africans were able to ascend to intellectual heights. Ferris also positioned Seme in the larger context of achievements by Africans and ancient civilisations in Africa, thereby disproving the theory of racial inferiority. Following his award, Seme was engaged by the New York Board of Education to deliver a series of public lectures on 'Life in Zululand'.[11] More than a hundred pupils turned up to listen to him speak at a public school, and many heard him at St Bartholomew's Lyceum Hall. The pupils were entertained by Seme's rhetorical flourishes at the same time as they viewed accompanying scenes from Zulu life through images projected by a stereopticon, an early slide projector.

Seme's speech promised that he would be one of the leading intellectual lights of his era. In June 1906, he completed his BA at Columbia University. While his experiences at Columbia shaped his intellectual growth, this university was not his first choice. He had wanted to study at Yale, and he was disappointed when his application was rejected; indeed, it was only in 1934 that South Africa had its first black graduate from Yale – Zachariah Keodirelang Matthews. Seme had also decided that he would study law, at Oxford University. Law, however, had not been his first choice: while at Columbia, he hoped to be a physician – like his brother, Lindley, who qualified in the United States. It was only in his final year at Columbia that Pixley Seme decided to pursue law.

First black South African at Oxford

While it is sometimes claimed that Seme held a law degree from the University of Oxford, this is not accurate information. Seme arrived on 13 October 1906 as a non-collegiate student. He registered as Pixley ka Isaka Seme, the fourth son of Sinono Isaka Seme, whose 'profession' is noted as 'member of Tribal Council'. His date of birth is recorded as 2 October 1882, at Inanda, Natal. His education is stated as having taken place at Inanda, Natal, Mount Hermon and Columbia University. Seme later 'migrated' to Jesus College on 22 January 1907, and was from that date a member of the college. The minutes of the board of the Faculty of Law state that his admission for the Bachelor of Civil Law (BCL) degree was approved on 19 June 1907. According to the archivist at Jesus College, the university holds no records that Seme actually qualified with the degree of BCL or any other degree at the university.[15] Significantly, when Seme later qualified as an attorney in South Africa, he did not claim any qualification from Oxford, though he did nothing to stop newspapers from referring to him as an 'Oxford graduate'.

Nevertheless, Seme's admission to Oxford was in itself a great achievement considering that, when he first went to study at Mount Hermon School in Massachusetts, USA, in 1897, his grasp of English was described as 'spattering'.[16] Like all Oxford students, Seme was allocated a tutor. The tutorial system is a feature of Oxford education. It takes the form of a dialogue between the tutor – either a lecturer or professor – and student, on an informal basis, outside of the classroom. Typically, a tutor is assigned between one and three students. While costly, it is an effective system which, as John H. Morgan suggests, has many virtues:

> The student comes once a week to the tutor's digs, a comfortable room or rooms with soft chairs, old carpet, usually a fireplace, and, at least in an earlier day, a pipe or two between them and a glass of sherry or port. The student reads a paper covering about a half to three-quarters of an hour, being intermittently interrupted with the tutor's questions, observations, suggestions, and clarifications.[17]

Seme's tutor was Alfred Ernest William Hazel, an accomplished barrister, academic and politician. Like Seme, he had been at Jesus College, where he gained a first in classics and law, and was awarded the Eldon Law Scholarship. In 1906, the year Seme entered Oxford, Hazel was elected as an MP for the Liberal Party,[18] which had won the election of 1906, beating both the Labour and the Conservative parties. While it came into power under typical liberal values of individualism and a limited form of government, the extent of poverty and inequality in the United Kingdom caused it to shift its position. Government intervention was clearly required to reduce widespread poverty, and welfare reforms were introduced.

These included the introduction of free school meals, health insurance, fair wage policy and old-age pensions; public works schemes such as road tarring and waterworks were also introduced. This phase is sometimes referred to as 'new liberalism'. There was a shift away from individualism to the need for state intervention to alleviate extreme human suffering, though with limits on state power regarding control over the economy and individual people's lives. Thus, the welfare state was born.

Hazel was among those who rejected liberal individualism in favour of a welfare state. Seme's tutor held a fellowship in law, and his areas of specialisation were constitutional law, law of evidence and criminal law. Given his eventual career trajectory, it may be assumed that he was a tough taskmaster: Seme would have been expected to submit essays on time, so that they could be considered before the tutorial, where he would have had to think on his feet and answer probing questions that tested the content of his essay. Seme would have received fair and equitable treatment, and his race would have been irrelevant to a man like Hazel. Like all other students, he would have had to fulfil his side of the bargain.

Hazel's liberal values and his concern for the less privileged are evident in a letter he wrote to a potential voter, Mr Jones, in January 1910:

> Dear Sir,
> May I make a final appeal for your vote at the poll on Monday next, Jan 17th. I would like to see every elector personally, but this is impossible. During the last four years I have done my best to stand by the Workers, who sent me to Parliament, and in this crisis I stand for the People against the Rich, who would take their food. I ask you to do your part towards returning a West Bromwich man to represent West Bromwich.
> I am, yours very truly,
> A.E.W. Hazel[19]

It may safely be assumed that Hazel's contribution to Seme's intellectual development was considerable, and the BCL degree he began was reputed to be rigorous. Despite this, letters he wrote to his African-American friend and fellow student, Alain Locke, make no reference to his academic endeavours at Oxford. Seme was beset with financial difficulties. In one letter, he wryly observes that he could no longer 'live like a Duke', and had therefore decided to simultaneously study at Middle Temple.[20] Seme's pride in being associated with Oxford, coupled with his failure to achieve a qualification, created something of a quandary for him. His letters to Locke express a fawning admiration for Oxford. Yet Locke, the first African-American Rhodes Scholar, who graduated with a PhD in 1918, was enamoured neither with the academic staff, nor with the cultural aspects of the university. Locke's candid letters to his mother reveal much about the life of a black student at Oxford in the early twentieth century. Upon arrival at Oxford, in 1907, Locke wrote that good locations had a lot to do with 'an entrée into social life'.[21] By this, he meant that good accommodation was available only to the socially connected few. Locke found it hard to tolerate the 'superficiality and insincerity' of Oxford academics and students.[22] His negative experiences evidently had to do with his race. Indeed, it is not clear whether the Rhodes Selection Committee that recommended him was aware that he was black, since interviews with candidates were at the time conducted through written correspondence.

Race aside, Locke faced another hurdle. Perhaps even more of a problem than race in Victorian England, with its puritan mores, was homosexuality. In an angry letter to his mother in 1909, Locke referred to the case of Oscar Wilde, where the disclosure of his homosexuality 'tarnished' his image. Describing Oxfordians as 'particularly stupid, priggish people', Locke wrote that '[t]hey don't seem to mind as long a man keeps his private life away from public knowledge and censure – for instance Oscar Wilde's defects were well known and the subject of risqué gossip while he was yet at Oxford – Swinburne they disowned because he was a confirmed erotic and drunkard'.[23]

Locke's disgust erupts when he complains about his roommate's reference to conduct deemed 'unmanly' and 'a break of friendship etiquette', an attitude reflective of the arrogance of the university where 'everything Oxfordian is right'.[24] He clearly found the general behaviour pretentious and discriminatory, and the atmosphere claustrophobic. The fact that Locke held a prestigious scholarship, and was a Harvard graduate, held little sway at Oxford. As a result, he gravitated towards the few black people at the university – these were mainly from the British colonies and Caribbean Islands, and they included Seme.

Alain Locke: a close friendship

Many of Seme's friendships were founded upon legal and political connections. With Locke, however, things were different. Their bond operated on another plane, with a unique level of personal and intellectual intensity. Seme's connection with Locke was established even before they met, and during their Oxford days it intensified, producing something of a mutual dependency. In 1908, Locke, who had just graduated from Harvard with an excellent academic record, became the first African American to be awarded a Rhodes Scholarship. The news reached Seme, who was impressed and pleased at the prospect of welcoming a fellow Ivy League graduate to Oxford. From the outset, the tone of their correspondence is warm and familiar, with Seme addressing Locke as a 'dear friend'. Seme took it upon himself to inform – and gently warn – Locke about life at Oxford: 'Rhodes scholars are simply a drop in the ocean here. They have no influence whatsoever.

You come to Oxford, the climax and inspiration of the university system of Great Britain and of the world.' Seme also provided counsel concerning the selection of a college: 'My best advice is that you should try more than anything else to postpone the final selection.' If that were not possible, Locke should seek admission to Christ Church College, Magdalene, New College, Brasnose and Trinity College.

Upon Locke's arrival at Oxford, he immediately struck up a friendship with Seme. They regularly invited each other to tea or lunch. In one note, Seme wrote, 'Please come and join us at coffee tomorrow 8 o'clock in my room. I expect Mr Harley also to come. Please ask Mr Downs to come at the same time Wednesday.'[25] In another note, which also mentions Mr Downs, Seme wrote, 'Please make it convenient to come and take coffee with me next Thursday at 8.15. I expect a lot of friends including three Americans in Jesus College whom I wish you to know. I have asked Mr Downs also to come.'[26] When Locke excused himself from a lunch invitation on 22 February 1908, Seme expressed regret and hoped that he could soon arrange a day when 'I shall have pleasure of your society at tea in my digs', signing off with 'good luck old man'. Apart from enjoying the occasional tea or lunch at each other's rooms, the two men also played tennis together.[27]

After registering at Middle Temple, Seme had to juggle two equally demanding responsibilities: studying for his BCL degree and training to be a barrister. This placed a strain on him, and he relied substantially on Locke for support. On 10 March 1908, giving his new address to Locke – 24 South Hill Park Gardens, Hampstead, London – he wrote: 'Of course you know what to do with it.' Inviting him to come over, he promised a game of billiards: 'There is a fine private table in the house.' Seme routinely asked Locke for books: while he had an account with several bookshops, Seme had left a trail of debt after leaving Oxford. Seme apologised that Locke would 'lead a strenuous life' on his account, and thanked him effusively for his kindness.

One of Seme's Hampstead housemates was a fellow South African, Alfred Mangena. Seme informed Locke of the accommodation problems, saying that 'this house is quite full now. I found Mr Mangena here. However he is contemplating on his past and future dignity in an attic chamber. He was complaining to me today that he could not sleep on account of the pigeons.' Since all the bedrooms were taken, the landlord had kindly cleared the sitting room, converting it into a bedroom for Seme. So, Seme said, he would not be inviting his dear friend to join him in the overcrowded accommodation, and instead suggested an alternative house, 'a very nice place'. He proposed that Locke should 'condescend to read the Daily Telegraph'; houses which also 'enjoy fine gardens' might be found on 'fair terms' in Elgin Crescent. Seme had a further request:

Let me ask you to kiss the following for me and in this order – (1) Roman – (2) Marsh – (3) Rev Williams (your tutor) – (4) Rev Barrows – (5) J. Archer LLB. BA. BD. If after this there is still more energy left, please then go about paying off my bills, beginning with my landlady's. Only don't call at the wine company. Enclosed please find a fiver.[28]

Seme also owed money for jewellery and clothing he had bought. In one letter, undated, but probably written around the middle of 1908, Seme expressed regret at abandoning his affairs 'in such a state'. His dependency on Locke is clear: 'where it not for the fact that you are there I certainly would have come back on my return ticket'. To make up for the inconvenience, Seme promised 'a good fat binge when you come down'. He asked Locke to bring with him items he had left behind, such as his pipe, a pouch, an amber kist and a postcard album. A piano, apparently unpaid for, needed to be returned to the music shop, and Seme promised that the bill would be paid 'at beginning of term'. As his financial problems piled up, Seme avoided his creditors and asked Locke to send everything on to him 'except summons'. A letter had arrived from 'his Majesty's office', which he had been reluctant to open, fearing it might be a creditor. As it turned out, the envelope contained a £20 note – which had been awaiting collection for a full three weeks. Seme humorously described his reaction to the discovery: 'Oh darn it said I. Let me go take a bath.' Then he promised 'Lockus' that he would be coming down to Oxford the following day, 'with the devil as usual'.[29]

It was Seme's final year at Oxford, but he had made little academic progress. He was aware of this, and it weighed heavily on him. On 26 August 1908, he wrote to Locke, telling him he was back in Oxford due to 'serious reflections in connection with the fact that this is the last year of my undergraduate life'. He would therefore be spending the remaining months in the 'closer study of law and literature'. He had now secured 'most comfortable and cosy lodgings in Blackhall near Keble College'. The accommodation was 'a rather fine' room in a fine house, and Locke would 'certainly approve' of his choice. He invited Locke to visit, telling him that he had played tennis the previous day. Apparently concerned that Locke had gained the impression that he was not studying enough, he told his friend that he could now 'study much better here'. He went on to express regret at being unable to meet Locke's mother during her visit to Oxford, but conveyed his 'very highest respects and wishes for a happy voyage'. Locke's admiration for Seme shines through in a letter he wrote to his mother at the end of November 1908. Seme, wrote Locke, 'is blossoming out in African exuberance into everything'. At this stage, the two friends were spending much time together. 'Seme is here often, almost every day,' Locke mentioned.[30] Later on, Locke would tell his mother of a 'wonderful performance of Coleridge-Taylor's Hiawatha' which he had attended together with Seme 'and a Gold Coast Negro by the name of Gibson who returned to Oxford to take his MA and BCL (think of that you Afro-Americans!)'. The show, which he had never seen before, had 'stunned' Locke. He found it 'strange' – perhaps intriguing – that Samuel Coleridge-Taylor, who had composed 'The Song of Hiawatha', 'is of African extraction'.[31]

Seme, having achieved little success at Oxford that year, began to spend more time in London. Towards the end of 1908, he was attending classes at Middle Temple in preparation for his Bar examinations. And by 1909 he appears to have completely abandoned his Oxford studies and moved to London to focus on qualifying as a barrister.[32] In an undated letter, presumably sent towards the end of 1909 (and after meeting with the South African delegation to London), Seme was contemplating life back in South Africa. This would inevitably mean separation from Locke, to whom he wrote: 'Locke, I miss you and Oxford.' Seme wrote that he had been advised to go to Holland in order to renew his acquaintance with the Dutch language. This, he said, would be important for his work in South Africa. Since the country was 'confronted by two official languages', it would be regarded by the Boers as 'a great compliment to talk with a pure accent', that is, the Dutch language as it was spoken in Holland. Dutch was spoken in court, he wrote, and also by learned clergy.

It was 1910, Seme had written his examinations, and he was now ready for admission to the Bar. His last letter to Locke – a further affirmation of the intimacy of their friendship – informed him as follows:

> I am coming to town tomorrow with the devil as usual. I am going to be called to the Bar on the 8th of June. Please come and spend that day with me. I wish you could come for a longer time. But this day you must come. I have news for you and briefly it is in this I wish to collect all my strength and courage to the African Union Society. Do drop me a line to the address below. With highest expectations and best wishes for your successes.[33]

Back in South Africa, the resistance to the formation of the Union of South Africa had reached a climax. In 1909, John Dube, whom Seme regarded as a family elder, was among the delegates to London to protest the exclusion of Africans. He had met with Seme, who by now was close to thirty years of age, and impressed upon him the necessity of returning home and immersing himself in the 'concerns of his people'. Seme had been spending an inordinate amount of time in London, and had left a mountain of debt and a host of creditors in Oxford. He could no longer afford to pay his rent. Indeed, in the three years he spent at Oxford, he had five known addresses: 7 Iffley Road, 168 Walton Street, 162 Walton Street, 3 Blackhall Road and 205 Iffley Road. In each case, he left either without paying his rent, or with money owed to the landlord. On 27 January 1909, one of his creditors, Joseph & Son, distributors of new and second-hand books, reminded him that their accounts had been 'rendered to him on very many occasions'. Their letter stated that the company was 'unable to allow this account to remain in its present state and must therefore request an immediate settlement'. If no payment was received, 'we shall be compelled to place the matter in the Solicitor's hands, a course we would have no wish to adopt'. No payment was made, however, and Seme candidly admitted to Locke that he was in London 'hiding over here from an overzealous Oxford trades man'. So numerous were Seme's debts that he had learnt the trick of fending them off – and boasted about it in a letter to his friend:

I fixed the old gentlemen the other day. Really they must be thick headed and foolish. You know Dr Reuner and Dr Scholes wished to be introduced to each other. I offered most gladly to perform the ceremony and [he suggested that] I should escort Dr Reuner to the mighty columns of the British museum and there and then seek the presence of the learned colleague and author. Then of course we three immortals should march to the Trocadero and take lunch. Well as you suppose both of them jumped to accept these generous suggestions and to my surprise they brought mighty appetites with them to the expensive and attractive table. I thought they came to lunch but they sat for dinner. Well I followed suit and would not be excelled in collecting fancy side dishes – indeed Ceres is witness to the fact that I feasted more than they all. But the Devil had it that I sat at the head of the table and the gracious waiter came to me for everything. Now he brings the wine list and now this and that … Imagine the chill down my spine when I had only a borrowed 7/6 in my pocket. Presently God inspired me to ask the illustrious to excuse me as I then asked for a lavatory and of course the waiter took me around the gold bright hall and in the corner I said this prayer within hearing of my waiter 'give the bill to the man on my right. Now don't forget, here is your six pence.' 'Alright sir.' Now Locke you have heard of English Bull dogs and their determination – this is nothing compared to the tenacity of an English waiter once he gets an idea in his unfrequented brain. The victim of this persistent attack was one friend Dr Reuner indeed a worthy man is he. But strange he did not wish to see it. For he did not want to pay it. I ran around to get the overcoats and silk hats. Dr Scholes could scarcely move for he had eaten so much dinner. Locke I wish you had seen him turn black and cold. The end of the story is that I went home with 7 bobs still in pocket. O I had fun about this. It worked well. Just fancy my paying for them … No news – best wishes.

Seme's financial predicament seems to have arisen from a combination of extravagance and the drying up of financial support from his South African sponsor. For reasons that are unclear, Reverend Pixley suddenly terminated his financial support for Seme. Pixley was an American missionary based in Zululand, and it was from him that Seme took his first name. He had taken a keen interest in Seme from a young age and helped pay for his studies in America, and also for a while at Oxford. When this financial support was terminated, Seme appears to have been unwilling to take on odd jobs to pay his way as a student. He saw himself, after all, as a 'Zulu prince'.[34] While in London, Seme regularly attended debates at the House of Commons, where he displayed keen interest, assessing each speaker and allocating scores on their public-speaking abilities. After one such occasion, on 18 March 1908, he missed his train and found himself without accommodation. He then called upon Locke, profusely apologising for the inconvenience, and asked if he could stay over that evening.

By now, it is likely that Locke had confided in Seme about his homosexuality. Seme's evolving ideas and beliefs are likely to have taught him tolerance of difference. He had, after all, spent his formative years in the broad multicultural spaces of America, where he had embraced Pan-Africanism. It was one of their achievements that, in the smaller, more isolated and isolating environment of Oxford, they were founder members of the African Union Society.[35] Long after the Oxford association, they were still in regular contact, writing to each other as they shared thoughts, fears and hopes for themselves and for their race. Seme eventually returned to South Africa a far more rounded person, becoming a pioneer in his country's path to liberation, while Locke's legacy in America as a thinker and writer continues to shape academic and popular discourses.

Unlike his time at Columbia, Seme's last days at Oxford ended not with the proverbial bang, but with something of a whimper. While his name appears on the list of examination candidates for the degree of BCL in Trinity Term 1909,[36] it is missing from the list of those who passed.[37] There is no record that Seme passed any examination at Oxford University, and no degree was conferred on him. He did, however, pass his legal training at Middle Temple, and he was admitted to the English Bar.

'A man of wig and gown'
On 2 October 1910, a steamer from England arrived on South African shores. Among those on board was Pixley ka Isaka Seme. There was a sense of elation upon disembarking, and also expectation. Since leaving for America thirteen years before, Seme had become an accomplished gentleman. Fluent in English, he was fully conversant in Dutch and French, played the piano, and enjoyed a game of snooker or tennis. He also held a BA degree from a prestigious Ivy League

university. And though he had not completed his BCL at Oxford, he had qualified as a barrister. By now, Seme was a man of the world, having lived in New York, Oxford and London, and visited Paris and Holland in 1909. His cosmopolitan outlook was formed by friendships and relationships he had developed in various parts of the world. Booker T. Washington was a mentor, and Seme counted Henry Sylvester Williams, the founder of Pan-Africanism, a friend. He could call upon Alfred Hazel, his former Oxford tutor, who was also at the heart of political action in the United Kingdom. Now, Seme's priority was to qualify as a lawyer, the culmination of a career many years in the making.

On 13 January 1911, Seme opened legal offices on the corner of Joubert and Anderson Streets in Johannesburg. At the time, the only other black law firm in Johannesburg was that of Alfred Mangena, also in Anderson Street.[38] Although Seme applied for admission as an attorney, he had hoped to practise as an advocate. This was not possible, however: unlike in the Cape, the profession of advocates in the Transvaal was reserved for persons of European descent. There is a clear undertone of annoyance in Seme's January 1912 letter to his former benefactor, Reverend Pixley, where he lampoons the practices of the barrister – 'a man of wig and gown':

It will be an evil day for [the barrister] when he starts brief hunting though he may be starving for lack of golden guineas. On circuit the watchful eyes of etiquette are always on him. Even for the sake of company he must be a sociable man, he must not travel there by any class but the first. Even his professional dress is regulated for him to the extent that he must not appear in court in any other coat but one of sober black, nor must he show his face in court if he is carrying the blue bag which may be his familiar companion in street and train. Unless he is entitled to carry a red bag (and this he must not buy – it must be given to him by some friendly senior), he must be content to make his appearance with his briefs and papers under his arm.[39]

For all his lightheartedness, Seme was aware that he had a mission to fulfil. The land he had left behind nine years before was not the place he had returned to. The Union of South Africa had been established as a country under British dominion. Natal and the Cape were no longer colonies, but provinces of South Africa, as were the two former Boer republics, the Transvaal and the Orange Free State. A new, though shifting, South African identity had been thrust on his people. Some had embraced it. And others not.

It is remarkable that, in all the years he spent at Columbia, Oxford and Middle Temple, Seme never once referred to any experience of race discrimination. But in South Africa it was different. Some two years after his return, Seme the black attorney was forced to spend a night in a stable. Returning from a visit to Swaziland on 17 October 1912, despite being the only passenger to disembark from the train, he was refused accommodation at a hotel, which was for 'Europeans only'. The African driver of a mail coach gave up the nearby stable for Seme to spend the night there, while the driver himself slept inside the coach – which had the misfortune of being robbed of £3 000 that very night. The distraught driver was discovered by the police in the morning, gagged and bound. Seme would encounter many such instances. Race continued to count against him, and not even his Ivy League and Oxford education spared him such indignities.

In the new political dispensation, Dube expected that Seme would 'find it convenient to stay in Natal to work in the new field of government's efforts for leading the native people to the new ideas of life that are to largely aid in consolidating the whole interests of the Union'. But Seme had a much grander vision: he would reject tribalism, ethnicity and provincialism in favour of a broad nationalism. He urgently needed to work towards a national political organisation, as envisaged by Jabavu.

The role of Seme in the history and formation of the ANC is a highly contested topic. As early as 1929, S.E.K. Mqhayi repudiated claims by Richard Victor Selope Thema, then secretary of the ANC, that Seme had founded the ANC:

> This gentleman says this assembly was founded by Dr Seme in 1912. It is on precisely this point that I wish to enlighten this young man so that he sees his way clearly, because what he is focusing on is a worthy story indeed. As an old man I would like to take him back to the year 1887, the year of Thung'Umlomo, Stitch the Mouth. In that year there was an effort here in the Cape to establish a major association with Mr Goda Sishuba in the chair and Mr J.T. Jabavu as secretary – but after a while, Mr Thomas Mqanda became chairman and Mr Jonathan Tunyiswa secretary. That association was named the SA Native Congress (Ingqungquthela).[40]

There are certain indisputable facts concerning the circumstances which led to the formation of the ANC. The South African Native Congress was already in existence by 1890. Between 1908 and 1910, the South African Native Convention existed, and its deputation went to Britain in 1909. Ironically, the seeds for a national organisation were first planted not by those who eventually became leaders of the ANC, but by Jabavu, who was opposed to the formation of its forerunner, the SANNC. Jabavu envisaged a new national organisation founded along non-racial lines. Echoing Jabavu, on 24 October 1911 Seme published an article in *Imvo Zabantsundu* in which he announced that 'several natives, leaders and chiefs' had asked him to 'write a full and concise statement on the subject of the South African Native Congress'.[41]

In the article, Seme argued that societal progress could only be achieved by cooperation 'among all races'. He believed that people 'everywhere in the world' bear mutual obligations to God and 'towards one another'. The implication was that people everywhere had a moral duty to the oppressed people of South Africa; this was Seme's unique contribution to the debate, and to the character of the new organisation. It was also a manifestation of Seme's internationalism and universalism, which he sought to infuse into the nascent organisation. The greatest success, he added, would come when 'man shall have learned to cooperate, not only with his own kith and kin but all peoples and with all life'. From the outset, the SANNC would not be limited by borders, and would cooperate with all the peoples of the world. Only thus could it achieve meaningful progress. The character of the organisation should be anti-tribal and non-racial, Seme urged:

> The demon of racialism, the aberrations of the Xosa-Fingo feud, the animosity that exists between the Zulus and the Tongas, between the Bantus and every other Native must be buried and forgotten; it has shed among us sufficient blood! We are one people. These divisions, these jealousies, are the cause of all our woes and of all our backwardness and ignorance to-day.

Seme's use of the term 'racialism' and his subsequent references to inter-tribal 'aberrations' and 'animosities' is intriguing. It is likely that he wished to distinguish racialism from inter-tribal conflicts. In his Columbia speech of 1906, Seme had used the term 'race' in distinguishing between Africans and Europeans – the 'African race' and the 'European race'. But 'racialism' was different – it was a demon that had caused too much bloodshed. The declaration that 'we are one people' is more significant than is generally acknowledged. First, it is a non-racial concept, which includes all South Africans, regardless of race. Second, it is a universal concept, rooted in a humanism which places at the centre 'all peoples' and 'all life'. Peace and unity should be available to all who live in South Africa. As such, the new country, founded on the idea of non-racialism and non-tribalism, would be a home for all.

While universalism and non-racialism were the guiding principles of the SANNC, it would be formed and controlled primarily by Africans. The South African Native Congress, Seme explained, was a 'voice in the wilderness bidding all the dark races of this sub-continent to come together once or twice a year' with the purpose of reviewing the past and rejecting 'all those things which have retarded our progress, the things which poison the springs of our national life and virtue'. It would enable Africans 'as members of one household to talk and think loudly on our home problems and the solution to them'. When Seme referred to 'national life', he was not speaking of tribes. For him, the concept of a 'nation' was close to that of 'race' – it encompassed Africans as a race, which included tribal differences. The thing that was 'poisoning' the national life and 'retarding' its progress had been identified – it was racialism. The cure was not further racialism. Rather, 'the key and the watchword' was cooperation, which would open the 'everlasting door which leads into progress and all national success'. The congress would therefore be formed by Africans. But it had to be guided by the principles of universalism and non-racialism.

There were immediate tasks ahead. One related to the government's adoption of a uniform policy with regard to questions affecting the native races. A key issue of the South Africa Act of 1909 was the extension of the right to vote. Previously, the South African Native Convention had unsuccessfully campaigned for the extension of the franchise beyond the confines of the Cape, now that South Africa was a unitary country. With the establishment of this new congress, there was hope that the government might yet be persuaded to adopt a single policy for the whole of the Union. The congress would be a point of contact between 'native thought' and the government, particularly those remaining African representatives in Parliament. Through the congress, 'the Native Senators in the Union House of Parliament will be able to live in close touch with the Natives of the whole country whose interest each Senator is supposed to represent'. The congress would then serve to filter the concerns of the people through to their own parliamentary representatives. Another sphere of concern was the communication of the views of Africans to the executive branch of government. Seme suggested that the government should 'also find a direct and independent channel of informing itself as to the things uppermost in Natives' mind from time to time', making it 'easier for the Union Government to deal with Natives of the whole of South Africa'. But the role of the congress should not be reduced to a mere conduit of the collective grievances of Africans. Instead, it should provide natives with 'the opportunity and means with which to influence the public opinion of this country'. This would, in turn, 'greatly assist the South African Statesmen who are working for peace, prosperity, and the development of this land'. Peace and prosperity were the watchwords, and even in the face of governmental aggression the vision had to be kept alive. Seme emphasised the importance of Africans maintaining the gains of 'civilisation' and progress thus far achieved. A militant approach would be regressive, if not destructive of the educational, spiritual and scientific progress made by Africans.

The realm of the chiefs was ambiguous and contentious. In the mid-nineteenth century, the destruction of the power of the chiefs in the Eastern Cape was seen as essential to the entrenchment of the colonial order. By the beginning of the twentieth century, indirect rule was becoming the norm. Having significantly weakened the influence of the chiefs, the imperial government now attempted to control vast tracts of land and the communities who lived there through the chiefs themselves. Through occupation, military action and the arbitrary expulsion of people from ancestral lands, Empire had succeeded in reshaping tribal identities and reorganising tribal affiliations. People who did not traditionally live together found themselves having to share living spaces. Chiefs were arbitrarily demoted and replaced. Existing geographic boundaries were ignored, and new and often unstable ones were created. Imperial political and economic exigencies were paramount.

Given the situation, the position of chiefs was a problematic issue for Seme and his colleagues. Should chiefs be rejected as incurably tainted by collaboration with colonial authorities, or should they be embraced on the grounds that they too were part of the oppressed? Ultimately, it was decided to accommodate the chiefs. Far from being an uncritical endorsement of the position of the chiefs, the decision was pragmatic. For, despite their diminution in status and power, the chiefs still enjoyed enormous public respect. Since the main goal of the SANNC was to influence public opinion, it was vital that it remained rooted among the chiefs. But there was more to the decision: one of the primary concerns of the new organisation was the raising of funds, and chiefs would be a useful means. Their position enabled them to collect funds from their constituencies, while the chiefs themselves received stipends and salaries from the government. It had long been government policy that chiefs should be 'employees' of the government, which was thereby granted leverage and power over chiefly power. For all these reasons, it was proposed that the chiefs be invited to join the organisation. With apparent delight, Seme announced that 'a Great Paramount chief'[42] had accepted the inclusion of his name on the list of delegates, and suggested that the congress 'should set their faces strongly against the jargon of racial feeling, the ebullition of the Xosa-Fingo element, and the excessive display of political partisanship'.

A general announcement was made to 'all the Native leaders, Societies and Editors' requesting them 'to explain this important news to the people at large, and to advise them to arrange for the sending of delegates so that every section of the people shall be represented' at a conference planned for December 1911. Leaders would be elected, and discussion topics ranged from the serious and urgent business of native labour, Native Courts, schools and churches to issues such as whether 'native beer' might be regarded as a national beverage. A 'vote of confidence' would also be held to establish whether Africans had confidence in the prime minister – this despite the fact that they had no representation in government, and were therefore unable to give effect to the outcome. Eventually, owing to logistical challenges and difficulties in raising funds, the conference was postponed to January 1912.

Seme urgently needed more funding, and so he turned to the chiefs. The call for chiefs to attend the conference was a resounding success. Not only did they provide financial support, their very presence had symbolic value to the growing resistance movement in the Southern African region. Among the royals who attended were Lewanika of Barotseland (today part of Zambia), Dinuzulu ka Cetshwayo of the Zulu, Letsie II of the Basotho, Marelane of the Mpondo, Khama of the Tswanas, Dalindyebo of the Thembu and Moepi of the Bakgatla. Rather than their names being put forward for election, they were made honorary presidents of the SANNC, owing to their status.

On 8 January 2012, at 3 p.m., Seme's dream was realised. Under the auspices of the Orange Free State Native Congress, the conference was opened in Mangaung, Bloemfontein. As Tiyo Soga's Christian hymn – *'Lizalis' idinga lakho Thixo Nkosi'* (God fulfil thy promise) – reverberated through the house, Seme was called to the stage. In accordance with a joint agreement between Alfred Mangena, George Montsioa and himself, Seme moved the motion for the 'formation and establishment' of the South African Native National Congress. Mangena rose to second the motion. There was no dissenting voice, and the motion was adopted. The draft constitution, which had been prepared by Montsioa, was approved. It provided for the nomination of officers, which was duly done. In the structure envisaged by Seme, chiefs occupied the Upper House, and served by virtue of their standing as chiefs, without nomination or election as such. The new national organisation was formed, and its new leadership installed. The president, John Dube, was elected in absentia.

At this point, Seme had no presidential aspirations, and was instead occupied with his legal practice. The Johannesburg–Pretoria area witnessed a period of expansion and economic development. Mining was at the centre of Johannesburg's thriving economy, while in Pretoria, where government administration was based, there was an urgent need for infrastructure. Agriculture, too, was a major source of economic activity. Labour, the bedrock of development, was in short supply. Hundreds of Africans left the native reserves in search of opportunities in the *'egoli'*, the city of gold. The expanding economy resulted in the handful of young black lawyers practising in Johannesburg being flooded with work. Initially, there were doubts as to whether sufficient legal work was available for 'native attorneys'. As things turned out, though, there was far too much to handle. The problem was exacerbated by their lack of financial and administrative experience. The result was that the energy and hope of a few years earlier turned into disappointment and despair. In the case of Seme, Swaziland would loom large.

Swaziland's land tenure system

The loss of land by the people of Swaziland was not the result of war or draconian legislation such as the South African Natives Land Act. The land was lost through a system of privately bargained 'concessions' between white settlers on the one hand and the native people on the other. White settlers comprised two groups, Afrikaner farmers and English-speaking businessmen. The system of concessions can be traced to the end of the Anglo-Boer War, when Britain annexed the Transvaal. The powers of the governor of the Transvaal extended to Swaziland, whose land and finances were placed under the control of the Transvaal. In 1906, as a result of an Order in Council,[43] Swaziland was placed under British protection. Yet the political and legal status of Swaziland oscillated between a dominion within the Empire, as South Africa was at the time, and a full protectorate, such as Bechuanaland. The land tenure system was equally complicated. Francis de Winton, who was resident commissioner in Swaziland in 1889, described the territory's land tenure system as 'probably without parallel' in terms of exploitation by 'adventurers':

> There are many instances where native rulers have given large and important rights to individuals and to corporations, but in Swaziland the late King [Mbandzeni] and his Council have parted not only with all their actual territory but with rights which should only belong to the Government of a country, to a lot of adventurers whose sole object was to make money by them.[44]

These remarks relate to the three kinds of concessions in existence in Swaziland. The first of these were trading concessions generally given to traders, which did not involve the allocation of land or rights to land. A trader could set up a store in order to trade, with no further expectation. Once the term lapsed, he lost the rights. The second kind of concession included agricultural rights, grazing rights, water rights and mineral rights. The third category was private revenue concessions. In theory, a private individual could give away their land rights to the state in exchange for payment. In reality, however, only one concession fell into this category. It related to private revenue collection for the benefit of the king of Swaziland – at the time, Mbandzeni sat on the throne. In exchange for giving away land for state use, the king received a specified amount per annum, while the rest of the revenue generated was allocated to the royal household. With the Transvaal in charge of Swaziland, it was now up to the representative of the imperial government, Lord Alfred Milner, to deal with the land question. Milner decided to expropriate all the trading concessions. He paid no compensation for this, and instead used monies raised through revenue collection in Swaziland. He accounted for these monies as 'loans'.

The land concessions were, however, not only numerous, they were also complex. Every piece of ground in Swaziland was accounted for by a land concession of some sort, whether this related to grazing, mineral or water rights. R.T. Coryndon, who was appointed resident commissioner for Swaziland in 1907, described the situation as follows:

> Practically the whole area of the country was covered ... by concessions of all sizes, for different purposes, and for greatly varying periods. In but very few cases were even the boundaries defined; many ... had been subdivided and sold several times ... In addition to this, concessions were granted for all lands and minerals previously unallotted, or which, having been allotted, might lapse or become forfeited. Finally, it must be remembered that over these three or four strata of conflicting interests, boundaries, and periods there had to be preserved the natural rights of the Natives to live, move, cultivate, graze and hunt.[45]

Amidst such 'complexity and chaos', Coryndon continued, it would be difficult to arrive at 'a solution which would preserve to the native his proper rights while securing to the concessionaire some equitable enjoyment of the privileges and rights he had purchased and which had been confirmed to him by responsible Courts'.

The problem was the familiar story of colonial occupation of Africa. European settlers, having acquired access to land as tenants, soon wanted to alter that relationship to become full owners. Africans resisted their efforts, arguing that they had never sold the land, which was in any case their spiritual and material heritage, and was, as such, inalienable. Conflict was inevitable. Sir Godfrey Lagden, a colonial administrator, wrote in a memorandum to the British government: 'it is paramount that a modus vivendi be found which, while not giving [concessionaires] political ascendancy, maintains their status as white men. If the natives on a land concession reject all reasonable proposals to compromise, the authority of Government should be fully exerted.' What Lagden proposed as a solution has a familiar South African ring to it: a clear demarcation between native and white areas. He reminded the Swazis that the 'assumption of direct control by His Majesty's Government does not give them the right to settle anywhere at will except on ground reserved into which white people are not admitted'. The Swazis also needed to know that 'the parental attitude of His Majesty's Government in taking the country under active protection involves certain obligations, chief of which are implicit obedience to laws and lawful orders'.[46] As with the Lagden Commission of 1903–1905 in South Africa, the problem would be resolved through the appointment of a commission – which was named the Concessions Commission.

Ultimately, the solution proposed by the Concessions Commission was partition, with two-thirds of the land being allocated to European settlers, and the rest being 'native reserves'. Swazis could be in undisturbed possession of the land, even if they could not be owners. On the European side, the concessionaires could own their portions of land. Where land was allocated for white settlement, Swazis would have no rights at all unless they were there as workers, though this itself was at the discretion of the white employer. To address the problem of land availability, whites would be required to cede portions of their land to Swazis – a system known as 'land partitioning'. But these recommendations were rejected outright by whites, who argued that being surrounded by native reserves would diminish the value of their concessions. Instead, they wanted a scheme that would push the natives into reserves that were labour reservoirs, as in South Africa. And so, Milner's Concession Commission and its recommendations came crashing down.

Yet resistance did not only emanate from whites. There were also objections to the concession-based land tenure system among the Swazi. They had initially viewed the concessions as purely arm's length transactions which could be terminated at any time. But now the concessions had assumed a different complexion and become a de facto form of land deprivation. The Swazi chiefs and their followers demanded an audience with the imperial government. While there was initial resistance from Lord Selborne, who was at the time high commissioner in South Africa and governor of the Transvaal, he eventually relented. A Swazi deputation then petitioned the imperial government in Britain, but it failed, with no changes being made to the land policy. Adding insult to injury, during the deputation's absence special commissioner George Gray[47] went ahead and partitioned the land in accordance with the wishes of the Transvaal government. At a meeting in March 1908, Chief Malunge, one of the minor Swazi chiefs, angrily complained: 'We know the ... Commissioner is at work but we have not agreed to it and we are not satisfied. It is Government work and we are not in it ... We only think it is being done because we are a different race.' Then he emphatically declared: 'The land is ours.'[48]

Some months later, on 29 December 1908, Gray published a report that totally disregarded the concerns of the Swazi people. They would only be allocated a third of the land. The report was met with widespread condemnation, but still Gray insisted that he had selected 'the most fertile portions' of the land for the Swazi. He argued that if the land was judged by its capacity to produce food, 'the value of the portions awarded to the Swazis as native area would be greater in value than the remainder of the country'. This was mere sophistry, since the central issue was the extent of the land taken from the people. The Swazi people needed the land for both residential and agricultural purposes. However, the fate of the people was sealed, and Swaziland would be governed by the ubiquitous and iniquitous concession system. That is, until Seme attempted to use the courts to upend the entire land tenure system of Swaziland, and to win back some ground for the Swazis. The case Seme took on presented a challenge to the legality of the very proclamations that underpinned and formalised the concession system. The final word would be spoken by the highest court in the British Empire – the Privy Council.

Sobhuza appeals to the Privy Council

While the British government may have believed that the land conflict was resolved by the Order in Council of 1906, the issue was in fact postponed. Shortly after his admission as an attorney, Seme established contact with Queen Labotsibeni, grandmother of Sobhuza II, through the agency of Richard Msimang. Seme would use that relationship to obtain funding to found a newspaper, *Abantu-Batho*. While some have suggested that this was intended to be an 'ANC mouthpiece',[49] this is not borne out by its content. Rather, the picture that emerges is one that broadly reflects black life in an era where race discrimination became official state policy. While there was manifest urgency in the dismantling of the racist order, ordinary black people went on with their day-to-day lives, holding on to dreams and aspirations. Stories about love, marriage and children often displaced politics from the front pages. Sports, leisure and social life were also important to people. The newspaper's role in the promotion of literature is often forgotten: Samuel Edward Krune Mqhayi's evocative poem *Ukutshona kuka Mendi* was published in 1926. Nontsizi Mgqwetho, the sole female Xhosa poet of the early twentieth century to commit her work to writing burst onto the national scene in the pages of *Abantu-Batho*.[50] The finding was in part the consequence of Seme's relationship with the royal family. As it solidified, he began to act as its legal advisor. A pressing problem was how to extricate the Swazi people from the unfair consequences of the concessions. Soon, a case presented itself to Seme: it hinged on interpretation of the terms of the concession agreements.

Deputations, representations and petitions

Seme had already earned his stripes in being party to deputations, representations and recourse to the British government. By 1921 he was ready to assist the Swazi royal family. At issue were long-standing disputes about the extent to which the king of Swaziland could exercise territorial sovereignty over the land. Several British proclamations and orders in council had severely restricted the ability of the Swazi king to exercise full control over the land. Not only was the king unable to exercise his powers, the Swazi people themselves were subject to the extremely precarious land tenure system. Especially problematic was the Order in Council of 1903. Under that order, the rights and powers of the Transvaal had by conquest passed to the British government. Further, under the Foreign Jurisdiction Act of 1890, the British government extended the jurisdiction of the Transvaal government over Swaziland. Revenues collected in Swaziland would be paid to the

Transvaal. Any appeals from Swaziland would be dealt with in the Transvaal. Lord Milner, acting in accordance with the Swaziland Order in Council of 25 June 1903, had issued a proclamation in terms of which all the laws of the Transvaal applied to Swaziland, which would be governed as if it were an extension of the Transvaal. Although there would be several later versions, the 1903 Order in Council was still essentially applicable in the 1920s. Sobhuza, having come of age, now wished to assert his authority, not only in relation to the territory of Swaziland, but vis-à-vis the British government. Seme was brought in to assist, and on 29 August 1921 he drew up a petition on behalf of the king of Swaziland. It called for the withdrawal of the Swaziland Order in Council of 1903, and the repeal of the proclamation that cancelled the king's private revenue concession and limited his control over the revenue and expenditure of the Swazi nation. Finally, the petition called for the recognition of the authority of Sobhuza as king of Swaziland, both within and outside of the territory. This was a radical stance. Swaziland was no longer willing to accept a position of subservience to the British government. It wanted autonomy and independence. It now viewed the actions of the British government differently. While at the beginning the British government had served as protector to the people of Swaziland, it had now assumed control of the land, the resources and the political authority of Swaziland. This had to stop – as Seme put it, the protector had become the usurper.[51]

On 19 December 1921, a local British representative, Arthur Frederick, replied. None of the demands contained in the petition would be entertained. Moreover, Sobhuza II could not refer to himself as 'King of Swaziland', as the appropriate title was 'Paramount Chief'. As such, it was hoped that in future correspondence no references to 'King' would be used. The battle lines were drawn. Not only were the requests rejected, Sobhuza had to be put in his place. For Seme and his clients, the British response did not signal the end of the matter. It simply highlighted the arduous road ahead. First, it was decided that an audience with the British government was more appropriate than a letter addressed by a representative in Swaziland. To this end, on 30 May 1922, Seme addressed a further petition to the resident commissioner in Swaziland. He asked for permission to send a deputation to England, accompanied by its advocates and attorneys. The petition repeated the demands of the Swazi royal family, with Seme ignoring Frederick by defiantly referring to Sobhuza as king of Swaziland. An audience was eventually granted, and on 22 December 1922, Seme, together with the king and members of his family, travelled to the United Kingdom.

The Aborigines' Protection Society, under the leadership of Ellis Ashmead-Bartlett and Lord Buxton, hosted the Swazi delegation and facilitated its meetings. On 29 January 1923, the deputation met with King George V at Buckingham Palace. There, Sobhuza pledged loyalty to the British government, but no further discussion took place. The matter would be attended to by the colonial office, which would in turn advise King George on an appropriate course of action. That meeting was held two days later. Sobhuza was curtly informed that he was a paramount chief 'of a British possession'. No recognition or autonomy would be granted to him as king. Accordingly, the proclamations would not be rescinded, and the applicable laws contained sufficient safeguards for the interests of the people of Swaziland. The British government, it was pointed out, had paid due attention to the report of the South African Native Affairs Commission. Its recommendations, which carried 'great weight', should reassure Sobhuza 'that the rights and interests of the natives of Swaziland would be protected as adequately under the Union Government of South Africa as they are now'.[52] The matter was at an end, and the wishes of the Swaziland deputation would not be accommodated. Seme had tried the non-confrontational route, but failed. He would now have to consider whether to persist with petitions, or to adopt a more aggressive stance. Since diplomacy had failed, the solution seemed to be litigation.

In 1925, Seme took on a case relating to the land issue: *Sobhuza v. Allister M. Miller and Others*. In a concession granted under the late King Mbandzeni, on 26 July 1889, John Thorburn and Frank Watkins were granted exclusive grazing, agricultural and planting rights for fifty years, with the right of renewal at an annual rental of £50. They agreed to respect all prior existing rights, and not to interfere with the rights of the native subjects of Swaziland. The king undertook to protect the concessionaires in the exercise of their rights under the agreement. A problem arose when Thorburn and Watkins began to evict Swazis from the land. The person who had negotiated the concession on their behalf was one Allister Miller, who doubled as an advisor to King Mbandzeni, and it was he who carried out the evictions. He had been asked to do this by Thorburn and Watkins, as the concessionaires. In his argument, Seme did not attack the evictions *per se*. He considered that the problem was a foundational one: it concerned the rights and entitlements of Sobhuza and the Swazis over land administered through the concession system. It had to be decided whether, on a proper interpretation of the applicable proclamations, the land was properly considered Crown land or whether the king of the Swazis had authority over the land. Seme's argument was that concessionaires had no right to evict a native Swazi from the land. The rights of native Swazis to occupy the land predated the arrival of whites. The concessions could not trump the rights of Swazis. If the court accepted the arguments, the radical proposition would effectively restore the full and unqualified entitlement of Swazis to occupy, exploit and benefit from the land. Most significantly, it would secure and entrench their tenure of the land. When the matter was presented before the Special Court of Swaziland, with Seme representing Sobhuza and his people, the argument was wholly rejected. The court held that the combined effect of the orders in council passed on 25 June 1903 and 2 November 1907 meant that

> [t]he ownership of the land had passed to the Crown, and that the effect of this
> was to extinguish any rights of use and occupation that were in the natives;
> and that the documents and circumstances showed that it was intended to
> extinguish all such rights. As a matter of fact, the natives were given instead sole
> and exclusive rights over one third of the land included in the concession and
> the concessionaires had been given such rights over the remaining two-thirds.

From the Swazi perspective, this was a questionable conclusion. In their view, it was not the case that native rights over the land, including their right to occupy and benefit from the land, were extinguished when the king concluded the concessions. Quite the contrary. The clause that concessionaires would respect existing rights was protection against interference with Swazi land use. Seme suggested an appeal. For him, the issue was not simply whether there was a reasonable prospect of success. There was a deeper concern: freedom. Writing to Locke on 10 June 1925, he mentioned his 'dream of trying to set my country free', and drew a connection between the goal of liberation and the law: 'The merit of the struggle is too deeply involved into legal phraseology.' This was in recognition of the fact that the use of the law was central to the struggle for freedom. Legal terms could be used to advance the struggle for freedom. Though Swaziland was a protectorate, this did not imply that the British government had full rights, 'either of property or of sovereignty'. Swaziland was suffering negative financial consequences: 'For instance, every money there is done under the authority granted by the Swazi King but we don't get the money for these royalties.' Swaziland had been guaranteed independence in 1881, and in 1912 it had asked for protectorate status to prevent encroachments on its land, but now, as Seme pointed out, 'owing to the discoveries of gold etc. we fear that the protector wants to become the usurper'.

'The notion of individual ownership is foreign to native ideas'
Seme's arguments underpinned the appeal petition to the Privy Council, which gave its ruling on 15 April 1926. The question, it noted, to be answered is: 'what is the meaning of a protectorate?' Relying on an earlier judgment,[53] the Privy Council noted that 'a manifestation by Orders in Council of the intention of the Crown to exercise full dominion over lands which are unallotted is sufficient for the establishment of complete power'. As 'an act of state', this was a 'method of peacefully extending British dominion'; as such, it was 'unquestionable'. Then, in an analysis of land rights, it held that 'the notion of individual ownership is foreign to native ideas. Land belongs to the community and to the individual.

The title of the native community generally takes the form of a usufructuary right, a mere qualification of a burden on the radical or final title of whoever is sovereign.' Significantly, the right of usufruct, or land use, 'may be extinguished by the action of the paramount power which assumes possession or the entire control of the land'.

In light of these arguments, the conclusion was predictable. But the question remained: who had sovereignty over Swaziland? According to the court, sovereignty over the territory of Swaziland was assigned to the Transvaal government, which was a British colony. By extension, the Swaziland territory was under the sovereign control of the British government. The argument put forward by Seme 'that the Crown has no powers over Swaziland, except those which it had under the conventions and those which it acquired by the consent of the South African Republic' was, accordingly, 'impossible to maintain'.[54]

For Seme's client, this was a double blow. First, evictions and the confinement of Swazis to overcrowded spaces while whites exploited much of the land, could not be prevented. Second, the sovereign status of Swaziland, which until then had been ambiguous and therefore politically negotiable, was now confirmed in a judgment of the highest court in the British Empire. Swaziland had lost all territorial and political sovereignty. It was a British possession. Its king was merely an extension of the British Empire. The case ended in courtroom defeat, but it also ended in acrimony between lawyers and clients. Senior counsel retained by Seme were not paid, and Seme's own invoices remained unpaid for a substantial period. Litigation ensued – this time against Sobhuza and Seme. Counsel that had been briefed in the matter instituted civil proceedings to recover their fees. Both Seme and Sobhuza initially opposed the proceedings, but subsequently they decided to raise money from donations of the long-suffering Swazis.

Although the case was lost, there were some notable successes. The question of Swaziland's sovereignty had been brought to the attention of the British public and its political class. And among the Swazis themselves, a new political awareness was emerging. Any hope that the British government would place their interests first had proven to be baseless. If Swaziland wanted political self-determination, its citizens would have to fight for it. Seme had also learnt some lessons, and though he had lost the case, he had gained valuable experience. He would now turn to the land struggles of South Africa. After making himself available for election in the ANC, he was able, as president, to appear on behalf of Africans in government forums, including commissions of inquiry. One of the most important of these was the Native Economic Commission, which began in 1930. Seme, who was now both lawyer and politician, would be the voice of the ANC.

'Equal rights to all civilised men'
Seme's testimony at the Native Economic Commission reveals the contradictions of the man. Discriminatory legislation must be scrapped, he proclaimed. If this were done, it would introduce a spirit of healthy competition among all races and sections of society. 'The whites would be told that they must qualify for the highest citizenship and for ultimate freedom.' Then, in an apparent criticism of what he referred to as 'native agitators', Seme argued that, by creating equality and removing discriminatory legislation, the case of the agitators 'would have its bottom completely knocked out'. It is possible that Seme was pandering to the white commissioners, yet his ambivalence about equality shines through in the following: 'Equal rights for all civilised men should be the goal of all legislation in this country.' As things stood, equal rights applied to a select few – 'all civilised men'. His point of reference was the United States, a country where 'discriminating legislation is illegal'. In that country, he argued, black people had developed their own schools and universities, and this created racial harmony because it eliminated competition between black and white. Seme's focus was, nevertheless, on the removal of discriminatory legislation, which, he argued, was doing South Africa more harm than good. For example, by making it criminal for black people to buy, distribute and consume alcohol in particular areas, the law had 'created a notorious class of criminals'. He tried to persuade the commissioners that, 'within a stone's throw of Marshall Square [a police station], no native is short of bottle [*sic*], Sunday or no Sunday' – the law had clearly failed.

The effects on labour of the Masters and Servants Act was also closely scrutinised. Seme submitted that the Act criminalised ordinary employment disputes, and that many magistrates who were property owners themselves were racially biased. The Act was harmful in that 'it interferes with freedom of contract between master and servant and, therefore, it interferes with the progress and prosperity of the country'. On farms, well-paid workers tended to be more productive, which in turn created a harmonious working relationship. As such, the law itself was not an instrument of productivity, which was attributable rather to economic circumstances. The problems on farms, he noted, should be understood in the context of the 1913 Natives Land Act. Seme went on to argue that, from his perspective, 'the court policy to follow [was] to encourage the native to own property wherever possible'. Doing so would encourage enterprise. And concerning influx control, rather than protecting white residents, it was creating a class of homeless black people. To avoid this, property-owning Africans should be permitted in urban areas. This would, furthermore, inspire 'other natives' and promote enterprise. The apparently incredulous chairman of the commission then enquired whether, 'in a country with people on different levels of civilisation', discriminatory legislation might not be reasonable. Seme's reply was frank: the correct approach was not to create discriminatory legislation, but to ensure that there were 'equal rights'. Still not satisfied, the chairman asked, 'You mean, we ought to aim at a condition under which discriminating legislation will not be required?' Simply and emphatically, Seme repeated, 'yes, will be unnecessary. If that principle is accepted by Parliament and opinion throughout the country, it will help to clear public feeling'. Pressed further on whether discriminatory legislation was necessary 'at present', Seme appeared to cede ground: 'I do realise at present there is a need for some discrimination to be made; but it is this present spirit that I am against.' Parliament was not moving towards the creation of equal rights for all, but in the opposite direction. The solution was not more discrimination. A practical step towards the attainment of equality was the extension of the franchise to Africans. But the chairman remained doubtful, suggesting that, despite their right to vote, African Americans hardly used the franchise. Seme's retort was that blacks living in the American North did in fact use their right to vote because they were as advanced as their white counterparts.

The difficulty in the American South was not the extension of the franchise *per se*, but its qualifications – which should not focus on race or skin colour but on factors such as education or property ownership. Seme was then asked to make a proposal about 'a sort of differentiation or discrimination' that would be acceptable 'so that people living on a lower level of civilisation should not con-tinually be undercutting people who are living on a higher level of civilisation'. Ignoring the bait, Seme replied that the mischief arose from laws which create the environment where an 'average policeman' believes that 'the native is some-thing below a human'. For this, Seme directly blamed Parliament, 'because it does not recognise for the natives the ordinary human right'.

On the question of distribution, he said that this should be done fairly. If black people were allowed sufficient land, that would go a long way towards a resolution of their grievances. When asked what he meant by 'sufficient' land, he replied that there should be sufficient land available for Africans to live on. The land should be partitioned, particularly because Africans outnumbered white people. There was no reason, as suggested by the commission, why this was not possible. Despite the fact that land had been taken by force, Seme did not envis-age that it should be given back 'gratis'. Instead, 'Parliament should say that the native can, through his own enterprise, be allowed to purchase up to his own half; it should not be given to him gratis, but it should be open to him, and not to restrict him to one tenth'. Discriminatory legislation not only restricted blacks from working freely, it also restricted the economic freedom and pros-perity of the country because it prevented ordinary commerce between Africans and Europeans. Seme said that this was 'very unprofitable', and declared, 'that is why I really am against it'. He did not accept the allegation that Africans were not making proper use of the land, since tribal land differed from land that was individually owned. He gave a number of examples where Africans had purchased farms and were making optimum use of the portions available to them. The problem, as he saw it, was in communal areas, which were often overcrowded. In such areas there was a need for the regulation of settlement and agricultural use of the land. As far as farmland was concerned, land use was the same, whether the farm was European-owned or African-owned. Indeed, experience had shown him that success depended on government support of the farmer. If the same privileges were extended to African farmers, he could not see why they would not succeed. Seme was critical of the government's system of tribal ownership, which stunted progress. Individual tenure was more conducive to growth, and he advocated a system of private ownership of agricultural land.

The rapid expansion of squatter areas in the towns was a result of land shortage. The solution was to build townships, where land could be purchased on an individual title basis. But instead, the government wished to preserve the towns and cities for white settlement. The chairman then raised an issue of concern to white South Africa: the race ratio. In America, he argued, 'there is about one black man to ten whites, whereas here there are more than three black men to one white'. If blacks were allowed to compete freely with whites, would that not spell doom for the white man? But Seme had no patience with this and replied, 'Well, if the inefficient white man does not help the country, he should be made to feel that he should pull himself up.' And if the argument was that discrimination was intended to protect inefficiency, then it should be removed because by removing it one would encourage efficiency. The argument was now turned on its head. In apparent agreement, the chairman then noted that the Land Bank gave white farmers 'money for nothing', to which Seme replied 'quite so'.

Seme questioned the economic logic of legislation that reserved certain occupations for whites: their labour was expensive, and, unlike the African, they refused to do menial tasks:

> The native, I think, is a better driver of the lorry – he will do more of the work of a driver than a white man will; the white man will require a boy to assist him, whereas the native driver alone will do all that is necessary; he will do the loading and offloading and all that; he will not ask for so many petty considerations.

The commission probed Seme regarding 'the fear of the Europeans' that Africa would 'swamp their civilisation'. Seme rejected the idea by arguing that Africans 'are attracted by civilisation and they improve themselves according to European standards; it is not vice versa; the white people do not revert to the native standard'.

It was the other way around, he said. Africans had become consumers of European products. Social and economic integration would not result in the dissipation of European culture, but rather in the marginalisation of African culture. Blacks would simply be 'greater consumers'. The fear of racial mixing was therefore baseless.

An issue that then arose concerned squatting. Seme argued for the repeal of the relevant laws, and went on to explain the practical implications of squatting:

> Each farmer is allowed to have five cows on his farm and he gets a certain class of labour from those natives. Now, so long as he sees many natives, he has no anxiety; he knows he will be able to live comfortably and he does not exert himself. Now, at the same time, he does not consider the comfort and the interests of the particular natives concerned; all that he desires is that they should be there and within call.[55]

Ever since the land dispossessions of the late nineteenth century, with their accompanying violence, 'squatting' had become rife. Across the country there were laws regulating such settlement, but it persisted. At its heart was government policy that prohibited blacks from owning land. Such prohibitions placed Africans living on farms at the mercy of farm owners. It became the norm that dispossessed Africans served as labourers for the land owners – hence the emergence of 'labour tenants' as a distinct category of farm dwellers. It was this practice that Seme decried. It encouraged indolence among the farmers, he argued, and it exploited workers. Seme called for the abolition of labour tenancy, an evil associated with squatting. No one should pay with their labour. Workers should be paid in cash or in kind. Where payment was in kind, 'there should be a definite cash basis, that [the farmer] will allow each native to plough so much land, the value of which will be so much in cash, or, if it is a beast, of such and such a value'. To prevent worker abuse, Seme proposed the registration of labour contracts. The notion that African workers were unwilling to sign contracts was false. They were willing to do so, provided that, in the negotiation of contracts, they were represented, so as to prevent workers from being cheated of their labour. The registration of contracts also served the purpose of monitoring and enforcement. The native commissioner's office generally refused to entertain complaints from farmworkers if they were unable to produce written contracts of service.

While it is clear that Seme's stature as a lawyer gave him unique access to structures of power, it is also the case that his notion of equality was restricted to the 'civilised' few. With the passing of a new law in 1927, the impact on individuals worsened as government was empowered to banish its political opponents. Seme took on a case that would become one of the most publicised of the era.

'Administrative exile'

The provisions of the Native Administration Act of 1927 included the draconian power to 'administratively exile' any African from any part of the country to any place in the country determined by the authorities. The power to banish has its origins in the Natal Code of Native Law, 1891, which was introduced on the dubious grounds that 'savages' could not be controlled by 'civilised law'.[56] The code entrenched the role of the governor of Natal as the supreme chief who 'exercised all political power over Africans in Natal'. He was able to rule by proclamation, with Africans having no recourse to the judicial process. In terms of section 37, the governor could, 'when deemed in the general public good, remove … any native from any part of the Colony or location to any part of the Colony or location, upon such terms and conditions as he may decide'. It was expected that the institution of the supreme chief would accustom Africans to colonial rule and also provide the government with a convenient and flexible administrative instrument. The president of the Transvaal was granted similar powers, enabling the arbitrary displacement of Africans residing in that province from their homes.

The system of banishment or administrative exile was not uniquely South African. In *Siberia and the Exile System*, George Kennan describes the 'administrative process' that he observed in 1891:

> The obnoxious person may not be guilty of any crime … but if in the opinion of the local authorities, his presence in a particular place is 'prejudicial to public order' or 'incompatible with public tranquillity' he may be arrested without warrant, may be held from two weeks to two years in prison, and may then be removed by force to any other place within the limits of the empire and there be put under the police surveillance for a period of from one to ten years.[57]

This system, often applied without trial or sentencing, was used against anyone perceived to be a political opponent of Tsar Nicholas I. One of its most famous victims was Fyodor Dostoevsky, who in 1849 was exiled to Siberia, and later recorded his prison experiences in *The House of the Dead* (1862). After visiting Siberia, Anton Chekhov described the appalling situation of exiles:

> The majority of them are financially poor, have little strength, little practical training and possess nothing except their ability to write, which is frequently of absolutely no use to anybody. Some of them commenced by selling, piece by piece, their shirts of Holland linen, their sheets, their scarves and handkerchiefs and finish up, dying in fearful penury.[58]

In South Africa, the Native Administration Act expanded the reach of the Natal Code of Native Law to apply to the whole country. Section 24(1) of the Act provided the governor-general with the despotic power to 'define and extend his own powers without any limits, and without going to Parliament'. He could also restrict the power of the courts to interfere in any of his decisions, thereby establishing an immense field of administrative decision-making that operated outside the jurisdiction of the courts. Tielman Roos, minister of justice at the time, defended the logic behind the provisions: 'Detribalised and exempted natives ... in many cases are the principal agitators in South Africa today. If you have the power to remove them from the one place where they do mischief to a place where they do not do mischief what a useful provision that would be.'[59]

Not all white politicians endorsed the powers of banishment, however. The member of Parliament for Tembuland, Thomas Payne – after whom the Mthatha township of KwaPayne is named – stated that it was 'grossly unfair that anyone should have the power to order a man to leave Cape Town for Durban, and that man should have no appeal'. And Deneys Reitz, a former Boer commando who founded a law firm, objected on the grounds that such power amounted to a suspension of *habeas corpus*. A prominent African objector was academic Z.K. Matthews, who objected on the grounds that the power of banishment was a political instrument intended to quell criticism.

One such victim was Mpafuri, who was exiled in terms of section 5(1)(b) of the Act. This section gave the governor-general the power 'whenever he deems it expedient in the general public interest' to 'order the removal of any tribe, or portion thereof or any native from any place to any other place within the Union upon such conditions as he may determine'. In *R. v. Mpafuri* it was argued on Mpafuri's behalf that the order could not be obeyed because it did not specify where he should be relocated to. The court agreed. While not disturbing the essential parameters of the Act, it nevertheless held that a valid management order should specify 'the place to which such removal is ordered'. Because the banishment order failed to do this, Mpafuri had been wrongly convicted. The judges were critical of the provisions of the Act, remarking that the Act could be 'despotically used by the Governor-General ... it is a matter which is entirely in his own discretion and he may exercise his discretion on informal evidence which is placed before him and not on such evidence as adduced in a court of law.'

Despite such criticisms, the government continued to exercise its power of administrative exile. But it was not until *Mpanza v. The Minister of Native Affairs and Others* that the loopholes in the provisions of the Act would be exposed and exploited. Prior to that, the attitude of the Supreme Court was that it was not up to the courts to decide the reasonableness or otherwise of the orders of the governor-general. It was enough that they had been issued in accordance with the provisions of the Act. The prevailing judicial attitude held that courts should not be concerned with personal hardships caused by application of the law. Their role was limited to applying the terms of the law as they found it. The case of *Mabi and 5 Others* v. *The Minister of Native Affairs and Others* exemplifies this approach. In 1935, Mabi and five others were served with orders banishing them from Rustenburg to various other places. When they refused to comply, they were charged under section 5(2) of the Act, which provided that any 'native who neglects or refuses to comply with' an order of banishment was guilty of a criminal offence and liable on conviction to a fine or to imprisonment for any period not exceeding three months.

Under section 5(3), the Act granted the power to any magistrate, native commissioner or assistant native commissioner upon the conviction of any person charged under section 5(2) to 'take all such steps as may be necessary to effect the removal in terms of the order'. It was argued on behalf of Mabi and the others that they were being banished without compensation, and to areas where there was neither accommodation nor water. It was unreasonable to simply banish them to any place, including being dumped in an open veld. The government, however, submitted that if the order was lawful it could not be invalidated on grounds of unreasonableness. Judge Fisher accepted that the banishment order could produce considerable harm to Mabi and his colleagues. But the terms of the Act were clear: they conferred almost unlimited discretion, and the court was not entitled to interfere with an order solely on the grounds of unreasonableness or hardship. It was then argued that there was a legal presumption that rights could not be taken away without compensation, and laws should be interpreted to promote individual liberty. Fisher shot this down too, and essentially washed his hands of the matter, by holding that:

> The court was always very astute to uphold these matters but we are not enti-
> tled on that account solely to override the unequivocally expressed intention
> of the legislature that the Governor-General should act in this manner. If the
> legislature had committed an injustice to the appellants and inflicted upon
> them hardship, the courts could do nothing about it.

Another case involved Sofasonke Mpanza, who resided in Orlando township; by 1944 it had become overpopulated with many people being drawn to the Witwatersrand. There was insufficient housing, and so the newcomers occupied vacant municipal land where they built informal housing using 'sticks, sacking, old tins, and maize stalks'. They were soon joined by 'thousands of other homeless persons [who] came to join them from other parts of the reef. Thus, was shanty town born.'[60] Mpanza became a leader of these people. His personal story appeared in the *African Sunrise* of March 1946:

> I, Sofasonke Mpanza, born May 15, 1889 … had many blows in my youthful days. At the age of 18 in 1908 I started working as an interpreter and clerk in a solicitor's office in Camperdown in Natal. In 1912 I got into serious trouble and was imprisoned for fraud. In 1914, while under the influence of strong drink, I committed murder and was sentenced to death, but was reprieved.
>
> In 1918 I had a vision: was converted to the Lord in the Cinderella Prison, Transvaal, and was born again. I began to testify for the Lord. I was given permission to preach to the prisoners and to teach a class about the spirit of the new birth and many prisoners were converted. After preaching thus for three years, a new Governor came to that prison and at his instance I was sent to Pretoria and, without any cause on my part, was put into solitary confinement for six months. It was there and then that a feeling of depression came upon me and I was convinced that I should make the Lord's message known to the world. I asked the Governor of the gaol for writing materials and this was my prayer at the time: 'O Lord, if I am given permission to write this book I will understand that I am sent by you. Be with me Lord.'
>
> I was given materials to write and I sat down and wrote. In 1927, after thirteen years imprisonment I was released on parole and placed with a Swiss Mission in Pretoria as a teacher. I served for three years as an Evangelist in that congregation under a devoted white missionary, a great believer, the Rev. P. Dourquin. I had a happy life there. I preached with success at the Mental Hospital, Leper Hospital and many other places, such as the Railway Location, Pretoria, Lady Selborne, etc. In 1930 I came to Bertrams and taught in Mr Light's private school. I remained here until the place was demolished.

Mpanza was a charismatic figure, whose followers regarded him as a prophet. They bought into his narrative about Godly visions and being the messenger of the Lord. His troubles with the law, which landed him in prison in the first instance, were forgotten. Now, he would lead them in their struggles against the authorities. 'Prophet' Mpanza had come to the attention of the Orlando residents by outmanoeuvring the local leaders of the ANC, who were perceived to be timid and unwilling to engage in direct confrontation with the government. These leaders included Dr Alfred Xuma, who had been president of the ANC until his removal in 1944. The residents of the settlement called themselves Sofasonke – we die together – and subsequently Mpanza organised them into the Sofasonke Party.[61] Even though the municipality had begun to tackle the problem of homelessness, it did not remove the residents. Nevertheless, Mpanza became a target for criminal prosecution as he was perceived to be influencing the residents. And so, on 6 February 1946, the governor-general issued an order pursuant to section 5(1)(b) of the Native Administration Act requiring Mpanza to 'remove himself from Orlando, Johannesburg, within three days of the service of the order to betake himself to the farm Coldplace in the district of Ixopo, Natal, and to reside at a place to be indicated by the Magistrate'.

He was further ordered not to leave Coldplace without the written permission of the secretary for native affairs. The order was served on Mpanza on 11 February 1946, but he refused to comply with it. Criminal charges were then brought under section 5(2) of the Act, and on 25 February 1946, he was convicted. Two days later, the native commissioner of Johannesburg issued an order stating that the police were authorised to 'immediately upon sight hereof ... take the said James Sofasonke Mpanza into custody and forthwith remove him under escort in terms of the said order of his excellency the Governor-General to the place indicated therein'.

Mpanza was put on the train to Natal on 28 February 1946 at 3:40 p.m. That afternoon, word reached Seme about Mpanza's relocation to Natal. Urgent papers were prepared seeking the immediate return of Mpanza to Johannesburg, pending an appeal against the removal order of the governor-general. Seme argued on behalf of Mpanza that the removal order could not be executed while there was a pending appeal. In reply, the state contended that the administrative act of removal or banishment from a home depended on a conviction. The court was therefore urged to assume that such orders would be made only in cases of great urgency, and it could not have been foreseen that the delay of an appeal might intervene between the date of the conviction and the date of the possible removal. But the court rejected this argument as irrelevant, pointing out that it was, moreover, fundamentally flawed. What would happen, the court asked, 'where a person has been removed, and thereafter an appeal against which his conviction succeeds?' In the absence of a convincing answer, the court stated that it could not assume that the legislature 'intended to lay down that the administrative machinery of forcible removal could be set in motion and carried into effect on a bad conviction'. It unequivocally declared that 'to hold this would be to fly in the face of common sense'. In any event, the court stated, the steps of interfering with personal liberty, forcible removal from one's home and business, and compulsory residence 'in some possibly remote place – in this case on a farm with an uninviting name of Coldplace in Natal – is a matter of the very gravest importance'. Bearing in mind these considerations, it would not be enough that a technical conviction is made. A full appeal had to be entertained before the order could come into operation. Mpanza was then granted a temporary reprieve. He would not be banished to Coldplace until such time as his appeal was decided.

On appeal, Seme found the main loophole in the state's case: it had wrongly assumed that Mpanza fell within the provisions of the Native Administration Act. But, properly interpreted, the Act did not apply to every African person. It only applied to those subject to 'native law'. Some Africans were excluded from the purview of native law either because of where they lived or due to exemption. If an African person was exempt from the application of the Act, the governor-general could not make an order of banishment applicable to them. Mpanza lived outside a native area, hence the Act did not apply to him. The argument was upheld. This was a blow to the government, which had hoped to use the provisions of the Act against 'detribalised and exempted natives'. Now the court had found in explicit terms that the Act could not be used against its very targets. Not only was this an important victory for Mpanza, it was a memorable piece of legal ingenuity on the part of Seme. Now, the government was forced to reconsider the entire scheme of the Act. It would take another two years before amendments were passed covering all Africans, including those living in 'native areas' and those in townships. Significantly, Seme had shown that loopholes in the legal system could be used to expand the liberties of individuals. The increasingly authoritarian government resulted in many people relying on the law. In turn, this created a large client base for Seme. But since there was only a handful of lawyers, the practice eventually became unmanageable. At the same time, certain cases presented a similar line of enquiry, and Seme resorted to a more systematic and cost-effective way of dealing with large numbers of clients similarly affected by the draconian laws.

The strategy of the 'test case'
The notion of the 'test case' is entrenched in human rights litigation. In the 1980s, the Legal Resources Centre, under its senior counsel, Arthur Chaskalson, used the strategy of the test case in a range of contexts. An example that is still cited as a model in human rights studies is *Komani N.O.* v. *Bantu Affairs Administration Board, Peninsula Area*.[62] It would be useful to give a brief overview of the political context of this 1980 case. A central element of the apartheid strategy was to denationalise Africans. What that meant was that Africans would not be citizens of South Africa, but of 'independent homelands' – which were a replication of the reserves established during the colonial era. The aim was to make South Africa a country for white people. But the demands of commerce and industry meant that there was a constant flow of Africans into the cities that were part of South Africa. To control this labour demand and to guarantee the political need to keep Africans out of South Africa, the government introduced influx-control laws. One of these was the Natives (Urban Areas) Act, 21 of 1923. It contained a clause, section 10(1)(a), which obliged a person from the homelands to seek the

permission of the authorities to live and work in the cities. Males, the backbone of the labour economy, were usually granted their section 10 permits. The problem was their wives. They too had to obtain permission from the government if they wished to visit their husbands in urban areas. The system worked on the basis that an employee – usually a man – would be granted permission to reside in the city for a period of twelve months, at the end of which he would be obliged to return to the homelands. The problem in the Komani case concerned a set of regulations implemented purportedly to give effect to influx-control legislation.

Arthur Chaskalson, in discussion with his then attorney Geoff Budlender, was consulted by a non-governmental organisation that focused on human rights, the Black Sash. Chaskalson was hesitant about the merits of the case. Nevertheless, he proposed that it be taken on as a 'test case'. This would enable them to test the impact of the regulations. Moreover, the case would enable them to gauge the views of the Appellate Division, at the time the highest court in South Africa, on 'this sort of litigation and we should take it on even if we were not going to win it'.[63]

The essential facts in the case were that Mrs Komani wanted to visit her husband, but the Labour Bureau rejected her application for a permit. When Chaskalson was briefed to take on the case, it appeared to concern the interpretation of the regulations and the powers of the Labour Bureau. However, as he began working on it, a different aspect emerged. He believed that the regulations could be challenged at source. The regulations were probably unlawful because they were inconsistent with the primary statute. In the end the case succeeded, with the Appellate Division affirming unanimously that the regulations were unlawful. The impact of the case was profound. Not only did it put the newly established Legal Resources Centre on the national and international stage, it set the tone for the judicial dismantling of influx-control regulations. Soon thereafter, in 1983, another case presented itself, run on the same lines and with similar success: *Rikhoto* v. *East Rand Administration Board and Another*.[64]

Such test cases became a strategy for litigation. Yet, what is generally unknown is that more than fifty years before the Komani and Rikhoto cases, black lawyers had already begun to conceptualise, strategise and litigate test cases, with Pixley Seme at the forefront. The circumstances that prompted Seme were not dissimilar to those that confronted Chaskalson and Budlender: in an oppressive legal system, and with limited legal resources, how might the law be used to ensure justice for the greatest number of people? At issue were the provisions of the Natives (Urban Areas) Act of 1923, the very same statute that Chaskalson had to contend with more than half a century later. In August 1930, black people living in the township of Waverley received summonses to appear before the Magistrate's Court for breach of the Urban Areas Act.[65] The charge was that, contrary to the provisions of the Act, they were living in an area designated for European settlement. More than a hundred people were affected. They were introduced to Seme, who agreed to take on their case. A fee of £2 and 10 shillings per head was agreed to. Seme proposed that, since it was likely that the matter would be lost in the Magistrate's Court, an appeal might be necessary to the Transvaal Provincial Division and to the Appellate Division. A fee of £3 per head was agreed to, and the case began on 30 March 1931. One of the accused was Koos Sheshele who, 'being a native, and not being in the *bona fide* employment of the owner, lessee, or occupier of the said land, did wrongfully and unlawfully reside upon or occupy a dwelling on such land'.

Seme acted for the accused. As soon as the trial began, Seme launched an attack on the fundamentals of the charge. Waverley was a township that had been occupied for many years by natives, he began, and then he said, 'Some of the natives residing at Waverley work in Innesdale. The Municipality itself employs a number of natives. We are a native compound.' In those three sentences, Seme exposed the fundamental flaw in the state's case: the charge was that the accused were not in *bona fide* employment of the owner, lessee or occupier of the said land, but nevertheless lived on the land. In pointing out the employment status of the accused, Seme was exposing the perversity of the charge. Not only were the accused in *bona fide* employment, they were employed by the municipality itself. In its reply, the state pointed out that the owner of the land, Mr Moffat, was not the employer of the accused. Seme's retort was that the purpose of the legislation was to prevent squatting. It was therefore sufficient that the accused were in *bona fide* employment, irrespective of whether this employment was provided by the owner of the land. In any case, the accused were *bona fide* and lawful tenants of the owner of the property. If they were committing a criminal offence by residing thereon, the owner was equally guilty of aiding and abetting a criminal offence – as was the municipality. There had in fact been an attempt to prosecute Mr Moffat, though he had been discharged of the crime. When the state pointed out that the accused had not been paying rent, Seme countered by showing that the accused had offered to pay, but Mr Moffat had not collected the money owing to harassment by the police. As such, the failure to collect the rent could not be blamed on the accused. The accused had in any event offered to buy individual stands on the property, but were prevented from doing so by the provisions of the Natives Land Act of 1913, which restricted the ability of black individuals to acquire land in their own names. Ultimately, the state rested its case on the argument that, as long as the accused was not employed by the owner of the property, a criminal offence had been committed under section 6 of the Urban Areas Act.

Seme, however, had a broader argument, which covered an entire class of persons. Section 6 of the Act had no application, he contended. The onus was on the state to prove that the accused had not obtained prior permission from the minister before residing on the property. It had failed to do so, he submitted. Moreover, because his clients had offered to purchase the land, they had to be regarded as prospective purchasers, protected under the schedule to the Natives Land Act. The 1913 Act had been amended in 1936 to include a schedule of land which would be available for purchase by Africans. However, before an African could buy the land, permission had to be granted by the authorities. That there had been delays in obtaining the requisite approvals from the authorities could not be blamed on his clients. These factors, taken cumulatively, meant that criminal conduct could not be proved.

The magistrate ruled that he appreciated the complexity and significance of the case: 'A number of cases have been brought before this court in regard to this property against owner and occupiers, and in October last year an occupier was charged with contravening section 6(1) Act 21 of 1923, as amended. This case was regarded as a test case and a great deal of evidence was taken.' The difficulty, said the magistrate, related to the wording employed by the Act. The ambiguity was caused by the fact that it was not clear whether or not section 6 applied to an instance where there was an existing lease agreement, orally concluded and renewed on an annual basis, or whether it required such lease agreement to be in writing. He then referred to the argument that the municipality, being the employer of some of the accused, had made no provision for a residential area for natives inside the municipal area, and therefore the Urban Areas Act could not be applied strictly. But these arguments were not persuasive, he said. While the magistrate claimed that he did not 'seek to impose any unnecessary hardship on any of' the natives, it was his view that they had been given enough notice to vacate: 'These men have been warned over and over again to leave the place and persist in refusing, and there are still some hundreds of natives living on the farm who have also to be moved.' The magistrate thereafter concluded that the accused were guilty of an offence under the Act, and imposed a fine to be paid forthwith, alternatively imprisonment of five days with hard labour, suspended for one month. As Seme had anticipated, he lost the test case. But the reasoning was woefully inadequate, he advised his clients. An appeal had to be brought.

On 15 June 1931, the Transvaal Provincial Division dismissed the appeal. Judge Krause concluded his judgment with the following significant observation: 'It would appear that the case against the accused was selected as a test case, as there were similar charges against some 30 natives, and it was agreed between the Crown and the accused that the legal points which would be raised and the evidence which would be led should be accepted as against all other accused.' The problem, the judge stated, was that Waverley had been occupied for many years by Africans working at Innesdale – their place of employment had no nearby native location.

Moreover, the Innesdale Municipality had made no provision for the residence of natives under the Urban Areas Act. Despite this, his interpretation of the Act was that it prohibited the occupation of land by natives without the permission of the owner. Because this permission could not be proved owing to the fact that the agreement was verbal, he was driven to the conclusion that the Act had been breached and therefore the accused persons had committed an offence. Nevertheless, the perversity and injustice of the outcome could not be ignored: 'It is true that in respect of the natives in this case the enforcement of the Act might lead to grave hardships and even injustices, and in the circumstances disclosed I have no hesitation in saying that, personally, one has great sympathy with the lot of these unfortunate natives, but the court has to apply the law as it finds it, whatever hardship may result.' He therefore dismissed the appeal, holding that the interpretation of the magistrate was correct, with his colleague, Judge Maritz, concurring.

Many negative consequences followed: the case had brought the municipality such negative publicity that it began assessing the employment of some of the accused, arbitrarily terminating it in certain instances. The owner of the land, Mr Moffat, had been subjected to intense persecution, with the result that he decided to terminate the lease agreements. As such problems mounted, there were increasing disagreements among Seme's clients about whether to proceed with the appeal. And it became clear that Seme was himself not fully available to take the appeal to the Appellate Division, having been elected president of the ANC in 1930, and with many demands on his time from the Swazi king. Unsurprisingly, Seme's clients began to turn on him.

Struck off the roll
Following the dismissal of the appeal by the Transvaal Provincial Division, Seme sought counsel's opinion on prospects of a further appeal.[66] The advice was unfavourable, and he conveyed this to his clients, who were not pleased with the news. But they had lost their employment, and they had no further funds to prosecute the appeal. They then accused Seme of collecting monies ostensibly to run a test case and after two court losses refusing to take on the appeal. Denouncing his clients, Seme refused to further engage with them. But this was a miscalculation, and the decision would cost him dearly. In a letter of demand from an attorney's firm, delivered on 17 July 1931, Seme was informed: 'We are instructed by the native community at Waverley to ask you for a statement of account showing how you have dealt with the monies which they contributed for the conduct of the above matter. They state that they have in all paid you an amount of several hundreds of Pounds.'

The letter went on to complain that Seme's conduct was open to 'the strongest criticism' and he was urged to give the matter immediate attention and to make sure that any overpayment was repaid. But this was not all. The letter accused Seme of negligence. It alleged that he had failed to institute the necessary appeal to the Appellate Division. When his clients approached a different firm of attorneys, by then it was too late, with the prescribed period of three weeks having run out. Seme did not reply to the letter. On 4 August 1931, he was threatened with a referral to the Transvaal Law Society. This prompted an immediate reply, and the very next day Seme responded. He argued that his clients had not instructed him only as an attorney, but also in his capacity as president of the African National Congress. This meant that he had to do more than would ordinarily be required of an attorney:

> I could foresee that the case might not end in the court below and that moreover I should fight their case politically and otherwise. I called them together and explained that I could use influence to reach the authorities politically but that I would require them to provide at least £100 for such expenses. They agreed and some of the money has been paid under this head too but not all. But I used the money for that purpose.

Seme explained that his political intervention included discussions with the minister of police, the provincial departments, the municipality of Innesdale and the Commission on Native Locations. The meeting with the minister took place in Cape Town, and some of the funds were disbursed during that trip. He denied the accusation of negligence pertaining to the lodgement of the appeal with the Appellate Division, and instead pointed the finger at his clients for failing to raise the necessary funds timeously. By this point, however, the relationship between Seme and his clients had hit rock-bottom. They referred him to the Law Society on a charge of unprofessional conduct. Without delay, the Law Society instituted proceedings to have Seme struck off the roll of attorneys.

This was not the first application to have Seme's name struck off the roll. In 1927 the Law Society had tried to have him removed from the roll of practising attorneys on the grounds of a criminal conviction. The first application likewise involved money. Seme had been a central figure in the establishment of the Native Farmers Association in 1913; as previously suggested, its prime object was the acquisition of land in areas designated for native settlement, in order to protect such land from the reach of the Natives Land Act. Soon afterwards, the association acquired some farms in Wakkerstroom in the eastern Transvaal. Its method was simple: the association acquired several farms in its own name. Once the farms were acquired, individual buyers could buy from the association. As its attorney, Seme took responsibility for the subdivision and registration of the properties.

Ndhlosi Manana was one of the individual buyers who deposited money with the association with the intention of acquiring a piece of land. He paid £100, which was handed over to Seme, as the attorney. Manana did not, however, receive the land. When he asked for his money back, it appeared that Seme had used the money for other purposes. A charge of theft was then laid against Seme. In the criminal trial before the Supreme Court, Seme ran his own defence. No dispute of fact was raised concerning the essential elements of the case of *R. v. Manana*. Even though Seme accepted that the money had been paid to him directly, he blamed the association. In the result, Seme was found guilty of theft and sentenced to a period of imprisonment of one year, which was suspended in full; he did not have to serve time in jail. It was those facts which the Law Society used to have him struck off the roll in 1927. In the hearing of the application, Seme was represented by W.P. Schreiner, who argued that the finding of guilt based on the charge of theft was not consistent with the facts. The case of the state had been that the money was paid to Seme to be held in trust for the benefit of Manana. Seme's argument was that the money was paid to the company established by the association and thus the money belonged to the association. This argument was upheld by Judge Greenberg who heard the application for the striking off. He found that it was not in those circumstances proved beyond a reasonable doubt that a crime of theft had been committed. Seme was therefore entitled to an acquittal. On those grounds, the court concluded that the application for his striking off was unwarranted, and as such dismissed it. The intricacies of the law were of no consequence to Manana, who had given money to Seme to acquire land for him. Now, he had neither money nor land. Seme had appeared to be a man who was concerned about black people who were at the receiving end of discriminatory laws. Yet he himself was exploiting the very people he claimed to be representing.

Five years later, on its second attempt at striking Seme off the roll, the Law Society had more conclusive evidence. Tom Ntuli, a resident at Waverley, made a statement under oath implicating Seme in improper conduct. The complaint was that Seme had collected substantial amounts of money, failed to account or provide receipts, had not disbursed the amount either to his correspondents or counsel, and failed to timeously prosecute the application for leave to appeal, all of which resulted in the lapse of the appeal. John Murray filed an affidavit in support of the Law Society's application, in which he confirmed that he had not been paid by Seme, and that he had therefore added Seme's name to a list of blacklisted attorneys. In his answering affidavit, Seme reiterated what had been stated in his correspondence. His mandate was not purely legal. He was asked to use his political standing. This was conveyed to his clients. Some of the funds had been used in connection with the necessary political intervention. Counsel and the correspondent attorneys would have been paid if the clients had raised enough money for the prosecution of the appeal before the Appellate Division. In fact, Seme had a point. In January 1931 he had, in his capacity as president of the ANC, addressed a letter to the minister for native affairs in which he suggested that a practical solution was to declare the township a native area. In his reply, the minister for native affairs pointed to the fact that the prosecutions were necessary to appease the white residents in the neighbouring area:

> Numerous petitions were received from European residents of Villieria and the neighbourhood pointing out that the position at Waverley constituted a source not only of annoyance but of positive danger to themselves and asking for the removal of the natives, while the township owner represented that he was powerless to secure the removal of the trespassers and appealed for government assistance to this end.

The minister had, however, declined the suggestion to intervene. He refused to acquire the property in order to have it converted into a native area.

The case was enrolled for hearing on 22 September 1932. Seme did not appear in court. No explanation was given. The Law Society then moved its application, and it was granted an order finding Seme guilty of 'unprofessional and dishonourable conduct' and conduct 'contrary to the dignities and duties of his office'. His name was duly struck off the roll, and he was prevented from practising as an attorney. He was directed to hand over his certificate of admission as an attorney to the Law Society. A later attempt at overturning the judgment on the grounds that he had not received adequate notice for appearance was turned down. For the next ten years, Seme would be prohibited from practising as an attorney. A career that began with so much promise had ended in ignominy. The test case that promised to usher him into the annals of legal history had, instead, planted the seeds of his downfall. Ten years later, he would, however, pick himself up again: Seme was reinstated as a practising attorney, and his legal career limped on.

The emergence of Anton Lembede

In 1942, the year of Seme's reinstatement, a young lawyer had just completed his LLB degree. His name was Anton Muziwakhe Lembede, and Seme took him on as an articled clerk. Seme had been practising for more than thirty troubled years, and this had taken its toll on him. He needed a partner to run the practice, and together with Lembede he took on some of the most complex and challenging cases of the day. One of those cases was *Albertyn* v. *Kumalo and Others*.[67] It established the principle that the court will come to the relief of one of the parties to an illegal contract where such a course is necessary to prevent injustice or to satisfy the requirements of public policy. Again, the facts raised the question of segregated settlements and the shortage of land for black people. In brief, what transpired was that a Cape coloured man named Albertyn entered into an agreement with an Indian man, Moonshi, to sell various plots of land to natives. There was a fallout between the applicant and Moonshi, with the applicant accusing the latter of engaging in systematic fraud. As for the natives, they had bought plots of land from Moonshi, and could produce deeds of sale and proof of payment of the purchase price. Because of the dispute between the applicant and Moonshi, the applicant asked for the ejectment of all the Africans who had bought property through Moonshi.

The question in court was whether or not the order of ejectment should be granted. The court refused to grant the ejectment order. The law was quite clear that no one was allowed to sell property to a black person when the area on which the property was designated was not designated for native settlement. That would mean that the entire scheme was illegal. But the court was not prepared to grant an ejectment order on that account alone. Since the scheme was fundamentally illegal, the black people who had bought the land did so in good faith and without any knowledge that the scheme might be illegal. They had therefore to receive the benefit of the doubt. As such, the court concluded, while the illegality of the scheme was under judicial consideration, the ejectment order would not be granted.

For young Lembede, this was a significant case. He had spent his years as an articled clerk engaged with the evidentiary material and statements from his clients, the squatters. The ultimate vindication in court gave a different complexion to the uses of law in a politically discriminatory world. One such case was that of *R. v. Miya*,[68] which concerned an ejectment. Miya was born in Tugela, Natal. At the age of six he went to live near Harrismith, where he registered as a taxpayer. Some seven years afterwards, he returned to Tugela. But upon his arrival, and for the sake of political expedience, the native commissioner gave notice ejecting Miya from Tugela and instructing him to return to Harrismith on the grounds that, having lived in Harrismith, he had lost his domicile of origin. But this was a mere smokescreen. Miya was a prominent political figure, and his presence in Tugela was considered undesirable by the authorities. He refused to comply with the order ejecting him from Tugela, and was accordingly criminally charged and convicted, whereupon a fine was imposed. On appeal, it was argued that Miya had never abandoned his domicile of origin. Even though he was in Harrismith out of economic necessity, he had never established a home there, and regularly visited Tugela, where he had a home and kept livestock. The prosecutor's case that the accused had acquired a new domicile and renounced his original domicile was rejected. The case confirmed the practical reality of many Africans, that because of residential segregation, most were compelled to maintain more than one place of residence – in the reserves as well as in the native areas closer to their places of work. For all intents and purposes, they could not be regarded as having abandoned their homes in the reserves when they went to seek employment in urban areas. The year after Miya's case was decided, Lembede suddenly and unexpectedly died. He was only thirty-three years old. He had by that stage signed a partnership agreement with Seme in terms of which he acquired the firm and retained the name Seme and Lembede. By now, Seme's own health was also deteriorating, and three years later, in 1951, he too died.

The memory of Pixley ka Isaka Seme as a founder of the ANC is firmly entrenched. However, it is clear that his contribution to the law, the legal system and to the emergence of black law professionals is considerable. Though he may have stumbled along the way at times, his legacy deserves full recognition. Together with Alfred Mangena, Seme founded the first law partnership of African lawyers. While that did not survive for long, he also founded the second, with Anton Lembede. With the formation of Seme and Lembede, he had planted the seed for the emergence of a new generation of black lawyers. The importance of establishing the law firms showed many aspirant lawyers that, even in conditions which negated and denied a person's very existence – as the dominant race theories of the time attempted to do – it was still possible to follow one's dreams. It was this relentless pursuit of a dream that enabled Seme and his generation to qualify as lawyers, against all odds. However, surrounded by injustices that resulted from white racism, Seme could not afford to focus solely on his legal practice. Hence, he threw himself heart and soul into the struggle for the elimination of the racial political order. Ironically, it was this very decision that precipitated his early demise as a lawyer. And while Seme was a product of his time, advocating for equality among only 'civilised men', it is to his vision that South Africa owes the existence of the ANC, which would continue to conduct the long struggle for racial, social and gender equality. The notion of equality is foundational to the country's legal order, and, as this chapter indicates, when the full history of ideas concerning equality is written, Seme's name will be writ large.

6

The unintended
legacy of King Leopold

The experiment [...] has been carried out very successfully. Friends appreciating [the principal's] efforts are beginning to subscribe liberally for enlarging the Institute so as to accommodate 50 boys. What I have seen of the boys and the teachers impresses me very much. As the latter does not confine itself to teaching them to read and write and to become Christians, but also teaches them to handle tools, until the boys have become skilful in carpentry and blacksmithing, etc.

– H.M. Stanley, 7 July 1891

The King of the Belgians, King Leopold II, is notorious for the genocide of ten million people and the relentless pursuit of spoils such as ivory and rubber in the Congo. For an entire decade he escaped condemnation, resorting to the old European excuse for the pillaging of Africa – civilisation. One of his 'civilising' projects was a little-known school in the obscure town of Colwyn Bay in Wales. The school was called the Congo Institute, though Leopold himself never set foot in Colwyn Bay. Today, more than a hundred years after the closure of the institute, Leopold's presence lingers on in the memory of the living. The school building still stands, though it is now a residential apartment block.[1] At the glass entrance door, a 2008 newspaper report announces the 'historic link' between South Africa and Colwyn Bay. During a visit, Nelson Mandela spoke of his fondness for a former student of the institute, D.D.T. Jabavu, who was later his professor at the University of Fort Hare.[2]

Two other students, George Montsioa and Ngcubu Poswayo, later became barristers at Lincoln's Inn, and went on to practise as attorneys in South Africa. Montsioa served as the first recording secretary of the South African Native National Congress; he was in that role for a limited period before concentrating on his legal practice and becoming involved in the affairs of the royal family of the Barolong, of which he was a member. Poswayo eschewed the political cause altogether. Upon his return to South Africa, he became an advocate of the Supreme Court for a period of three months, before removing his name from the roll of advocates in order to practise as an attorney. His admission as an advocate was in itself significant. Before him, no black South African had been admitted to practise law as an advocate. While the more liberal laws of the Cape allowed him admission to the Bar, they could not protect him from the professional consequences of racism – a fact that had led Henry Sylvester Williams before him to abandon the Bar. As with his colleagues – Seme, Mangena and Msimang – Montsioa was occupied with cases that exposed the precarious position of blacks in relation to the land.

Though Leopold did not found the Congo Institute, he was in many ways a strong influence. The man who established it, William Hughes, had been a Baptist missionary in the Congo during the rule of Leopold in that region. Hughes was determined that the only hope for the Congo was the education of its children into the European way of life. Yet his motive was not to free them from the grip of Leopold and his local enforcers, but to 'civilise' them, thereby liberating them from their 'barbarous' ways. He needed a patron, and so he approached Henry Morton Stanley, Leopold's agent in the Congo, with whom he had become friends. The king was only too happy to oblige: the venture would enable him to continue exploiting people and resources, under the guise of 'civilisation' – a subterfuge that generally underpinned European activities in Africa at the time. Leopold's name appears in most of the annual reports as the founding patron of the institute; he made many promises of financial support, which, typically, were not kept.[3] Despite this, upon hearing of the king's death, on 17 December 1909, the institute paid tribute to him: classes were suspended, and there was a procession and prayers, just as Leopold would have wanted it. His name and his deeds were praised. Among those present were Ngcubu Poswayo and George Montsioa. They may not have known much about the Belgian king's activities in the Congo, but when they returned to South Africa with an education obtained under the aegis of Leopold, they would defy the peculiarities of the colonial experience. The experiences of their forebears in the colonial era, and indeed their own marginalisation in foreign lands, may well have driven them to feel antagonistic towards European peoples. Yet instead they used their knowledge and experience to imagine a new and inclusive world.

Ngcubu Poswayo: All Saints mission station

The story of Ngcubu Poswayo begins at the All Saints missionary school in Ngcobo, a village in the Eastern Cape. The idea to establish the school originated not with missionaries, but with the residents of the village of Nyanga. They approached the Anglican church in Grahamstown to open a mission for their community. Only a few kilometres away, at Clarkebury, there was another mission station run by the Methodists. But Ntshacile Poswayo, the founder of the community of Nyanga and the grandfather of Ngcubu, wanted a separate mission for his people. In the event, the Anglicans obliged after enabling Ntshacile to learn basic English and to read the Bible over a period of about six months. The All Saints mission school opened in 1889. Ngcubu's uncle, Thomas Poswayo, had donated the land, provided labour for the building of the classrooms, as well as funds for school materials and teachers' salaries. The boys in the boarding school stayed free of charge. By 1891, there were twenty-two boarders, including Ngcubu. Five years later, in 1896, a girls' school was opened, with financial contributions from the community of All Saints. In his 1896 annual report, the resident magistrate, Walter Stanford, reported to the government that 'the Qwati section of the Thembu tribe occupying this district have contributed £135 towards the erection of a native girls' training institution to be built at All Saints mission station'. Thus, the education of the Thembu people living at Ngcobo was initiated by the Poswayo family. After completing his studies at the Congo Institute, Ngcubu was tempted to return to his village to take up a teaching position. But he was persuaded by his friend, Montsioa, rather to pursue a career in law.

Ngcubu Poswayo spent three years at Zonnebloem College in Cape Town. While there, he developed an interest in cricket, becoming an effective batsman. He was among the first generation of Africans that played the sport. In 1904, an article appeared in *Imvo Zabantsundu* promoting a school for African children in Colwyn Bay, North Wales, which Poswayo read with interest. On a promotional visit to Natal and the Cape, Hughes had made an impression on a number of students at Zonnebloem. Poswayo, together with fellow student Montsioa, were among the group chosen to study at the Congo Institute.

This was not the first such institute established in Europe for the training and teaching of African children. The first was established in 1828: Don Mazza, a Catholic priest in Verona, established an institute for the Christian education of African girls. In 1832 a similar one was founded for young African boys. Both institutes housed slave children ransomed from Africa.[4] In the Congo, young children were often taken without parental consent and sent to the Institute Des Jeunes Noirs (the Institute for Young Black People), in Malta, to be trained in medicine and taught about Christianity. The Congo Training Institute followed this tradition.

In the Congo, Hughes was in charge of the Bayleston mission station, where a few black children were employed as servants.[5] He decided to set up a school there in 1882; two boys, Kinkasa and Nsakala, became preachers, spreading the gospel among the natives. With his health deteriorating, Hughes was advised to return home, and in September 1895 he left for Wales, together with Kinkasa and another boy from the Congo, Nkanza. By then he had decided to set up the institute and to raise funds. Hughes believed that the only practical way of promoting Christianity in Africa was to train Africans in Europe so that they could then return home and convert other Africans. Soon after its establishment, however, the Congo Institute became an object of ridicule and the target of bitter criticism: 'they have black ones at Colwyn Bay from Africa, whom they will blind and change the colour of the inhabitance of our land.'[6] In Hughes's opinion, there was no need for the teachers to understand the native languages of the students they taught. Also, industrial education was especially important for African children. Reflecting the prejudices of the era, he argued that the 'natives of Africa do not honour work, the men shirk work and despise the work; they generally force the women to do the menial work, fetch water, cultivate the ground, build their huts'.[7]

Hughes outlines his motivation for establishing the institute in a work titled *Dark Africa and the Way Out: or, a scheme for civilizing and evangelizing the Dark Continent*.[8] In this book, he claims that Africa needs evangelising and enlightenment, and that the institute should be based in Europe as 'the African is able to endure both European and African climates better than Europeans'. Africans themselves should spread the gospel, as they will 'naturally have more influence over their own countrymen than foreigners will'. For the project to succeed, African students had to be kept 'away from the surrounding superstitions and evil influences of their people'; they needed to be exposed to the institute's 'high moral, spiritual, and industrial training'. Living in Europe and witnessing the way of life of Europeans would 'create in them a desire to evangelise and civilise their own countrymen'.[9]

Hughes believed in cultural conversion through Christianity, but he also believed in the self-reliance of Africans – as long as it was done along Christian lines. Accordingly, African preachers should be responsible for African churches. In his view, it 'ought to be the first duty of every missionary when he enters a foreign field to look for native preachers to take the place of himself'; this was 'the natural way of giving every country kindred home missionaries'.[10] Perhaps projecting the nationalistic conceptions of the Welsh, Hughes continued: 'The Africans, like every other nationality, desire that their teachers shall come from amongst themselves, and who can blame them for what is reasonable and natural?' He preferred his mother tongue for communicating with God, and he wished the same for Africans. Essentially, Christianity need not negate African beliefs. The two were complementary.

While the institute began as a school for boys, Hughes soon opened it to African girls. The first to be admitted was Ernestina Francis, who had a Congolese mother and a Belgian father. The students spent four or five years studying an industrial apprenticeship before returning to Africa as missionaries, school teachers and tradesmen. The first year was dedicated to learning English; in subsequent years they learnt a trade while focusing also on mathematics, teaching methods and the basics of medicine. Since the school was largely funded from private donations, Hughes was able to promote the school throughout Africa on the basis that it would place no financial burdens on parents. Students were taught trades, becoming wheelwrights, carpenters, printers or blacksmiths. By contrast, the education of female students appears to have been more expansive, as it included mathematics, medical training (which qualified them to become assistant medical missionaries), music, teaching and arts. The institute's annual report of 1909 boasted that it was the only place in the world that could train 'native girl children' to qualify as medical missionaries.[11] The training took place by means of apprenticeship for a specified period, after which they were tested and certified as qualified. The same applied to medicine, where students learnt by assisting doctors. Students were required to write exams, and reports were sent to the committee of the Congo House.

Leopold's 'philanthropy'

In 1878, Stanley entered into an agreement to serve Leopold II as his agent for a term of five years. During this period, the king agreed to raise funds for the Congo Institute. However, Stanley's claim that he was promoting African interests was dubious. When he travelled to the Congo in 1879, Stanley was in fact scouting for territory on behalf of Leopold II. That year, he built outposts and a road along the Congo River. He travelled up and down the river by steamboat, and using a mixture of gifts, deception and brute force, he succeeded in making a number of African chiefs sign away rights to their land. As Hughes later put it, this 'opened up that vast and wealthy country'.[12] In 1885, at the Berlin Conference, Leopold II devised a cunning plan to make the Congo his personal property. The Congo Free State, as it was called, would belong to no European country. Instead, it would be turned into an oasis for free trade. Every European country would be free to enter it and conduct business without any restrictions. But while the European countries were looking away, preoccupied with the new possessions they had gained, Leopold reneged on his promises, one of which was to 'civilise' the barbarian races of the Congo. He did this by sending in a private army of 20 000 men who included Belgians and local Congolese. Equipped with rifles, cannons and machine guns, they enforced the terms of the 'contracts', 'treaties' and 'agreements' that Africans had concluded with Stanley. The Africans were no match for Leopold's army. By 1908, when the true extent of Leopold's atrocities were exposed to the world, ten million Congolese had been killed, tortured, displaced and enslaved in pursuit first of ivory, and later rubber.[13]

Leopold attempted to justify his plunder of the Congo, and argued that he was in fact 'civilising' the Congolese 'heathens'. Stanley was central in providing legitimacy to Leopold's official explanation, and the Congo Institute became a flagship project, validating the king's 'civilising' mission. Its location in the United Kingdom provided it with symbolic value: the British, who were sceptical of Leopold's intentions in the Congo, could now see for themselves the extent of the king's altruism.

It was on 7 July 1891 that Stanley had first written to Leopold, soliciting patronage for the institute:

> Sire, I have been requested to bring to your Majesty's notice the work of Reverend W. Hughes of Colwyn Bay – North Wales.
>
> Mr Hughes was formerly a Baptist missionary at Bayleston on the Congo. Finding that his health suffered greatly in Africa, and yet feeling great interest in Congo natives, he conceived the idea of bringing Congo natives to Wales and educating them there.
>
> The experiment [...] has been carried out very successfully. Friends appreciating his efforts are beginning to subscribe liberally for enlarging the Institute so as to accommodate 50 boys. What I have seen of the boys and the teachers impresses me very much. As the latter does not confine itself to teaching them to read and write and to become Christians, but also teaches them to handle tools, until the boys have become skilful in carpentry and blacksmithing, etc.
>
> I am asked therefore as Mr Hughes' efforts are directed to the improvement of some of your Majesty's subjects, to intercede with your Majesty that he will permit the use of your royal name as patron of the Institution. This does not involve any subscription, but Mr Hughes believes that by your royal patronage it would acquire rank and merit in the eyes of many Christians in his neighbourhood.
>
> I have the honour to enclose for your inspection the last report of the Institute issued by Mr Hughes.
>
> I beg to remain your Majesty's most devoted servant.
>
> To his Majesty, King Leopold II.
>
> H.M. Stanley[14]

Leopold wasted no time, replying a week later, 'I have to acknowledge the receipt of your letter of 7th July 1891 in accordance with which I have decided to grant my patronage to the institution of Mr Hughes for the education of African natives.' Stanley duly informed Hughes of Leopold's 'gracious permission' to serve as patron of the institute. At that point, however, Leopold's genocidal pillaging of the Congo had already been exposed in the United States. The African-American journalist George Washington Williams had written a letter to the president of the United States. He also wrote an open letter to Leopold. Williams had travelled to the Congo and witnessed first-hand 'the deceit, fraud, robberies, arson, murder, slave-raiding, and general policy of cruelty of your Majesty's Government to the natives'. Drawing a telling contrast, he described 'their record of unexampled patience, long-suffering and forgiving spirit, which put the boasted civilisation and professed religion of your Majesty's Government to the blush. During thirteen years only one white man has lost his life by the hands of the natives, and only two white men have been killed in the Congo.'[15]

Presumably ignorant of the full extent of Leopold's activities in the Congo, Hughes wrote a letter of appreciation on 4 August 1891, in which he thanked the king for his patronage:

> May it please your Majesty to allow me on behalf of the Committee of the above Institute to convey their most sincere thanks for your Majesty's greatest patronage, with which our work has recently been so highly honoured. The following is the resolution which was unanimously passed by the Committee after the receipt of your gracious letter.
>
> That we desire most gratefully to acknowledge the great honour conferred upon our institution, by his most excellent Majesty, Leopold II, King of the Belgians, for becoming its patron, which gracious act, we are confident, adds much weight and influence to the success of a scheme destined to accomplish so much good in central Africa.
>
> May it please your Majesty to accept the enclosed report of our work. I have the honour to remain, with the profoundest respect, your Majesty's most faithful servant. W. Hughes.

Leopold's reputation as a philanthropist was now secure. African children would be the means to restoring it. Hughes extolled the king's virtues, describing him as 'a prince in his philanthropic ideas'.[16] Leopold had, he said, 'expended millions on the banks of the Congo, in order to give the light of civilisation to his 40 million dusky subjects'; he went on to quote the king, who described the Congo as his 'hobby', the place where he had decided to spend his money. It is significant that Hughes dedicated his book to King Leopold, and 'to the noble work accomplished by your Majesty on the Congo'.[17] Plainly, Hughes was seduced by the royal connection with Leopold. All the while, Stanley was helping to polish Leopold's image overseas, and the model of a school for African children was a perfect fit for the deception.

The South African connection

Ngcubu Poswayo arrived at the institute in 1904. By this time the student body was more diverse, accommodating students from across the African continent, including women. Leopold II was due to pay a visit to Liverpool. Hoping to meet the king, Hughes wrote – rather unctuously – on 18 May 1903:

> May it please your Majesty to accept this letter from me on behalf of the annual conference of the African Institute, which was held here on Saturday last.
>
> … Colwyn Bay being only about three hours sail from Liverpool it occurred to us that your Majesty might graciously grant us the honour of a visit at this beautiful society resort, where your Majesty would see about 25 African students, in whose race your Majesty has taken such deep and practical interest in the past. I can assure your Majesty that the friends of our institution, like Sir H.M. Stanley and Sir Alfred Jones, are too well acquainted with your Majesty's philanthropic spirit and interest in Africa, to believe that the atrocities reported from the region of the Congo River, if true, have, in any way, your Majesty's approval.[18]

By now Leopold's atrocities in the Congo were commonly known and had been widely denounced by Protestant missionaries in the United Kingdom. Yet Hughes found it hard to resist the lure of royal endorsement. As things turned out, Leopold did not visit Liverpool, though he did acknowledge receipt of the letter, and said that a decision on the visit had been postponed. Writing again on 4 June 1903, Hughes repeated that a 'great honour' would be conferred upon the institute by the king's visit. The political campaign against Leopold was, however, gaining momentum, and the king responded that the visit would have risked public humiliation in the British press. He had decided to cancel the trip altogether. Though disappointed, Hughes retained Leopold as patron of the institute. He knew that the financial position of the institute had entered a precarious state. In a 1902 circular, he wrote that he was forced to appeal for funds 'because of the injury done to our funds by the disastrous strike which took place a few years earlier in South Wales, the war in South Africa, the Indian famine'.

Notwithstanding such difficulties – of which only Hughes seemed to be aware – the South African students at the institute were thriving. They included Montsioa, Poswayo, Mabel Gabashane, who would later become a teacher in the Orange Free State, and young Davidson Jabavu. After failing to gain admission at Dale College in the King William's Town area, Jabavu had come to the institute. Dale College had rejected his application on the basis that to admit him would have been in conflict with the race policy of the Cape Colony. Jabavu senior took his son to the United Kingdom instead. There, Jabavu excelled, gaining a first-class pass for mathematics, as well as passing the London matriculation exam and achieving a qualification from the College of Preceptors. In 1906, Jabavu was the overall best student at the institute. He also learnt to play the piano and the cello. Praising Jabavu's talents and character, Hughes wrote:

He also is a good preacher and musician. He is passionately fond of music, and has always a book in his hand. When at this Institute these students were monitors in turn and were carrying the food of one week each from the kitchen to the tables. Jabavu always brought his book to the kitchen with him, when fetching the food, in case it would not be quite ready. This and early rising account for their great success in studying side by side with the young man of our land and in passing successfully our severe examination. Jabavu will prove a bright star in South Africa, and by his genius and geniality will help his father and other clever and good natives to break down the 'colour bar' and to prove to their white brethren that they are equal to them in intellect and high purposes at all times, granting that they always receive the same advantages.[19]

In 1912, D.D.T. Jabavu obtained a BA degree specialising in English at the University College, London. Two years later, in 1914, he studied for a teaching diploma at the University of Birmingham. During that year, he spent three months at the Tuskegee Institute in Alabama, USA. Upon his return to South Africa, he was appointed as one of the first black professors at the South African Native College in the Cape Province (later the University of Fort Hare), where he encountered a young student named Nelson Mandela,[20] and wrote extensively about racial segregation.[21]

Among Jabavu's fellow students who excelled was Ngcubu Poswayo. Apart from his academic studies, Poswayo distinguished himself on the cricket field. In 1903, a local newspaper reported the following:

On Wednesday last (17 June) the African students played a cricket match at Llandudno with the county school. The bowling of the Africans was too good for the Welshmen, who only mastered 13 runs between them, and the match resulted in a victory for the Africans by 21 runs. They continued their victorious career at Abergele on Thursday, when they beat the county school by 33 runs, the scores being Abergele, 41; Africa Institute, 74.[22]

In the following years, the institute played against local teams such as Rhos College, Mr Underhill's 11, Colwyn Bay and Mr Dares' English 11. The best ever performance of the institute was in 1905, when they defeated Rhos College by 124 runs to 30. Their best bowler was Ladipo Oluwole, from Nigeria, and best batsman was Poswayo. He helped his team beat a Welsh team named Plas-Y-Coed, and in 1907 he hit fifty runs off a Colwyn Bay team.[23] Montsioa, on the other hand, was an all-rounder. But he was also a talented musician, and in 1905 he rendered a song at a garden party organised by the Young Men's Christian Association, where he was 'vociferously cheered' for his performance.[24] He was also active in the affairs of the Student Society, and in December 1905 he organised a YMCA jumble sale where, together with a student from Sierra Leone, he manned an African curio stall.[25]

Poswayo graduated in 1909. By that stage he had decided to pursue a legal career. The annual report of the institute (1910 to 1911), which has his picture on the cover, notes that he had been accepted at Lincoln's Inn. The following year the institute closed down. It had run out of funds, and Hughes was blamed for mismanagement. But there was another factor: the weekly newspaper *John Bull* had published two scurrilous articles by H. Bottomley, on 16 and 23 December 1911. Bottomley, who had never been a supporter of the institute, had managed to rally society against it by exploiting prevailing prejudices. He had hinted at a scandal, suggesting that there was 'intimate contact between English ladies and negros' at the institute.

Barrister

After passing his exams at Lincoln's Inn in 1913, after three years of pupillage training, Ngcubu Poswayo returned to South Africa. When he arrived at his home in Ngcobo, there were wild celebrations. Several beasts were slaughtered and traditional beer was brewed. It was a joyous occasion all round. On the day after the celebrations, Poswayo surprised the community by donning his wig, gown and bib. Some, looking on from a distance, wondered whether he had grown a white man's hair after all the years he had spent in the United Kingdom.[26] Poswayo now considered his options in the light of the fate of three other lawyers with whom he had crossed paths at Lincoln's Inn. Upon returning to South Africa, they were admitted as attorneys, not advocates. But here in the Cape, things would be different, he believed: there was no discriminatory legislation prohibiting black lawyers from practising as advocates.

On 1 August 1913, Poswayo applied for admission as an advocate of the Supreme Court of South Africa, Cape of Good Hope Provincial Division, based in Cape Town. His application, heard by Judge Searle, was duly granted. *Imvo Zabantsundu* was pleased to note that another black person had been admitted as an advocate of the Supreme Court, in the Cape Province. However, the reaction from white media such as the *Cape Times* and the *Cape Argus* was muted, and the significance of the event was ignored. For, of course, not only had Poswayo been admitted as a barrister in the United Kingdom, he was also an advocate of the Supreme Court of South Africa. In the event, Poswayo contemplated setting up chambers in Cape Town, but was discouraged from doing so as a result of numerous accounts of racial discrimination in the Cape. He consulted senior political leaders, including Dr Rubusana and J.T. Jabavu, both of whom would have recalled the fate of Henry Sylvester Williams. Although no record of their advice exists, it may be inferred from the decision Poswayo took. He considered opening chambers: some ten years earlier, in 1903, a Bar had been opened in Grahamstown.

Attorney

Poswayo hoped to practise as an advocate in Grahamstown. Although he met the formal requirements and qualifications, it soon became apparent that, not only would he be unwelcome from a social point of view, trying to make a living as an advocate in Grahamstown would be economic suicide. He would receive no briefs, no collegiality and probably no civility from the bench. While the Cape generally projected the image of being a crucible of racial harmony, the reality was quite different. While a person's education might promise entry into a professional world, racial pigmentation was a barrier.

Upon his return to Ngcobo, Poswayo visited a firm of attorneys called E.W. Carey; he discussed his difficulties in securing chambers and a place to practise as an advocate in the Eastern Cape. Carey advised Poswayo to remove his name from the roll of advocates and rather practise as an attorney. Many 'native litigants' did not have an attorney who could speak their language and who shared their social and cultural background.[27] An African attorney, steeped in the traditions and cultures of the community, would therefore be most welcome. But Mr Carey himself was unable to offer him a position as an articled clerk. He undertook to speak to his friend, also an attorney, who had a practice in nearby Cofimvaba. Appreciating the practical sense of Carey's advice, in October 1913 Poswayo briefed an attorney in Cape Town to instruct counsel to prepare a petition for his removal from the roll of advocates. He now wished to practise as an attorney. His application, dated 21 November 1913, stated:

1. That your petitioner is an advocate of this honourable court and was duly admitted and enrolled to practise as such as will appear from the annexed certificate of admission and enrolment which bears date the first day of August 1913.
2. That your petitioner is the person referred to in the said certificate.
3. That your petitioner's name is still on the roll of advocates of this honourable court, and that your petitioner has never been struck off such roll or removed therefrom, nor has your petitioner been suspended from practise, nor to the best of your petitioner's knowledge and belief is there any proceeding pending against him for his suspension or his removal from such roll.
4. That your petitioner is desirous of entering into articles of service with

an attorney of this honourable court and to such end your petitioner is
desirous of having his name struck off or removed from the roll of
advocates of this honourable court.

On 25 November 1913, the matter came before court and Poswayo's request was
granted. Thus, little more than two months after Poswayo was enrolled to practise
as an advocate in the Cape, and after about a month of practice, his career as an
advocate came to an end. It would take another fifty years, with the registration
of Dumalisile Nokwe, for another African to apply to be admitted and be granted
such application as an advocate of the Supreme Court of South Africa. Turning
his gaze, Poswayo now wished to be signed up as an articled clerk to qualify as an
attorney. Unlike in the Transvaal, the law in the Cape was that admission as
an advocate did not necessarily qualify the person to practise as an attorney.
Required to undergo a period of two years of articles of clerkship, Poswayo
signed up with an attorneys firm in Cofimvaba, after which he registered his own
law firm, Poswayo Solicitors, in Ngcobo in 1915. While there had been other
Africans before him who practised as law agents, he was the first to practise as
a fully qualified solicitor or attorney. He became the first black person to register a
law firm in his name in the Cape Colony.

His practise as an attorney was an instant success. A genial soul, kind and gentle
with clients, Poswayo was generally well liked. The primary concerns affecting
his clients were criminal matters that were adjudicated in the Magistrate's Court
or in the Native Court. His first appearance in the Magistrate's Court was noted
by the *Tembuland Advertiser*, which regularly reported on cases in that court as
well as the Supreme Court, which usually sat on circuit in Queenstown and in
Cala. Poswayo soon rekindled his relationships with Msimang and Mangena,
whom he had met up with in London. He was also associated with *Abantu-Batho*,
the SANNC-aligned newspaper published in Johannesburg, and he played an
active role organising for the SANNC in the Tembuland area. By 1916 preparations were underway to send a delegation to the United Kingdom to protest the
introduction of the Natives Land Act, but Poswayo was reluctant to take an active
part in a political formation. He did, however, agree to assist in the collection of
evidence pertaining to the effects of the Natives Land Act in the Tembuland area.
At that stage, property-owning black men were permitted to vote in the Cape.
Under the Cape of Good Hope Constitution Ordinance of 1852, neither race nor
colour, but property ownership or property occupation for a period of at least
one year, or salary or wages of at least £50 per annum, served to qualify the right
to vote. Similarly, the Franchise and Ballot Act 9 of 1892 did not introduce race
or colour into the franchise equation. But in addition to property and salary, it
required literacy as an additional qualifying criterion. However, the Glen Grey

Act 25 of 1894 – instigated by the government of Cecil John Rhodes – sought to curtail these rights of franchise. When Rhodes introduced the Bill on 30 July 1894, he commenced by noting that 'the natives are children. They are just emerging from barbarism. They have human minds, and I would like them to devote themselves wholly to the local matters that surround them and appeal to them.' It was on this premise that he had no qualms about depriving them of any form of land ownership, stating the following:

> There is the payment of quitrents, and there is that of alienation with consent of the government. Some newspapers have said that the whole object of the Bill is to get land into the hands of the white man, and I simply refer to the title to refute this. Again, we hear the argument that after five years these people will sell out to the white man. My idea is that the natives should be kept in these native reserves and not be mixed with the white man at all. Are you going to sanction the idea, with all the difficulties of the poor whites before us, that these people should be mixed up with white men, and white children grow up in the middle of native locations? In the interest of the white people themselves we must never let this happen. White labour cannot compete with black labour in this country – physical labour I mean.[28]

From this, it would seem that the later Natives Land Act was based on the Glen Grey Act. But in relation to the qualifications for franchise, the Glen Grey Act excluded land held on a communal basis and land held under the quitrent[29] – a perpetual rent system – from counting as qualifications for franchise. This meant that only land held via outright title would qualify a person for the right to vote. This, coupled with restrictions on capacity to earn and restrictions on education, meant that very small numbers of Africans were in fact able to vote. Consequently, by 1905 there were a meagre 8 000 black voters out of a possible 140 000. It is therefore clear that, although the 'progressive' policy of the Cape allowing franchise for blacks has generally been extolled, the reality was far from praiseworthy. Nevertheless, as Poswayo experienced in the Tembuland area, by 1916 there was administrative self-government by means of district councils, which were appointed by the government.[30]

The next year would prove to be a particularly busy one for Poswayo. It was also the year he married Beatrix Kule, a local teacher at All Saints, who had qualified at Healdtown and become the first African female teacher at the mission school. At the time, the law did not allow married women to work as teachers, so Beatrix was forced to resign. However, she continued to run classes for elementary phases of schooling and for adult learners who wished to acquire literacy and numerical skills. She also acquired a farm at Saint Marks mission station where she grew fresh produce and kept livestock, and this developed into a full-scale farming operation. Today 'UMam' is remembered by many locals not only for her intellect and industry, but also for her generosity and constant willingness to advise people who approached her with their problems. She gave her full support to her husband, enabling him to focus on his legal practice, which grew as quickly as his influence spread.

Accessing justice in the Magistrate's Court

In April 1917, Poswayo was appointed to serve on a commission of inquiry investigating access to justice by black people in relation to the lower courts. The government was concerned at the lack of uniformity in the manner in which the Magistrate's Court Act applied justice to black people. Poswayo was the only African on a commission comprising five members, including the resident magistrate of Mthatha.

Their conclusions, contained in a 100-page volume, pointed to five areas that prevented access to the legal system, thereby contributing to the lack of uniformity between the Magistrate's Courts and the Native Courts. The first was the question of language. Black people, the report reasoned, found it easier to approach the Native Courts because the language used was familiar to them, and there was no need for interpreters. Though an attempt had been made in the Magistrate's Courts to employ interpreters, the problem of language accessibility persisted. The interpreters themselves were sometimes not adequately qualified, or the terms being translated did not sufficiently correlate to enable a proper and meaningful interpretation of concepts, words and events. It was therefore proposed that the Magistrate's Courts should use native languages, so as to make proceedings more accessible to Africans. The second area concerned the use of assessors in both criminal and civil courts. It was noted that many persons accused in criminal cases or with civil claims felt that justice would more likely be done if there were people sitting together with the magistrate – invariably a white man – whose backgrounds were familiar to them. In the Native Courts, it had long been the practice that a presiding officer was accompanied or assisted by assessors. The commission therefore recommended that the use of assessors be extended to the Magistrate's Courts so as to create a representative and legitimate system. The third concern was the matter of legal representation, which was in many instances absent, in the Native Courts as well as in the Magistrate's Courts. This was not only due to lack of funds, but was also a result of ignorance. Magistrates, it was recommended, should not preside over cases where there was a likelihood of imprisonment without informing accused persons that they should secure the services of an attorney for their particular case. Fourth, the question of the Supreme Court and its accessibility was raised: it sat in Cape Town and in Grahamstown, while the Tembuland area was only visited on circuit. The concerns were lack of frequency as well as the distances people had to travel when the Supreme Court was on circuit. It is noteworthy that this request seems only to have been brought into practice some ten years later. On 12 March 1926, the *Tembuland Advertiser* carried the following article on the 'Cala Circuit':

> Almost every household in Cala who was not exempted from serving as a juror received the well-known Sheriff's notice telling him that he was required to attend before the Supreme Court, 'to be holden at Cala on the 16th day of April, 1926' writes a Cala correspondent to the *Dispatch*. And though every man who received a juror's notice put up the usual grouse it was more from force of habit than discontent. For we are all very glad (you should see some of the dresses the ladies are having made for the ball, which is being given to entertain the judge and barristers) that the Circuit Court is coming back to Cala again. It is years since the Circuit Court was held here, and we were beginning to wonder if it would ever be held here again; though we wondered much more why it had been taken away. Engcobo cases will be tried here in future, and so will those from St Marks, as the district has been taken away from Queenstown and again added onto Cala. The Elliot cases, which used to be tried here, will now be tried in Dordrecht, I suppose because the railway makes this more convenient, but when you come to think of it Cala is that many miles further of the line than Dordrecht, and it is many miles closer to Elliot by rail or road than Dordrecht.

The final recommendation of the commission concerned the issue of lack of properly qualified interpreters. It was suggested that the government should consider appointing more interpreters, from among the ranks of native teachers in particular (the Poswayos usually offered their services in the Native Courts). In any event, there was unlikely to be a shortage of interpreters, since many of those employed in the Native Courts did the interpretation without any expectation of reward. The commission believed that this system could be extended to the Magistrate's Courts.

The Mpondo and the SS *Mendi*

An incomplete 1923 file provides a glimpse into the legal practice of Poswayo. The matter concerned claims of the Mpondo, which related to the sinking of the SS *Mendi*. At first glance, the file is somewhat confusing. But considering the events of five years before, in 1917, this may be understandable. Towards the end of the First World War, Britain was forced to recruit soldiers from across the British Empire, including the Cape. In this way, the South African Native Labour

Contingent was formed; it included several recruits from the Eastern Cape, Pondoland in particular. They were to be transported by ship from Cape Town to France. And so, the SS *Mendi* left Cape Town for France on 16 January 1917, with more than 800 African recruits on board.

They included chiefs from Pondoland, among them Henry Bokleni, Dokota Richard Ndamase and Mxonywa Bangani; Reverend Isaac Wauchope Dyobha was also on board. On 21 February, another ship, the SS *Darro*, rammed into the *Mendi*, which sank in less than twenty minutes. Legend has it that, as the ship was sinking, Reverend Dyobha cried out:

> Be quiet and calm, my countrymen, for what is taking place is exactly what you came to do. You are going to die ... but that is what you came to do ... Brothers, we are drilling the death drill. I, a Xhosa, say you are my brothers, Swazi's, Pondo's, Basotho's, we die like brothers. We are the sons of Africa. Raise your war cries, brothers, for though they made us leave our assegais in the kraal, our voices are left with our bodies.[31]

The captain ordered everyone to abandon ship and many threw themselves into the sea. After an explosion was heard and the lights went out, there was panic and confusion. Many were too afraid to jump, and were still on board when the vessel sank. The captain, who would later testify at an inquiry, said: 'I had a life belt on. There were hundreds of boys around me after the wreck. They died from exposure. They all had life belts on ... it was a very cold, dark, damp, miserable night ...'[32] The news of the tragedy eventually reached the South African Parliament on 19 March 1917, and members rose as a token of respect. While there is no clear reference to the sinking of the *Mendi* in Poswayo's file on the Mpondo, the possibility remains that some family members never received compensation, and were forced to seek the services of an attorney to receive compensation from the government. Indeed, the dispensation for the compensation of the recruits who perished on the *Mendi* was racially inequitable. The British government set up a compensation fund to cover families for loss of support. White officers who died during the war received payments in the region of £300, with sometimes more being paid. But there was a standard payment of £50 for Africans who perished on the *Mendi*.[33]

Whatever the case, it is nevertheless true that, by the time Poswayo died at a relatively young age, in 1926, he had accumulated a fair number of assets. Among these was a farm that became the subject of litigation between him and his cousin, Thomas, ultimately causing divisions in the family of this legal pioneer. But Beatrix and their two children were left with a sizable estate. His grave, located in the village of Nyanga, stands out as the only one with a marble headstone.

George Montsioa: legal activist

George Montsioa, who was a great friend of Poswayo, completed his studies at the Congo Institute in August 1906. On 24 October of that year, he registered at Lincoln's Inn, noting that he came from 'Mafeking, Bechuanaland, South Africa (20) first son of Nche Montsioa of Mafeking aforesaid chief of Montsioa's country'.[34] Although he graduated on 8 June 1910, he only returned to South Africa in January 1911; it is unclear why he chose to remain in London for the six-month period.

After being admitted as an attorney of the Supreme Court, he was requested, together with Seme and Mangena, to assist the preparatory committee of the SANNC, which was working towards a launch of the organisation in January 1912. In addition to his chiefly connection, he also had links with the royal Molema family, and with his education as a lawyer, Montsioa was especially attractive to the political elite at the SANNC. At its founding, he was appointed recording secretary, an onerous task that involved record-keeping of all congress decisions. It is a tribute to Montsioa that most of the records of the SANNC, from its founding on 8 January 1912 until it was renamed the African National Congress in 1923, still survive, providing clear insights into the activities of the organisation.

Four years after returning to South Africa, Montsioa decided to get married. But two years later, in 1918, tragedy struck when his wife and two-year-old son succumbed to an illness.[35] Two years afterwards, Montsioa remarried, this time to the daughter of Marcus Gabashane, founder of the African Methodist Episcopal Church of South Africa. Montsioa had met his future sister-in-law, Mabel Gabashane, at the Congo Institute. Montsioa did not have any other children, though his niece, Molili, lived with him and Mabel.

Montsioa opened a law practice in Johannesburg, with an office in Pietersburg, where he and Mabel lived for a while. A third office, in Middelburg, was also opened. Later, however, as he became increasingly busy, Montsioa closed the Pietersburg office and concentrated on his Johannesburg office in Anderson Street. His work largely concerned the struggles of black people in relation to land.

Natives and the Magistrate's Courts

In 1916 Montsioa took on a case that brought to the fore the intricacies of the jurisdiction between Magistrate's Courts and Native Courts.[36] *Makoti v. Madupi*[37] involved a claim for the return of *lobola*, or bride price. The plaintiff had paid cattle to the defendant, who was the father of the woman who was to be married to the plaintiff. But the marriage did not take place. The plaintiff sued the defendant for the return of the cattle. The defendant approached Montsioa, and the matter went before the Magistrate's Court. Montsioa took exception on the grounds of lack of jurisdiction, arguing that in the area of Potchefstroom there were Native Commissioner's Courts, and according to Transvaal Law No. 4 of 1885, cases between natives had to be tried by a native commissioner, unless there was no native commissioner in the district, in which case the magistrate would assume jurisdiction.

The court agreed, but the plaintiff appealed. On appeal, before the Transvaal Provincial Division, the finding as to lack of jurisdiction was overturned. Two reasons were provided by Judge Mason, who presided over the case together with Judge Curlewis. He noted that, textually, the law that created the jurisdiction of magistrates, proclamation 21 of 1902, did not explicitly preclude the jurisdiction of magistrates in relation to natives, but gave jurisdiction to the magistrate in respect of a certain limited class of cases, and in respect of persons resident within the jurisdiction of the Magistrate's Court in all civil disputes: 'The Magistrate's jurisdiction within those limits is not restricted in any way with reference to classes of persons or classes of cases. It is, within the limits set forth, as complete as the jurisdiction conferred upon the Superior Courts.' Still, this conclusion did not give a full answer to the question raised. Laws passed subsequent to 1902 recognised 'the position of native administrators as judicial officers in connection with cases between natives'. By implication, therefore, were such cases not excluded from the jurisdictional ambit of the Magistrate's Court? The court preferred to leave the question open, simply noting that *prima facie* 'native cases would come before both courts'. In any event, it was not necessary to disturb something that had been a practice in the Transvaal, namely that Native Commissioner's Courts and Magistrate's Courts had concurrent jurisdiction in respect to civil disputes among Africans. Therefore, the finding by the magistrate was overturned, and Montsioa lost the case. But an important principle was established. Civil disputes among Africans could also be decided in the Magistrate's Court. They were not outside the legal system, but rather within the legal system. If the government wished to exclude them, it had to pass a specific statute.

This was not an edifying outcome. Native commissioners were clearly civil servants, whose powers of administration over the affairs of natives were of a generic nature. In addition to their administrative functions, they were given judicial authority. But magistrates were also civil servants, though their primary function was judicial, and they had the authority to try cases regardless of the race of the parties appearing before them.

Law as resistance

The enforcement of the Natives Land Act of 1913 was not uniform. Although many Africans ejected from farms in the Transvaal complied, and were deprived of their rights of occupation, those who could resist did so. Since resistance by force was generally not an option, the law was used as an instrument of resistance. The 1923 case of *R. v. Kana*[38] became a rallying point around which certain Africans could resist their ejectment from farms. Reported in black newspapers such as *Abantu-Batho*, the case was widely discussed and hailed as a victory for tenants who had no security of tenure on farms. The appellant, Dirk Kana, had been charged with violating section 7 of law 21 of 1895 in that 'he did wrongfully and unlawfully disobey an order of court given under the hand of P.C. Dalmahoy, Native Commissioner for the district of Lydenburg, on the first day of March, to wit the said accused was in the said order instructed that he had to remove from the farm aforesaid by the 7th March, 1923, which order he failed to obey'.

Though Kana pleaded not guilty to the charge, he was convicted and fined £25 or three months' imprisonment. Law 21 of 1895 was also known as the Squatters Law Act. The effect of violating that law was that a person was liable not only to an ejectment from a farm, but also to a criminal conviction. The ambit and parameters of that law were put to the test: the Natives Land Act of 1913 had introduced a different dimension to the application of the Squatters Law Act. If a person was not a squatter, but an annual tenant, he would not be liable to an ejectment before his period of tenancy had lapsed. Furthermore, the Natives Land Act had suspended the provisions of section 7 of the Squatters Law Act of 1895 until Parliament decided or introduced a different law. At the time the case was brought, Parliament had not yet replaced the provisions of section 7 of the Squatters Law Act of 1895. Two arguments were made on appeal. According to the first, Kana was not a squatter as such, but an annual tenant. To counter this, the land owner, the Berlin Missionary Society, argued that he could not be a yearly tenant because he had been in arrears with his rent for three years. Kana admitted to this, but argued that during the First World War, he had done work for the German mission for which he had not been paid. Consequently, he had a counterclaim for the non-payment of rent in the amount of £23. Until that claim was settled, the contention was that he could not be liable for the unpaid rent. The native affairs commissioner had made an enquiry into this, but the report was fraught with complication. The Supreme Court elected not to decide this question. It was for Parliament to resolve. As the law stood, however,

> no native residing on any farm in the Transvaal or Natal shall be liable to penalties or to be removed from such farm under any law, if at the commencement of this Act, he or the head of his family is registered for taxation or other purposes in the Department of Native Affairs as being resident on such farm, nor shall the owner of any such farm be liable to the penalties imposed by Sec. 5 in respect of the occupation of land by such native; but nothing herein contained shall affect any right possessed by law by any owner or lessee of a farm to remove any native therefrom.

As a resident on the farm owned by the Berlin Missionary Society, Kana was registered for taxation. Therefore, on the face of it, he was protected by the law. The court noted that it had previously held that the Squatters Law Act could not be used either for purposes of punishing a native living on the land, or for purposes of removing one. The state made a further argument, submitting that the law did not affect the right of an owner or lessee of a farm to eject a native. But this too was unpersuasive, and the judge ruled as follows:

> I do not wish to state all the rights that an owner possessed by law, but he certainly possesses the right by law that if he wishes to remove a native from his farm he can sue him for ejectment. The native in this case was on the farm on annual lease, and he is in arrears with his rent; if the owner wishes to contend that the native has no right there, and wishes him removed, he can sue the native for ejectment. If he does that, the native can set up any defence he wishes, such as the defence before the Native Commissioner in the first instance, when he said he had not paid the rent because the German Missionary owed him a large amount of money.
>
> I think the Magistrate erred in this matter. In giving his reasons he stated that his attention had not been directed to sec. 6(c) of law 27 of 1913 when the case was before him; I take it that it was due to this that he gave the judgment he did. In my opinion, he has erred.

The appeal was thus upheld, and the conviction and sentence were set aside. Montsioa's client was free, and an important point of principle had been set. People on annual leases were exempt from ejectment. Nor could they be convicted for committing a crime simply on account of being on a farm without payment of rental. But as soon as the news of the court victory spread, land owners terminated leases and ejected at will, thereby depriving tenants of legal recourse. Montsioa was undaunted, however, and continued to challenge the law.

Limiting the powers of landlords

An important case that immediately followed that of Kana was a response to its findings that natives on long-term annual leases were exempt from ejectment in terms of the Squatters Law Act. *Ntsobi* v. *Berlin Mission Society*[39] remains the authority for the proposition that where a landlord wishes to terminate a lease, such termination must be clear and unequivocal in order to be effective. Ntsobi, a tenant on the premises of the Berlin Missionary Society, was represented by Montsioa. He was sued for the amount of £2, rent that was alleged to be due between July 1922 and June 1923, and ordered to leave the premises. Ntsobi argued that the missionary society should have sent a person to the farm to collect the rent, but had failed to do so, and therefore the rent was not due. When the matter came to court, Montsioa tendered the payment to the court. In relation to the notice to vacate the premises, Ntsobi submitted that he had received no notice to leave the premises. A judgment was entered against Ntsobi, and he appealed. On appeal, it was common cause that the lease was an annual lease terminating on 30 June each year. Montsioa had submitted that a proper notice of termination would be one year, which had not been given. Citing a similar case,[40] he argued that an annual lease required an annual notice to be effective.

The court did not express an opinion on that argument, noting that 'it does not necessarily follow that all yearly tenancies do require a years' notice, special circumstances may show that a shorter period of notice is a proper notice'. Instead, it decided the case on the assumption that a yearly notice was a proper notice. The question to be decided was whether the notice given was effective. Turning to the facts, the court noted that the person who had given the notice, S. Wedemeyer, had testified that he had been on the farm in July 1921, when he had 'informed the residents that from the 1st July, 1921, they had to pay the increased rent'. At a meeting of all the residents of Draaihoek, he had 'informed them that from then they had to pay £3 per annum and £1 for every 16 head of cattle or portion thereof. They refused to pay the increased rent. I told them that if they refused to pay the increased rent, they had to quit the farm.' Wedemeyer testified further that, on 27 August 1921, the defendant had paid his rent for the year 1920 to 1921. He had informed him that 'in future' he had to abide by the new terms or quit the farm. In deciding this point, the court, in reference to an earlier decision, noted that: 'the notice to be effective must be clear and unequivocal'. Having considered Wedemeyer's evidence, the court was 'uncertain what exactly he intended to convey when he gave the alleged notice which is now relied on'. Moreover, it was not clear whether the instructions were merely an intention or an attempt to extract an increased rent, or whether the intention was for the 'tenants' to leave the premises forthwith. Under those circumstances, 'it is hardly to be wondered at that the tenant was left in doubt as to whether he was being told to quit the farm unconditionally or merely being warned or threatened. My view, therefore, is that the language used in the notice was so obscure that the tenant was not obliged to act upon it and treat it as a notice.' The appeal was upheld and the ejectment order of the magistrate was overturned. Montsioa had claimed another victory for justice.

Montsioa lived a long and productive life. When he died in 1953, three friends were at his bedside. They included two medical doctors and a teacher: Dr Alfred Xuma, former president of the ANC; Dr Modiri Molema, former secretary of the ANC, who was also a relative; and John Beaver Marks. In the years following Montsioa's return to Johannesburg, he had been persuaded to turn to the tribal politics of the Barolong, whom he served as an informal legal advisor. His cousin,

Sebopioa Molema, who was also a lawyer, was secretary to Chief Montsioa. Together, they provided strong legal advice to the royal family. This formed part of his broad contribution as a legal activist.

The legal cases that Montsioa and Poswayo were involved in may have been few in number, but their significance was immense. Their skills were pitted against enormous power. The colonial state was enforcing its imperial vision by means of legislation, laws crafted with the aim of constructing a subordinate class of citizens based on race. Courts were presided over by white men, and there was merely the promise and the appearance of justice. Judicial officers – traditionally the guardians of justice – were embedded in the institutions of a race-obsessed colonial state. But the legal rules they enforced underwent fundamental transformation when applied in practice. As *Ntsobi* v. *Berlin Mission Society* proved, a legal rule might on the face of it appear neutral. But its application can have harsh consequences for the people concerned. The challenge for lawyers such as Poswayo and Montsioa was to articulate the concerns of their clients when confronted with the harsh laws of the day. The law was not solely the instrument of Empire: when wielded by colonial subjects, the law itself could function as a weapon against oppression. Yet the migration of law – and of legal practice – from the colonial centre to the periphery inhabited by 'natives' would not have been possible without particular actors. George Montsioa and Ngcubu Poswayo may be said to have occupied two worlds – Belgium and Britain – which intersected in terms of race, yet also collided. For, while they shared the common goal of colonisation, they clashed in relation to the way they pursued that goal. The British press was only too pleased to be able to expose the atrocities of Leopold in the Congo. While this was admirable, it tended to obscure – and even whitewash – the more banal, though equally evil, realities of the European project of creating colonies in Africa. Reconciling the different traditions of Empire was an experience unique to these two black South Africans. However, as with their entire generation of lawyers, they resisted the temptation to view the law as merely colonialist.[41] For them, the law was not simply and always an instrument of colonial domination. It could also be an ally in the fight for freedom. Then, as now, its usefulness was contingent, depending on individual actors, context and circumstances. And so, Montsioa and Poswayo formed a 'band of brothers'[42] who bravely took on an apparently invincible enemy by using its own laws against it, thereby revealing its hollow centre. Leopold's subterfuge may well have been successful in establishing a school for African boys and girls in Wales for the purpose of perpetuating colonial conquest and economic exploitation. But in adulthood, those same boys and girls would demand the return not only of their country, but also of their continent, with its rich resources. It is a satisfying irony that they achieved this by using the very tool they had gained in Wales: education.

PART III

LEGACIES

7

Visions of equality
in a divided Union

'Without the land, the natives are absolutely compelled to starve.'
— Percy Alden, 13 May 1908

The Treaty of Vereeniging of 1902 incorporated the vanquished Boer republics of Transvaal and Orange Free State into the British Empire. Until then, its sovereignty had extended over the colonies of the Cape and Natal, but now, all of South Africa was made up of British colonies. But this would be short-lived. On 12 October 1908, representatives from these colonies met in Cape Town in what became a defining moment in South Africa's history. Uppermost on the agenda was the forging of a Union of South Africa – a policy long favoured by the imperial government. Lord Henry de Villiers, chief justice of the Cape, chaired the meeting, which became known as the South African National Convention. M.T. Steyn, C.R. de Wet and Barry Hertzog represented the Orange River Colony, while Louis Botha and Jan Smuts represented the Transvaal. John X. Merriman and J.W. Sauer came on behalf of the Cape, and the Natal delegates were F.R. Moore and Thomas Watt. At stake was the status of the white population of South Africa; to ensure its dominance, discussion centred on issues such as language, the economy, the 'native problem', labour sources, and the structure of government and of the judiciary.

The outcome was the South Africa Act of 1909. For the first time, South Africa would be a political entity, with a unified Parliament, a single executive and an overarching judiciary, whose apex would be the Bloemfontein-based Appellate Division. Section 4 of the Act confirmed the creation of a new government for the 'united' South Africa:

> It shall be lawful for the King, with the advice of the Privy Council, to declare by proclamation that, on and after a day therein appointed, not being later than one year after the passing of this Act, the Colonies of the Cape of Good Hope, Natal, the Transvaal, and the Orange River Colony, hereinafter called the Colonies, shall be united in a legislative union under one Government under the name of the Union of South Africa. On and after the day appointed

by such proclamation the Government and Parliament of the Union shall have full power and authority within the limits of the Colonies, but the King may at any time after the proclamation appoint a Governor-General for the Union.

Pretoria was designated the seat of the executive, while the legislature would be housed in Cape Town. Elected office such as the senate, the executive or Parliament, was restricted to 'British subjects of European descent'.[1] The qualification for franchise confirmed the supremacy of the white race. Except for the Cape, Africans in the other three provinces were excluded from voting, though even in the Cape, the qualified African franchise hung by the barest of threads. Clearly, 'race or colour' was a central consideration in section 35 of the Act, and the franchise depended on approval by the whites-only Parliament:

(1) Parliament may by law prescribe the qualifications which shall be necessary to entitle persons to vote at the election of members of the House of Assembly, but no such law shall disqualify any person in the province of the Cape of Good Hope who, under the laws existing in the Colony of the Cape of Good Hope at the establishment of the Union, is or may become capable of being registered as a voter from being so registered in the province of the Cape of Good Hope by reason of his race or colour only, unless the Bill be passed by both Houses of Parliament sitting together, and at the third reading be agreed to by not less than two-thirds of the total number of members of both Houses. A Bill so passed at such joint sitting shall be taken to have been duly passed by both Houses of Parliament.

(2) No person who at the passing of any such law is registered as a voter in any province shall be removed from the register by reason only of any disqualification based on race or colour.

On the face of it, the Act forbade 'disqualification based on race or colour', but ultimately the African franchise was subject to the whim of white people. Unsurprisingly, the Act sent shockwaves among Africans. Contrary to the promises of the Anglo-Boer War, there would be no place for black people in the Union of South Africa. Sampie Terreblanche[2] explains that during the Anglo-Boer War, the British colonial authorities did not only promise Africans, but 'assured' them that 'equal laws, equal liberty' would be granted to all population groups after a Boer defeat. But during the negotiations for the drafting of the Treaty of Vereeniging, 'the British imperial politicians reneged on these promises by making a crucial concession to the Afrikaners'. The concession was that the African franchise would be postponed until after the restoration of self-governance to the former Boer republics. Indeed, clause 8 of the treaty expressly reserved 'the question of granting of Franchise to Natives' until after 'the introduction of Self-Government'. Thus, having vanquished the Boers, the British focused on placating them, at the expense of their erstwhile allies, the Africans. With self-government having been attained, franchise, equality and liberty for Africans remained elusive.[3] The news of the Act reached Pixley Seme and his colleagues in London. Alfred Mangena, who had barely returned to South Africa, was immediately aware of discussions around the Act. A few months before his final return to Trinidad, the land of his birth, Henry Sylvester Williams expressed his views concerning the future of South Africa. Together with Alfred Mangena, Williams regularly attended meetings of the Africa Society in London, and it was there that he argued that the possibility of a new South African state where natives were relegated to second-class status was repugnant to the standards of 'British civilization'. As for the future, South Africans, 'regardless of race, colour or caste ought to combine to make the country exemplary – morally and politically'.[4] Mangena shared these sentiments, telling his colleagues that South Africa's future harmony hinged 'on a law which must give due and equal recognition to the rights of all races inhabiting the land'.[5] While the consolidation of white political power as manifested in the Act of Union was a betrayal of African loyalty, it did not signify the end of African hope in the ability of the British government to guarantee equal rights. The response of the Africans was a familiar one: petitions, deputations and delegations. Two of the petitions drawn up in protest against the Act of Union indicate that Africans remained hopeful of British intervention to secure their political rights.

The first claim by the Africans, as embodied in the petition of 22 October 1908, was representation in the institutions of government of the newly formed Union of South Africa. On that date, the Transvaal Native Congress, writing on behalf of the 'aboriginal natives of South Africa, resident in the Transvaal' called for Africans to be granted 'representation in the Parliament of a United South Africa'. It asked for political equality between the white and black races of South Africa, calling for the extension to Africans of 'the full political privileges as may be granted to the European population in the constitution'. Embedded in the notions of representation and equality was the extension of franchise rights, an old African demand, and a long-standing practice in the Cape, the petition argued. Typical of educated Africans of the time,[6] the writers of the petition were infatuated with the language of 'progress' associated with the enjoyment of rights. They attributed the 'advancement in prosperity, contentment, and loyalty, which is such a marked characteristic of the natives of Cape Colony, to the generous policy which has permitted themselves as citizens, and to enjoy the privileges of citizenship'. It was their hope, they submitted, that 'the same happy result' would be achieved if franchise was extended throughout South Africa. Though recognising that some might not qualify for franchise, the petition observed that this would not constitute justification for exclusion from representation in governmental structures. Accordingly, it pleaded that those who did not qualify for franchise should be protected in the form of separate representation. Speaking against the Bill in March 1909, the South African Native Convention requested that references to 'race or colour' be excised from the Bill.[7] Confirming African loyalty to the Empire, the petition recognised the principle of a united South Africa among 'His Majesty's subjects' to be 'essential, necessary, and inevitable'. Proclaiming Africans as 'loyal subjects' of the imperial government, it asserted an obligation on the part of government towards the native and coloured races of South Africa. The 'King and Empire owe good and just government to every class of their subjects'. This would not be possible if one class of subjects was abandoned at the mercy of another, being 'absolutely deprived of the right of equal representation'. It was with these motivations that the petition demanded an amendment to the phrase 'European male adults' in clause 33, to read 'European male adults and native and coloured voters'. Declaring that the colour bar was a 'real vital basic wrong and injustice', the petition called for a law recognising that all persons within the Union were entitled to full and equal rights and privileges, subject only to the conditions and limitations established by law, and applicable to all citizens, irrespective of class, colour or creed.[8] In June 1909, African chiefs from the Transkei addressed a petition to the governor of the Cape Colony. They too emphasised their devotion and loyalty 'to the throne and person of His Most Gracious Majesty the King'. Their fear, they argued, was that the limited rights of franchise which were enjoyed under the 'benign and fostering' rule of the British Empire were threatened by the Act of Union. With 'great apprehension' they also protested the use of race and colour in parliamentary selection, as this excluded the great majority of South Africans from participating in the affairs of 'their country'.[9]

When the pleas fell upon deaf ears, the South African Native Convention decided to approach the imperial government directly. The resolution to send a deputation to London threw the South African government into a state of confusion. General Louis Botha hastily organised a meeting with John Dube, where he tried unsuccessfully to dissuade him. Dube politely informed the prime minister that the decision was out of his hands. The suggestion was duly rejected, and all the provincial congresses went ahead with the plan to send deputations to plead their cause in London. Their spokesperson was former prime minister William Schreiner, who was now an MP and senior advocate at the Cape Bar. Schreiner, an anti-imperialist, had earned the trust of the Africans as a Cape representative of Africans at a time when they still enjoyed limited franchise rights. Also, instead of representing the Cape at the South African National Convention of 1908, he chose to represent the Zulu king, Dinuzulu ka Cetshwayo, in a trial which many saw as a political trial arising out of the Bambatha uprising. In that trial, Schreiner gained the acquittal of King Dinuzulu on all but three of twenty-three counts of high treason and sedition; Dinuzulu served a brief prison term and was released in 1910 by Prime Minister Botha.

The South African Native Convention considered Schreiner's close association with the Cape administration advantageous, and if anybody were to be listened to, it was him. It was resolved that Seme and Mangena – the latter was also officially mandated by the Transvaal Native Congress – would link up with the delegation in London. Two other students, Richard Msimang and D.D.T. Jabavu, who were in London at the time, also joined the delegation.[10]

'Without the land, the natives are absolutely compelled to starve'
Mangena and Seme informed the South African delegation of their optimism that the British government would most likely reject the racial clauses in the South African Union Bill. They had good reason for this. The Bill had in fact originated in the British House of Commons. On 13 May 1908, a debate on 'native affairs in South Africa' was introduced by Mr Percy Alden, MP for Tottenham.[11] He moved a motion for the recognition of the growing opinion in the colonies of South Africa 'in favour of safe-guarding the rights and future of the natives in any scheme of political unification or Federation'. He proposed that the imperial government should welcome the adoption of provisions calculated to render possible 'the ultimate inclusion of the whole of British South Africa in federal union'. He explained that he intended no criticism of the South African British colonies, and that, as a member of the Liberal Party himself, he supported the decision to give self-government to the Transvaal and the Orange River Colony. While the imperial government should not dictate the form of the federation or Union, or indeed interfere in its internal affairs, it nevertheless had a 'direct responsibility for the natives of South Africa'. The natives, he argued, should not be denied elementary principles of justice by the new Union. Rather than enforcing order, a 'right solution' had to be found. In support of his proposal, Alden quoted Lord Selborne:

> No reasonable man can live in this country and doubt that the existence here
> of the white community must, from first to last, depend upon their success or
> failure in finding a right solution of the coloured native questions or, in other
> words, upon the wisdom they can show in determining the relative places
> which the white, coloured and native population are to fill. It would, indeed,
> be a hideous error to suppose that the white people of this country are dis-
> charged of responsibility by perfecting an arrangement for enforcing order
> among the native population. The mission they have undertaken is of a far

higher and more difficult nature than that, and one which calls for the inspiration of the statesman rather than that of the soldier.[12]

A 'hideous error' should be avoided. Alden went on to propose that the native question could not be regarded as a Natal or Transvaal question, but as a South African question. The natives were not 'tools', but men, and anyone who did not see this would likely cause disruption in the Empire. Bearing in mind that Africans were the numerical majority, whites 'had somehow or other to assimilate the blacks' in the government if the desired consolidation had any prospect of succeeding. Blacks could not be driven into the sea. The prevailing assumption that natives were only good to work for the white races was a 'dangerous doctrine', not only for the whites in South Africa but for the Empire as a whole. Alden referred to the 1905 report of the South African Native Affairs Commission, which noted the concern among Africans that they were governed solely to serve the interests of the white population. Arguing that administrative reforms could not be carried out in an atmosphere of racial antipathy, exclusiveness and selfishness, Alden stated that 'the natives were correct that in the past they had suffered from many breaches of faith on the part of the white population'. It was essential to restore confidence in the rule of the imperial government and South African whites. The commission also rejected the belief that 'the native must be treated somewhat harshly because he was incorrigibly lazy and because the future of South Africa depended upon his being compelled to work'. The gender stereotype was also dismissed: 'The labour of tilling the soil is shared but no means exclusively performed by native women, and the representation of the native living at his own village, a lazy, luxurious life supported by his wife or wives, is misleading.'[13]

Alden's counter-argument was that the 'lazy' African was 'as lazy as a good many men in England who had the opportunity of work and failed to do it'. Any perceived reluctance to work in occupations such as mining could be attributed to conditions of employment: 'the native who worked in the mines often had to walk hundreds of miles before performing his irksome duties', for a small sum of money, and in 'very unpleasant occupations'. Moreover, natives were subjected to harsh and unjust treatment. Africans should not be regarded simply as a source of unskilled labour. Rather, they had to be integrated into the political, social and economic fabric of the new society.

Another contentious issue concerned the allocation of land to dispossessed Africans. Alden's conception of land was an expansive one, encompassing both physical and metaphysical elements. Thus, land was not simply a piece of ground. Through it, Africans were connected to their own systems of government and cultural identity, and it also ensured economic well-being. In short, land was life.

The taking away of land meant the negation of entire societies, cultures and modes of being. In making the point, Alden was not breaking new ground. A similar conception about land prevailed among the Scottish. Alden argued that the effect of land policies relating to the creation of reserves and the expulsion of Africans from their traditional homes resulted in 'a disintegration in the tribal system', which 'undoubtedly contained the germs of unrest'. For Africans, 'the struggle for land [was] simply the struggle for life' – a fact that held good for England and Scotland too: 'without the land, the natives were absolutely compelled to starve. It was no use saying the natives did not know the value of land, and did not make the best use of it. As a matter of fact, that was the reason put forward for alienating their land.' Alden argued that this was an 'extremely dangerous' justification, and pointed to a resolution in Natal that constituted nothing more than an attempt to 'grab the land for European occupation'. Africans, he submitted, had been dispossessed of their land on the dubious grounds that 'a higher civilisation must come in and compel them to work'. This argument was false and self-serving, because 'it was well-known that whenever self-interest led any race to do an injustice to another race they generally found some good moral or religious excuse for doing it'. Alden offered a solution: the fair allocation of land to Africans. Land, Alden proposed, was inevitably linked to the question of franchise for Africans. As such, the 'safest and the best way of ensuring that the natives would not lose their present tenure of the land and to ensure that they should be safeguarded in their rights in holding it, was to give them some form of representation and some form of franchise'. Since this policy was already applicable in the Cape Colony, other colonies could follow suit. But the franchise should be limited to an educated few property holders, and the pretext of insufficient education should not be used to prevent natives from exercising the rights of franchise. Instead, Alden argued, there should be greater investment in the education and the improvement of the standard of living of the natives.

Alden went on to address the issue of martial law. Two years earlier, in 1906, the Bambatha uprising had forced the British Parliament to consider its policy on martial law, and now it should be considered in relation to the proposed South African Union. Alden argued for the urgent release of the Bambatha detainees, as there was no longer any necessity for martial law, and no evidence to justify large-scale detentions. Indeed, the source of the problem lay elsewhere. Evidence showed that 'martial law, native floggings, and the imprisonment of Dinuzulu' were the cause of social and political instability. Peace could be achieved by stopping these, not escalating them. He rejected a proposal that there should be a Bill of Indemnity, arguing that 'illegal acts made possible by reason of Martial law imposed against the wish of the British Government' had to be punished even if the perpetrators were British. The sporadic rebellion had been caused by 'continued and repeated breaches of faith in Zululand on the part of the Natal Government'. Alden called for the release of Dinuzulu, demanding to know how long he would remain in prison on vague charges of high treason. He concluded by moving

> That this house, recognising signs of a growing opinion on the part of the self-governing colonies of South Africa in favour of safeguarding the rights and future of the natives in any scheme of political unification or federation, expresses its confidence that his Majesty's Government will welcome the adoption of provisions calculated to render possible the ultimate inclusion of the whole of British South Africa in federal union.[14]

Both Mangena and Seme were present as the debate unfolded, and Sir Charles W. Dike, MP for Gloucestershire, rose in support of the motion. Emphasising the necessity for a resolution of the native question, he said that race should not be used to distinguish who was entitled to vote and who was not. Indeed, the importance of resolving the native question was pivotal to the British Parliament's decision to invite South Africa to consider the establishment of the Union. Four central issues were: franchise for the Africans; alienation and dispossession of the land; the use of martial law; and forced labour.

Mangena immediately wrote to his colleagues in the Cape, Natal and Transvaal, expressing the urgency of a direct approach to the House of Commons in the light of the 'positive sentiments expressed' relating to matters of concern among the 'natives of South Africa'. Though it is unclear whether any of the delegates that eventually went to the House of Commons represented the Native Convention, it is notable that there was a change of strategy subsequent to the May 1908 debate at the House of Commons, with correspondence now being addressed directly to the British government, rather than the South African government.

Sir George Grey: 'father of the idea of South African Union'
The apparently positive attitude displayed by the House of Commons was to be short-lived, however. Jan Smuts, who was colonial secretary in the Transvaal government at the time, began lobbying in the Union debate. His position was clear: there would be no native franchise, regardless of education or property holding; the coloured position remained unchanged, though subject to parliamentary override; and no commitments would be made on the land or labour front. Those questions would be dealt with by separate legislation, after the adoption of the Act of Union. Similarly, the question of martial law would be a domestic issue which the British government should not interfere with. Smuts had prepared the draft constitution for the formation of the Union. What he wanted for the

white races was 'a national Parliament, a national executive'. The native races had to trust these institutions 'for a solution of those questions that have troubled us in the past'.[15]

At the same time that Smuts was drawing up a constitution entrenching racial separation and the supremacy of the white race, J.T. Jabavu was drawing up a petition to the House of Commons calling for racial equality. The petition contained a prophetic statement: 'The only practical and efficient means whereby fair and just administration and legislation can be attained, peace, harmony, and contentment secured, is by granting equal political rights to qualified men irrespective of race, colour, or creed.'[16] Matters came to a head in London on 27 July 1909. The South African delegates presented the outcomes of the 1908 National Convention to the House of Commons in the form of a draft Bill – the South Africa Bill of 1909.[17] Before it was read, the Earl of Crewe, secretary of state for the colonies, invoked Sir George Grey:

> The man who might be described as the father of the idea of South African Union was that very distinguished colonial governor, Sir George Grey. When Sir George Grey was there in 1858 the Orange Free State made advances towards some system of federation or union – advances which he, the man on the spot of whom we have heard so much since, was in favour of meeting. But in those days, as I have said, the idea of such union was not very palatable at home.[18]

The 1909 Bill marked a culmination, he suggested, as he gave credit to 'the remarkable band of statesmen in South Africa' that represented 'all parties and both races'. The secretary noted that there were two major motivations behind the formation of the Union: imperial considerations, and local and practical considerations that included a functional economy and a pragmatic political system. Rather than dealing with four separate administrations, the imperial government preferred dealing with only one. Concerning the controversial issue of the franchise, the secretary was not prepared 'to take the responsibility for the possible wrecking' of the Union 'by a provision of this kind', i.e. the expansion of the native franchise beyond the Cape. If there were to be a change in this regard, it must be made in South Africa by South Africans themselves, and it was not possible to force the issue. The secretary had clearly ignored the fact that the South Africans before him were not representative, and that the unanimity they claimed represented only a small section of the population – this despite the fact that the previous year Parliament itself had expressly noted that Union would not be possible without the accommodation of the natives. When the secretary spoke of 'both races', he clearly had in mind the English and the Afrikaners, excluding Africans. Instead of increased rights following the war, the limited rights enjoyed by Africans were threatened, something which the secretary was keen to address. He expressed the hope that the South African government would not disenfranchise a class of persons that had until then held the right to vote; any such action would be viewed 'with very deep disappointment' by the British. Disenfranchisement, he warned, 'is always an odious stain in itself', and its application in the Cape 'would assume a somewhat especially odious form'. And then, in a seeming dismissal of any such possibility, he described disenfranchisement as 'a purely abstract question'. The secretary concluded on a positive note: this union of colonies, he remarked, constituted 'a great advance in the fusion of the races which inhabit South Africa'. Its inhabitants – 'some of British, some of Dutch, and some of French Huguenot descent' – had forebears who had suffered and fought for freedom over many years, and it would be one of 'the most tragic ironies of all history if men descended from such races as those had remained permanently estranged'. He proposed that they be joined in a free Union under the British Crown, and on that rhetorical flourish – which ignored the Africans – he proposed that the Bill be read.

Having seconded the Bill, Lord Northcote proposed that the concerns of the 'coloured races in Cape Colony', which had been brought to their attention by Schreiner 'and other distinguished signatories in South Africa', be addressed. He issued a blunt reminder of what, in his view, lay behind the concept of the formation of the Union: 'the determination to have white rule and white responsibility for the conduct of public affairs'. In contrast with its overseas dominions, there was no risk in the United Kingdom that the white races would be 'swamped by an influx of coloured races'. Therefore, the British government was determined to preserve, at least, the administration of public affairs by white people.

Another member, Lord Courtney, rejected such claims, arguing that there was no proper basis for the exclusion of the native races of Natal, Transvaal and the Orange River Colony from the franchise, or for subjecting the franchise to parliamentary amendment in the Cape. Moreover, there could be no functioning government that excluded the overwhelming majority of citizens from participating in governance. Regarding education, statistics proved that there were many native children at school and many qualified men and women in various professions, including barristers. It could not be argued, he said, that those natives involved in the professions were unable to appreciate their entitlement to vote. Bearing in mind that the proportional representation system had been removed from the draft of the Bill, he suggested that there should be permanent representation of natives in Parliament. Complicating matters was the use of concepts such as 'European descent', which were incapable of any precise definition, and he remarked that, 'it would be interesting to know what proportion of blood renders a person European'. Aware that his proposals would be unlikely to find favour, Lord Courtney nevertheless issued a reminder that parliamentary representation tends to unify people, 'to make society one'. And so, voter eligibility 'ought to be cherished if we really wish to build up a society which will hold together as one society in Africa'.

Following this discussion, the Bill was passed. Not a single word was changed. For Jabavu, 'the blow had fallen'. Confronted with a new and painful reality, South Africans would need to unite and take bold action:

> The Native and Coloured people must now realise that an entirely new chapter in South African history is opening, in which they will to depend on themselves and their South African European friends for the securing and maintenance of their civil and political rights. They must become united politically and, refusing to cling to any of the present political parties, must work for the creation of a new political party in the State which will unite the religious and moral forces – European and Natives – of South Africa upon lines of righteous legislation, justice and fair play irrespective of race and colour.[19]

The dream of equality had not died, Jabavu declared, as he urged Africans to have faith in the justice of their cause. For now, they had to accept 'the crumbs of justice' falling from the new constitution. But they would continue 'mentally and constitutionally claiming our full heritage'. This idea of claiming one's 'full heritage' – embracing concepts of the land as well as culture – first proposed here by Jabavu, would underpin much subsequent thought about politics and the law among African intellectuals. A law, founded on justice, should have been the foundation of South Africa, but as Mangena pointed out, the problem with the South Africa Act was that it was not based on 'that which is just'.[20] As a result, it 'failed to qualify as a law'.[21] Significantly, the notion that a law which is not founded on justice is not law at all recalls Cicero, whom Seme regularly quoted in his letters to Locke:[22] 'for there is but one essential justice which cements society, and one law which establishes this justice. This law is right reason, which is the true rule of all commandments and prohibitions. Whoever neglects this law, whether written or unwritten, is necessarily unjust and wicked.'[23] Cicero's notions of justice were important to Seme not least because of the context in which they were developed – the period when Greece was under Roman occupation. And while no direct parallels could be drawn with the South African situation, the abiding lesson for Seme, as he would later point out,[24] was that the call for justice – a justice which 'cements society' – is not necessarily suspended in a situation where there is an unjust occupying force. Most importantly, justice could not be limited to a fortunate few.

Race, gender and the judiciary

The period 1910 to 1920 marked the institutionalisation of the racial order flowing from the Act of Union. This entailed the fundamental transformation of all aspects of society, reflective of the prejudices of the influential leaders of the day: Smuts, Hertzog and Botha. While they had their disagreements about the future of South Africa, their opinion on the native question was clear: South Africa belonged to the white man. A key institution that legitimated the racial political order was the judiciary. Judgments delivered by the superior courts of the time reveal the consolidation of the racial political order by the judicial system. Some judgments were nothing other than mere reflections of the prevalent political attitudes. Though some statutes did not contain explicit racial language, their interpretation by judges produced segregation that accorded with the implicit intentions. One example is *Moller* v. *Keimos School Committee*,[25] which concerned racial segregation in state schools. White parents objected to their children attending the same school as black children. No statute sanctioned racial separation in public schools. But Chief Justice Henry de Villiers, who in 1908 had chaired the whites-only South African National Convention which negotiated the Act of Union, considered race to be a relevant consideration in judicial interpretation, holding that 'pre-possessions' or 'prejudices' of a community are a relevant consideration in judicial determination. Hence, given the prevailing attitudes of the community, white parents could not have been consenting parties 'to an Act by which European parents could be compelled to send their children to a school which children of mixed origin could also be compelled to attend'. Hence, from that moment, and without any compelling legislation, state schools would be segregated.

Racial discrimination was extended with the support of the judiciary to other aspects of life also. In *Williams and Adendorff* v. *Johannesburg Municipality*,[26] the legal issue was whether the law allowed racial segregation in the use of tramcars. One of the judges, Judge Leonard Syer Bristowe, was of the opinion that, bearing in mind the 'feelings and sensitiveness, even the prejudices and foibles of the general body of reasonable citizens', the law should be interpreted to allow racial segregation in the use of tramcars. Another member of the court, Judge John Stephen Curlewis, who would later become chief justice, supported the approach, noting that the use by natives of the ordinary tramcars 'would be so distasteful and revolting to the rest of the community that the council as a common carrier would be justified in refusing to carry them as passengers in the same cars as Europeans'. When racial segregation regarding the use of counters at post offices came up for judicial determination in *Minister of Posts and Telegraphs* v. *Rasool*,[27] Chief Justice James Stratford held that the race of the person likely to use the postal services was relevant. He concluded that the division of the community on the grounds of race or language was *prima facie* 'sensible' as it would result in the convenience and comfort of the public as a whole. He justified this conclusion by holding that officials should be conversant with the 'customs requirements and language of each section' of the public that they would likely serve.

Race aside, this period also saw the entry of women into the legal profession impeded by stereotypes in the judiciary. The most notorious such case is *Incorporated Law Society v. Wookey*.[28] Madeline Una Wookey, a white woman from the Cape, applied under section 20 of the Cape Charter of Justice for registration as an articled clerk to qualify as an attorney. Although a law firm was willing to take her on, the secretary of the Cape Incorporated Law Society refused to register the articles. Litigation ensued, and in the court of first instance, the Law Society was ordered to register the articles. In its appeal, debate centred around the meaning of the term 'persons' employed in section 20 of the Cape Charter of Justice, which provided that any person suitably qualified could apply for admission as an attorney. Did the term 'person' include women? An earlier ruling by the Transvaal Supreme Court, *Schlesin v. Law Society*,[29] had decided against the admission of women to practise as solicitors on the grounds of the 'long practise which has prevailed not only in this country, but in Holland and in England too, not to admit women to be solicitors'. In refusing the admission, Judge Bristowe held that if an 'innovation' was to be made, the correct place would be the legislature, not the judiciary. Schlesin's application for enrolment as an attorney was thus declined. While judges had been willing to admit black attorneys, they would, however, refuse to do the same for women.

In Wookey, the full bench of the Cape Supreme Court, led by Chief Justice Rose Innes, refused Wookey's application for registration of her articles of clerkship, holding that the term 'person' excluded women. The law had to be interpreted in a manner consistent with the practice in England and Holland, where the court's view was that women were not allowed to practise law.[30] Such views were prevalent in the legal profession too. In 1914, the *South African Law Journal* published an article titled 'Women as Advocates and Attorneys'[31] written by R.P.B. Davis, who would later be appointed judge of the Supreme Court in the Cape. Davis referred to an American court decision which found that women were temperamentally unsuitable for the legal profession: 'nature has tempered women as little for the juristical conflicts in the courtroom as for the physical conflicts of the battlefield'. Davis concluded that women should not 'mix professionally in all the nastiness of the world which finds its way into courts of justice; on the unclean issues, all the collateral questions of sodomy, incest, rape'. Deepening the negative stereotype, M. de Villiers argued that women were 'conspicuously unfitted' for the law because they 'have no idea of relevance, or analogy, or evidence'.[32]

Clearly, racism and sexism filtered into the courtroom, which in turn reinforced negative stereotypes. In relation to the status of women as legal practitioners, change would emanate not from the judiciary, but from the legislature. On 26 March 1923, South Africa passed the Women Legal Practitioners Act 7 of 1923.[33] In section 1, the statute proclaimed that 'women shall be entitled to be admitted to practise and to be enrolled as advocates, attorneys, notaries, public or convey-ancers ... subject to the same terms and conditions as apply to men'. Three years later, Constance Mary Hall became the first woman to be admitted as an attorney in South Africa, and Gladys Steyn became the first female advocate to be admitted to the Bar. The position of black women, however, remained unchanged. While there was no statutory bar to their admission as attorneys or advocates, it was only in 1962 that Zainunnisa Gool was admitted as an advocate at the Cape Bar. Gool was the daughter of Dr Abdullah Abdurahman, champion of coloured people's rights in the Cape. Having been admitted late in life, at the age of sixty-four, Gool died the following year after only a few months of practice. Four years later, in 1967, Desiree Finca of Mthatha became the first African female to be admitted as an attorney after serving her articles under Godfrey Pitje, one of the few black attorneys practising in Johannesburg at the time.

The last days of petitions, delegations and deputations
Racial segregation was institutionalised by the Act of Union of 1910. Later statutes moved beyond the formal state institutions into the social sphere, with the result that segregation spread to schools, modes of transport and living areas. Yet, as argued above, the allocation of land along racial lines did not become entrenched until the passing of the iniquitous Natives Land Act in 1913, which strength-ened the pillars of the whites-only country. The SANNC launched a campaign to oppose the Act by petitioning Prime Minister Louis Botha. On 14 February 1914, the *Cape Argus* carried the full petition of the SANNC. Signed by SANNC president John Dube, the petition spoke on behalf of 'all of the native tribes of South Africa'.

The petition began on an uncomfortable note for Botha, an Afrikaner nation-alist, informing him 'that money is now being raised to send a deputation to England to the King against the injustice of the Native Lands Act'. Dube con-tinued: 'You are reported to have said that a political question of this kind would be better settled here, with which we entirely agree.' But the problem, Dube argued, was that the political system which excluded Africans from institutions of power rendered this moot. Though they attempted to prevent the passing of the Bill, 'scarcely any notice was taken of our representations'. In the event that it was said that they had not exhausted every possible means to secure redress for their grievances, the SANNC was now making an appeal to Botha. To assuage Botha and his segregationist followers, Dube explained that they 'made no protest against the principle of separation', provided that it could be 'fairly and practically carried out'. However, racial separation was not practical: 'We do not see how it is possible for this law to effect any greater separation between the races than obtains now.' Accordingly, the law had to be seen for what it was: an instrument 'to compel service by taking away the means of independence and self-improvement'. In this sense, Dube was paraphrasing Msimang, who had written about the effects of the Act in depriving Africans of cattle, restricting their ability to acquire land and compelling them into service contracts with white farmers. The petition stated: 'This compulsory service at reduced wages and high rents will not be separation, but an intermingling of the most injurious character of both races.' When the Act was promoted, its supporters claimed that it would protect Africans living in areas designated for African settlement from evictions. But, as Dube noted, this was of no help at all. The law did not prohibit Europeans holding land in native areas from selling the land. Moreover, Africans were not protected from landlords 'who take advantage under the law to charge high rents, knowing we cannot move away with our stock or find admittance to any other farm as rent-paying tenants. We are more at the mercy than ever we were before.' The solution, Dube proposed, was that there should be no prohibition on the sale of land to Africans until after the report of the Beaumont Commission and after the promised extension of the native reserve areas.[34]

Predictably, the petition fell on deaf ears. Not even an acknowledgement was received. The next step was to approach the imperial government directly. In June 1914, 'An appeal to the Imperial Parliament and Public of Great Britain' listed grievances such as the Act's prohibition on land purchase by Africans, and the 'condition of slavery' resulting from a provision which 'encourages the farmer to exact unpaid service from the native tenants'. As 'loyal subjects of his Majesty the King', the SANNC, which had no voice in legislative councils, felt compelled to send a delegation to the United Kingdom directly.

Unlike the Schreiner delegation of 1909, the 1914 delegation, under Dr Walter Rubusana, was not well received. The Anti-Slavery and Aborigines Protection Society, the human-rights watchdog of the times, showed little sympathy for their cause. On 8 July 1914, the society wrote to the colonial office, noting its dissatisfaction with the presence of the SANNC in London. The society's view was that the discontent over the land question should be resolved in South Africa, not in the United Kingdom. The lack of support by the society must have stung the SANNC, as historically the society had sided with the natives of South Africa.[35] Its impatience with a South African delegation is clear from a newspaper article[36] in which it refers to the representation by Richard Msimang, which, it alleges, 'ends with a threat, for it repeats a statement of the deputation that if their mission failed, they would return and advise our people that the King, like the Union

Parliament, did not care for their welfare'. The society concluded with the following statement, which lays bare its contempt:

> As we have already said the determination of the deputation to visit England was bad enough, but this sort of language puts it out of court completely. Nor do we see any use in circulating stories that these natives were unable by the ordinary means to obtain passages to England. Unfortunately for their cause, the fact remains that they came. Having received the useful advice which they will get from the Colonial Office, their best plan will be to lose no time in returning to their native country, then to assist in the advancement and enlightenment of their race by the many legitimate means which are available.

Ignored by the British government, and abandoned by its erstwhile supporters, the SANNC faced a choice. They could press ahead with their mission or return to South Africa. In deciding the latter, another problem emerged. They had no money to travel home, and it was to the society that they turned. They were advanced a loan which they agreed to repay upon their return. One of the members of the delegation, Sol Plaatje, stayed behind. He engaged in a public campaign, denouncing the Act and the failure of the British government to intervene. The society was not pleased, and they tried to get him to return to South Africa. But Plaatje stayed on until 1916, when the book he had been working on for the past two years, *Native Life in South Africa*, was published in London.[37]

When the SANNC delegation returned to South Africa, the world was in a state of war. That war – the First World War – pitted global powers against each other: Germany versus Britain. The allegiances of the Dutch- and English-speaking people of South Africa were split down the middle. Botha's decision to occupy the German territory of South West Africa cost him the support of many Afrikaners. While their sympathies lay with Germany, the overwhelming Dutch sentiment was for South Africa to remain neutral in the war. The SANNC pledged 5 000 men to fight on the side of Britain, but this was rejected by Botha 'on the grounds that this War was waged between white people only'. Thousands of Africans were instead sent to German South West Africa as drivers to assist in rail construction for military purposes. When the Afrikaners rebelled in 1914 against the seizure of German South West Africa, the SANNC remained neutral. Seventeen thousand Africans served under General Smuts in the 1916 campaign in German East Africa (now Tanzania), with many dying from malaria and fever, and suffering 'severe hardships and privations'. Lastly, the SANNC 'heartily responded' to the call by the imperial government for 25 000 Africans to do manual work in the French docks.

As a result, '615 of our men sank in the SS Mendi while in the service of your majesty and the Empire'.[38]

At the end of the war in 1918, African expectations were again raised. And once again, on 16 December 1918, the SANNC penned a petition, this time to King George V, reminding the monarch of the 'active part played by ourselves' in the war. As 'loyal subjects of His Majesty', they asked for 'equality *under* British rule in South Africa'. Quite clearly, the anti-imperialist position of the SANNC was not yet established. While equality was a demand, imperialism would be accepted. A deputation was sent to meet British prime minister David Lloyd George in Versailles, France, in June 1919. They were unable to do so, and instead they met the prime minister in July 1919, in London. But they returned home empty-handed. The prime minister made no commitments. Britain's policy was self-government for South Africa. It would not interfere in the country's domestic affairs. Thus, after five petitions and five deputations, Africans finally realised that the British imperial government would not fight on their behalf. From this time onwards the strategy of deputations, begun ten years earlier, would gradually but surely be abandoned.

For its part, the nascent South African state was about to commence with an aggressive legislative scheme of segregation. It began with an obnoxious piece of law, the Native (Urban Areas) Act of 1923, through which it would control the 'influx' of blacks into urban areas. The basic aim of the statute was the division of the country into 'native areas' and 'urban areas'. Native areas were the reserves, which were created by the 1913 Natives Land Act, while urban areas were reserved for whites only. The movements of Africans into and outside of urban areas was strictly regulated through the pass system, the terms of which included that every black person in an urban area had to be in employment. With the pass system now in place, the Union government had put the lives of all Africans under its complete control. There would be no participation of Africans in government; they would hold no land in their own name; and their movements would be policed by the state.

Upholding its fidelity to a rights-based political dispensation, the ANC's response to the renewed state onslaught on the rights and freedoms of Africans was 'The African Bill of Rights (1923)'.[39] This was adopted at the annual conference of the SANNC held on 28 May 1923. The document declared that, as human beings, the 'Bantu inhabitants' of the country have the 'indisputable right to a place of abode in this land of their fathers'. As 'sons of the soil', Africans have the right to 'unrestricted ownership of this land, the land of their birth'. Yet, while a system based on human rights appeared inevitable and necessary for South Africa's future, the notion of allegiance to the British government was not rejected. To the contrary, it was hoped that the rights enjoyed by British citizens would extend to the natives of South Africa. Turning Rhodes's imperialist argument on its head, the document proclaimed:

> [Natives'] legal and moral rights to claim the application or extension to them of Cecil Rhodes' famous formula of 'equal rights for all civilised men south of the Zambezi', as well as the democratic principles of equality of treatment and equally of citizenship in the land, irrespective of race, class, creed or origin.[40]

Accordingly, the 'great European races of the Union' were urged to take the rights of the natives into 'serious consideration'. The ANC document called upon Parliament to amend the South Africa Act in order to make provision for the representation of all the 'non-European races domiciled within the borders of the Union of South Africa' both in Parliament and in the provincial councils.

As with previous attempts, these pleas were ignored. The British government would not be drawn into the domestic affairs of South Africa. Hence the British government, which had once promised to ensure equal rights for all British subjects, had turned foe. But this was not all. Blacks would now face a new and additional threat to their freedom: the growth of Afrikaner nationalism.

The rise of Afrikaner hegemony

J.B.M. Hertzog remains the symbol of Afrikaner nationalism. He founded the National Party in 1914, the year the First World War broke out. As a dominion of the British Empire, South Africa was expected to support Britain against Germany. But with his slogan 'South Africa first', Hertzog opposed any involvement in the war, and embraced a policy of neutrality. After Prime Minister Botha offered Britain military assistance, South Africa was asked to seize the German territory of South West Africa. General De la Rey, a senior member of Botha's South African Party, who also opposed the war, began to agitate for an Afrikaner republic. There was a minor rebellion, but it was crushed. In December 1914, the leaders of the rebellion faced a firing squad. The next year, others were tried, convicted, and imprisoned or fined. Despite the eventual triumph of the British and the seizure of South West Africa, the days of Botha's South African Party were numbered. During the campaign of 1917, he faced accusations of being a traitor. In 1919 he died and was replaced by Smuts as prime minister. Hertzog seized the moment. The South African Party suffered huge electoral losses in 1920, and to remain in power Smuts entered into a coalition with the arch-imperialist Unionist Party. It was clear that it was only a matter of time before Hertzog would ascend to the highest office – and by 1924 he was prime minister. The stage was set for the rise of Afrikaner nationalism. Hertzog had two primary goals. The first was to undo South Africa's subordination to the imperial government and to move towards self-government, under the political leadership of the Afrikaners. Together with the prime ministers of other dominions such as Australia, New Zealand and Canada, Hertzog attended the seventh Imperial Conference in October 1926. His primary goal was to destroy the vestiges of the Treaty of Vereeniging,[41] as it subordinated South Africa to the British monarchy.[42]

Britain had by 1919 begun to loosen its shackles over dominions as its focus shifted to economic reconstruction, including paying off a war loan.[43] Furthermore, as arch-imperialist Lord Milner acknowledged, the 'only possibility for the continuance of the British Empire is a basis of absolute, thoroughgoing equal membership between England and the Dominions'.[44] After his electoral losses in 1920, Jan Smuts, once 'the handyman of Empire',[45] expressed apparent support for the 'virtually unanimous' view that the British Empire could only exist 'on a basis of complete freedom and equality' with its dominions.[46] After initial resistance, Britain could no longer contain the rising sentiment of Afrikaner nationalism, and gave in to Hertzog's demands. In 1926, Lord Arthur Balfour, a conservative British politician and former prime minister, chaired the Imperial Conference in London. Its resolutions, hammered out during 'a fortnight of private discussion',[47] with Hertzog at the centre, acknowledged: 'autonomous communities within the British Empire, equal in status, in no way subordinate one to another in any aspect of their domestic or external affairs, though united by a common allegiance to the Crown, and freely associated as members of the British Commonwealth of Nations'.[48]

In the meantime, however, Hertzog sought to achieve his second important goal: the formalisation and entrenchment of white control over Africans. In the aftermath of the miners' strike of 1922, a primary focus was the protection of white workers. The Wages Act was passed in 1925, permitting government to decide wage rates in specific industries. But the Act excluded agricultural and domestic workers, who were mainly black, with the result that employers were able to decide on their wages. The Mines and Works Amendment Act was passed in 1926, making the 'colour bar' lawful in the mining industry. By then, Hertzog's 'civilised labour policy' was in full motion. Its central tenet was the displacement of Africans by white workers, often at higher wages. In the town of Smithfield, in the Orange Free State, Hertzog had delivered his views on the native question in November 1925. What the government wanted to achieve, he announced, was the removal of Africans from the common voters' roll in the Cape, in order to achieve a uniformity of policy across the Union. Africans would be represented in Parliament by a selected number of white representatives, and local 'native councils' would be established, with the role of government being primarily advisory. In return for Africans giving up their franchise at the Cape, Hertzog promised that 'development funds' would be made available for 'native' areas. He presented his proposals through the Native Bills in 1925.

The success of the Hertzog government and the aggressive tone of its administration presented a profound challenge, though at a moment when the ANC was at its weakest organisationally, politically and also ideologically. Moreover, the ANC was short of funds. It had previously relied on the support of chiefs, but this was drying up. Its political structures were weak, as it was still grappling with its identity, whether it was a party of the African elite or a mass-based party. Ideologically, it was squeezed between the vicious nationalism of the Afrikaners and the continuing – though weakened – imperialism of Britain. This accounts for the ambiguity in ANC messages that called for equality, while simultaneously pledging loyalty to Empire. At its national conference held on 31 May 1924, the ANC did not denounce the government outright. It passed a resolution expressing 'appreciation' of the decision by the Union government 'in summoning periodical conferences of chiefs and representatives of the Bantu population for the purposes of ascertaining the sentiments of the Bantu people in regard to legislative measures affecting the native people of the Union'. Noting the ineffectiveness of conferences with the government, the ANC nevertheless recommended that 'steps be taken' to ensure that African people, through their chiefs and their existing political, industrial and agricultural associations, elected their own representatives to government conferences. Promising a 'vigorous campaign' for the removal of the colour bar in the Union of South Africa Act, there were, however, no practical steps for the achievement of this goal, other than the necessity for the cooperation of all black associations. Regarding education, it was resolved that it would be in the interests of African people for 'educational facilities' to be brought within the reach of every child; furthermore, education should be placed directly under the control of the government. Also, the 'cynical shooting of the Bantu people in various parts of the country' was decried.[49] The final resolution was, typically, an ineffectual statement that the ANC could no longer tolerate such a state of affairs.

By this time, the political space had been taken up by the All Africa Convention under the forceful and persuasive leadership of Davidson Don Tengo Jabavu, son of John Tengo Jabavu. Incorporating a broad spectrum of African opinion, the AAC aimed to promote the rights of African people. D.D.T. Jabavu was among the delegates called to the government's Native Conference held in Pretoria in 1925. There, Hertzog laid out his plan for territorial separation of Africans from Europeans. He accepted that, for geographic segregation to be implemented, there should first and foremost be sufficient land. But he could not offer concrete proposals as to the amount of land that would be made available for African occupation. He gave vague and ambiguous promises that Africans would be allowed to 'purchase' and 'lease' land, though without describing the precise location of such land, bearing in mind that the 1913 Natives Land Act expressly prohibited the purchase of land by Africans in designated areas. Denying that native councils would effectively reinstate tribal boundaries, he explained that such councils were, instead, an essential part of native policy:

> Within a Native area, a Native ought to feel at home. So far as he is concerned therefore, there should be no limitations within his area except those which exist in a well-managed community. As I have already said, it is my object that, so far as the Native is capable to do so, he will himself lay down the rules according to the demands of civilisation, which will suit him. I do not only desire that he shall be his own legislator within his own house, but he must also control his administration by means of Native effort. Within these areas there will be opportunity for the Native statesman as well as the Native civil servant. The employment of the European must be the exception, and as a general rule no white person shall be employed for work for which a native can [be] found. In the European areas conditions will naturally be the opposite to a certain extent. While the European is almost wholly excluded from doing work in Native Areas it would not be right to place the European in his own area in a position of unrestricted competition on the part of the native. Both have a right to protection; and the question to me is to give this protection in such a manner that justice shall be done to both.[50]

This was a ruse, however, and Jabavu suggested as much in describing segregation as 'a mere catchword'. Segregation was not possible in South Africa. The reason was simple. There was not enough land to accommodate Africans. In any event, it was impossible to disentangle Africans from the economic structure of South Africa. They were integral to the economy of the country and therefore to the needs of white people. It was thus impossible to separate them in a physical sense. Similarly, Hertzog's notion that black and white should 'develop along their own lines' was ambiguous and impractical. As Jabavu noted, the fact was that Africans could not be divorced from 'institutions of modern civilisations'. In the first place, there was no substitute for such 'institutions' in ordinary tribal life. Furthermore, Africans wished to live in an economic system where new needs that arose from ordinary development, such as schools, homes with furniture and clothing, could be met. These things were generally regarded as necessary for any civilised people, regardless of their race: 'Civilisation involves ability to do things, to control one's environment, mastery and efficiency, and has no relation to nationality or race.'[51] Apart from material needs, there was also a need for freedom and autonomy.

African responses to the Hertzog Bills
In 1926, another ANC conference was held. Although there was much heated discussion, no coherent plan of action to resist Hertzog's Native Bills[52] emerged.

The conference opened with a proposal from Reverend Pitso of Winburg that the congress should place on record 'its sincere and hearty appreciation' of Hertzog's courage in dealing with the 'vexed question known as the native problem' in a practical and sympathetic manner. In so doing, Pitso implied that Hertzog was a statesman, while dismissing the race issue and the right of Africans to solve their own problems. Though some delegates expressed dismay, the ANC president-general, Reverend Z.R. Mahabane, seconded the motion, noting that the ANC would not be committed to the prime minister's proposal, but was merely thanking him for placing it in the open. Previous prime ministers, Mahabane argued, had not declared their true intentions in the fear of losing votes, but Hertzog had taken a different stance. This was like 'a snake that has come out of the grass'. Mahabane explained that this act of thanks would enable him to approach Hertzog in a 'tactful manner'.

In a fiery speech, conference delegate Clements Kadalie said that previous prime ministers had been spoilt by compromise. There was no point in being tactful or beating about the bush, he continued, since it was widely known that Hertzog wanted to remove the 'native franchise'. Therefore, the prime minister and the white people had to be told that their proposals were rejected. Kadalie wanted it placed on record that Africans would not allow white people to relegate them to a position of inferiority in the land of their birth. He declared that there was no such thing as a 'native problem' – instead, there was 'a European problem of weakness, greed and robbery'. White people had robbed the aboriginal races of South Africa of their inheritance, and for this, Kadalie concluded, they could not be thanked or congratulated. His speech was greeted by thunderous applause, and his proposal to reject the Hertzog Bills was carried unanimously after Pitso withdrew his motion in the face of defeat.

A call was made for the amendment of the South Africa Act to make provision for adequate representation of Africans in Parliament and in the provincial councils. The native franchise of the Cape, it was noted, was inadequate. The government had to be urged to take steps to extend such franchise to the northern provinces of the Union. Political and industrial racial segregation was equally deplored. It was proposed that 'a solution that is likely to be acceptable to all parties concerned will be found if a round table conference of an equal number of representatives of the Union government and the African National Congress' could be called as early as possible. Since the Hertzog Bills were on their way in Parliament, the ANC elected a deputation to attend the parliamentary proceedings to watch and advise on further steps to be taken. Moreover, the council system, which constituted the cornerstone of the native administration system, was equally rejected.

Despite the absence of an effective black opposition, Hertzog still failed to pass the Native Bills: he failed to secure the necessary majorities required by law. Both Jan Hofmeyr, an Afrikaner liberal member of Parliament, and Sir James Rose Innes, former chief justice of the Cape, strongly opposed the Bills, arguing instead for the retention of the Cape native franchise. In 1935, having received a fresh electoral mandate, Hertzog dusted off the Bills and made another attempt. He consulted directly with representatives of African opinion. A central figure in consolidating and articulating such opinion was D.D.T. Jabavu of the AAC. In 1935 he produced a comprehensive response to the Bills that contained not only his personal reflections, but also the views of African organisations. Published by Lovedale Press in 1935 as *Criticisms of the Native Bills*, Jabavu's book is testament to his extraordinary ability to exercise linguistic restraint in the face of provocation and abrasiveness. Yet he is always forthright and clear, as this statement from the introduction demonstrates: 'Perhaps there are many citizens of South Africa and abroad who are unaware that the primary object of these draft native bills is nothing but the abolition of the Cape native vote.' The Hertzog Bills had been presented as a package. All four touched upon issues of governance, which, Jabavu noted, were included in the hope that parliamentarians would not pay attention to their substantive effects. Regarding the abolition of the native franchise, Jabavu put forward a cogent argument. At the time, there were more than 800 000 qualified white voters, and only 10 000 qualified black voters. The idea that Africans should be removed from the common voters' roll because they posed a threat to white interests was clearly unfounded. As Jabavu put it, 'the suggestion is unreasonable and almost amusing'. He went on to observe that in 1913 Parliament had admitted that the area set aside for natives, which constituted 12 per cent of the entire area of South Africa, was inadequate, and a promise was made that more land would be made available to Africans by means of legislation. But this had not been forthcoming. 'The present Bill, instead of implementing that old standing undertaking is ... only a promise to redeem another promise made long ago and a promise that cannot be contingent upon any change in the possession of the franchise.'[53]

Jabavu had long been a critic of segregation and separate development. In '"Native disabilities" in South Africa', published by Lovedale Press in 1932, he had written about the colour bar in the South Africa Act. He pointed out that, when put into practice, segregation results in the repression of all non-Europeans, in every conceivable manner. The separation of races was 'being used as a lever to curtail native freedom and movement, to deny the natives the rights of trading in their areas, to cripple their education grounds, and generally to deny them their common human rights and privileges of equality and opportunity in economic development, undermining all fair play'. Jabavu proved not only to be an effective opponent to the government; he also represented a threat to the growth of the ANC.

Contesting the space for African hegemony: AAC versus ANC

Under Jabavu's leadership, the agile and vociferous AAC represented strong competition to a faction-ridden ANC, for whose survival Seme had fought in the early 1930s. Jabavu's proposal for the transformation of the AAC into a mass-based organisation was accepted at the 1937 AAC annual convention, where it was agreed that membership should be recruited directly from branches. By making the proposal, Jabavu aimed to guarantee the status of the AAC as the sole representative of Africans in the country. Hitherto the AAC did not recruit individual members, but was instead a federal structure comprising various affiliated African organisations. The ANC was one of these affiliating organisations. Unlike the AAC, the ANC's mode of recruitment depended primarily on individual affiliation. Tribal chiefs, however, could affiliate on behalf of entire tribes. Seme participated in the discussions within the AAC on behalf of the ANC. Supported by the older generation of ANC leaders, he opposed the proposal to allow the AAC to recruit individual members. Considering the organisational weaknesses of the ANC during the Seme presidency, with Seme himself questioning whether it was 'dead', it is almost certain that the ANC would have been decimated by the AAC.[54] Seme's refusal to allow the AAC to move into the organisational spaces of the ANC rescued his organisation from a potential terminal collapse. Still, the AAC remained a national structure, though with fewer affiliations on a regional level, and as such its broad penetration made it difficult for the ANC to recruit, raise funds and sustain itself. Up to then, the strength of the ANC was its branch organisation, which by now was considerably weakened.

While Seme had saved the ANC from possible extinction, he was unable to save his own position. By 1936, he was already being blamed for the organisation's stagnation. The small group of critics included Reverend James Calata, who was at the time president of the ANC in the Cape. In his view, if the ANC were to regain national support, sharpen its focus and provide a platform for confrontation with the government, then Seme's lethargic presidency had to be terminated. By 1937, Calata had garnered enough support to push this motion – but no replacement had yet been found. However, later that year, in November, a familiar name cropped up – Reverend Zaccheus Richard Mahabane. Well versed in the politics of the ANC, Mahabane had, between 1924 and 1927, been president-general of the organisation. He was also experienced in political intrigue, as, together with Seme, Mahabane had successfully plotted the removal of his successor, Josiah Gumede. Since his own ousting, Mahabane had become a firm ally of Seme, who became president in 1930, taking over from Mahabane's nemesis, Gumede. Whether rightly or wrongly, Gumede had been accused of communist leanings after his 1927 visit to the Soviet Union.[55] His alleged Soviet sympathies gave his detractors the perfect excuse, and a mere three years after his election, they successfully campaigned for his removal, and Mahabane was reinstated as president-general.

With Mahabane's election as ANC president-general in 1937, the wheel had turned full circle. Seme's friend had now turned enemy. Yet Mahabane himself would not last very long in the position. The ANC was in urgent need of organisational overhaul. Its vision of national unity was not reflected in its own political culture. Its original structure had become dysfunctional, bureaucratised and institutionally weak. As the next chapter reveals, Mahabane's successor would not only modernise the ANC, he would set the most comprehensive vision yet conceived for South Africa.

8

The birth of constitutionalism[1]

Many of the Bantu feel and rightly too that the laws of the land are not
made for Black and White alike.   — Charlotte Maxeke, 1930

Of all the presidents of the ANC, few are as maligned as Dr Alfred Bitini Xuma. What historians have yet to engage with, however, is Xuma's commitment to human rights. While he was not the originator of the idea that human rights play a central role in South African society, he was the inheritor of this notion, and also a powerful interlocutor. Xuma occupied a transitional position, between the founding generation of the ANC, which first located the struggle for freedom in the notion of human rights, and what may be termed the liberating generation of the 1950s.

A brief glance at his history is helpful in understanding what drove Xuma, a man who abandoned politics and returned to the obscurity of his medical practice, eventually dying in 1962, an isolated man in a country he could no longer recognise. Born at Manzana in the Ngcobo district of the former Transkei in 1893, Alfred Bitini was the son of illiterate parents who were Wesleyan converts. In 1911, he qualified as a primary-school teacher at the Clarkebury Institution. After teaching for two years in the Eastern Cape, he left for the United States where he qualified as a medical doctor at Northwestern University in Chicago, in 1926. His decision to study medicine in the United States was influenced by another son of Ngcobo, Ngcubu Poswayo, who had qualified as a barrister in London some years before.

Upon Xuma's return to South Africa in 1927, he set up a medical practice in Johannesburg. In a period before the evictions of the Group Areas Act, he lived in the suburb of Sophiatown in a comfortable home that he named Empilweni (place of health). Xuma was soon able to afford several properties, and he also made personal donations to the ANC. It was his work as a black doctor in a racist society that drew him to politics. In the 1930s, he occupied an executive position in the All Africa Convention, which continued to grow as the ANC declined under the presidency of Seme. Some time later, though, Xuma was recruited to contest the 1940 election for the position of ANC president-general – a position that he won.

Birth of the Youth League and the demise of Xuma

Xuma stands accused of having a 'pompous English style' and being obsessed with 'delegations and telegrams'.[2] Nelson Mandela is similarly critical, and in his auto-biography, *Long Walk to Freedom*, he mentions two encounters with A.B. Xuma, the first of which occurred in 1943. At the time, Mandela formed part of a young leadership group that included Anton Lembede, Ashby Mda, Walter Sisulu and Oliver Tambo.[3] Xuma had already been president for three years when Mandela and his comrades sought his approval for establishing a youth league, under the wing of the ANC. The five young leaders expressed concern about the possible demise of the moribund ANC, believing that it needed to change tactics and adopt a more radical policy: mass mobilisation. Xuma, one of South Africa's first black medical doctors, had been educated at universities in America and at Edinburgh. Given this background and the tenor of the times, it is perhaps unsurprising that Xuma dismissed their ideas. Africans, he argued, were 'too unorganised and undisciplined to participate in a mass campaign'.[4] He offered a compromise by suggesting that the league 'should be a more loosely organised group and act mainly as a recruiting committee for the ANC'.[5] By facilitating the establishment of the Youth League, Xuma paved the way to fresh ideas, new energy and the radicalisation of the ANC.

Exploiting the opportunity thus opened to them, Mandela and his colleagues organised a small youth committee. Their intention was to launch a fully fledged and autonomous youth league, which would be a vehicle for mass mobilisation and direct confrontation with the white government led, once again, by Jan Smuts.[6] The goals were the same as those spelt out by the ANC in 1912, and foremost was the urgent task of resisting government encroachment on African liberty and land. What distinguished the ANC Youth League from its mother body was strategy rather than substance. The age of 'decorous protest'[7] had come to an end. It was time for mobilisation, agitation and confrontation. However, when, in 1944, the youth leaders met to elect their inaugural executive, it was not Nelson Mandela whom they appointed as president. Instead, they chose a young lawyer, an LLB graduate, who was perhaps the most intellectually gifted of his generation: Anton Muziwakhe Lembede. An articulate spokesperson, Lembede did not focus solely on confrontation; instead, he sketched a new order, a vision of a 'non-racial' future for South Africa. His friend and colleague Ashby Mda gave a fitting tribute when Lembede later graduated with an MA degree: 'This significant achievement is the culmination of an epic struggle for self-education under severe handicaps and almost insufferable difficulties. It is a dramatic climax to Mr Lembede's brilliant scholastic career.'[8] While serving as president of the ANC Youth League, Lembede also served articles of clerkship to Pixley Seme. When, in 1947, Lembede suddenly and unexpectedly died of natural causes, his deputy, Ashby Mda, replaced him as president of the Youth League. Though Lembede himself had passed away, his vision of a non-racial South Africa lived on.

The second encounter with Xuma, as recounted by Mandela, occurred in 1949. By that stage, the Youth League had drawn up its militant 'Programme of Action'. Its mission was to drive the politics of the ANC towards radical confrontation, and so, rather than the youth merely organising within the ANC, the ANC itself had to be reimagined. The young leaders of five years before – with the exception of the now deceased Lembede – once again approached Xuma. This time, they had a threatening message for him. If he failed to support the Programme of Action, they would, at the next elective conference, organise for his removal as president. But Xuma would not be blackmailed, and he refused: he was confident in his position and prospects of re-election. For the Youth League, though, the task of radicalising the ANC as a liberation movement was urgent. The previous year, D.F. Malan had been elected prime minister, and his electoral platform was clear: South Africa would become a white man's country. Apartheid was now the official and unequivocal policy of the government. Yet, Xuma reasoned with the young leaders, Malan's electoral success was no more than a natural extension of the colonial and Union governments. No special measures were necessary to confront Malan's government. Any strategy of mass mobilisation was 'premature and would merely give the government an excuse to crush the ANC'.[9] The youth leaders ultimately accepted that Xuma would not be persuaded. Not only was he admired by traditional leaders, he also had special relationships with cabinet ministers and had a thriving medical practice. Though critical of Xuma's 'air of superciliousness', Mandela noted somewhat approvingly that 'everything was done in the English manner, the idea being that despite our disagreements we were all gentlemen'.[10] At first, the Youth League did not have a candidate to oppose Xuma. After unsuccessfully approaching the legal academic Z.K. Matthews, they then turned to Dr James Moroka, even though Mandela claimed he was not a member of the ANC because he constantly referred to it as the African National 'Council'. Moroka was pleased to accept the nomination.

Xuma's looming defeat was evident from the start of the conference on 17 December 1949.[11] In Xuma's opening address, he called for unity in the struggle against apartheid, though he rejected any militant response to the situation. This received 'meagre applause'.[12] Seizing the moment, a youth leader named Dilizintaba Mji, who was at the time a medical student at the University of the Witwatersrand, called for a vote of no confidence in Xuma. 'A shockwave went through the hall,' Mji would later recall. 'Never before had an ANC president been openly criticised.'[13] The Programme of Action and the Statement of Policy of the Youth League were adopted by the ANC at the conference.[14] The 'fundamental principle' of this policy was the desire to achieve 'national freedom', which meant 'freedom from White domination and the attainment of political independence'. This implied the rejection of 'segregation, apartheid, trusteeship or white leadership'. The ANC confidently declared: 'African people claim the right to self-determination.' Yet the right of a people to self-determination would itself be subject to a Bill of Rights which protected individual freedoms and liberties. A most important right was the right of 'direct representation in all the governing bodies of the country – national, provincial and local'. The ANC also resolved 'to work for the abolition of differential institutions or bodies specifically created for Africans'. The Programme of Action was a rejection of tactics that had hitherto been favoured by the ANC. Now, a new programme focused on mobilisation and confrontation was on the table. High on the agenda was the creation of a 'national fund to finance the struggle for national liberation'. While the usual media, including newspapers and newsletters, would be employed for 'propaganda' purposes, the ANC needed to establish 'a national press'. Also, 'a council of action' should be formed whose function would be 'to carry into effect, vigorously and with the utmost determination' the Programme of Action by, for example, seeking 'the abolition of all differential political institutions', calling boycotts, strikes and civil-disobedience programmes, and planning a national one-day work stoppage 'as a mark of protest against the reactionary policy of the government'. Education was vital, and there should be a 'common educational forum' where 'intellectuals, peasants and workers' could work towards the 'common good'. There had to be 'national centres of education' to train and educate African youth and to provide 'large-scale scholarships' for overseas education.

Following Moroka's defeat of Xuma, the Youth League of Mda, Mandela, Sisulu and Tambo established its role as kingmaker in the politics of the ANC. For a short while, Xuma remained in the National Executive Committee of the ANC, but a year later he was pushed out and replaced by the young Nelson Mandela. Despite his criticism of Xuma, Mandela acknowledged the role that Xuma played in making the ANC a cohesive, functional organisation. The first step was getting the finances in order. Xuma controlled these with an iron fist, and during his tenure the ANC coffers grew fivefold. He centralised operations so that power was concentrated in the National Executive Committee. Related to this was the introduction of a new constitution in 1943, which abolished the upper house of chiefs and traditional leaders. The ANC would henceforth be an egalitarian organisation where office-bearers held their positions through election rather than inheritance. Donations were sought from individual members as well as foreign funders. This ANC, as reimagined by Xuma, continued into the future, up to the present moment.

'Without women, we cannot go far'
When the SANNC was formed in 1912, its position in relation to women members was somewhat ambivalent. Direct membership by women was not allowed,[15] so,

for example, they were denied the right to elect leaders or serve in elected office. Yet women could be 'auxiliary members', permitted to participate in certain women-related activities of the organisation. Peter Limb suggests that certain male leaders may have regarded women as 'tea and cake ladies', when it came to the heartland of politics, expecting them to be responsible for the logistical aspects of political events such as arranging venues and preparing food for delegates.[16]

It was in this environment that Charlotte Manye Maxeke nevertheless emerged as a leading force and an articulate spokesperson advocating the rights of women, both inside and outside of the Congress movement. Having been an activist in her own right for more than a decade after her return from Wilberforce University in 1901, she was the sole voice representing women at the SANNC's founding conference in 1912. In May and June of the following year, she played a central role in the women's anti-pass campaigns in the Orange Free State. One of these protests took place on 2 June in Winburg.[17] In July 1913, *Abantu-Batho* reported on the drama that had unfolded on the steps of the Winburg Town Hall on the day of the protest:

> The Town Hall was reached. A clerk appeared, and the women demanded to see the Superintendent of the Location. He was soon found, and when he appeared he said. 'Oh! You people almost frightened me. What's wrong?'
>
> 'We've brought your passes: we don't want them anymore', spoke one of the leaders, showing the little bundle.
>
> The Superintendent said: 'I don't want the dirty things!'
>
> 'Where shall I put them?' asked the same woman, and then threw the bundle down at the door, whereas the Superintendent had pointed to some other direction where to put the 'dirty' papers. But eventually he called a clerk or official to pick the bundle up, and commended him to burn it at the yard yonder ... Thus, in the presence of the Superintendent and before all the women, the 'dirty' passes were burnt into ashes! To an outsider it was an amusing little ceremony, but to the women it meant much and more than the Superintendent realized.[18]

The march had an immediate effect, as the superintendent announced the decision to revoke the use of passes by married women, limiting its application to unmarried women. But this too was challenged, with the protesters arguing that their daughters should equally not be required to carry passes. A promise was made that the grievances would receive the attention of the Winburg town council. When the editor of *Abantu-Batho* enquired about the women's next steps, one of their leaders replied: 'we won't carry passes, and we are determined to go to Edenburg [jail] and to reduce the Pass Law into ashes, as we did the "dirty papers"'.[19]

The success of this anti-pass campaign was not replicated elsewhere in the Orange Free State, however. In many towns, such as Waaihoek location, where Maxeke was present at a protest, the police cracked down, creating a combustible atmosphere which was then used as justification for mass arrests. These protests triggered a women's movement, with one of its earliest organisations, the Orange Free State Native and Coloured Women's Organisation, being launched in July 1913.[20] The pass laws remained a key concern of the women's movement through-out the decade. When the Transvaal provincial council proposed a motion to enforce pass laws for native women in the Transvaal, Mrs A. Serrero and Mrs C. Mallela, two leaders of the women's organisation, declared it a 'war of extermin-ation on native women'.[21] The women subsequently formed the 'Native Women Leagues for the purpose of fighting against these brutal laws whose aim is to destroy the dignity of womenfolk', and called upon 'every native woman in the Union to strive for the liberation of our womenfolk from that slavery badge known as the "pass".[22]

In 1917, Charlotte Maxeke launched the Bantu Women's National League, serv-ing as its inaugural president. The immediate challenge, she said, were the pass laws 'which have turned thousands of [our] beloved sons into criminals, and which today seek to degrade the honour of [our] womanhood. It is high time the voice of the Bantu women was heard. They must get themselves ready for the struggle.'[23] There were loud cheers when she declared that 'in the building of this nation, women must lead'. The league would later collaborate with the Transvaal Native Congress, a branch of the SANNC. Its vice-president, Daniel Lentaka, who spoke at a meeting of the league in January 1918, admitted the failure of the Congress movement in bringing women into the fold, and conceded that 'women are organizing themselves without the aid of Congress because [it] has failed to do its duty'. The relationship of autonomy and mutual cooperation forged in the Transvaal between the SANNC and the league persisted throughout the 1920s.

Over the years, the league focused on struggles faced by African women in social as well as political spheres. At the conference of European and Bantu Christian Student Associations held from 27 June to 3 July 1930, Maxeke gave a comprehensive analysis entitled 'Social Conditions of African Women'.[24] For 'Bantu women in urban areas', she began, 'the first thing to be considered is the home, around which and in which the whole activity of family life circulates'. In the household, she continued, 'the woman, the wife, is the keystone of the house-hold'. Yet despite this, Bantu women faced many problems, which 'disturb the peaceful working of our homes'. The most important factor was the absence of men. 'Men leave their homes, and go into big towns ... where they get a glimpse of a life such as they had never dreamed existed.' Similar opportunities were not available to black women who were then compelled to make a living.

Maxeke was, however, aware of the structural reasons for the absence of black men from their families. It was the conditions of employment in 'large towns' like Johannesburg, where 'male Natives' were mistreated by Europeans 'only pushing him further and further down in the social scale, forgetting that it was he and his kind who brought these conditions about in South Africa, forgetting his responsibilities to those who labour for him and to whom he introduced the benefits, and evils, of civilization ...'[25]

Quite apart from employment opportunities that were only available in the cities, another problem was the Natives Land Act, which, Maxeke argued, had disrupted the family structure. It had restricted the land available to blacks, and limited their ability to acquire land without governmental approval. Even the limited land available was 'shrinking daily owing to increased population, and to many other economic and climatic causes'.[26] The Act was a reflection of a broader pattern of the government's failure to pass just legislation. 'Many of the Bantu,' she argued, 'feel and rightly too that the laws of the land are not made for Black and White alike.' As an example, she referred to the pass laws, which produced hardships for black people. Blacks were forced to look for work because that was their only means of survival. Yet there was no work available, thus exposing many Africans to the risk of arrest: 'The poor unfortunate Native, fresh from the country does not know of these rules and regulations, naturally breaks them and is thrown into prison'. In conclusion, she stated that the social conditions of natives had driven her to believe that 'there are two Gods, one for the White and one for the Black'.[27]

In 1930, Dr A.B. Xuma wrote a biography titled *Charlotte Manye (Mrs. Maxeke): 'What an Educated African Girl Can Do'*.[28] In this book, he makes the important observation that Maxeke 'inspired her countrymen for education'.[29] One of these was D.D.T. Jabavu, founder of the AAC, which permitted women delegates to attend its opening conference in 1935.[30] Charlotte Maxeke was one of them. The AAC passed a resolution approving the establishment of a women's organisation affiliated 'on the lines similar to those of the national councils of other races, in order that we may be able to do our share in the advancement of our race'. Jabavu and Xuma were elected president and vice-president respectively, but Maxeke did not stand for a leadership position, presumably because she was at the time president of the Bantu Women's National League. She would nevertheless be an active member of the AAC, attending both its 1936 and 1937 national conferences, and placing the interests of women at the forefront of the struggle for equality and justice. She died in 1939, the year before Xuma, her long-time admirer and a supporter of women's rights, assumed the presidency of the ANC.

Xuma initiated the recognition of women as full members of the ANC, and he helped to establish a women's league, the successor to Maxeke's Bantu Women's

National League. He saw the need for 'the organisation of the women into the African Women's League of the Congress', since 'without women we cannot go far'.[31] In another letter, to A.G. Champion, president of the ANC in Natal, Xuma wrote: 'the African National Congress cannot progress far as a men's organisation only'.[32] Thus, he requested that women be given the opportunity of having their own section in the organisation, and to meet up at mass meetings and annual conferences. Xuma's wife, Madie Hall, an African American, served as the first president of the ANC Women's League. It had taken over thirty years for the ANC to recognise women as full members, and though Maxeke was no longer alive to attend the meeting of 1943 in which this became a reality, her views loomed large in discussions that led to this historic event. From now on, Xuma's ANC would focus on the formalisation of international human-rights standards as the fulcrum of its politics.

The Atlantic Charter and its paradoxes

Xuma's idea of modernising the ANC was an integral aspect of his vision for the future, which should itself be viewed from the perspective of the period. For the greater part of his presidency, from 1940 to 1949, the world beyond South Africa was in a state of upheaval as competing ideologies fought for dominance. In this context, Xuma perceived the election of the National Party as the inevitable elevation of the 'aristocracy of the white colour of the skin', which had been established through the colonial and Union governments, to becoming 'the emblem of supremacy'.[33] He denied that 1948 marked a turning point in history. He had seen enough in his lifetime to know that history could not be reduced to a single event, but constituted a continuum of trajectories. Yet, one event was so significant for him that he seriously entertained the prospect of 'common citizenship of all races' in South Africa, where there would be respect for human rights and fundamental freedoms for all 'without distinction as to race, sex, language or religion'. That event took place on 14 August 1941.

At the height of the Second World War, Franklin D. Roosevelt and Winston Churchill, the leaders of the United States and the United Kingdom, held a series of meetings. They agreed on a set of 'common principles' on which they based their hopes 'for a better future for the world'. These were laid down in the 'Declaration of Principles issued by the President of the United States and the Prime Minister of the United Kingdom', known as the Atlantic Charter. It contained eight principles to which the United States and the United Kingdom committed themselves. Among these principles was a pledge to 'seek no aggrandisement, territorial or other'. No territorial changes would be made to countries falling under the sphere of either the United States or the United Kingdom unless these accorded 'with the freely expressed wishes of the people's consent'. There was a further commitment to 'respect the right of all peoples to choose the form of government under which they will live', and to restore 'sovereign rights and self-government ... to those who have been forcibly deprived of them'.

Economic prosperity was important to ensure world peace. Therefore, '[a]ll states, great or small, victor or vanquished', should be guaranteed 'access, on equal terms, to the trade and to the raw materials of the world'. Economic cooperation was necessary to secure improved labour standards, economic advancement and the social security of each country. After the destruction of Nazi tyranny, peace should be established, giving 'assurance that all the men in all the lands may live out their lives in freedom from fear and want'. There should be freedom of movement, with people being able to cross the oceans 'without hindrance'. Finally, the use of force should be abandoned in settling disputes, and there should be 'a wider and permanent system of general security' that might result in the disarmament of nations which 'threaten, or may threaten aggression outside of their frontiers'.

There was, however, a paradox in all of this. In 1941, the entire African continent was occupied by European countries, as had been the case ever since it was carved up into colonies at the 1884 Berlin Conference. While South Africa was not strictly a colony, it occupied an ambiguous status as a British dominion with a growing movement to become an independent white republic. Rather than ushering in a new world, the Atlantic Charter promised a set of new normative principles that would underpin government within and between states. For Africans in South Africa, whose position of subservience had been entrenched in the South Africa Act of 1909, what resonated most were principles 2 and 3 of the Charter. Principle 2 stated that no territorial changes should be made within states unless they were consistent with 'the freely expressed wishes of the peoples concerned'. Principle 3 promised to 'respect the right of all people to choose the form of government under which they will live'. Self-government would be restored to those who had forcibly been deprived of it.

The emptiness of these hopes was exposed by D.D.T. Jabavu, an articulate critic of the Smuts government at the time. The original terms of the Charter, he argued, were 'couched in grandiose language that easily satisfies complacent communities that find this world a fairly comfortable place to live in'. In the case of Africans in South Africa, the Charter could be epochal if 'given a close and conscientious interpretation' by the government. By the same token, however, it constituted 'nothing more than empty words' if the government refused to extend its promises to Africans.[34] He went on to ask pointed questions: Does the Charter apply to people who fall under the control of imperial countries by reason of imperial wars? Will the Charter cater for the inclusion of Africans when the terms of peace are negotiated? Are Africans included under principle 3, namely the right of people to choose the form of government under which they live? In short, Jabavu asked, would the Charter spur the movement towards the abandonment of racial discrimination? It was only if these questions were satisfactorily answered that the Charter could be said to be meaningful for Africans. Otherwise, so far as Africans were concerned, the Charter was just an 'empty shell'.[35]

Roosevelt may well have intended these principles to apply globally, without exception, as an antidote to Nazi aggression. In fact, he told Churchill[36] that he could not believe that two nations engaged in war against fascism would be opposed to ending colonialism. But Churchill would hear none of this. For him, the focus was on the fascism of Adolf Hitler. Roosevelt pressed the point further: peace was not possible if the colonies remained under European control. That they were being robbed of their raw materials with nothing given back to them would simply plant the seeds for escalation of conflict within the colonies. Churchill's stance merely stiffened. He would not be moved. In the end, the statements of the Atlantic Charter were left hanging, with no recommendations as to the colonies. Roosevelt, however, made his position plain at a press conference held in 1941: 'There has never been, there isn't now, and there never will be any race of people on earth fit to serve as masters over their fellow men ... we believe that any nationality, no matter how small, has the inherent right to its own nationhood'.[37]

Not so for Churchill, social Darwinist and disciple of Thomas Carlyle, a racial theorist of Victorian England.[38] Responding to the massacres of the Mau-Mau people in Kenya, Churchill advocated use of even greater force: 'It's the power of a modern nation being used to kill savages. It's pretty terrible. Savages, savages? Not savages. They're savages filled with ideas – much more difficult to deal with.'[39] When concentration camps were built in South Africa, mainly for Boers, he said they produced 'the minimum of suffering' – despite the deaths of 26 000 women and children. And although 14 000 Africans also died in the British camps, Churchill merely noted his 'irritation that Kaffirs should be allowed to fire on white men'. He would later boast of his experiences in the early days of the Anglo-Boer War, before it 'degenerated': 'It was great fun galloping about.'[40] Later still, as an MP during the Second World War, Churchill demanded an escalation of hostilities, based on his belief that 'as civilised nations become more powerful they will get more ruthless, and the time will come when the world will impatiently bear the existence of great barbaric nations who may at any time arm themselves and menace barbaric nations', adding that 'the Aryan stock is bound to triumph'.[41] In 1942, while making grand pronouncements on the world stage about self-determination and equality as contained in the Atlantic Charter, Churchill was instrumental in causing the Bengal famine that killed more than three million Indians, arguing that the Indians were 'a beastly people with a beastly religion' who 'bred like rabbits'.[42]

It is not surprising that, when asked whether the Atlantic Charter would apply to Africans, Churchill replied in the negative. After all, he said, 'I have not become the King's First Minister in order to preside over the liquidation of the British Empire.'[43] On 9 September 1941, he addressed the House of Commons, dispelling any doubts. The Atlantic Charter would not apply to British colonies:

> At the Atlantic meeting, we had in mind, primarily, the restoration of the sovereignty, self-government and national life of the states and nations of Europe now under the Nazi yolk, and the principles governing any alterations in the territorial boundaries which may have to be made. So that is quite a separate problem from the progressive evolution of self-governing institutions in the regions and people which owe allegiance to the British Crown. We have made declarations in these matters which are complete in themselves, free from ambiguity, and relate to the conditions and circumstances of the territories and peoples affected. They will be found to be entirely in harmony with the high conception of freedom and justice which inspired the joint declaration.[44]

Once again, the ANC had been let down by the British government. Churchill's view that equality was good for some, but not all, was a familiar response of the British government. Yet the ANC was acutely aware that, in order to break white domination over blacks in South Africa, a new course of action had to be charted on the domestic front. The adoption of a basic set of norms, founded on equality, had been urged throughout the period of Empire, but this had come to nothing. And now, inspired by the universal vision of the Atlantic Charter, the ANC saw the opportunity of reimagining the foundations of the legal system. Leading African intellectuals would be approached to draw up South Africa's first Bill of Rights. For Nelson Mandela, the Charter reaffirmed 'faith in the dignity of each human being and propagated a host of democratic principles'.[45] While 'some in the West' saw the Charter as empty promises, Mandela said, 'those of us in Africa' were inspired by its terms. Directly arising from the Atlantic Charter, South Africa's first Bill of Rights was thus born.

South Africa's first Bill of Rights

At the December 1942 conference of the ANC, Xuma devoted a substantial part of his address to the Atlantic Charter. The freedoms promised by the Charter, such as freedom from fear, freedom from want and freedom from oppression, were vital and fundamental, Xuma declared. Also, 'They have a special meaning and significance to the Africans in South Africa. With police raids, mass arrests, landlessness, homelessness, low wages, pass laws and other restrictions and disabilities, there are no such freedoms for them.'[46]

To translate the promises of the Atlantic Charter into a reality, it was necessary, Xuma said, to develop an 'Atlantic Charter for Africans of the Union of South Africa'. But no charter should be applied selectively, on the grounds of race: 'The test of the people is their aim, not their colour.' He closed his address with the proposal that an Atlantic Charter for Africans be drawn up; this was unanimously endorsed at the conference. So, too, was the recommendation regarding its universal application. While the first thirty years of the ANC had been spent opposing the race-based policies of the Union government, the years that followed would focus on mobilising around a common set of principles, crystallised in the envisaged Charter for Africans.

A committee comprising twenty-eight influential Africans was tasked by Xuma with formulating this Charter. It included three lawyers, and it was chaired by Z.K. Matthews, an attorney and the first African to obtain the LLB degree at the University of South Africa. On the advice of Johannesburg attorney Deneys Reitz, who was also a prominent member of the South African Party, Matthews had chosen to become an attorney rather than an advocate; the Transvaal rules of court did not require the holder of a law degree from a South African university to serve articles before being admitted as an attorney. However, soon after being admitted as an attorney, Matthews decided to make a change, as the black lawyers he knew – Seme, Msimang, Montsioa, Mangena and H. Bikitsha – did not appear 'to have a particularly distinguished career at the Bar'.[47] He took up a scholarship at Yale University in 1932, and two years later graduated with a master's degree in anthropology before attending the London School of Economics for further specialisation. When he returned to South Africa in 1936, Matthews took up a lectureship at the University of Fort Hare, where he taught anthropology as well as native law and administration, before becoming the first black man in the country to be appointed professor of law. Another member of the committee was Lionel Mtimkulu, the first African to graduate with a law degree from the University of Cape Town,[48] who was at the time practising as an attorney in the Eastern Cape – only the second African attorney to do so in that area. The venerable Seme, who had recently been reinstated as a lawyer, was also a member of the committee.[49]

The task was completed the following year, in November 1943, and adopted at the ANC conference in December. Two documents were produced. The first, called 'Africans' Claims in South Africa', began by acknowledging the significance of the Atlantic Charter which had 'aroused hopes and fired the imagination of all peoples' about the new world order it envisaged.[50] For South Africa, the Charter held special significance because of its endorsement by Smuts, who had pronounced that the post-war world would be based on principles contained in the Charter. Deneys Reitz, by now a minister in the Smuts government, had declared

THE BIRTH OF CONSTITUTIONALISM

at the Sixth Session of the Native's Representative Council in December 1942 that the freedoms in the Charter were also intended to be applicable to the African people of South Africa. This view was shared by at least twenty-six other signatories to the Charter who had announced that the freedoms must be realised by the Allied powers 'in their own lands as well as other lands'. If there was a degree of ambiguity in this, South African blacks responded with a comprehensive statement prepared by the Africans' Claims Charter Committee. It was headed 'The Atlantic Charter: From the standpoint of Africans within the Union of South Africa'.[51] Although the Atlantic Charter promised an end to territorial expansion, concerns remained of explicit as well as subtle forms of territorial control such as economic strangulation 'under veiled forms of assistance'. Turning to Abyssinia as an example, assurances were sought about the status and independence of that country and her right of sovereignty. Any political or economic assistance that might be required in Abyssinia should take place freely and in accordance with the free expression of the wishes of the people of Abyssinia.[52] A war aim of the Allied nations had been to liberate territories and peoples under foreign domination. To fulfil this, the Africans' Claims urged the liberation of colonies, and the provision of security.

As one of the two countries that had drawn up the Atlantic Charter, Britain was urged to reconsider the South Africa Act of 1909, as 'Africans were not contracting parties' to the arrangements concluded under that Act, and did not regard its contents 'as morally and politically' acceptable to them. The declaration that territorial changes could only take place if they accorded with the freely expressed wishes of people was especially important to the Africans' Claims Charter Committee. While they recognised that this was initially intended to refer to territorial changes in Europe caused by military aggression, other parts of the world were affected too. Here, the argument was forthright. Africans were concerned about territorial changes that related to the African continent. While the most invasive territorial organisation and reorganisation of Africa had taken place in 1884, fresh territorial changes in respect of West Africa, East Africa and Southern Africa were currently being contemplated by Smuts. It was imperative, the committee submitted, that any such changes should not take place without the freely expressed wishes of the people in those areas. To do otherwise would be to repeat 'the mistakes of the past whereby African people and their lands were treated as pawns in the political game of European nations'. A specific demand regarding colonisation was made: self-government for colonial people had to be actively pursued as a matter of international concern. Undoubtedly, the most important principle for Africans was the right to form one's own government, or the right to self-determination, whose genesis could be traced to the 'Fourteen Points' of President Woodrow Wilson in 1918. For Africans, self-determination would not be confined to states, but extend to the political rights of minorities and oppressed peoples within states. On the African continent, 'European aggression and conquest had resulted in the establishment of Alien governments which, however beneficent they might be in intention or in fact, are not accountable to the indigenous inhabitants.'[53]

By according Africans 'sovereign rights and to establish administrations of their own choosing', the Allied nations would prove their commitment to the principles of the Charter. However, even as such principles were being articulated, the ANC was reluctant to ask for full liberation from white rule in South Africa. Instead, it sought to draw a distinction between those African countries where full sovereignty was possible and others where 'there are the peculiar circumstances of a politically entrenched European minority'. In those instances, such as the Union of South Africa, full independence might not be possible, yet Africans could be given 'full citizenship rights and direct participation in all the councils of the state'.

Colonialism had, furthermore, turned Africa into a vassal, a mere supplier of raw materials, even though the Atlantic Charter promised free trade in raw materials, without distinction between the victors and the vanquished. The ANC believed that Africa faced the risk of economic exploitation, to the detriment of the indigenous inhabitants and the advantage of foreigners. The freedom to trade could, however, only take place if accompanied by meaningful political freedoms. After all, the primary obligation of any government is to promote the economic advancement of the peoples under its charge, and any obligation, agreement, contract or treaty in conflict with its primary obligation should not be countenanced. The improvement of labour standards should be applied to African economies, and include the removal of the colour bar, the training of Africans in skilled occupations, remuneration according to skill rather than race, a living wage across the board, and proper and adequate housing for all workers, regardless of race. While Nazism had to be destroyed, this was not enough: 'All forms of racial domination in all lands, including the Allied countries' had to be completely destroyed. The use of force had to be abandoned. But the South African case deserved special attention. Here, the committee indicated force was frequently resorted to as a means of supressing 'the legitimate ventilation' of grievances of oppressed, unarmed and disarmed sections of the population. Only if the principle extended to cover that scenario would it be legitimate.

The second document that the committee prepared was a 'Bill of Rights, Full Citizenship Rights and Demands'; part of the Africans' Claims, it was also adopted at the 1943 conference. Its contents are testament to the talent and the farsightedness of its members. The rights are listed under seven headings: Full Citizenship Rights and Demands; Land; Industry and Labour; Commerce; Education; Public

Health and Medical Services; and Discriminatory Legislation.[54] Racial discrimination, as exemplified by a racially based franchise, should be outlawed, with voting being extended 'to all adults, regardless of race'. The right to vote and to be elected to Parliament, provincial councils and other representative institutions should not be based on race. Courts should dispense equal justice to all. Freedom of movement and freedom of residence should be guaranteed, and restrictive laws such as the Natives Land Act and the Urban Areas Act had to be scrapped. A significant demand was '[t]he right of freedom of the press': it was, of course, an important platform for the expression of African views in a repressive system, and some of the leading figures of the era were either owners or editors of newspapers such as *Abantu-Batho, Umteteli Wabantu* and *Native Advocate*.[55] The Bill recognised 'the sanctity and inviolability of the home as the right of every family'. Everyone, regardless of race, should have the right to 'own, buy, hire, lease and occupy land' or any other form of property, with restrictive laws being repealed. The right to engage in any occupation, trade or profession, without discrimination, was demanded. Employment in the public service should be open for all. Every child had the right to 'free and compulsory education', and 'admission to technical schools, universities and other institutions of higher learning'. Yet it was recognised that, unless employment opportunities were open to all, without regard to race, access to schools and universities would be meaningless. Hence the related demand for equal pay for equal work, and equal opportunity. Most importantly, the document ended with a demand for the repeal of discriminatory clauses in the constitution, as well as the repeal of laws which it listed, and the abandonment of unfair policy and practices.

The Bill of Rights was endorsed at the ANC's 1943 conference. From that moment, it was official policy, informing the ANC's vision for a new South Africa. When, soon afterwards, Xuma sought a meeting with Smuts to discuss the Africans' Claims document, Smuts summarily dismissed it as propaganda and said he was 'not prepared to discuss proposals which are wildly impracticable'.[56] History has shown, however, that white supremacist attitudes were powerless against the movement towards a new foundation for South Africa. In a post-democratic South Africa, the enduring nature of the Africans' Claims continues to be recognised. Kgalema Motlanthe, the former deputy president of the ANC, has drawn parallels between the Africans' Claims and South Africa's Bill of Rights, noting the 'continuity of both the aspirations of our people and their loyalty to a particular world view'.[57] He is correct in doing so. Nearly half a century later, in 1989, another group of ANC-aligned lawyers[58] drew up the ANC's 'Constitutional Guidelines for a Democratic South Africa'.[59] They did not do so from a position of ignorance. Their guiding light was the Africans' Claims of 1943 – a document that weathered the storms of colonialism and apartheid. Today, the spirit of its founders lives on in the Bill of Rights that forms part of the Constitution of South Africa. And so, when the 'Eurocentric origins' of the country's constitutional order are called into question, it is illuminating to investigate its unfolding history. We might then discover the truth that history 'is not a calculating machine'; instead, as Basil Davidson suggests, 'It unfolds in the mind and the imagination, and it takes body in the multifarious responses of a people's culture, itself the infinite circle mediation of material realities, of underpinning economic fact, of gritty objectivities.'[60]

In South Africa, the colonial encounter was particularly violent and disruptive. Invading European settlers took the land that Africans lived on, and by depriving them of their cattle they forced local people to become labourers on farms and mines. Yet as colonialism mutated into imperialism, it assumed a totalising form – transforming the cultures, languages, religions and ways of being of entire peoples. South Africa, with its apartheid pathology, became a typical case of colonialism transmogrifying into a form of imperialism. Black responses to conquest here and elsewhere have varied over time. As this book has tried to demonstrate, there is no necessary development from conquest to resistance to liberation. Rather than linear, this is a complex, sinuous story, one where Africans who accepted European ways came to play a leading role in the liberation of communities which initially viewed them with suspicion. While Western education and conversion to Christianity was once seen as a negation of one's being by many Africans, this gradually changed. It soon became a common-sense notion that one could be both African and Christian. As European culture permeated African culture, it also became indispensable to the survival of Africans. In this process, African identity was never completely obliterated. For Africans retained a certain distance from their colonisers even as they adopted elements of their culture. The 1913 Natives Land Act was the most visible manifestation of colonial conquest, as it formalised dispossession. The lives examined in this book demonstrate the response to such legislation by a particular group of Africans – those who had acquired, and mastered, Western legal training.

Contrary to the explicit desire of European settlers, Western education did not produce a docile class of black elites, willing transmitters of colonial culture. Rather, its products were prepared to stand up to the system, using the very tools of Western legal training in confronting its inequities. But in order to be effective – as many cases discussed here have proved – this training had to be anchored in the daily struggles and experiences of blacks. Having lost the land through conquest, the law and the courts became a new frontier for the pursuit of justice. However, as the black lawyers soon learnt, the entire edifice of the judiciary operated as an extension of Empire. Although their call was for the rule of law,

African lawyers recognised that, without equality before the law, the rule of law could be turned into an instrument for rule by the powerful. And so, individual actors, such as the lawyers dealt with in this book, were indispensable to the just functioning of the rule of law.

While the focus of this book has been on certain individuals, they should be viewed as part of a greater whole, for their lives were shaped by a range of circumstances and other individuals. And though the critique of colonialism has generally been viewed through the lens of the Western-educated black man,[61] women are also seen to have featured in unexpected ways, and from surprising quarters. Alice Victoria Kinloch emerges as the woman who placed South Africa on the agenda of the Pan-Africanist movement. It was Charlotte Manye Maxeke who was the inspiration behind Alfred Mangena's decision to study law. There were female pioneers in other fields: Mangena's wife, Anna Mcobela, a nurse, and Poswayo's wife, Beatrix Kule, a teacher. These neglected figures stood alongside the big men of the times, bolstering the critique of Empire.

In focusing on the past, this book attempts to understand the complexities of present-day South Africa. But it is not solely a history of actual events. It has also traced the development of the ideas that underpinned these events, and which have helped shape the country. By examining the forgotten origins of constitutionalism, South Africa may be better equipped to imagine a shared future based on equality.

Acknowledgements

My name is on the cover of this book, but it has taken a village to write it. I must therefore name and thank the members of the village who have made the writing possible through their material, emotional and intellectual support. Although I had entertained the idea of researching the stories of black lawyers since I was a student at the University of Transkei in the late 1990s, I only made the decision . to write a book in 2009. I had been asked by the South African Law Reform Commission to speak at the award ceremony for the Ismail Mohamed Law Reform Essay Competition, named after the former chief justice of South Africa. While researching for my speech, I came across the name of Alfred Mangena, one of the first black lawyers in South Africa. Years of intensive research and writing, including two trips to London, followed. By 2015 I had collected enough material to consider converting the research into a book. Many people made this possible. In London, the archivists of Lincoln's Inn, Middle Temple Inn, the British Library and the British Parliament were most helpful. In Wales, the librarians of Bangor University proved invaluable. My work was made infinitely easier by archivists at the National Archives of South Africa in Johannesburg, Pretoria, Cape Town and Pietermaritzburg, and the librarians and archivists at the universities of the Witwatersrand, Cape Town and KwaZulu-Natal were always willing to help.

A number of individuals deserve special mention. My late father has been a huge influence in my life. I was seven years old when I decided to study law. This was after I learnt that at the time of his death, in 1983, my father was a law student at the University of South Africa. In a sense, my dream has been to fulfil his. But my greatest debt of gratitude is owed to my mother Nomsa and my aunt Vuyelwa. They taught me patience, kindness and perseverance, attributes without which life is meaningless. I had to draw on these during the many days and nights of solitude that I spent writing this book.

I was fortunate to have access to some eminent historians with whom I could discuss my ideas. I met Professor Geoffrey Bisson and Dr Brian Willan in 2015 when I visited Queen's College, Somerset, in the United Kingdom. Not only did they provide me with excellent leads, but it was also their infectious enthusiasm for the project that convinced me I was on the correct track. Brian also took time to read an early draft of the manuscript and provided me with encouraging feedback. Professor Hermann Giliomee was a pillar of strength in the final two years of writing. He read the whole manuscript and kindly invited me to spend a day at his beautiful Stellenbosch home to discuss the book. Professor Bill Nasson also read the manuscript and gave me excellent feedback.

My friends and colleagues – Dr Lwazi Lushaba, Lwandile Sisilana, Janice Bleazard, Professor Xolela Mangcu, Sithembile Mbete (I hope we shall be calling her Dr Mbete soon!) and Dr Mcebisi Ndletyana – all read different chapters and provided comments for which I am eternally grateful. A word of thanks also goes to Vauldi Carelse, who recorded the interviews with the Molema and Montsioa families in Mafikeng – I can't wait for the documentary on South Africa's first black lawyers that she is producing! I also benefited from the research assistance of Fikile Masikane. My secretary, Diana Morais, was meticulous in typing up the first draft of the manuscript. My former pupil Yanela Ntloko helped to check some of the chapters for silly errors. Phakamisa Ndzamela and Dr Bongani Ngqulunga served as my soundboards to the many ideas and personalities I came across when writing the book.

Finally, a big thank you to the Penguin team: commissioning editor Melt Myburgh who saw the potential in my idea, managing editor Robert Plummer who oversaw the project from start to finish, and my editor Lynda Gilfillan for spending many nights polishing the rough drafts I produced. To everyone who has contributed to making this book possible, I say *Ukwanda kwaliwa ngumthakathi!*

TEMBEKA NGCUKAITOBI
DECEMBER 2017

Notes

Introduction

1. See *Myers and Misnum* v. *Rex*, 1907 Transvaal Supreme Court Reports, p. 760.
2. Kader Asmal, David Chidester and Cassius Lubisi (eds), *Legacy of Freedom: The ANC's Human Rights Tradition* (Johannesburg: Jonathan Ball, 2005), pp. 47–51.
3. Albie Sachs, *We, the People: Insights of an Activist Judge* (Johannesburg: Wits University Press, 2016), pp. 12–13.
4. See http://www.anc.org.za/content/constitutional-guidelines-democratic-south-africa.
5. Asmal et al., *Legacy of Freedom*, p. 60. The preamble of the Freedom Charter states: 'South Africa belongs to all who live in it, black and white, and that no government can justly claim authority unless it is based on the will of the people.' The balance of the charter is a blueprint for a bill of rights. What had been achieved at the 1943 conference of the ANC was reinforced at the Congress of the People in 1955. For the role of Z.K. Matthews in the Congress of the People and the Freedom Charter, see Isie Maisels, *A Life at Law* (Johannesburg: Jonathan Ball, 1998), pp. 129–216.
6. House of Commons Debates, 13 May 1908, vol. 188, cc 1215259, British Parliamentary Archives, London.

Chapter 1: How the land was lost

1. See William Gqoba, 'Isizathu sokuXhelwa kwe Nkomo ngo Nongqawuse', in *Isigidimi sama Xhosa*, 1 March 1888. Gqoba was the editor of the newspaper.
2. For an account of the origins of the War of Mlanjeni, see Jeff Peires, *The House of Phalo: A History of the Xhosa People in the Days of their Independence* (Johannesburg: Ravan, 1981), pp. 153, 190–91. The first written account of this war seems, however, to have appeared in John Henderson Soga, *The South-Eastern Bantu: Abe-Nguni, Aba-Mbo, Ama-Lala* (Johannesburg: Wits University Press, 1930).
3. See, for example, Timothy Keegan, *Colonial South Africa and the Origins of the Racial Order* (Charlottesville: Virginia University Press, 2006), pp. 233–40; C. Crais, *White Supremacy and Black Resistance in Pre-Industrial South Africa: The Making of the Colonial Order in the Eastern Cape, 1770–1865* (Cambridge: Cambridge University Press, 1992), pp. 175–188.
4. Peires, *The House of Phalo*, pp. 22–24.
5. Jeff Peires, *The Dead Will Arise: Nongqawuse and the Great Xhosa Cattle-Killing of 1856–7* (Johannesburg: Jonathan Ball, 2003), p. 37.
6. Taken from a letter written by a British settler, in Roger S. Levine, *A Living Man from Africa: Jan Tzatzoe, a Xhosa Chief and Missionary, and the Making of Nineteenth-Century South Africa* (New Haven: Yale University Press, 2010), p. 185.
7. Ibid.
8. Ibid.
9. Peires, *The Dead Will Arise*, p. 37.

10. Noël Mostert, *Frontiers: The Epic of South Africa's Creation and the Tragedy of the Xhosa People* (London: PIMLICO, 1992), p. 1221.

11. See Alan Lester, *Imperial Networks: Creating Identities in Nineteenth-Century South Africa and Britain* (London: Routledge, 2001), p. 182.

12. Peires, *The Dead Will Arise*, p. 37.

13. Ibid.

14. William Gqoba, 'Isizathu sokuxelwa kwenkomo ngo Nongqawuse', in *Isigidimi sama Xhosa*, 1 March 1888, pp. 22–23. The following translation is by A.C. Jordan, with my explanations inserted: 'You are to tell the people that the whole community is about to rise again from the dead. Then go on to say to them that all the cattle living now must be slaughtered, for they are reared with defiled hands, as the people practise witchcraft. Say to them there must be no ploughing of lands, rather must the people dig deep pits [granaries], erect new huts, set up wide, strongly built cattlefolds, make milksacks, and weave doors from barka roots. The people must give up witchcraft on their own, not waiting until they are exposed by the witchdoctors. You are to tell them that these are the words of their chiefs – the words of uNapakade [Forever], the son of Sifubasibanzi [The Broad-chested one].'

15. See also A.C. Jordan, 'The Tale of Nongqawuse', in A.C. Jordan, *Towards an African Literature: The Emergence of Literary Form in Xhosa* (Berkeley: University of California Press, 1973), p. 111.

16. Ibid., p. 112.

17. With the death of Sarhili's youngest son at the age of twelve, Sarhili had lost all his heirs.

18. Peires, *The Dead Will Arise*, p. 124.

19. Mostert, *Frontiers*, p. 1214.

20. Heidi Holland, *African Magic: Traditional Ideas that Heal a Continent* (Johannesburg: Penguin, 2001), Ch. 5.

21. See Lester, *Imperial Networks*, p. 182.

22. From the *King Williams Town Gazette*, 12 December 1857, in Mostert, *Frontiers*, p. 1218.

23. Mostert, *Frontiers*, p. 1218.

24. See A.C. Stuart Donald, 'Henry Tempest Waters 1819 to 1883, Anglican, South Africa', in *The Dictionary of African Christian Biography*, http://www.dacb.org/stories/south africa/waters-henry.html.

25. Lester, *Imperial Networks*, p. 183.

26. Stuart Donald, 'Henry Tempest Waters'.

27. Lester, *Imperial Networks*, p. 184.

28. The conference introduced the principle of 'effective occupation', which permitted powers to acquire rights over colonial lands in Africa, on condition that they possessed them, i.e. if they had signed treaties with local leaders, and if they had established an administration to govern the territory and to keep order. The colonial power could then use the colony for economic purposes.

29. See http://genocide-namibia.net/wp-content/uploads/2017/01/Class-Action-Complaint .pdf, par. 41, p. 12.

30. Ibid.

31. Ibid.

32. Article 22 provided as follows: 'To those colonies and territories which as a consequence of the late war have ceased to be under the sovereignty of the States which formerly governed them and which are inhabited by peoples not yet able to

stand by themselves under the strenuous conditions of the modern world, there should be applied the principle that the well-being and development of such peoples form a sacred trust of civilisation and that securities for the performance of this trust should be embodied in this Covenant.' However, insofar as South West Africa (Namibia) was concerned, the covenant recorded that, given the territory's proximity to the powers of Europe, it should be governed by South Africa: 'There are territories, such as South-West Africa and certain of the South Pacific Islands, which, owing to the sparseness of their population, or their small size, or their remoteness from the centres of civilisation, or their geographical contiguity to the territory of the Mandatory, and other circumstances, can be best administered under the laws of the Mandatory as integral portions of its territory, subject to the safeguards above mentioned in the interests of the indigenous population.' See http://avalon.law.yale.edu/20th_century/leagcov.asp.

33. South Africa had brought the German atrocities in German South West Africa to the attention of the world in 1915. Yet when that country was incorporated into 'Crown lands of South West Africa', thereby enabling occupation by white South African settlers in 1921, the oppression of the indigenous population continued unabated. See David Olusoga and Casper W. Erichsen, *The Kaiser's Holocaust: Germany's Forgotten Genocide* (London: Faber & Faber, 2010), pp. 364–347.

34. Peires, *The House of Phalo*, p. 12.

35. Veit Erlmann, *Music, Modernity, and the Global Imagination: South Africa and the West* (Oxford: Oxford University Press, 1999), p. 17.

36. Ibid., pp. 17–18.

37. Marshall Berman, *All that is Solid Melts into Air: The Experience of Modernity* (London: Verso, 1982), p. 21.

38. Ibid.

39. Ibid, p. 22.

40. See Martin Legassick, *Towards Socialist Democracy* (Pietermaritzburg: University of Natal Press, 2007).

41. When Benjamin Disraeli became prime minister of the United Kingdom in 1868, he proclaimed that he had reached the 'top of the greasy pole'. See Adam Kirsch, *Benjamin Disraeli* (London: Nextbook, 2008), p. 96.

42. Letter to William Thomas Stead, editor, *Review of Reviews*. See Liz Stanley and Andrea Salter, *The World's Great Question: Olive Schreiner's South African Letters, 1899–1920* (Cape Town: Van Riebeeck Society, 2014), p. 58.

43. Stanley and Salter, *The World's Great Question*, p. 59.

44. Ibid.

45. The Anglo-Boer War is now referred to as the South African War, in acknowledgement of the role played by all South Africans.

46. Jack Simons and Esther Simons, *Class and Colour in South Africa, 1850–1950* (London: Penguin African Library, 1969), p. 52.

47. Stanley and Salter, *The World's Great Question*, pp. 142–143.

48. Milner's Papers, Vol. XXXIV, *Miscellaneous Correspondence* (D, E, F 1901–1905), Bodleian Library, University of Oxford.

49. Ben Magubane, *The Political Economy of Race and Class in South Africa* (New York: Monthly Review Press, 1979), p. 51.

50. Stanley and Salter, *The World's Great Question*, pp. 171–172.

51. John Buchan, *The African Colony: Studies in the Reconstruction* (Edinburgh: William Blackwood & Sons, 1903), p. 289.

52. Ibid., p. 290.
53. Ibid.
54. See http://archive.spectator.co.uk/article/29th-august-1903/23/the-gold-mining
-industry-of-the-witwatersrand.
55. Ibid.
56. Walter Nimocks, *Milner's Young Men: The Kindergarten in Edwardian Imperial Affairs* (Durham: Duke University Press, 1968), p. 11.
57. *1903–1905 South African Native Commission Report*, p. 66. See https://archive.org/details/southafricannatioosout.
58. Ibid., p. 67.
59. Joseph Daniel Reilly, *Teaching the Native: Behind the Architecture of an Unequal Education System* (Pretoria: HSRC Press, 2016), p. 109.
60. Ibid.
61. See Denis Martin, *Coon Carnival: New Year in Cape Town, Past and Present* (Cape Town: New Africa Education, 2000), p. 86.
62. *Cape Argus*, 1 July 1890, in Martin, *Coon Carnival*, p. 87.
63. Ibid.
64. Veit Erlmann, *Studies in Black South African Performance* (Chicago: University of Chicago Press, 1991), p. 39.
65. *The Transvaal Advertiser*, February 1891.
66. Allen D. Callahan, *The Talking Book: African Americans and the Bible* (New Haven: Yale University Press, 2006), p. 165.
67. Erlmann, *Studies in Black South African Performance*, p. 43.
68. *Imvo Zabantsundu*, 16 October 1890.
69. The university, the first to be run by African Americans, is in Wilberforce, Ohio. Its roots lie in the notorious history of slavery. When slavery was abolished in America, new universities opened to provide tertiary education to black students. Wilberforce, founded by the African Methodist Episcopal Church, opened in October 1856, with the idea that 'the colored man must, for the most part, be the educator and elevator of his own race in this and other lands', and with the explicit goal 'to educate and thoroughly train many of them for the professional teachers, or for any other position or to pursuit in life to which God, in His providence, or by his Spirit, may call them'. Nelson T. Strobert, *Daniel Alexander Payne: The Venerable Preceptor of the African Methodist Episcopal Church* (New York: University Press of America, 2012), p. 77. Though Wilberforce experienced financial difficulties, by the time the South African students arrived, it was a sprawling campus, offering a range of subjects.
70. Erlmann, *Music, Modernity, and the Global Imagination*, p. 80.
71. 'Libini tsa Africa', *Leselinyana*, 1 November 1891. The original articles in *Leselinyana* are written in seTswana. I have relied on the translations provided by Erlmann in *Music, Modernity, and the Global Imagination*, which I have amended where I considered it necessary to do so.
72. Ibid.
73. See http://www.ric.edu/faculty/rpotter/temp/noblesav.html.
74. Ibid.
75. Erlmann, *Music, Modernity, and the Global Imagination*, p. 85.
76. Ibid. The quotation is taken from a dialogue between Marlow and Kurtz in Conrad's novella (first published in 1899), *Heart of Darkness* (London: Hesperus, 2002), p. 9. Marlow is imagining how England might have appeared to the conquering Romans – a savage place that was simultaneously appalling and enthralling.

77. Ibid.
78. Sebopioa Molema, 6 July 1904. The letter was addressed to his uncle, Modiri Molema. See http://www.historicalpapers.wits.ac.za/?inventory/U/Collections&c=A979/I.
79. See http://www.historicalpapers.wits.ac.za/?inventory_enhanced/U/Collections&c=199527/R/A979-Ac1.
80. Thozama April, 'Rethinking the Frontiers of the Eastern Cape', paper read at Humanities Seminar Room, Rhodes University, 8 June 2016, p. 10.
81. Ibid., p. 7.
82. Ibid., p. 11.
83. W.E.B. Du Bois, 'The Talented Tenth', in *The Negro Problem: A Series of Articles by Representative American Negroes of To-Day* (New York: James Pott, 1903), pp. 33–34.
84. See Peter Limb (ed.), *A.B. Xuma: Autobiography and Selected Works* (Paarl: Van Riebeeck Society, 2012), pp. 244–275.

Chapter 2: 'Fair play and no favours'

1. Of the early proponents of Pan-Africanism, more is generally known about Marcus Garvey and W.E.B. Du Bois than about Henry Sylvester Williams, despite the latter's pioneering role in the conceptualisation of Pan-Africanism.
2. The African Association was the predecessor to the Pan-African Association, which was established in 1900.
3. J.R. Hooker, *Henry Sylvester Williams: Imperial Pan-Africanist* (London: Rex Collings, 1975), p. 52.
4. Figures taken from Misha J. Charles, '*Soort soek soort*': *The American Negro Population in Cape Town until 1930*, MA dissertation, University of Cape Town, 2004, pp. 36–38. Charles bases her figures on the censuses conducted in 1875, 1891 and 1904. See https://open.uct.ac.za/handle/11427/7986.
5. Robert Trent Vinson, *The Americans are Coming! Dreams of African American Liberation in Segregationist South Africa* (Ohio: Ohio University Press, 2012), pp. 22–23.
6. C.L.R. James, 'Discovering Literature in Trinidad: The 1930s', in *Spheres of Existence: Selected Writings* (Connecticut: Westport, 1980), p. 238.
7. Vivian Bickford-Smith, *Ethnic Pride and Racial Prejudice in Victorian Cape Town: Group Identity and Social Practice, 1975–1902* (Cambridge: Cambridge University Press, 1995), pp. 32, 86.
8. Ibid., p. 86.
9. Vinson, *The Americans are Coming!*, p. 23.
10. Marika Sherwood, *Origins of Pan-Africanism: Henry Sylvester Williams and the African Diaspora* (New York: Routledge, 2011), p. 5.
11. Ibid. Comments such as these should be understood in the light of racist attitudes that were prevalent in Nova Scotia at the time.
12. See David Killingray, 'Rights, Land and Labour: Black British Critics of South African Policies before 1948', *Journal of Southern African Studies*, 35(2), 2009: 375–398.
13. *Yorkshire Herald*, 5 May 1897, p. 4.
14. *Manchester Guardian*, 6 May 1897, p. 12.
15. Sherwood, *Origins of Pan-Africanism*, pp. 42–44.
16. A.V. Alexander, *Are South African Diamonds Worth their Cost?* (Manchester: Labour Press, 1897).
17. Sherwood, *Origins of Pan-Africanism*, p. 44.
18. *The New Age*, 13 January 1898, in David Killingray, 'Significant Black South Africans

in Britain before 1912: Pan-African Organisations and the Emergence of South Africa's First Black Lawyers', *South African Historical Journal*, 64(3), 2012: 405.

19. Ibid., p. 404.

20. Ibid.

21. Ibid., p. 405. Incidentally, Killingray notes that Kinloch often used other pseudonyms such as 'a friend of South Africa' in her correspondence.

22. See for instance *The Liverpool Mercury*, 27 April 1899, which reported that the aims of the African Association were to take steps to 'influence public opinion on existing circumstances and conditions affecting the welfare of the natives under British rule, principally in South Africa, West Africa and the West Indies'.

23. See Sherwood, *Origins of Pan-Africanism*, p. 99.

24. Ibid., p. 42. Hooker expands on the reasons for the formation of the African Association in *Henry Sylvester Williams*, pp. 26–27.

25. See Sherwood, *Origins of Pan-Africanism*, p. 42.

26. See Killingray, 'Significant Black South Africans in Britain', p. 403.

27. The quote is taken from Joseph Conrad's character Marlow's description of colonialism: 'The conquest of the earth, which mostly means the taking it away from those who have a different complexion or slightly flatter noses than ourselves, is not a pretty thing when you look into it too much.' *Heart of Darkness* (London: Hesperus, 2002), p. 7.

28. *Western Mail*, 20 April 1899.

29. See Ian Knight, *Zulu Rising: The Epic Story of Isandlwana and Rorke's Drift* (London: Pan Macmillan, 2010).

30. For further information on the APS, see James Heartfield, *The Aborigines' Protection Society: Humanitarian Imperialism in Australia, New Zealand, Fiji, Canada, South Africa, and the Congo, 1837–1909* (New York: University of Columbia Press, 2011).

31. *The Aborigines' Friend*, August 1900, p. 529.

32. Ibid.

33. Ibid., November 1899.

34. House of Commons Debates, 4 May 1899, vol. 70, cc1302–4 1302, British Parliamentary Archives, London.

35. *Pall Mall Gazette*, 4 May 1899.

36. *Galveston Daily News*, 20 August 1899, p. 3.

37. Hooker, *Henry Sylvester Williams*, p. 25.

38. Ibid., p. 26.

39. Sherwood, *Origins of Pan-Africanism*, p. 62.

40. Hooker, *Henry Sylvester Williams*, pp. 28–29.

41. *The Glasgow Herald*, 1900.

42. Sherwood, *Origins of Pan-Africanism*, p. 87.

43. For conference proceedings, see http://credo.library.umass.edu/view/full/mums312-b004-i321.

44. Ibid.

45. Hooker, *Henry Sylvester Williams*, pp. 35–36.

46. Ibid., p. 37.

47. Ibid.

48. See M. Adhikari and L. Switzer, *South Africa's Alternative Press: Voices of Protest and Resistance, 1880s–1960s* (Cambridge: Cambridge University Press, 1979), pp. 127–128.

49. Stowell Kessler, *The Black Concentration Camps of the Anglo-Boer War* (Pretoria: War Museum of the Boer Republics, 2012).

50. Ibid.
51. Thomas Pakenham, *The Boer War* (Johannesburg: Jonathan Ball, 1997), p. 575.
52. See Erlmann, *Music, Modernity, and the Global Imagination*, p. 71.
53. Ibid.
54. Ibid., p. 72.
55. See link to the essay 'The Talented Tenth', in W.E.B. Du Bois, *The Negro Problem*, http://isites.harvard.edu/fs/docs/icb.topic1443192.files/DuBois_The%20Talented%20Tenth.pdf.
56. Ibid., p. 45.
57. Ibid., p. 61.
58. See Thomas Karis and G.M. Carter, *From Protest to Challenge: Protest and Hope, 1882–1934*, Vol. 1 (Johannesburg: Jacana, 2014), p. 7.
59. Ibid., pp. 7–8.
60. Ibid., pp. 102–118.
61. Ibid., p. 105.
62. See, for example, *Imvo Zabantsundu*, 23 March 1887.
63. Hooker, *Henry Sylvester Williams*, p. 65.
64. Ibid., pp. 65–66.
65. Ibid.
66. *Cape Argus Weekly*, 16 December 1903.
67. Owen Charles Mathurin, *Henry Sylvester Williams and the Origins of the Pan-African Movement, 1869–1911* (Connecticut: Greenwood, 1976), p. 126.
68. *Van Boom* v. *Visser* 1904, 21 SC 360.
69. Sherwood, *Origins of Pan-Africanism*, p. 154.
70. *Imvo Zabantsundu*, 16 August 1904.
71. Williams also claimed that a large number of his friends and acquaintances were Zulu. See 'The Black Peril: Why the Zulus are Threatening Rebellion', in *Manchester Daily Dispatch*, 5 December 1907, p. 4.
72. Henry Sylvester Williams, *The British Negro: A Factor in the Empire* (Brighton: W.T. Mouton, 1902).
73. Ibid., p. 6.
74. Ibid., p. 8.
75. Walter Rubusana, *Zemk'inkomo magwalandini* (Alice: Lovedale Press, 1906). The title may be translated as 'The cattle are being taken while you sleep, you cowards'.
76. *Tsewu* v. *Registrar of Deeds* 1905 TS, p. 130.
77. In 1910 Tsewu became president of the Transvaal Native Farmers Union. He was also part of the 1914 SANNC delegation to the United Kingdom to protest the effects of the 1913 Natives Land Act.
78. *Tsewu* v. *Registrar of Deeds* 1905 TS, pp. 130–131.
79. See Harvey Feinberg, *Our Land, Our Life, Our Future: Black South African Challenges to Territorial Segregation, 1913–1948* (Pretoria: University of South Africa Press, 2016), pp. 10–11.
80. Transvaal Colony, Department of Native Affairs, Annual Report, 1907–1908.
81. Ibid., p. 30.
82. Ibid., p. 35.
83. Feinberg, *Our Land, Our Life, Our Future*, p. 11.
84. Mathurin, *Henry Sylvester Williams*, p. 133.
85. See 'The Royal Aquarium', *The Standard*, 6 June 1892.
86. *The Scotsman*, 5 January 1907.

87. John J. Stevens, *Fuelling the Empire: South Africa's Gold and the Road to War* (London: John Wiley & Sons, 2003), pp. 138–139.
88. See report titled 'Declaration', 25 March 1908, enclosed in 'Report on a West Indian Negro named H. Sylvester Williams', 10 April 1908, National Archives of South Africa, Pretoria.
89. See 'Report on a West Indian Negro named H. Sylvester Williams', 10 April 1908, in National Archives of South Africa, Pretoria.
90. The intelligence report titled 'West Indian Negro named H. Sylvester Williams' dated 10 April 1908 does not appear to have been followed up by the colonial authorities, National Archives of South Africa, Pretoria.

Chapter 3: 'We don't want to swamp the white man in Africa'

1. The notion of the *Mfecane* (the crushing) is a highly contested topic. The dominant school of thought perceived it as a period of internal wars in the early part of the nineteenth century, driven by the emergence of a unified and powerful Zulu kingdom under King Shaka. These wars were believed to have caused ruptures within groups living in Zululand, causing rapid outward migration and dispersal of thousands of Zulu-speaking people. This view has, however, been challenged. Julian Cobbing argues that the idea of a 'Zulu explosion' which triggered a series of internal wars is a colonial myth. At the heart of the disruption and external migration from the land of the Zulu were raids for slaves, fuelled by the Delagoa Bay slave trade, and the demands for labour from Cape settlers, in 'The Mfecane as Alibi: Thoughts on Dithakong and Mbolompo', *Journal of African History*, 29 (1988): 487–519. See also Carolyn Hamilton (ed.), *The Mfecane Aftermath: Reconstructive Debates in Southern African History* (Johannesburg: Witwatersrand University Press, 1995).
2. *Natal Papers Relating to the Case of Mr Alfred Mangena*, Parliamentary Papers, Cd. 4403, 1908 (London: Darling & Sons, 1908), Government Publications, p. 57.
3. Ibid.
4. A point made by James Stewart, the founder of Lovedale Missionary College, the centre of missionary education in the mid-nineteenth century Cape. Stewart dedicated the book *Lovedale, South Africa* (Edinburgh: David Bryce & Son, 1894) to Sir George Grey. In the preface, he stated that it was owing to Grey that the 'industrial section' of the school commenced. The 'main features' of Grey's 'wise and humane native policy' were 'to combat superstition by promoting Christianity; to shake native faith in witchcraft, and those who practiced it by skilled medical aid; to overcome ignorance by native schools; and to counteract indolence by industrial training in various trades, and by employment on works of public utility'. Stewart's rendition of Grey's mission obscured its imperial design. Grey, as argued in Chapter 1, ultimately wanted to create a labour force. His criticism of the 'bookish' nature of missionary education for blacks was fundamentally animated by his imperial policies, and not by any humanity towards the native races of the land.
5. *Natal Papers Relating to the Case of Mr Alfred Mangena*, pp. 32–33.
6. Ibid., p. 34.
7. Cape of Good Hope 'Report and Proceedings, with Annexures, of the Cape Peninsula Plague Advisory Board, appointed to advise the Government on matters connected with the suppression of Bubonic Plague, 1901' [G 61 – 1901]. Hereafter referred to as 1901 Plague Report.
8. 1901 Plague Report, p. 6.
9. Ibid., p. 8.

10. Ibid., p. 9.
11. See Myron Echenberg, *Plague Ports: The Global Urban Impact of Bubonic Plague, 1894–1901* (New York: New York University Press, 2007), p. 286.
12. Rhodes introduced the Glen Grey Act to the Cape Parliament on 30 July 1894. For his speech, see http://www.sahistory.org.za/archive/glen-grey-act-native-issue-cecil-john-rhodes-july-30-1894-cape-house-parliament.
13. Echenberg, *Plague Ports*, p. 291.
14. Ibid., p. 287.
15. Ibid., p. 285.
16. Ibid., p. 288.
17. *The Reminiscences of Sir Walter Stanford 1850–1885*, Vol. 1 (Cape Town: Van Riebeeck Society, 1962), p. 213.
18. Ibid.
19. Ibid., pp. 214–215.
20. Ibid.
21. Ibid., p. 214.
22. Ibid.
23. *South African News*, 19 March 1901.
24. Gandhi's view regarding the inferiority of Africans remained constant throughout his life. In 1894, he wrote: 'A general belief seems to prevail in the Colony that the Indians are little better, if at all, than savages or the Natives of Africa. Even the children are taught to believe in that manner, with the result that the Indian is being dragged down to the position of a raw Kaffir.' See *The Collected Works of Mahatma Gandhi*, Vol. 1, p. 193, http://gandhiserve.org/cwmg/VOL001.PDF. In 1902, complaining about 'anti-Indian' laws of the Transvaal, Gandhi wrote: 'All the anti-Indian laws in both the Colonies are in full force; under them, in the Transvaal, the Indians cannot own land or trade except in Locations, and must, like the Kaffirs, hold travelling and other passes.' See *The Collected Works of Mahatma Gandhi*, Vol. 2, p. 453.
25. Echenberg, *Plague Ports*, p. 295.
26. Ibid., p. 296.
27. 1901 Plague Report, pp. 39–40.
28. *R. v. Radas*, *Cape Times* Law Reports, 21 April 1903. All such reports are held in the Special Collections Section, University of Cape Town Library.
29. John Austin sought to explain the role of law in the ordering of social relations through what he referred to as the 'command theory'. According to this theory, the ultimate source of all law is the sovereign Parliament – an assembly of the people. When judges interpret and apply the law, they do not exercise original command power, they possess only delegated powers, which flow from the sovereign power. See *The Province of Jurisprudence Determined* (Amherst: Prometheus Books, 2000).
30. See *The Records of the Honourable Society of Lincoln's Inn: The Black Books* (London, 1841–1920), https://archive.org/details/blackbookrecord01lincuoft.
31. These numbers declined after the First World War, when less than 40 per cent of admissions were from outside the United Kingdom.
32. Clause 2 and 14, Poll Tax Act No. 38 of 1905.
33. The urgent demand for African labour on the mines and on farms is evident, for example, in the Transvaal Colony Annual Report of the Department of Native Affairs of 1904, University of South Africa Archives, Pretoria.
34. Petition by Alfred Mangena, *Ilanga Lase Natal*, 19 October 1906.

35. Shula Marks, *Reluctant Rebellion: The 1906–8 Disturbances in Natal* (Oxford: Clarendon Press, 1970), p. 193.

36. Quoted in Shula Marks, *Reluctant Rebellion*, p. 175.

37. This references Thomas Gray's famous poem, 'Elegy Written in a Country Churchyard', which celebrates the bravery of John Hampden, a hero of the English civil war. Mangena was probably referring to the line: 'Some village-Hampden, that with dauntless breast'. See https://www.saylor.org/site/wp-content/uploads/2011/01/Elegy-written-in-a-Country-Courtyard.pdf.

38. *The Logan's Poet Daily Reporter*, 31 July 1906.

39. *Natal (Execution of Natives) Petition to His Majesty in Council 1906* [Cd. 2927] (London: Wyman and Sons, 1906).

40. Ibid., p. 5.

41. The judgment is reported as *Mgomini and others. The Governor of Natal (Natal)* [1906] UKPC 22 (2 April 1906).

42. *The Star*, 21 April 1906.

43. *The Logan's Poet Daily Reporter*, 31 July 1906.

44. *Ilanga Lase Natal*, 19 October 1906.

45. See Ronald Hyam, *Elgin and Churchill at the Colonial Office 1905–1908* (London: Macmillan, 1968), p. 241.

46. Ibid., p 242.

47. As reported in *The Scotsman* of 24 October 1908.

48. *Alfred Mangena* v. *Sir William Arbuckle* K.B. 1906 M. No. 2882 KwaZulu-Natal Provincial Archives, Pietermaritzburg. The letter is annexed as No. 96 on page 98. It is notable that by 1906 Mdolomba had been appointed as Wesleyan chaplain to the Natal Mounted Horse Police, which was specifically raised to crush the Bambatha rebellion. See *The Bideford Weekly Gazette*, 29 May 1906.

49. *Alfred Mangena* v. *Sir William Arbuckle* 1906 M. No. 2882. See note: 'interrogatories on behalf of the above named Plaintiff Alfred for the examination of the above named Defendant', KwaZulu-Natal Provincial Archives, Pietermaritzburg.

50. Ibid.

51. *Ilanga Lase Natal*, 2 August 1907.

52. Ibid., 19 October 1906.

53. An informal term referring to a major difficulty faced by a person.

54. *Mangena* v. *Wright* [1909] Kings Bench Division Law Reports, p. 958.

55. *Mangena* v. *Lloyd* [1908] 99 Law Times Reports, p. 824.

56. *Izwi Labantu*, 11 August 1908.

57. For Mangena's application for admission, see Supreme Court of Transvaal, *Alfred Mangena In re: Application for Admission as an Attorney* Ref. 8/4 Case No 123/1910, pp. 444–447, National Archives of South Africa, Pretoria.

58. See *Mangena* v. *Law Society of Transvaal* 1910 Transvaal Supreme Court, p. 649.

59. *Ilanga Lase Natal*, 4 February 1910.

60. Mweli Skota, *The African Who's Who: An Illustrated Classified Register and National Biographical Dictionary of the Africans in the Transvaal* (Johannesburg: Central News Agency, 1965), pp. 90–91.

61. 'Appearance of Attorneys, Advocates and Agents in Sub-Commissioner's Courts', Department of Native Affairs File No. F, 25 November 1910, National Archives of South Africa, Pretoria.

62. For further information, see Charles R. DiSalvo, *M.K. Gandhi, Attorney at Law: The Man before the Mahatma* (California: University of California Press, 2013).

63. See https://archive.org/stream/papersoninterracoouniviala/papersoninterracoouniviala_djvu.txt.
64. 'Ummeli uMangena noMlungukazi eGoli', *Ilanga Lase Natal*, 9 April 1913.
65. Robert Knox, *Dissecting the Races of Man* (London: Henry Renshaw, 1850).
66. *R. v. Johannes & 46 others*, National Archives of South Africa, Pretoria, Vol. 405, pp. 1–159.
67. Attorney-General to Secretary of Native Affairs Department, 20 August 1902, National Archives of South Africa, Pretoria.
68. Secretary for Native Affairs Internal Memorandum, NA 1285/08/1616/08, National Archives of South Africa, Pretoria.
69. Ibid.
70. Ibid.
71. Secretary for Native Affairs to Lord Selborne, 1208/08/SNA/1617/08, National Archives of South Africa, Pretoria.
72. Anne Applebaum, *Gulag: A History* (New York: Doubleday, 2004).
73. See typescripts of interviews in 'Selby Msimang's Autobiographical Notes', in Selby Msimang Papers, Alan Paton/PC14/1/2/2, 1971–1972, Alan Paton Centre and Struggle Archives, University of KwaZulu-Natal, Pietermaritzburg.
74. Meghan Healy, 'A World of Their Own: Community, Power, and Resilience at an American School for South African Women, 1869 to Recent Times', History and African Studies Seminar, University of KwaZulu-Natal, Durban, 29 October 2008. See http://www.kznhass-history.net/files/seminars/Healy2008.pdf.
75. Martin J. Lunde, *An Approach to Medical Missions: Dr. Neil Macvicar and the Victoria Hospital, Lovedale, South Africa, circa 1900–1950*, PhD dissertation, University of Edinburgh, 2009, p. 24.
76. Skota, *The African Who's Who*, p. 91.
77. Christoph Strobel, *The Testing Grounds of Modern Empire: The Making of Colonial Racial Order in the American Ohio Country and the South African Eastern Cape, 1770s–1850s* (Oxford: Peter Lang, 2007), p. 130.
78. For information on the Xhosa of Zimbabwe, see Hleze Kunju, *IsiXhosa ulwimi lwabantu abangesosininzi eZimbabwe: ukuphila nokulondolozwa kwaso (IsiXhosa as minority language in Zimbabwe: its survival and continued usage)*, PhD dissertation, Rhodes University, Grahamstown, 2017.
79. Terence Ranger, 'Traditional Authorities and the Rise of Modern Politics in Southern Rhodesia, 1898–1930', in Eric Stokes and Richard Brown (eds), *The Zambesian Past: Studies in Central African History* (Manchester: Manchester University Press, 1966), p. 180.
80. Ibid.
81. Petition to the King, 10 March 1919, A3/18/18/6, British Parliamentary Archives, London.
82. See Complaint of Hokolo, Section 70 of Proclamation 28 of 1902, 30 September 1918, National Archives of South Africa, Pretoria.
83. See 'Complaint against Native Attorney Mangena: Cases of Hokolo and Ephraim Mogorosi', November 1916, National Archives of South Africa, Pretoria.
84. Msimang, 'Autobiographical Notes', Ref. PC14/1/2/2.1.
85. 'Umfi Adv. Alfred Mangena', in *Imvo Zabantsundu*, 30 September 1924. D.D.T. Jabavu had taken over the editorship from his father, John Tengu Jabavu.

Chapter 4: The 'most gentlemanly' Richard Msimang

1. Anton Chekhov, *The Complete Short Novels*, trans. Richard Pevear and Larisa Volokhonsky (New York: Penguin Random House, 2004), p. xviii, introduction.
2. During the Anglo-Zulu War of 1879, the residents of Edendale – usually referred to as *Amakholwa* (Christian converts) – sided largely with the British. A memorial stone with the inscription 'Johannes Mgadi killed in action July 4th 1879' still stands in Edendale's Methodist church, built in the 1860s, as testament to the support for the British. It was not the first time that Christian converts had participated on the side of the British – in the 1874 Langalibalele uprising, the Christians of Edendale had fought on the British side – and it was not the last. Decades later, during the rebellion of Bambatha in 1906, the African Christian converts also fought on the side of the British. See Sibongiseni Mthokozisi Mkhize, *Class Consciousness, Non-racialism and Political Pragmatism: A Political Biography of Henry Selby Msimang, 1886–1982*, PhD dissertation, University of the Witwatersrand, Johannesburg, 2015, pp. 40–52.
3. Msimang, 'Autobiographical Notes', Ref. PC14/1/2/2.2.
4. Ibid.
5. Heather Hughes, *First President: A Life of John L. Dube, Founding President of the ANC* (Auckland Park: Jacana, 2011), p. 95.
6. Ibid., p. 96.
7. Albert Luthuli, *Let My People Go* (New York: McGraw-Hill, 1962).
8. Usually referred to by the Anglicised term 'Fingoes'.
9. Trevor Webster, *Healdtown Under the Eagle's Wings: The Legacy of an African Mission School* (Salt River: Methodist Publishing House, 2013).
10. One of its notable alumni is John Widgery, who became lord chief justice of England and Wales between 1971 and 1980.
11. School Register, 1904, Queen's College, Taunton.
12. Interview with Geoffrey Bisson, history teacher, Queen's College, Taunton, UK, 22 March 2016.
13. *The Wyvern*, Autumn 1905, p. 5. The Queen's College magazine contains much information on Msimang as a young man.
14. *The Wyvern*, Autumn 1904, p. 4.
15. *The Wyvern*, January 1905, p. 6.
16. Msimang, 'Autobiographical Notes', p. A24.
17. *The Wyvern*, January 1905, p. 10.
18. Ibid., p. 3.
19. 'Law Society of England and Wales Examination Results for 2nd and 3rd May 1906, list of candidates for preliminary examinations', Institute for Advanced Legal Studies, London.
20. *The Wyvern*, April 1907, p. 10.
21. Ibid., p. 21.
22. *The Wyvern*, July 1907, p. 139.
23. 'One of the Most Gentlemanly Players that Ever Donned a Jersey: the English Rugby Career of Richard Msimang, 1907 to 1912', *Quarterly Bulletin of the National Library of South Africa*, 66(3), July–Sept 2012: 5.
24. *The Courier*, 11 November 1908.
25. *The Courier*, 1 April 1908.
26. *The Courier*, 30 December 1908.
27. *The Gazette*, 28 September 1907.
28. *Western Daily Press*, 23 September 1907.

29. *The Wyvern*, Spring, 1910, p. 6.
30. *The Western Daily Press*, 23 September 1907.
31. See 'The New Native Solicitor', *Imvo Zabantsundu*, 16 December 1912: 'Mr Richard Msimang the New Native Solicitor arrived in South Africa last week by the *Armadale Castle* and his people welcomed him back heartily.'
32. Msimang, 'Autobiographical Notes', p. A24.
33. An attorney represents a client in court when pleading or defending a case. A solicitor (a term used mainly in Commonwealth countries) deals with conveyancing, the drawing up of wills and other legal matters. A solicitor may also conduct litigation in court on behalf of their client, but may not plead cases. An attorney may do both. A barrister (or advocate, in South Africa) specialises in pleading cases before courts, and deals with clients through a solicitor (attorney).
34. Msimang, 'Autobiographical Notes', p. A30.
35. Ibid., p. A26.
36. See R.W. Msimang (comp.), *Natives Land Act 1913: Specific cases of evictions and hardships, etc.* (Cape Town: South African Library, 1996,), p. 4. See also http://www.sahistory.org.za/sites/default/files/natives_land_act_1913_specific_cases_of_evictions_and_hardship.pdf.
37. Ibid., p. 5.
38. Ibid., p. 7.
39. For an explication of the concept, see Giorgio Agamben, *Homo Sacer: Sovereign Power and Bare Life*, trans. Daniel Heller-Roazen (Stanford: Stanford University Press, 1998), p. 99.
40. Papers of the Anti-Slavery Society, A.7.2.d, Union of South Africa, 1911–1914, Bodleian Library, University of Oxford.
41. For the proceedings, see Sol Plaatje, *Native Life in South Africa* (Johannesburg: Pan Macmillan, 2007), Ch. 16.
42. The commission referred to is the Beaumont Commission, which presented its findings in 1916.
43. South African Native Affairs Commission, 1903–1905, *Report of the Native Affairs Commission*, I (Cape Town, 1905), pp. 35–39. See http://www.historicalpapers.wits.ac.za/inventories/inv_pdfo/AD843/AD843-S40-4-001-jpeg.pdf.
44. Union of South Africa, *Report of the Natives Land Commission* (Cape Town, 1916), pp. 6–7. See http://www.historicalpapers.wits.ac.za/inventories/inv_pdfo/A1655/A1655-Da3b-01-jpeg.pdf.
45. Terence Ranger, 'The Rise of Modern Politics in Southern Rhodesia', in E. Stokes and R. Brown (eds), *The Zambesian Past: Studies in Central African History* (Manchester: Manchester University Press, 1966), pp. 188–189.
46. Karis and Carter, *From Protest to Challenge*, Vol. 1, p. 249.
47. Msimang, *Natives Land Act 1913*, p. 8.
48. The appeal case is reported as *Rex v. Ralulime*, 1929 Transvaal Provincial Division Law Reports, p. 176.
49. Ibid., p. 177.
50. *Rex v. Mpafuri*, 1928 Transvaal Provincial Division Law Reports, p. 609.
51. *Rex v. Ramkumba*, 1929 Transvaal Provincial Division Law Reports, p. 143.
52. 'The New Medical Act', *Umteteli Wabantu*, 22 December 1928.
53. On 18 May 1934, the native commissioner noted the following: 'Selby Msimang appeared before me today and states that to the best of his knowledge and belief the late R.W. Msimang, his brother left no property at all. That certain property

which deceased inherited from his late father's estate in Natal was sold when the late R.W. Msimang went insolvent. That he, Selby Msimang, knows of no property at all which belongs to deceased estate.' Estate Late R.W. Msimang, File No. DNC. 4/1630, National Archives of South Africa, Pretoria.

Chapter 5: 'In all races, genius is like a spark'

1. See Z.K. Matthews: 'he was … one of the founding members of the African National Congress. The moving spirit in the founding of this body which had as its aim the protection and the promotion of the rights of Africans in their homeland was Advocate Seme, the second African to enter the legal profession in this country.' In 'Our Heritage Series', *Imvo Zabantsundu*, 3 June–1 November 1961.
2. Montesquieu, *The Spirit of the Laws* (Cambridge: Cambridge University Press, 1989), p. 16.
3. Ibid., p. 22.
4. A.V. Dicey, *Introduction to the Study of the Constitution* (London: Palgrave Macmillan, 1978), pp. 120–121.
5. See, for instance, evidence given by Seme in *Report of Native Economic Commission 1930–1932*, Evidence and Memoranda, University of the Witwatersrand Historical Research Archive, Inventory No. AD. 1438, Box 8, p. 7404. Seme's view was that the land should be divided 'equally' between 'Natives' and 'Europeans'.
6. See, for example, Bongani Ngqulunga, *The Man Who Founded the ANC: A Biography of Pixley ka Isaka Seme* (Cape Town: Penguin, 2017).
7. 'Izulu e Oxford' (a Zulu in Oxford), *Ilanga Lase Natal*, 23 November 1906.
8. See Anti-Slavery and Protection of Aborigines Society, Bodleian Library of Commonwealth & African Studies, University of Oxford, A.9.1, Aborigines' Protection Society, 1906–1910.
9. Ibid.
10. Unidentified newspaper cutting, 1906, titled 'Zulu of King's Race a Prize Orator'. See Richard Rive and Tim Couzens, *Seme: Founder of the ANC* (New York: Africa World Publishers, 1993), p. 85.
11. Unidentified newspaper cutting, 16 April 1906, in Rive and Couzens, *Seme*, p. 88.
12. For a fuller discussion, see Walter Rodney, *How Europe Underdeveloped Africa* (London: Bogle-L'Ouverture Publications, 1972).
13. Pixley ka Isaka Seme, 'Regeneration of Africa', *Journal of Royal African Society*, 1905–1906, Vol. 5: 404–408.
14. Steve Biko, *I Write What I Like: A Selection of His Writings* (Johannesburg: Pan Macmillan, 1996), pp. 46–47.
15. Information provided in email from Chris Jeens, Jesus College archivist, 12 June 2015.
16. Unidentified newspaper cutting, 16 April 1906, in Rive and Couzens, *Seme*, p. 88.
17. John H. Morgan, 'Re-Inventing the Tutorial in an Internet World: An Enhancement of an Old English Tradition', *Journal of Alternative Perspectives in the Social Sciences* 5(3), 2013: 522–532.
18. Hazel lost his seat in 1910, though that year he was appointed reader in constitutional law at the Inns of Court. In 1915, he was appointed university lecturer on criminal law and the law of evidence at Oxford, a post he held until 1922, when he was appointed reader in law at All Souls College. In 1925 he was appointed principal of Jesus College.
19. According to the *Birmingham Mail* of 14 September 2014, the letter remained unopened for 103 years. See http://www.blackcountrybugle.co.uk/west-bromwich

-mps-election-address-unopened-103-years/story-20149147-detail/story.html#vzsftWJ
j8GLRuGe2.99.

20. I am grateful to Professor Robert Edgar of Howard University, and to Dr Bongani Ngqulunga, Seme's biographer, both of whom provided me with copies of the correspondence between Seme and Locke, from which I have extensively quoted.

21. See Leonard Harris and Charles Molesworth, *Alain L. Locke: The Biography of a Philosopher* (Chicago: University of Chicago Press, 2008), p. 59.

22. Ibid., p. 62.

23. Ibid.

24. Ibid.

25. Note from Seme to Locke, 25 January 1908, Locke Papers, Manuscript Division, Howard University. Hereafter Locke Papers.

26. 7 February 1908, Locke Papers.

27. Undated letter from Seme to Locke, inviting him to a game of tennis, Locke Papers.

28. Seme to Locke, 23 March 1907, Locke Papers.

29. 'The devil' was a term used by Locke and Seme to refer to alcohol.

30. Quoted in Jeffery Green, *Black Edwardians: Black People in Britain 1901–1914* (Oxford: Frank Cass, 2005), p. 150.

31. Locke to his mother, Mary Locke, 26 November 1908, Locke Papers. Samuel Coleridge-Taylor was born in Sierra Leone. The full title of his work is 'Scenes from The Song of Hiawatha by Henry Wadsworth Longfellow'.

32. Christopher Saunders, 'Pixley Seme: Towards a Biography', *South African Historical Journal* 25 (1991): 196–217, 204.

33. The letter is undated, but was probably written between May and June 1910, Locke Papers.

34. Until his marriage to Dinuzulu's daughter, Harriet, Seme had no blood links with the Zulu royal family.

35. Pamela Roberts, *Black Oxford: The Untold Stories of Oxford University's Black Scholars* (Oxford: Signal Books, 2013), p. 51. Seme and Locke were also among the founders of the Oxford Cosmopolitan Club, a group of international students; Seme served as treasurer.

36. *Oxford University Gazette*, 8 June 1909, p. 769. See https://www.ox.ac.uk/gazette/.

37. Ibid., 3 August 1909, p. 891.

38. Mangena was a friend of West African Akilagpa Osabrampa Sawyerr, who, like Mangena, had qualified at Lincoln's Inn as a barrister in 1907. They also collaborated in instituting proceedings against the Natal colonial government in relation to the Bambatha rebellion. Afterwards, Sawyerr returned to his native country, becoming active in the movement that eventually gained Ghana its independence in 1957.

39. *Imvo Zabantsundu*, January 1912.

40. See Xolela Mangcu, 'The ANC is Much Older than it Thinks', *City Press*, 8 March 2015.

41. In fact, the article had been developed jointly with Alfred Mangena (for further information on Mangena, see Ch. 3).

42. Most likely King Dalindyebo ka Ngangelizwe of the abaThembu, great-grandfather of King Buyelekhaya Dalindyebo.

43. This is a regulation issued by the sovereign, on the advice of the Privy Council.

44. Report by Colonel Sir Francis de Winton, commissioner appointed by the British government to enquire into the affairs of Swaziland, CO 879/33/1, 25 February 1890, UK National Archives, Kew, London.

45. Sir Robert Thorne Coryndon's papers, Ref. MSS. Afr.s., 633, Bodleian Library, University of Oxford.
46. See Godfrey Lagden papers, Ref. MSS. Afr.s., 142–214, Bodleian Library, University of Oxford.
47. Not to be confused with Sir George Grey, governor of the Cape Colony.
48. See report from Coryndon to Selborne, 7 March 1908, enclosing a report of a meeting of 'natives' held at Mbabane on 6 March 1908, where Chief Malunge spoke, in Records of Colonial Office Minute 417/456, UK National Archives, Kew, London.
49. See, for example, Saunders, 'Pixley Seme', p. 208.
50. Jeff Opland, 'Abantu-Batho and the Xhosa Poets', in Peter Limb (ed.), *The People's Paper: A Centenary History and Anthology of Abantu-Batho* (Johannesburg: Wits University Press, 2012), pp. 201–255.
51. Letter to Alain Locke, 10 June 1925, Locke Papers.
52. Quoted by Ronald Hyam, *The Failure of South African Expansion 1908–1948* (London: Holmes & Meier, 1972), p. 99.
53. See *Re: Southern Rhodesia* (1919) Appeal Court Reports, p. 211. See http://www.bailii.org/uk/cases/UKPC/.
54. See *Sobhuza v. Alister M. Miller and Others*, Privy Council Appeal No. 158 of 1924, p. 7. See http://www.bailii.org/uk/cases/UKPC/.
55. Native Economic Commission 1930–1932, Evidence and Memoranda, University of the Witwatersrand Historical Papers Research Archive, Johannesburg, pp. 7375–7444.
56. Saleem Badat, *Political Banishment under Apartheid: The Forgotten People* (Johannesburg: Jacana, 2012).
57. Quoted by Applebaum, *Gulag*, p. xxx.
58. Ibid., p. xxxii.
59. Quoted in Badat, *Political Banishment*, pp. 28–29.
60. Edward Roux, *Time Longer than Rope: A History of the Black Man's Struggle for Freedom in South Africa* (Madison: University of Wisconsin Press, 1966), pp. 322–323.
61. Ibid, p. 324.
62. *Komani N.O. v. Bantu Affairs Administration Board*, Peninsula Area 1980 (4) South African Law Reports, p. 448 (A).
63. Interview with Arthur Chaskalson. See www.historicalpapers.wits.ac.za, p. 9.
64. *Rikhoto v. East Rand Administration Board and Another*, 1983 (4) South African Law Reports, p. 278 (W).
65. *R. v. Koos Seshele and others*, Case No. A. 332/1931, Magistrate's Court for the District of Pretoria, National Archives of South Africa, Pretoria.
66. *Pixley ka Isaka Seme v. The Incorporated Law Society of the Transvaal*, 1932 Transvaal Provincial Division, National Archives of South Africa, Pretoria.
67. *Albertyn v. Kumalo and Others*, Witwatersrand Local Division Reports, p. 529.
68. Brought before the Supreme Court of Natal. See 1946 Natal Provincial Division Reports, p. 793.

Chapter 6: The unintended legacy of King Leopold

1. Local historian Charles Eaves showed me the location of 'Leopold's school' during my visit to Colwyn Bay on 24 April 2016.
2. Upon recognising my accent, the receptionist at the hotel where I was staying proudly informed me: 'Mr Mandela was here, in this building.'
3. It is worth noting that the Congo Free State, as the Congo was then known, was founded on a promise made by Leopold under the aegis of the Belgian International

Association for the Exploration of and Civilization of Africa. The countries that met at the Berlin Conference in 1885 agreed that the Congo would be a zone for free trade, where all the countries of Europe would have unfettered access to trade. At the outset, Leopold betrayed this promise when, in April 1885, the Belgian government permitted Leopold to be the 'chief' of the Congo Free State, though the relationship between Belgium and the Free State 'shall be exclusively personal'. In effect, this meant that Congo Free State would fall under the personal control of Leopold. It would not be a zone of free trade, as promised. Conditions akin to slavery were rife. George Washington Williams wrote an open letter to the president of the United States of America on 14 October 1891: 'Although the State of Congo promised the Powers of Europe to use all its abilities to suppress the slave-trade, the traffic goes on beneath its flag and upon its territory. At Stanley-Falls slaves were offered to me in broad day-light; and at night I discovered canoe loads of slaves, bound strongly together.' The letter contains a litany of promises made and breached by the Congo Free State, see http://www.blackpast.org/george-washington-williams-open-letter-king-leopold-congo-1890.

4. More such institutes followed: in 1856 Ludovico Casoria started the Collegio Dei Moretti in Naples, and three years later the Collegio Delle Morette was opened for black girls. In 1867, another college was opened in Verona.
5. Child labour was widespread in the Congo Free State. Hughes's intention was to establish 'child colonies', which would supply the state with soldiers. Catholic missionaries were at the forefront of establishing such colonies, and actively supported Leopold's scheme. See Adam Hochschild, *King Leopold's Ghost: A Story of Greed, Terror and Heroism in Colonial Africa* (Boston: Houghton Mifflin, 1998), p. 134.
6. Christopher Draper and John Lawson-Reay, *Scandal at Congo House: William Hughes and the African Institute, Colwyn Bay* (Colwyn Bay: Gwasg Carrey Gwalch, 2012), p. 152.
7. Congo Institute Annual Report 1892–1893, p. 7, African Studies, Library Archives, Bangor University, Wales.
8. W. Hughes, *Dark Africa and the Way Out: or, a Scheme for Civilizing and Evangelizing the Dark Continent* (London: Sampson Low, Marston & Co, 1892).
9. Congo Institute Annual Report 1892–1893, p. 8.
10. Ibid., p. 9.
11. Africa Training Institute, *The Twenty First Annual Report*, 1909–1910, p. 30.
12. Hughes, *Dark Africa*, p. 10.
13. For a description of these atrocities, see Hochschild, *King Leopold's Ghost*.
14. Congo Institute Annual Report 1892–1893, p. 2.
15. See http://www.blackpast.org/george-washington-williams-open-letter-king-leopold-congo-1890.
16. Hughes, *Dark Africa*, p. 12.
17. Ibid., pp. 12–13.
18. Quoted in Draper and Lawson-Reay, *Scandal at Congo House*, pp. 161–162.
19. Africa Training Institute, *The Twenty First Annual Report 1909–1910*, p. 10, Bangor University, Wales.
20. In 2013, a local Welsh newspaper described Jabavu as the most influential student of the institute, who, as a university lecturer, counted a young student named Nelson Mandela among his disciples. 'Colwyn Bay's historic link with Nelson Mandela', *North Wales Daily Post*, 12 December 2013.
21. His writings were published as *The Segregation Fallacy and Other Papers: A Native View of some South African Inter-racial Problems* (Lovedale: Lovedale Press, 1928).

22. *The Weekly News and Visitors' Chronicle for Colwyn Bay Colwyn Llandrillo Conway Deganwy and Neighbourhood*, 28 July 1903.
23. Report in *The Welsh Coast Pioneer and Review for North Cambria*, 15 August 1907.
24. Draper and Lawson-Reay, *Scandal at Congo House*, p. 170.
25. Peter Lobengula was a performer in the controversial show, 'Savage South Africa', in 1899. His elopement with a white woman resulted in a demand that the show be closed. Lobengula went on to marry Florence Kate Jewel, 'the attractive daughter of a Cornish mining engineer', but the couple were divorced and in 1902 he married Lily Magowan, an Irish woman. In 1907, Lobengula turned up at the Africa Institute in Colwyn Bay where, together with his Irish wife, he enjoyed a game of cricket, watching as Poswayo and Montsioa helped the institute to beat Colwyn Bay by 121 runs. By 1912 he was described as a 'frail-looking negro' claiming entitlement to vote in West Salford, as 'the oldest son of King Lobengula of Matebeleland'. By the time he contracted tuberculosis as a result of working in the English coal mines, he had four children – a fifth had died in childbirth. When his cause was made public, it was taken up by the British government and arrangements were made for his pension. See Ben Shepard, 'A Royal Gentleman of Colour', *History Today* 34 (4 April 1984).
26. Interview with Thukela Poswayo, nephew of Ngcubu Poswayo, 24 April 2015, Ngcobo, Eastern Cape.
27. See W.D. Cingo, *Ibali laba Tembu* (Pondoland: Palmerton Mission Printing Press, 1927), pp. 82–83.
28. See http://www.sahistory.org.za/archive/glen-grey-act-native-issue-cecil-john-rhodes -july-30-1894-cape-house-parliament.
29. Defined as 'a rent paid by the tenant of the freehold, by which he goes quit and free'. See http://legal-dictionary.thefreedictionary.com/Quit+rent.
30. Govan Mbeki was highly critical of this system of administrative 'self-government': 'The Bunga came into the Transkei as a natural consequence of the extension of the Glen Grey Act passed by Cecil Rhodes in 1894. Amongst other things this Act recognised the law of primogeniture, provided for local "self-government" by District Councils, which form the building material of that most prized (in Government circles) pyramidical structure whose apex is the Bunga. In the latter provision we meet with an Administrative form which resembles, on a miniature scale, the system of Indirect Rule in the British African Colonies. Even at this stage it is necessary that we are cleared of every doubt with regard to the use of the word "self-government." Correctly speaking, there is no self-government of the inhabitants of the Transkei by their own people. Even the vestigeal power which is apparently still wielded by the chiefs and headmen is but an eye-wash.' *Transkei in the Making* (Durban: Verulam Press, 1939), p. 3.
31. S.E.K. Mqhayi wrote: 'those who were there say that [Wauchope] was standing to one side now as the ship was sinking! As the chaplain he had the opportunity to board a boat and save himself, but he didn't! he was appealing to the leaderless soldiers urging them to stay calm, to die like heroes on their way to war.' See 'The late Rev. Isaac William Wauchope', in *Abantu Besizwe: Historical and Biographical Writings, 1902–1944*, ed. and trans. Jeff Opland (Johannesburg: Witwatersrand University Press, 2009), p. 478. See also John Gribble and Graham Scott, *We Die Like Brothers: The Sinking of the SS Mendi* (London: Historic England, 2017), pp. 126–127.
32. Gribble and Scott, *We Die Like Brothers*, p. 109.
33. Ibid.

34. See the records of the Honourable Society of Lincoln's Inn: The Black Books (London: 1841–1920).
35. I have unfortunately been unable to locate records of their names.
36. Native Courts were special courts established to hear disputes between African litigants. They fell under the Magistrate's Courts, which could hear appeals from Native Courts.
37. *Makoti* v. *Madupi*, 1916, Transvaal Provincial Division Reports, p. 393.
38. *R.* v. *Kana*, 1923, Transvaal Provincial Division Reports, p. 243.
39. *Ntsobi* v. *Berlin Mission Society*, 1924, Transvaal Provincial Division Reports, p. 378.
40. *Tiopaizi* v. *The Bulawayo Municipality*, 1923 Appellate Division Reports, p. 317.
41. A point made by Antony Angie about international law. See 'On critique and the other', in Anne Orford, *International Law and its Others* (Cambridge: Cambridge University Press, 2006), p. 394.
42. A well-known phrase referring to soldiers bravely uniting against a powerful enemy. See William Shakespeare, *Henry V* (Act IV Scene iii 18–67).

Chapter 7: Visions of equality in a divided Union
1. Section 44(c) of the South Africa Act.
2. Sampie Terreblanche, *A History of Inequality in South Africa, 1652–2002* (Scottsville: University of KwaZulu-Natal Press, 2012), p. 245. See also Anne Simpson, *Britain, South Africa and the East African Campaign, 1914–1918: The Union Comes of Age* (London: I.B. Tauris, 2007), pp. 109–110.
3. For Treaty of Vereeniging, see http://www.sahistory.org.za/archive/peace-treaty-vereeniging-original-document.
4. Sherwood, *Origins of Pan-Africanism*, p. 154.
5. Minutes of African Students Society, February 1909, London School of Economics, London.
6. See, for instance, Olúfémi Táíwò, *How Colonialism Preempted Modernity in Africa* (Indiana: Indiana University Press, 2009), pp. 91–92.
7. The convention met at Bloemfontein from 24 to 26 March 1909, with delegates from the Cape Colony, Natal, Transvaal, Orange River Colony and Bechuanaland. Their specific goal was to discuss 'those clauses of the Draft Act of the South African National Convention relating to Natives and Coloured people'. Karis and Carter, *From Protest to Challenge*, Vol. 1, p. 148.
8. Ibid., pp. 148–149.
9. Ibid., p. 149.
10. Ibid., p. 20.
11. House of Commons Debates, 13 May 1908, vol. 188, cc 1215259, British Parliamentary Archives, London.
12. Ibid.
13. Ibid.
14. Ibid.
15. Richard Steyn, *Jan Smuts: Unafraid of Greatness* (Johannesburg: Jonathan Ball, 2015), p. 57.
16. Karis and Carter, *From Protest to Challenge*, Vol. 1, p. 151.
17. House of Lords Debates, 27 July 1909, vol. 2, CC 753297, British Parliamentary Archives, London. The Bill was ratified by the British Parliament on 31 May 1910.
18. Ibid.
19. Karis and Carter, *From Protest to Challenge*, Vol. 1, p. 154.

20. Minutes of a meeting of the African Students Society, London School of Economics, February 1909.
21. Ibid.
22. During the period Seme was a student of constitutional law at Middle Temple, students were expected to be familiar with Cicero's thought. Seme's reference to Cicero appears in at least two letters to Locke, one dated 8 December 1910, and an undated letter, probably sent in about 1922, when Seme was engaged by the Swaziland government. Locke Papers, Moorland-Spingarn Research Center, Howard University, Washington DC.
23. Cicero, *De Legibus (On the Laws)*, Book I, Section 42. See http://media.bloomsbury.com/rep/files/Primary%20Source%201.3%20-%20Cicero.pdf.
24. See Seme's pamphlet, 'The African National Congress – Is it Dead?', in Karis and Carter, *From Protest to Challenge*, Vol. 1, pp. 539–543.
25. 1911 Appellate Division Reports, p. 635.
26. 1915 Transvaal Provincial Division Reports, p. 106.
27. 1934 Appellate Division Reports, p. 167.
28. 1912 Appellate Division Reports, p. 623.
29. 1909 Transvaal Supreme Court Reports, p. 363.
30. See *Hall* v. *Society of Law Agents*, Scottish Law Reporter, Vol. 38, p. 776.
31. *South African Law Journal* 31 (1914): 383.
32. M. de Villiers, 'Note', *South African Law Journal*, 34 (1917): 343.
33. Better-known by its Dutch title: Vrouwen Wetspraktizijnswet 7 of 1923.
34. Karis and Carter, *From Protest to Challenge*, Vol. 1, pp. 176–178.
35. See Brian Willan, 'The Anti-Slavery and Aborigines' Protection Society and the South African Natives' Land Act of 1913', *The Journal of African History* 20(1), 1979: 83–102.
36. *South Africa*, 20 June 1914.
37. Karis and Carter, *From Protest to Challenge*, Vol. 1, p. 44.
38. Ibid., pp. 229–235.
39. Kader Asmal, David Chidester and Cassius Lubisi (eds), *Legacy of Freedom: The ANC's Human Rights Tradition* (Jeppestown: Jonathan Ball, 2005), p. 45.
40. Ibid.
41. Hertzog was one of the signatories to the Treaty of Vereeniging.
42. See clause 2, which provided for the acceptance by 'burghers' of their position as 'subjects of HIS MAJESTY KING EDWARD VII'. See http://www.sahistory.org.za/archive/peace-treaty-vereeniging-original-document.
43. The loan was eventually repaid in 2015, following an announcement by the chancellor of the exchequer, George Osborne, on 3 December 2014: 'We can, at last, pay off the debts Britain incurred to fight the First World War.' See http://www.bbc.com/news/business-30306579.
44. Oswald Pirow, *James Barry Munnik Hertzog* (Cape Town: Howard Timmins, 1958), p. 102.
45. Steyn, *Jan Smuts*, p. 85.
46. Pirow, *James Barry Munnik Hertzog*, p. 103. In May 1920, Smuts's South African Party lost the elections by three seats to the Nationalist Party. He was compelled to form a coalition with the ultra-imperialist Unionist Party. His change of stance with regard to Britain may therefore be viewed in terms of shoring up his position. See also Steyn, *Jan Smuts*, p. 101.
47. H. Duncan Hall, 'The genesis of the Balfour Declaration of 1926', *Journal of Commonwealth Political Studies* 1 (1962): 169–193.

48. This came to be known as the Balfour Declaration. It set the framework for future relations between Britain and its dominions regarding the principle of equality.
49. Karis and Carter, *From Protest to Challenge*, Vol. 1, pp. 482–483.
50. Ibid., pp. 325–351.
51. Ibid.
52. Four Bills were introduced: the Native Trust and Land Bill (to extend native reserves created under the 1913 Natives Land Act), the Native Council Bill (to establish councils which would be responsible to collate native opinions to be channelled to the government, after their removal from the voter's roll), the Natives Representation Bill (to deprive Africans in the Cape of their right to vote), and the Coloured Persons Rights Bill (to give coloured people in the Orange Free State and Transvaal the right to elect one white person to represent their views in Parliament).
53. Karis and Carter, *From Protest to Challenge*, Vol. 1, pp. 325–351.
54. In the pamphlet 'The African National Congress – Is it Dead?', Seme acknowledged that the ANC had almost ceased to exist as an organisation, although he denied that he had killed it. To revive it, however, he proposed concentrating powers in the position of president-general, suggesting that the latter should 'be obeyed and followed by his Cabinet as he is responsible for their failures.' Karis and Carter, *From Protest to Challenge*, Vol.1, p. 540.
55. Apparently oblivious to the growing totalitarianism in the Soviet Union under Joseph Stalin, Gumede proclaimed on his return: 'When I left South Africa, I was under the impression that in Russia people were not safe. But what I saw there surprised me. I saw a new Jerusalem. I found people happy, contented, and prosperous. The government of Russia is the government of the working classes. Today in Russia the land belongs to the people.' See: http://www.sahistory.org.za/archive/chapter-7-gumede-keeps-bright-fire-burning-1928-29. The proceedings of the annual conference of the ANC of 1930 are reported in *Umteteleli Wabantu*, 3 May 1930. When Gumede spoke in support of communism, his speech was roundly rejected, and the delegates made it clear that he did not speak on their behalf.

Chapter 8: The birth of constitutionalism

1. This chapter draws on a previously published article: Tembeka Ngcukaitobi, 'South Africa's First Bill of Rights: Our Magna Carta Moment', *The Advocate* 30(2) (August 2017): pp. 21–28.
2. Anthony Sampson, *Mandela: The Authorised Biography* (London: HarperCollins, 1999).
3. Ashby Mda, Anton Lembede and Oliver Tambo went on to qualify as lawyers.
4. Nelson Mandela, *Long Walk to Freedom* (London: Abacus, 1995), p. 113.
5. Ibid., pp. 112–113.
6. Smuts served as prime minister from 1919–24, and again from 1939–48.
7. Mandela, *Long Walk to Freedom*, p. 132.
8. See Robert R. Edgar and Luyanda ka Msumza (eds), *Freedom in Our Lifetime: The Collected Writings of Anton Muziwakhe Lembede* (Cape Town: Kwela, 2015), p. 21.
9. Mandela, *Long Walk to Freedom*, p. 131.
10. Ibid., pp. 112–113.
11. Mandela was not present at this conference. See Mandela, *Long Walk to Freedom*, p. 113.
12. Sampson, *Mandela: The Authorised Biography*, p. 55.
13. Ibid.

14. See http://www.anc.org.za/content/38th-national-conference-programme-action -statement-policy-adopted.

15. See Peter Limb, *The ANC's Early Years: Nation, Class and Place in South Africa before 1940*, Hidden Histories Series (Pretoria: Unisa Press, 2010), p. 119.

16. Asmal, Chidester and Lubisi (eds), *Legacy of Freedom*, p. 53. This discrimination was not, however, confined to the SANNC, it was widespread throughout the South African political class. White women were only granted the right to vote in 1930, as a political manoeuvre by white politicians to neutralise the impact of the 'coloured vote' in the Cape. By granting women the right to vote, the numbers of white voters were immediately doubled. When one takes into consideration the property and education limits imposed on coloured voters, the doubling of white votes through women votes undermined the significance of the coloured votes. See Limb, *The ANC's Early Years*, p. 119.

17. Limb, *The ANC's Early Years*, p. 121.

18. See 'Native Women's Brave Stand', *Abantu-Batho*, July 1913, in Limb (ed.), *The People's Paper*, p. 343.

19. Ibid., p. 344.

20. Limb, *The ANC's Early Years*, p. 121.

21. Limb (ed.), *The People's Paper*, p. 391.

22. 'A Resolution: Native Women Pass Law', *Abantu-Batho*, 6 December 1917, in ibid., p. 391.

23. 'The National League of Bantu Women (Transvaal Province): Stirring Speech by Mrs Maxeke', *Abantu-Batho*, 20 December 1917, in ibid., p. 393.

24. Ibid., p. 48.

25. Ibid.

26. Ibid., p. 49.

27. Ibid., pp. 50–51.

28. See Limb (ed.), *A.B. Xuma*, pp. 244–275.

29. Ibid., p. 253.

30. For conference report, see Karis and Johns, *From Protest to Challenge*, Vol. 2 (Johannesburg: Jacana, 2015), pp. 117–132.

31. Letter to J.J. Maruma, March 1944, in Limb (ed.), *A.B. Xuma*, pp. 99–100.

32. Letter to A.W.G. Champion, 6 May 1946, in ibid., p.107.

33. Karis and Johns, *From Protest to Challenge*, Vol. 2, pp. 368–372.

34. Ibid., p. 255.

35. Ibid.

36. See Richard Toye, *Churchill's Empire: The World that Made Him and the World He Made* (New York: Henry Holt & Co, 2011), p. 245.

37. As quoted in David D. Newsom, *The Imperial Mantle: The United States, Decolonization, and the Third World* (Indiana: Indiana University Press, 2001), p. 50.

38. Thomas Carlyle, an influential figure in Victorian England, was the author of the notorious 1849 paper, 'Occasional Discourse on the Negro Question'. He argued that England should not have abolished slavery as black people were inherently inferior and suited to menial tasks under the supervision of whites. However, John Stuart Mill's rebuttal, also titled 'The Negro Question', rejects the notion that 'one kind of human beings are born servants to another kind' as a 'damnable doctrine'. For Thomas Carlyle's views on race and empire, see John Marrow, *Thomas Carlyle* (London: Hambledon Continuum, 2006), pp. 125–133. See also Richard Reeves, *John Stuart Mill: Victorian Firebrand* (London: Atlantic, 2007), pp. 123–128.

39. Toye, *Churchill's Empire*, p. xi.
40. David Jablonsky, *Churchill and Hitler: Essays on the Political-Military Direction of Total War* (Oxford: Routledge, 2013), p. 66. The quote is attributed to his physician, who noted: 'the P.M. likes to go back to the Boer War when he is in good humour. That was before war degenerated. It was great fun galloping about.'
41. Toye, *Churchill's Empire*, p. 81. As colonial secretary in the 1920s, Churchill unleashed the infamous Black and Tans on Ireland's Catholic civilians, and when the Kurds rebelled against British rule, he said: 'I am strongly in favour of using poisoned gas against uncivilised tribes … [It] would spread a lively terror.' See Warren Dockter, *Churchill and the Islamic World: Orientalism, Empire and Diplomacy in the Middle East* (London: I.B. Taurus, 2015), p. 113.
42. Toye, *Churchill's Empire*, p. 227.
43. Roy Douglas, *Liquidation of Empire: The Decline of the British Empire* (New York: Palgrave Macmillan, 2002), p. 1.
44. House of Commons Debates, 9 September 1941, vol. 374, CC 67–156, British Parliamentary Archives, London. See also http://hansard.millbanksystems.com/people/mr-winston-churchill/1941.
45. Mandela, *Long Walk to Freedom*, p. 110.
46. Karis and Johns, *From Protest to Challenge*, Vol. 2, pp. 270–272.
47. Z.K. Matthews, *Freedom for My People: The Autobiography of Z.K. Matthews: Southern Africa 1901 to 1968*, with a Memoir by Monica Wilson (Cape Town: David Philip, 1986), p. 92.
48. His father, Reverend Abner Mtimkulu, had approached the University of Cape Town in 1923 to enquire whether 'Lionel could be allowed to attend lectures in medicine in the University' – a career his son decided not to pursue. A copy of the letter is held at the University of Cape Town Library, Special Collections.
49. By this time, Seme's legal career had turned full circle. After being struck off the roll of attorneys in 1932, ten years later, on 14 April 1942, he had once again set up a legal practice.
50. It was presented at the ANC annual conference held on 12–16 December 1943. See Karis and Johns, *From Protest to Challenge*, Vol. 2, pp. 272–283.
51. Ibid., p. 272.
52. Ibid., p. 274.
53. Ibid., p. 275.
54. Ibid., p. 276.
55. In 1912, Alfred Mangena, together with Sefako Makgatho (who later served as president of the SANNC from 1917–1924), started the newspaper *The African Native Advocate*, which closed within months of its launch. The editor was Alan Kirkland Soga, who, despite having gained legal qualifications from Edinburgh University, did not practise law in South Africa. Instead, Soga played an active role in the Cape-based South Africa Native Congress, and was editor of the influential black newspaper, *Izwi Labantu*. See Les Switzer, 'Introduction', in Les Switzer (ed.), *South Africa's Alternative Press: Voices of Protest and Resistance, 1880–1960* (Cambridge: Cambridge University Press, 1997), p. 30.
56. Ibid., p. 278.
57. Kader Asmal and Cassius Lubisi, *Legacy of Freedom: The ANC's Human Rights Tradition* (Cape Town: Jonathan Ball, 2005), p. vii.
58. They included Albie Sachs, Penuell Maduna, Zola Skweyiya and Kader Asmal. Sachs was a judge of the Constitutional Court from 1994–2009; Maduna served as minister

of justice and constitutional development from 1999–2004; Skweyiya served as a cabinet minister from 1994–2009; and Asmal served as minister of water affairs from 1994–1999, and minister of education from 1999–2004.

59. See http://www.tandfonline.com/doi/abs/10.1080/02587203.1989.11827765.
60. Basil Davidson, *Africa in Modern History: The Search for a New Society* (London: Allan Lane, 1978), p. 200.
61. See, for example, *Aimé Césaire, Discourse on Colonialism*, trans. Joan Pinkham (New York: Monthly Review Press, 2001), which remains a classic text in anti-colonial discourses; also Franz Fanon, *A Dying Colonialism* (New York: Grove Press, 1965); and Steve Biko, *I Write What I Like* (Johannesburg: Picador Africa, 2017).

Index

Tambo, Oliver 5, 258
Tantsi, James 37
Taunton Rugby Club 115, 127–129
Taylor, Moses 84
Teatea, Simon 138
Tembuland Advertiser 218, 221
Terreblanche, Sampie 232
'test case' strategy 196–200
Thema, Richard Victor Selope 174
Thembu people 178, 209
Theo, John 84
'third university of England' 82–85
Thorburn, John 184
Tilonko, Chief 86–88
Times, The 47, 93
Tindall, B.A. 100
Tindall, Judge 146
Tolanku, Phillip 101
tramcars 242
Transvaal 22–26, 64–66
Transvaal Chamber of Mines 22, 25–26
Transvaal Law No. 4 of 1885 224
Transvaal Law Society 100–101, 114, 117, 131, 152, 159, 201–203
Transvaal Native Congress 97, 99, 233, 235, 262
Transvaal Supreme Court 64, 243
Treaty of Vereeniging 23, 231, 232, 249
Trespass Act of 1906 150–152
tribal affiliations 19, 144–146, 155–156, 160, 175–178
Trotha, Lothar von 20
Tsewu, Edward 64–65
Tshatshu, Dyani 45
Tshidi Barolong 35
Tuskegee Institute 119, 215
Twala, Rev. R. 131

Uitvlugt 77–79, 117
Ukutshona kuka Mendi (poem) 182
Umteteleli Wabantu 271
Umteteli Wabantu 153
Unionist Party 248
Union of South Africa, establishment of 2, 6–7, 56, 170, 231–232
United Kingdom *see* Britain
United States 27, 33–34, 36–38, 187, 264–267
unity 58
Universal Races Congress 104–105

universities for black people 27, 31–34
University College, London 215
University of Birmingham 215
University of Cape Town 268
University of Fort Hare 207, 215, 268
University of Oxford *see* Oxford University
University of the Witwatersrand 115, 259
Urban Areas Act *see* Natives (Urban Areas) Act
US *see* United States

Van Boom v. *Visser* 60–61
Van Pittius, Gey 152
Victoria Hospital 109
Victoria, Queen 33, 48, 53–54, 74
Vinson, Robert 42
Visser, Mr 60–61
voting rights *see* franchise

Wages Act 249
Wakani, Machine 81–82
Wales 207–208
Washington, Booker T. 43, 46, 119, 173
Watkins, Frank 184
Watt, Thomas 231
Waverley township 197–200
Wedemeyer, S. 227
Welverdiend 117–118
Wernher-Beit 55
Wesleyan Church 75, 78, 116, 121–122
Western Daily Press 127
West Indians living in Cape Colony 41–42, 56–57
We, the People 5
Wilberforce University 31, 34–38, 261
Wilde, Oscar 167
Wilkinson, Advocate 81–82
Willan, Brian 127
Williams, Agnes 59, 62
Williams and Adendorff v. *Johannesburg Municipality* 242
Williams, George Washington 212–213
Williams, Henry Sylvester
  early years 42–43
  Alfred Mangena and 37–38
  Alice Kinloch and 43–47
  Aborigines' Protection Society 48
  Cecil John Rhodes and 49–50
  'Savage South Africa' 49
  Pan-African Conference 51–52, 54